The MU Alumni Association was established to promote and further education in the global marketplace. Alumni are in a unique position to provide advice and counsel to strengthen MU's mission of teaching, research and service.

*Mission Statement*
The MU Alumni Association proudly supports the best interests and traditions of Missouri's flagship university and its alumni worldwide. Lifelong relationships are the foundation of our support. These relationships are enhanced through advocacy, communication and volunteerism.

*Guideposts to Excellence*
DISCOVERY ~ DIVERSITY ~ PRIDE ~ RESPECT ~ RESPONSIBILITY ~ TRADITION

Much like the stones which give strength to six beloved columns, these six values are supported only by the degree of excellence which they embody. The Association recognizes the special worth that the pursuit of excellence creates and strives to bond our alumni together using excellence as the foundation.

To learn more about the MU Alumni Association visit www.mizzou.com , call 1-800-372-MUAA(6822) or write to MUAA, 123 Reynolds Alumni Center, Columbia, MO 65211.

# TRUE SONS

## A CENTURY OF MISSOURI TIGERS BASKETBALL

by Michael Atchison

Foreword by Norm Stewart

THE DONNING COMPANY PUBLISHERS

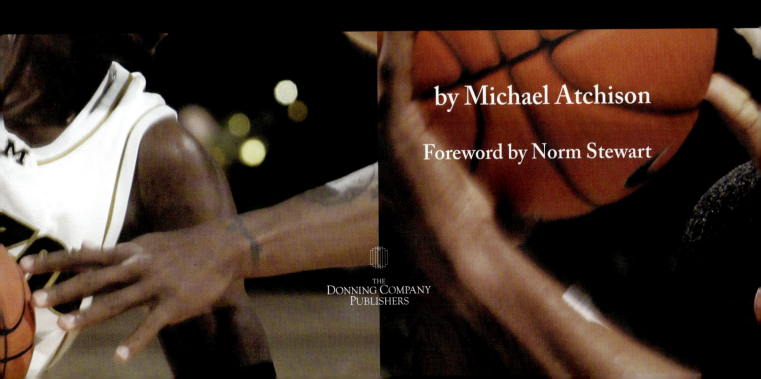

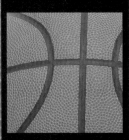

Copyright © 2006 by Michael Atchison

All rights reserved, including the right to reproduce this work in any form whatsoever without permission in writing from the publishers, except for brief passages in connection with a review. For information, write:

The Donning Company Publishers
184 Business Park Drive, Suite 206
Virginia Beach, VA 23462–6533

Steve Mull, General Manager
Barbara Buchanan, Office Manager
Kathleen Sheridan, Senior Editor
Lynn Parrott, Graphic Designer
Amy Thomann, Imaging Artist
Scott Rule, Director of Marketing and Cover Design
Stephanie Linneman, Marketing Coordinator

*Ed Williams/Steve Mull, Project Directors*

**Library of Congress Cataloging-in-Publication Data**

Atchison, Michael, 1968-
 True sons : a century of Missouri Tigers basketball / by Michael Atchison ; foreword by Norm Stewart
   p. cm.
 Includes index.
 ISBN-13: 978-1-57864-361-5 (alk. paper)
 ISBN-10: 1–57864–361–9 (alk. paper)
 1. University of Missouri—Basketball—History. 2. Missouri Tigers (Basketball team)—History. I. Title.
 GV958.U5294A86 2006
 796.323'630977829—dc22

2006009513

**Printed in the United States of America by Walsworth Publishing Company**

# CONTENTS

| | |
|---|---|
| Foreword by Norm Stewart | 6 |
| Introduction | 8 |
| THE EARLY YEARS | 10 |
| THE 1920s | 34 |
| THE 1930s | 56 |
| THE 1940s | 78 |
| THE 1950s | 104 |
| THE 1960s | 130 |
| THE 1970s | 154 |
| THE 1980s | 184 |
| THE 1990s | 218 |
| THE 2000s | 252 |
| Acknowledgments | 280 |
| Index | 281 |
| About the Author | 288 |

# FOREWORD

Do you like basketball? Do you like history? Do you like reading about the history of the Missouri-Kansas basketball rivalry? Do you like to read about a specific year in basketball at Missouri? If you do, you will love Michael Atchison's *True Sons, A Century of Missouri Tigers Basketball*.

When I was reading this account that has been well documented, it became apparent to me — even with my age, historical knowledge, and close contact with the Missouri program for fifty-three years—that the book brings out historical facts, individual situations, and games that I found interesting, amusing, and educational. For instance, did you know that Missouri was judged to be the best team in the country in the days before the national championship was decided by a tournament?

For those of you with some age (like me), you will be reminded of names of players and coaches and you may even remember some of the particular games. I was particularly pleased to read about the beginning history of basketball at Missouri when Brewer, Meanwell, and Ruby were the top names in basketball across the nation.

The first twenty years gave me more insight into the history of Missouri basketball. From the '26 period on, it was a renewal of names that I had the good fortune to know, not just at Missouri, but at the other institutions. Some of those faces I still see and am fortunate enough to have a cup of coffee with on a regular basis. I must admit that with all the enjoyment and appreciation I left a tear on some of the pages.

For the Tiger fan it will bring you back to your days at Mizzou and some great memories of your college experience. For the young fan it will make your future involvement with Tiger basketball more interesting and intense.

I feel, personally, that it is so important to chronicle your history. Michael Atchison has done an outstanding job in doing so about the history of Missouri basketball. This book should give every reader a feeling of belonging to a special part of the University of Missouri.

*Norm Stewart*

# INTRODUCTION

It's hard to imagine it in color. The mind conjures up sepia-toned images of young men, rail-thin and short-haired, wearing canvas sneakers and shooting a brown ball with white laces. They flip it from their waists or push it from their chests, two-handed, and they hit their target only occasionally. Their new gymnasium is an echo chamber. The sound of each bounce of each ball careens off the walls that stand so near the court, a million resounding booms, like cannon fire, adding fanfare to otherwise humble proceedings.

A draft flows through in the dead of winter, but the boys don't mind. They've been hardened by a full season of football, complete with wind, rain, and snow. Anyway, they warm up quickly, running up and down the court, colliding with one another far more than the rules intend. This new game is exotic even to them, but they are getting the hang of it, and they'd better, for they are the University of Missouri basketball team, and their season—their first season—has begun.

Hard to imagine or not, this scene is, in fact, relegated to the realm of imagination. A few black and white stills remain, but there are no sound recordings, no moving pictures, and no survivors. Those who were there are long gone, their memories gone with them. Contemporaneous written descriptions are tantalizing in their incompleteness. It's clear that something happened on those cold Columbia nights, but it's often hard to tell just what, apart from the final scores. The reports are brief and rendered in jargon that is less than descriptive. Beyond that the play was "fast" or "clean" or "hard," we typically know little about any given contest.

So you fill in the gaps in your mind's eye. But before you do, recognize that the game of 1907 bears little resemblance to the one you know today. There was no three-point line, no shot clock, no ten-second rule, and no prohibition on goal-tending. The backboards were wooden, the players were walk-ons, and in an age when prejudice was policy, all of them were white.

One player could shoot all of his team's free throws, which were awarded not only for fouls but for violations like traveling. While he was shooting, the clock continued to run. It always ran, even during the jump balls that followed every single basket. And because a jump ball followed each basket, it behooved a team to have a tall player, say six feet two inches, or better yet, a six-foot-four giant.

Fast-forward one hundred years to a game exploding in colors and sounds. The tiny gym has given way to a massive arena, single paragraph newspaper stories have been replaced by nonstop Internet coverage, and contests that once played to crowds of two hundred can now be seen simultaneously by millions around the world. Over the course of the century as the game has changed, one constant has remained. The proud players in black and gold have been Missouri Tigers.

From the moment Lee Coward sank a three-pointer at the buzzer to beat Kansas in my freshman year at the University of Missouri, I was hooked. I had known Missouri basketball before, especially Norm Stewart's great teams of the early 1980s, with names like Frazier,

Stipanovich, and Sundvold, but nothing prepared me for the overwhelming thrill of being among thirteen thousand frenzied fans as the Tigers upset the Jayhawks and then surged to an unexpected Big Eight title. During those heady days of Mizzou hoops, I'd look into the Hearnes Center rafters and see the retired jerseys and NCAA Tournament banners, and wonder about the program's history. Veteran fans often recalled the brilliance of John Brown and Willie Smith, but rarely did anyone talk about the deeper past. Time and again, I would hear it said that Missouri's tradition began and ended with Norm Stewart. And despite my great admiration for the Tigers' towering basketball legend, I could never believe that was true. Surely there must have been good stories about great players and teams that had receded into history's dark corners. Years later, when I began to dig, a compelling past emerged. There was the day in 1917 when the University hired college basketball's most accomplished coach and watched as his revolutionary style turned the Tigers into the nation's best team. There was the season of 1944 when a kid too young for the draft led a war-torn team into the NCAA Tournament. And there was the night in 1950 when the Tigers marched into Madison Square Garden and routed the reigning national champs, only later to learn that something much darker had happened that evening in New York.

The stories begged to be told, so here they are, tales from each of the first one hundred seasons of Missouri Tigers basketball. Taken together, they reveal a thread that begins in Rothwell Gymnasium in 1907 and winds all the way through the century, connecting men separated by generations. That thread also connects everyone who ever rooted for the Tigers, whether they kicked up dust in Brewer Field House or kicked up their heels in Mizzou Arena, all singing the University of Missouri's great fight song and sharing the values it celebrates—community, hope, and the spirit of competition:

*Every true son, so happy hearted,*
*Skies above us are blue,*
*There's a spirit so deep within us,*
*Old Missouri here's to you,*
*When the band plays the Tiger war song,*
*And when the fray is through,*
*We will tramp, tramp, tramp around the columns,*
*With a cheer for Old Mizzou!*

So here's to all the true sons and daughters of Mizzou—players, coaches, fans—who have built and supported the basketball program, who have shared your joy and tears through heart-stopping wins and heartbreaking losses, and who have kept the faith through a fascinating and sometimes difficult history. This book is for you.

From modest beginnings came magical things. Inside a little gymnasium on the edge of campus, a few young men formed a team and founded a tradition that would provide a century's worth of thrills. The rich history of Missouri Tigers basketball begins with them, players who toiled for little more than the pride of their school and a love of the game, but whose efforts would come to mean more than they could ever have imagined.

# THE Early Years

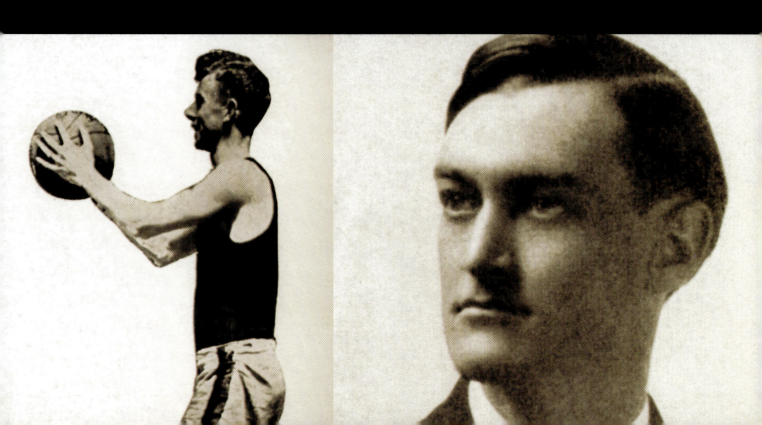

## 1906–07

Though the first Missouri basketball team was formed in Columbia, its seeds were planted 235 miles to the southwest, where Hezekiah "Zeke" Henley, Carl "Curly" Ristine, and John Gardner were teammates on the Joplin YMCA squad. When the freshmen arrived on Mizzou's campus in 1906, they persuaded Clark Hetherington, the university's first athletics director, to sanction a men's basketball team, which would be coached by Isadore Anderson, a graduate student and former Tiger football player who had briefly played in a Kansas City basketball league at the turn of the century. Joined by fellow Joplinites William Driver, William Stava, Albert Moore, and Frank "Pete" Burress and by Fred Bernet (who had played at St. Louis Central High), they became the first men to represent the University of Missouri on the hardwood.

First men, not first students. In 1907 basketball was a minor sport, and most of the hale and hearty Missourians who thought of the game at all considered it a feminine pursuit. Women had been playing basketball at the University of Missouri, or Missouri State University, as it was also known, since 1898. But the game that would be played by men throughout the heartland was anything but ladylike.

By 1906 two sets of rules had evolved. The YMCA game was pure finesse, with prohibitions on physical contact and dribbling; teams moved the ball solely by the pass. But the college game was rough and tumble, often played by men like Ristine and Driver, fresh off the football field. In those primordial days of collegiate hoops, players could rack up a limitless number of personal fouls without disqualification, and they did.

Though several of the Tigers were basketball veterans, they were new to this sort of organized violence, and they had little time to acclimate to it. After a mere week of "intensive limbering up exercises," the inaugural edition of the Missouri Tigers debuted on January 12, 1907, at state-of-the-art Rothwell Gymnasium, whose construction had been completed just months before. Their opponents were the young men of Central College in Fayette, Missouri.

Izzy Anderson settled on a lineup of Henley, Ristine, Bernet, Driver, and Gardner, which could hardly have been more dominant that first day. The Tigers trounced their overmatched opponents 65–5, still one of the most lopsided scores in school history.

Within the starting five, Zeke Henley and Curly Ristine emerged as stars. Ristine typically played center with Henley (a rare one-handed shooter) at forward in the primitive scheme that resembled more modern hockey and soccer formations. Forwards stayed forward and concentrated on offense. Guards stayed back and protected the goal. And the center played in between, forming the link between offense and defense. In the Missouri scheme, Henley and Ristine scored the overwhelming majority of the points, both from the field and by taking turns as the Tigers' designated free throw shooter.

Despite the showing in their first game, the Tigers stumbled early in the season. After the first rousing victory, Missouri lost to Washington University, Kansas City Athletic Club, and Baker University, though Ristine grabbed the attention of the Kansas City press by sinking a game-high seven field goals against KCAC ("the only player [in the game] who did anything exceptional," they said). But from there, the Tigers proved potent. Though a pair of losses was mixed in, they reeled off a

*Isadore Anderson, Mizzou's first coach*

*Rothwell Gymnasium, Missouri basketball's first home*

series of impressive wins, including a 43–18 romp over Warrensburg Normal and a 66–6 demolition of the Fort Riley team. In fact, the Tigers were good enough to merit consideration for a mythical title in their first season of play.

In this time before conference affiliations and national collegiate tournaments, the lone title to play for was that of unofficial state champions. In their first season, the Tigers staked a claim to that title, or at least a share of it. They won five of eight against in-state competition, and in the season's home stretch the Tigers defeated Washington University, Kansas City Athletic Club (a 46–26 thrashing), and Missouri Athletic Club, the only Show Me squads to defeat them during their inaugural campaign.

More than just statewide bragging rights were at stake that first season. The Tigers also battled a new and fierce rival. Though intercollegiate athletics were in their relative infancy, the University of Missouri already had become embroiled in a heated rivalry with the University of Kansas in track and especially football. The Tigers and Jayhawks first met on the gridiron on Halloween 1891, establishing one of the nation's longest-running series. Seven weeks after that first football game, in a gymnasium half a continent away, a gentleman named James Naismith presided over the first game of basketball, an activity he conjured up at the Springfield, Massachusetts, YMCA. Seven years after that, Naismith accepted a faculty appointment at the University of Kansas and organized the first Jayhawk basketball team. His ninth and last season as KU's coach coincided with Missouri's first with a basketball team. And in that final season, Missouri was Naismith's final opponent.

The Jayhawks invaded Columbia for a pair of games. As had been the case all year, Henley and Ristine carried the offense. The first contest, close throughout, was tied late in the game. But a Missouri field goal followed by a Ristine free throw capped a 34–31 Tiger triumph, a game in which Missouri's two stars combined for thirty points. Naismith's swan song came the next day. Again, it was close—for a while. The Tigers led 10–7 at halftime. But the second half, like Missouri's season, belonged to Henley and Ristine. Zeke scored sixteen, and Curly added nine in the Tigers' 34–12 victory. The win left Missouri 2–0 all-time against the game's inventor and helped launch one of the fiercest rivalries in all of sports.

*The inaugural Missouri Tigers basketball team, flanked by Isadore Anderson (left) and Clark Hetherington. Back row: John Gardner, Carl Ristine, William Driver and an unidentified player, likely Frank Burress or William Stava. Front: Fred Bernet, Hezekiah Henley, and Albert Moore.*

*Mills Ebright*

## 1907–08

On January 12, 1907, the same day the Tigers played their very first game, athletics director Clark Hetherington presided over a meeting that helped shape the course of college sports in the Midwest. Though bookish and a tad antisocial, Hetherington possessed a penchant for rules and order and a vision of how the region's top schools could work together for the benefit of all. His idea, almost certainly inspired by the formation of the Big Ten or "Western Conference" a decade before, was to organize the preeminent athletics programs across the plains. And so he called a meeting at Kansas City's Midland Hotel. After some squabbling over rules, including mandates making freshmen ineligible for varsity competition and limiting eligibility to three seasons, the University of Missouri, along with Washington University of St. Louis and the Universities of Kansas, Nebraska, and Iowa, formed the Missouri Valley Conference. Though Iowa's membership proved fleeting, Iowa State and Drake soon joined the Valley and became stable members. When the Tigers began preparations for their second basketball season, their goal was to win a conference title.

Those preparations came under the eye of Mills Ebright, Mizzou's baseball coach, who took on the additional duty when Hetherington assigned Izzy Anderson to lead the university's intramural program in hopes of developing varsity basketball talent. Ebright's work was made easier when the previous team returned almost entirely intact (exit Albert Moore, enter Dorcet Grimes), including all five starters. The Tigers' experience paid dividends when they started the season with five straight wins over nonconference foes, including a 75–11 destruction of Rolla's Missouri School of Mines. Despite the success, the ambivalence with which basketball was initially greeted is reflected in the January 17, 1908, entry in the year in review printed in the *Savitar*, Mizzou's yearbook: "Tigers beat Rolla at basketball along here sometime; everybody too busy to notice." The Tigers actually had met the Miners more than a month earlier than that.

If the students failed to take the team seriously, the press at least made an effort, though not always much of one. In those days, sports got a page in the newspaper, not a section, and games got a paragraph, not a series of stories. Unlike today, when beat writers devote themselves entirely to a single team, newspapers relied on telegraph messages from spectators or school officials, messages that could be a bit inaccurate, as illustrated by the *Columbia Daily Tribune*'s coverage of Missouri's January 30 game against Iowa. In a four-sentence story, the *Tribune* reported that the Tigers "had it their way from start to finish" in a 16–6 victory, but noted that St. Louis papers reported a 46–15 defeat. Unfortunately, the St. Louis papers had it right.

The Iowa loss was the second game in a terrible skid. The Tigers, who had won twelve of thirteen games dating to the previous season, failed to beat any of their new conference rivals in eight tries. Four of those losses came against a Kansas team coached by a twenty-two-year-old Missouri expatriate who replaced James Naismith. Forrest C. "Phog" Allen, Jamesport native and Independence High graduate, had played for Naismith at KU. Though his first stint as Jayhawk coach would be brief, the fiery Phog would prove to be Missouri's greatest nemesis for nearly half a century.

# 1908–09

Changes were afoot in Columbia. After helping to grow enrollment to more than twenty-three hundred, longtime MU President Richard Jesse, for whom the university's signature building is named, retired in summer 1908. Then, in September, the university's new journalism school began holding classes. Shortly thereafter, when basketball practice started, a new man took charge. Out went Mills Ebright, who moved to Kansas to become the Jayhawks' baseball coach. In came Guy Lowman, who replaced Ebright on the diamond and the hardwood.

It also was a time of passage for Missouri's basketball players. At a time when players provided more stability than did coaches, Zeke Henley and Carl Ristine had been stalwarts. Henley and Ristine also brought honor to the university through other pursuits. They teamed up to win the Missouri Valley tennis doubles title, and Ristine, a six-foot, 168-pound center, captained the Tigers to a 7–0–1 record and the 1909 Valley football championship. Henley went on to become a high school teacher and coach, while Ristine enjoyed a successful law practice that eventually took him to Washington, where he served as assistant attorney general of the United States.

The Tigers appeared formidable in the final season for Henley, Ristine, and fellow charter members Gardner, Bernet, and Stava, a quintet that had the benefit of years of experience playing together. The promise was evident after three wins to start the year, the third coming in a 53–14 whipping of Iowa State, then better known as Ames College. From there, the Tigers topped all competition save for Washington University (the Tigers lost two on Washington's tiny court) and conference champ Kansas, which took three of four from Mizzou. The rivalry with Kansas helped raise interest in a game that previously had been so vigorously ignored. Fans packed temporary bleachers and dangled from the overhead track that ringed the Rothwell Gymnasium court. Though the fans

*Guy Lowman was Missouri's third coach in three seasons.*

were disappointed with the first of two contests in Columbia, they were thrilled by the second, a 37–21 trouncing of Kansas that marked the first time the Tigers had beaten Phog Allen and the last time they would face him for several years. At age twenty-three, Allen left coaching to study osteopathic medicine. He would return.

The Tigers wrapped up their year—and the careers of The Originals—with two games against Washington University in Rothwell. The Pikers had done much to derail Mizzou's hopes in the Valley race by sweeping a pair in St. Louis a month earlier. The Tigers aimed to return the favor against the only team with a chance to catch Kansas for the conference crown. In the first game, Zeke Henley starred with fourteen points in a 36–16 victory. Carl Ristine, who would be named All-Valley at season's end, took his turn the next night. As Henley fouled out of the last game of his career, Curly picked up his brother in arms, scoring sixteen in a hard-fought 28–21 triumph that gave Mizzou eleven wins on the year, the highest total in the team's brief history. But with the Joplin gang headed toward graduation, it would be like starting over for the Tigers of 1910.

### 1909–10

Coach Guy Lowman came back for a second season, but most of his key players were gone. Herman Cohen and Frank Burress returned, and they were joined by Ted Hackney, Tiger football star. Despite the turnover, the season started well as Mizzou won seven of its first nine, setting up two important games with 8–0 Kansas.

The series came two and a half months after the football season finale, the most important game to date in the border pigskin rivalry. Both teams entered the Thanksgiving battle undefeated, Missouri at 6–0–1 and Kansas at 8–0. Recent history favored the Jayhawks, who had not lost to the Tigers in their previous seven contests (six wins, one tie). But Missouri reversed the tide that day at Kansas City's Association Park. Kansas quarterback Tommy Johnson played brilliantly, but Hackney, Mizzou's all-conference back, played hero. His two dropkick field goals helped propel the Tigers to a 12–6 victory, a Valley title, an undefeated season, and bragging rights over the Jayhawks.

When the schools renewed the rivalry on the hardwood, Hackney and Johnson were in uniform. They picked up where they left off in November, with Hackney tackling Johnson in the first game and rough play prevailing throughout. It was a far cry from the game James Naismith invented, one that emphasized finesse and forbade physical contact. One story, perhaps apocryphal, has Naismith attending the second contest and exclaiming, "Oh, my gracious! They are murdering my game!" as he took in the carnage. Unfortunately, bumps and bruises were all the Tigers had

*Carl "Curly" Ristine, Mizzou's first all-conference basketball player*

*Frank Burress captained the Tigers in 1909–10.*

to show for their efforts. Kansas, behind Johnson's standout play, won both meetings en route to its third straight Valley title.

The Kansas series marked a jarring turning point in Missouri's season. Though they would beat Drake in their next outing, the Tigers would not win after that. They dropped seven straight to close the season and the brief Lowman era.

# 1910–11

In the early twentieth century, coaches were like carpetbaggers, moving from one job to the next, rarely staying long. After the 1910 season, Guy Lowman went from Missouri to Alabama to Kansas State and then to somewhere else—and probably somewhere else after that. Rarely did a coach establish roots in a community. Chester Brewer was different. Through two stays as athletics director and an even longer stint on faculty, Brewer would weave himself into the fabric of Mizzou.

A four-sport star at the University of Wisconsin, the Michigan-born Brewer returned to his native state in 1903, serving as athletics director and coach of football, baseball, and basketball at Michigan Agricultural College (now Michigan State). Then in 1910 at age thirty-four, he arrived in Columbia, where he filled the same four roles for the University of Missouri. His warmth, leadership, and vision (among other achievements, Brewer invented homecoming) provided stability and ushered in a remarkably successful era for Missouri athletics.

As Missouri's basketball coach, Brewer had decent talent with which to work, including seniors Herman Cohen and Frank Burress (each an All-Valley performer) and a savvy, broad-shouldered sophomore guard from Kansas City named George Edwards, an excellent defender who was just beginning a long and storied relationship with Mizzou.

The Tigers' schedule was unlike any before or since. It featured a total of twelve games against just three teams, four contests apiece with Kansas, Iowa State, and Nebraska. More than anything, the limited slate proved that the Tigers weren't as good as league champion Kansas, which swept the season series, extending its winning streak against Missouri to eight straight games and fifteen of the previous sixteen. Mizzou took three of four from a quality Nebraska squad and split with Iowa State, each team defending its home court. All in all, Chet Brewer's first season at Mizzou was unremarkable, his team posting a 5–7 record. That would turn out to be Brewer's career mark at Missouri.

*Chester Brewer arrived at the University of Missouri in 1910, the beginning of a long and storied career.*

*Herman Cohen*

## 1911–12

After a year of coaching three sports and running the athletics department, Chester Brewer turned basketball and baseball coaching duties over to young O. F. Field, Missouri's fifth coach in six seasons. Not only did the Tiger players have to introduce themselves to their new coach, they had to introduce themselves to each other. When practice commenced in the fall of 1911, team captain Joe Parker, a forward, was the only hold-over from the previous squad.

The new men formed a cohesive unit and appeared ready when the season tipped off before fans who paid thirty-five cents for admission (fifty cents for reserved seats) at Rothwell Gym to see Mizzou take on Washburn, coached by original Tiger William Driver. Missouri center Harry Snodgrass starred in a rough affair won by the home team 26–17. A two-game sweep of Ames put Missouri at 3–0 as the Tigers got off to their typical hot start.

Then came the equally typical turn. The Tigers traveled to Washington University and got waxed twice just before a three-week break between semesters. They got some good news over the hiatus when George Edwards returned to school after taking a semester off. Unfortunately, his return paid no immediate dividend as three losses in three days (one to Warrensburg, two to Kansas) extended Missouri's slide to five games. Some stiff defense helped Mizzou win two of its next three, as did the shooting of emerging star George Taaffe, a sophomore forward. The reversal in fortunes was short-lived.

*George Taaffe was a gifted shooter.*

Missouri dropped its final four games by mostly lopsided scores to finish with a 5–10 mark, the Tigers' third straight losing season.

## 1912–13

Coach Field came back to try to reverse the losing trend. He was joined by two contributors from the previous squad, one offensive standout, George Taaffe, and one defensive stopper, George Edwards, each of whom would make the All-Valley team. Three newcomers rounded out the starting lineup: Milton Bernet, an offensively skilled center; Cleo Craig, a forward and the team's third scoring option; and George "Pip" Palfreyman, whose great speed and agility made him a uniquely gifted defender.

Again the Tigers opened the season with a winning streak, taking four games from three opponents before hosting the Valley's newest member, Kansas State Agricultural College. Former Tiger mentor Guy Lowman led the Aggies into Columbia and handed Mizzou its first two losses of the season. In past years, such a stumble inevitably led to a downward spiral, and there was reason to expect it to happen again. After opening with six straight home games, the Tigers embarked on their only road trip of the season, a grueling stretch that saw them cover twelve hundred miles and play seven games in eleven days. But first, Coach Field took advantage of a break in the schedule and traveled to Grand Rapids, Michigan, where he took a bride, marrying Miss Ida Childs. The nuptials seemed to bring the team some luck.

The first stop was St. Louis, where the Tigers faced Washington, which had beaten Missouri seven straight times on its home court. But the Tigers rolled, winning by eighteen in the first contest and twenty-five in the second. Next came Ames, Iowa, where Mizzou again prevailed by a lopsided score in game one, routing the Cyclones 33–13. Game two was more competitive and controversial. When the second half ended, the official score showed the game tied at 23 apiece. But before the overtime period began, an Ames mathematics professor "came down from the bleachers and stated that he had kept score and that Ames was ahead by one point. After much discussion the referee announced that the professor's word could not be doubted so the game was given to Ames by the score of 24 to 23."

Field's squad moved on to Manhattan for a rematch with the Kansas Aggies. The Tigers prevailed by a point, earning their fourth win in five tries on the road. Then they headed for their final stop, Lawrence, Kansas.

The enmity that had become the central feature of the Missouri-Kansas rivalry reared its head again. Throughout the two games, Kansas players complained of being fouled by the Tigers, but the officials had none of it. Unsatisfied with the referees' response, Kansas engaged in some frontier justice, as one Jayhawk knocked Palfreyman from the game with an elbow to the gut—a maneuver greeted with cheers from the home crowd. Led by the brilliant Ralph "Lefty" Sproull, Kansas took both contests, extending its winning streak against Mizzou to fourteen games. Still, the Tigers returned home with some hopes of winning the Valley's southern division (over Kansas, Kansas State, and Washington). The overall title was conceded to undefeated Nebraska, a team not on the Tigers' schedule.

Mizzou opened the final home stand by taking three straight—two from Washington University and one from William Jewell—to set up the season's final series, a pair of games with nemesis Kansas. Pip Palfreyman, with a one-hander from close range, opened the scoring in the first game as Missouri rushed to a 6–0 lead. The Tigers maintained that six-point lead through much of the game, which featured a head-to-head match-up between George Edwards and Jayhawk Loren "Red" Brown, erstwhile teammates at Kansas City's Central High. Edwards got the better of Brown, and Mizzou got the better of Kansas, winning by a final 26–20 score and setting up a climactic finale.

The Tigers entered with a chance to tie Kansas for southern division honors, but the Jayhawks were in no mood to share. In fact, the Jayhawks seemed to be in an overall foul mood, as demonstrated by Red Brown, who was held out of game two because of his rough play the previous night. While seated at the scorer's table, his demonstrative behavior drew heckles from the Mizzou partisans. On the court, the Jayhawks opened up an early lead in the year's roughest game. Mizzou rallied in the second half, but Kansas held on to win 34–26.

At 12–6 overall, Missouri enjoyed its best record in four years and finally emerged as a contender in the Valley. But taking the next step would be hard without George Edwards, who completed a stellar career. His defensive effort kept the Tigers, a team lacking great firepower, in games throughout the year. Without him, George Taaffe, who led the team with 9.9 points per game, and the rest of the Tigers would have to try to outscore the opposition. As they would discover, that would be a tall order.

*Speedy George "Pip" Palfreyman*

*A standout player, George Edwards became one of the most enduring figures in Missouri basketball history.*

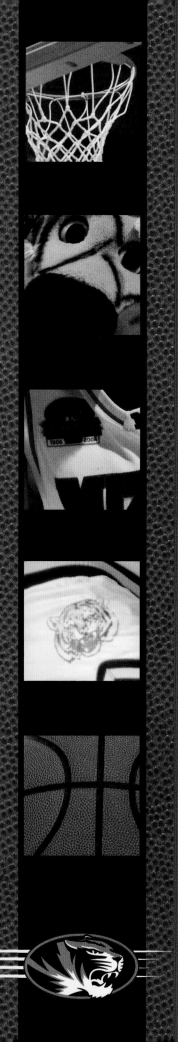

## 1913–14

The University of Missouri celebrated its seventy-fifth anniversary in 1914, at the end of a quarter century that had seen it come into its own as an institution, growing from five hundred students to thirty-four hundred in just twenty-five years. Chester Brewer's football Tigers jump-started the diamond jubilee by capturing the 1913 Missouri Valley championship. A similar feat by the basketball team would have pushed mere celebration to sheer hysteria. Unfortunately, they missed the title by a country mile.

Thank goodness for Ames. The Tigers, in Coach Field's final season, won just four of sixteen starts—and three victories came against Iowa State. Two of those were in the season's opening series, wins that might have caused spectators to mistake the Tigers for contenders. George Taaffe tallied ten first-half points in the opener as Missouri won 32–19. The next day, John Cheek and Francis Brodie, two young men from Kansas City, which had supplanted Joplin as fertile ground for future Tigers, starred in a 36–9 trouncing of the Cyclones. Mizzou moved to 3–0 with a nine-point victory over Washington University, but the seeds of disaster had been sown. The Tigers played without Taaffe and Brodie, who had been declared ineligible for the remainder of the season. Taaffe was Missouri's best player, and Brodie was a solid contributor. The Tigers had little depth even with those players; without them, the team appeared headed for trouble.

They found it at every turn. Milton "Snooks" Bernet assumed the captaincy vacated by Taaffe, and he went down with the ship. The decline began with the second Washington game, a 23–15 loss, then a pair of single-digit losses to Kansas. The second time the Jayhawks beat Mizzou, they exploited the Tigers' paltry depth; though Missouri had led most of the way, Kansas sped past the Tigers in the closing minutes after Bernet and Pip Palfreyman fouled out. The Tigers then traveled to Ames and split a pair

*An early Missouri-Kansas meeting in Rothwell Gym*

*The 1913–14 Tigers, coached by O. F. Field (back row, far right)*

with the Cyclones, but they would not win again. Over a span of eleven days, Kansas State took four games from Mizzou, while Kansas twice whipped the Tigers in Lawrence. Missouri closed the year with two sound defeats at Washington's hands, making eight straight losses, the longest streak—winning or losing—in the program's history to date. By almost any measure, the 1914 season was the worst one yet for the Tigers. But the arrival of two men, one a coach and the other a player, would help to create an abrupt change in Mizzou's fortunes.

# 1914–15

First and foremost, he was an athlete. His three collegiate letters in both track and football testified to that. But his physique was tailor-made for basketball, his six-foot-two-inch, 220-pound frame nearly perfect for a center. In fact, he was among the nation's finest players at any position. And when he stepped onto the court for his first practice as Missouri's coach, he commanded his team's attention.

Eugene Van Gent's first job out of college was as head coach of the Missouri basketball team. Despite his youth, the Ottumwa, Iowa, native possessed an impeccable resume. In his three seasons at the University of Wisconsin, the Badgers won forty-four games against just one loss and captured three Big Ten titles. For his part, Van Gent twice was named all-conference, and as a senior, he was the most outstanding player on the nation's most outstanding team. But perhaps his most impressive credential came from playing for a uniquely brilliant coach. Van Gent's three years at Wisconsin had come under the tutelage of Walter Meanwell, who helped transform the game by introducing an offense that featured short, precise passing and that wore down defenses not used to such disciplined maneuvering. It also

*Upon arriving from Wisconsin, Eugene Van Gent turned the Tigers into winners.*

produced far better shots than conventional schemes that relied on long passes and thirty-foot heaves toward the basket. In addition to this revolutionary offense, Van Gent brought a thoroughness of preparation previously unseen in the Valley when he introduced advance scouting to the league.

The futility of the 1914 season might have suggested otherwise, but a fair collection of talent awaited Van Gent and the "Wisconsin style," as it was known. Though George Palfreyman spent the first semester at home recuperating from typhoid fever, several others returned in good health, including forwards John Wear and Manuel Drumm and junior guards Jake Speelman and Harley Hyde, a flamboyant player oft described as "dashing" and "reckless." Still, Missouri's fortunes hinged on a newcomer, a player Van Gent could mold in his own image. Sophomore center Fred Williams possessed a combination of size and athleticism unlike any previously seen in Columbia but similar to the traits his coach displayed at Wisconsin. A gifted long-range shooter, Mizzou's new center was a high jumper on the Tiger track team, and his vertical leap would prove invaluable, with jump balls following every basket.

The Tigers quickly absorbed Van Gent's teachings, but the new style confounded onlookers. And though they might not have fully understood the Wisconsin style, they became intrigued when Van Gent unveiled it in a scrimmage between the varsity and freshman squads, a contest taken 50–11 by the A team. Though local scribes lamented that "some mighty good chances look to be passed up by this style of play," they did acknowledge its effectiveness.

Van Gent's official debut came when the Tigers hosted Tarkio College. Even without Palfreyman, Missouri overwhelmed its guests by using short passes to navigate the defense for point blank shots en route to a 20–2 halftime lead. The new coach cleared his bench in the second half as the Tigers cruised to a 29–11 victory behind ten points from John Wear. The next day, Mizzou completed its nonconference schedule with a 39–23 triumph over Central College, two of the Tigers' points coming when a disoriented Central player deposited the ball in his own goal. The Tigers, on the other hand, maintained their wits and opened up the offense, unleashing some long cross-court passes to Wear and Drumm for easy baskets.

With Palfreyman back in the fold, the Tigers won their first four Valley contests, including a pair against the Kansas Aggies, en route to an 8–6 record. Fred Williams

*The dashing and reckless Harley Hyde*

excelled in those wins over Kansas State while Jake Speelman put on an exceptional defensive display in Manhattan. But the most valuable Tiger at Nichols Gymnasium was John Wear. When the final gun sounded at the end of the second game, Missouri led 20–19. But referee Ernest Quigley called a double foul as time expired and awarded each team a free throw. When Wear sank Missouri's shot—the last of his team-high eleven points—the Tigers clinched a 21–19 victory. The Tigers also demolished Washington University 52–18, their first fifty-point effort in six years. Four of Missouri's six losses were routs at the hands of a dominant Kansas team led by three-time Valley scoring champ Ralph Sproull. Those defeats left the Tigers 4–30 against Kansas all-time as the Jayhawks made a mockery of the rivalry between the schools.

## 1915–16

When Van Gent returned for his second season, his team included a mix of savvy veterans and precocious youngsters. Three seniors—Speelman, Wear, and Hyde—provided stability, while two sophomores—Jesse "Mule" Campbell and Sam Shirkey—infused the team with talent and energy. But Missouri's linchpin was prodigiously skilled junior Fred Williams. In 1916 the Tigers would travel as far as Williams could carry them.

Graduation had taken George Palfreyman from the team, but not from the game. When the season opened, Pip sat on the opposing bench with the Maryville Normal School team. More than any other rival coach, Palfreyman understood Missouri's novel offensive scheme, and Maryville trailed by just three points at intermission. But Sam Shirkey added a new dimension to the Tiger attack, though one not in keeping with the spirit of the Wisconsin offense, when he sank a pair of thirty-footers en route to twelve points in a 49–25 win.

When the Tigers opened the conference slate before two thousand fans in Rothwell Gym, they began to make a habit of over-

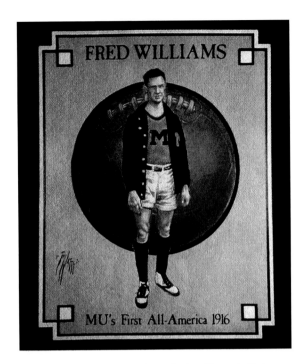

*The brilliant Fred Williams (here depicted by artist Ted Watts) became Missouri's first All-American.*

whelming opponents. Missouri held Washington without a first-half field goal before cruising to a 44–21 victory behind sixteen points from Fred Williams. Then, after picking up two relatively easy wins at Ames, Mizzou returned home for a stretch of games that announced Van Gent's men as serious contenders in the Valley.

They began by rolling to a 24–2 halftime lead against Central College before the reserves came in to close out a 44–19 victory. Mizzou's dominant play "made it seem that there were twice as many Tigers on the court as Central players." Then, after a lengthy semester break, Missouri hosted Kansas, which had thoroughly dominated the Tigers for eight years.

Mizzou got its long-awaited win (by the score of 30–24) in the first of a two-game series, but it was the effort on day two that inspired the *Columbia Daily Tribune* to run one of history's giddiest leads: "Playing the scrubs against Kansas! Fond dream, thou art real at last!" With Hyde and Speelman keying a relentless defensive effort, Missouri raced to a 25–5 halftime lead, after which the starters remained on the bench while the reserves cruised in a 42–20 win. More than at any other time since Van Gent's arrival, the Kansas thrashing opened the eyes

of Missouri's followers to the possibilities of the Wisconsin style. Wrote the *Tribune*:

> So fast and breathless was the play that time was taken out to tie shoe laces and adjust knee pads (and incidentally to gulp some air) twice in the first half. The Missourians, using the rapid fire, short pass game introduced here by Eugene Van Gent, wore down the antagonists, forced Kansas to the defensive, and hammered the defense till it cracked and opened avenues of attack undreamed of by the fondest rooters.

With the Tigers still undefeated in the Valley and with the season's end just two weeks away, thoughts turned to the Nebraska problem. When it came to basketball, the University of Nebraska was the most enigmatic member of the MVC. Nebraska's court at Grant Memorial Hall, narrow and obstructed by pillars, gave the Cornhuskers the conference's greatest home court advantage, an edge that had helped them win three of the previous four Valley titles. In the 1916 season, Nebraska tried to milk that advantage for its full worth. While agreeing to travel to play Drake and Ames, Nebraska refused to play the league's better teams away from Lincoln. Kansas and Kansas State capitulated, eventually agreeing to play on Nebraska's floor without return engagements. But Missouri, stubborn as the state's symbolic mule, refused. Accordingly, when the conference schedule came out, it failed to include any Missouri-Nebraska contests. Normally, no significant consequences would flow from that quirk in the slate, but as Missouri made its march through the Valley, Nebraska matched the Tigers win for win, creating the possibility that the conference race would end in a most unsatisfying tie.

*John Wear captained Missouri's 1915–16 squad.*

Before they could win that title, the Tigers would have to put forth an exceptional effort over the season's final six games, all on the road against Washington, Kansas State, and Kansas. The Tigers crept closer to a perfect Valley record with two wins over Washington in St. Louis and set up a grueling five-day swing through the Sunflower State, where Mizzou would play the season's final four games. With Nebraska continuing to feast on cream puffs, Missouri would almost certainly need a sweep to stake a claim to Valley preeminence. Unfortunately, hopes for such an outcome were dashed immediately in Manhattan when Kansas State held the Tigers scoreless until Fred Williams sank a field goal twelve minutes into a contest that Mizzou ultimately lost 27–19. But the resilient Tigers rebounded the next day for a 22–10 win that kept a sliver of hope alive. Though no longer in the driver's seat, Mizzou remained defiant when it came to the question of running Nebraska's obstacle course of a court in a playoff. The Tigers expressed interest in playing, but not on the Huskers' terms.

After the K-State series, Van Gent and company got just one day off before facing their archrivals in Lawrence. During that brief respite, they seemed to find the offense that had gone AWOL in Manhattan. In game one, Fred Williams scored twenty-four as Mizzou whipped Kansas in a 41–10 triumph that inspired students to spill into Columbia's streets to celebrate when the result reached campus by wire. But the Tigers' offense again abandoned them the next day. Missouri made just three field goals in a shattering 31–19 loss.

After completing the season with two losses in the Valley, Mizzou held little leverage in trying to force a playoff with Nebraska, which completed a perfect record in conference play. Nonetheless, the athletic department sent a letter to Lincoln to gauge the Cornhuskers' interest in a best-of-three series. A terse reply came back: "Our season is over and we do not care to schedule additional games." Nebraska's decision forced Mizzou to settle for second place.

Despite coming up short, Missouri's tenth basketball season proved to be its best. Fan interest surged, and the Tigers netted a $600.52 profit for the season, more than double the money made the previous year. The fans who filled the coffers were drawn inside Rothwell by the finest assemblage of talent yet to wear the black and gold, a fact recognized when Hyde and Campbell earned second team All-Valley honors, while Speelman made the first team and Williams became Mizzou's first All-American. Indeed, in the eyes of those who followed the league, the sensational Williams was "undoubtedly the best individual player in the Missouri Valley Conference, if not in the west." With Williams, Campbell, and Shirkey set to return the next season and with the Wisconsin system so fully implemented, the Tigers seemed on the verge of capturing the long-elusive title. But just as the season came to a close, Missouri's hopes for the future took a startling blow.

## 1916–17

On March 2, 1916, just two days after Missouri completed its best season ever, Eugene Van Gent, the architect of the Tigers' success, resigned, lured to the University of Texas by a $2,500 salary and the chance to serve as athletics director and coach of the basketball, football, and track teams. Mizzou turned to John F. Miller, a former athletics director at Kemper Military Academy, who had briefly played professional baseball. Miller, also a baseball assistant and freshman football coach, picked up where Van Gent left off.

The schedule favored the Tigers, with only six games away from Rothwell—two apiece at Kansas, Nebraska, and Washington University. For the first time in five years, Mizzou's itinerary did not include a trip to Manhattan, Kansas. The Tigers' only meeting with the Aggies would be a two-game set in Columbia just before season's end.

Fred Williams kicked off his senior campaign with twenty-one points in a 47–21 win over Central College. While that effort was sensational, his next was heroic. The Ames Cyclones blew into Rothwell Gym to open Valley play and took a 17–14 lead to intermission. In the second half, though, Williams overcame a badly sprained ankle to score six points in the closing minutes of a 28–25 victory.

*Coach John Miller*

The pain proved too much the next night. With their star on the bench, the Tigers failed to muster much offensive punch. The Cyclones' 24–21 victory dealt an early blow to Missouri's title hopes. A week later, despite fears that the sprain would continue to shelve him, Williams scored sixteen points against Washington. Harry Viner also proved valuable in the 36–22 rout, burying long shots and disrupting Washington's offense.

Over the next several weeks, Mizzou was nearly unbeatable. A one-point loss at Kansas was the only stumble through the middle part of the schedule, a stretch that saw the Tigers thrice beat the Jayhawks while sweeping a pair from Nebraska in Lincoln. But the Tigers suffered some attrition. Paul "Deerfoot" Vogt, a lanky forward/center who tallied eighteen points in a rout of Kansas City Polytechnic, fell ill in February and was lost for the season's duration.

Still, the Tigers, paced by Williams, a member of the All-Valley team and the league's leading scorer, and Jesse "Mule" Campbell, a long-armed forward who starred in wins over Kansas, remained formidable—so formidable that as the season snaked toward its climax, the Tigers and the Kansas Aggies were locked in a race for the championship. And Missouri held an advantage. The season's penultimate two-game series, the Tigers' only confrontation with the Aggies, would be in Columbia.

Referee Ernest Quigley called it "the best game on [the Rothwell] court for a long time." It was a fast, physical affair with many trips to the free throw line and several stoppages to allow players to gather their wits. And though the caliber of play was high, the result was disappointing. Despite fourteen points from Williams, the Aggies took a 26–22 win and command of the MVC race. To have any chance at the crown, the Tigers would need to win game two. For a while, it looked like they would. As always, Missouri relied on Williams's scoring touch,

*Missouri's "Mule," Jesse Campbell*

using it to optimum effect in building a 20–13 halftime lead. But Kansas State's defense turned oppressive in the second stanza. The Aggie guards overwhelmed Missouri's forwards, forcing wild shots from near midcourt. Kansas State clinched the title by racing past the Tigers in the final twenty minutes en route to a 32–27 win. It was the first in a series of disappointments the Tigers would suffer at the hands of their second fiercest rival.

Still, excitement built in Columbia. The teams of 1915, 1916, and 1917 had produced the first consecutive winning seasons the basketball program had known. Their accomplishments, however, were but prologue to the stunning success of the next five seasons— arguably the best five-year run in Missouri history.

## 1917–18

Few athletes are as largely forgotten as those who played basketball before World War II. Everyone knows legends from other fields of play: Babe Ruth, Red Grange, Joe Louis. But ask even a knowledgeable basketball fan to name a handful of great prewar players and you're likely to receive a blank stare.

There are good reasons for this, not the least of which is basketball was a second-tier game in those days, far less popular than baseball, college football, or boxing. It also lacked a national stage, with the NIT and the NCAA Tournament coming into existence only in 1938 and 1939, respectively. Finally, and no less important, players from that era have been eradicated from the record books. Slower play, shorter seasons, and freshman ineligibility guaranteed this. Players simply could not score enough points during games, seasons, or careers to compete with more recent athletes, and statistics like rebounds and assists were not officially kept. This amnesia is unfortunate, especially for Missouri basketball loyalists, because the Tiger players of that era rank among the most accomplished in school history.

Yet more anonymous than the players of that era are its coaches, even the great ones. As evidence, try asking Missouri fans to name a coach who took over the Tiger program in his early thirties. Some will pick Quin Snyder, who arrived in Columbia in 1999 after serving as an assistant at Duke. Others might choose Norm Stewart, who returned to his alma mater in 1967 after six years as head coach at the State College of Iowa. But few—probably none—will mention Walter Meanwell, who became Missouri's coach in 1917 at age thirty-three. That is more than a little ironic because while Snyder and Stewart came to Columbia looking to build legacies at a major program, Meanwell arrived already established as the finest coach in the brief history of college basketball.

Born in England but raised in Rochester, New York, Walter Meanwell earned a medical degree and a Ph.D. by age thirty-one. A diminutive man with a winning smile, a fierce temper, and a salty vocabulary, the Little Doctor first made his mark in sports as a champion amateur boxer and wrestler. He never played basketball. Nonetheless, after an apprenticeship limited to teaching the game to poor Baltimore youth, he assumed the role of head basketball coach at the University of Wisconsin in 1911 at age twenty-seven. His inexperience was neither uncommon nor detrimental. Basketball was still new, and few coaches were truly schooled in the sport. The game tended to be chaotic. It featured long passes, half-court shots, and little teamwork. But when Meanwell turned his scientific eye toward the rough-and-tumble game, he quickly displayed the trait that would make him one of basketball's earliest legends—the ability to create order out of chaos.

Doc Meanwell's philosophy was built on a simple premise: it is better to shoot from near the basket than far away. Though this now seems indisputably true, it was an unorthodox approach in the game's early days. At a time when the prevailing wisdom called for players to hone their shots from twenty-five feet or more, Meanwell devised strategies to work the ball close to the basket and to find shots from five or ten feet. In so doing, Meanwell's inexperience with basketball actually may have been a benefit. Unbound by convention, he looked to sports he knew—boxing, wrestling, gymnastics—and injected their movements into the newer game. Thus, he revolutionized basketball by having all five of his players participate in an organized offense, controlling the ball, setting screens, making short passes, and working the ball through a pivot player in the center of the floor. These devices, combined with crisscross weaves, allowed Meanwell's offenses to break down opposing defenses and create better shots. In contrast, his defensive schemes—Meanwell was a pioneer of the zone—pushed opposing offenses farther and farther from the basket.

This brave new style paid immediate dividends. Meanwell's Wisconsin team won the Big Ten conference title in 1912, his second season, and again in 1913, 1914, and 1916. Even more impressive, historians have unanimously declared the 1912, 1914, and 1916 teams mythical national champions. Meanwell's Badgers posted a remarkable 102–9 record from 1911 to 1917. One historical observer notes that "by the end of Meanwell's third season at Wisconsin, there was no longer any doubt that he had not only the best team in the country but the best system yet for playing the game."

Even during his years at Wisconsin, Meanwell's influence pervaded the Missouri program, beginning in 1915 when his protégé, Eugene Van Gent, took over as Tiger coach and implemented the Wisconsin short passing game. Meanwell's influence, though powerful, was nothing compared with his presence, which helped propel Missouri into college basketball's elite.

"The best man in the world." That's how Chester Brewer described his newly named successor after Brewer decided to return to Michigan Agricultural College. Doctor Walter E. Meanwell arrived in Columbia in 1917, lured from the University of Wisconsin by the chance to replace Brewer as Missouri's director of athletics as well as assume duties as the Tigers'

basketball coach. John Miller, after one season as at the helm, focused on his many other duties in the athletic department, which would soon include being head coach of the football team.

Miller left behind a core of players, including Mule Campbell, Clyde Slusher, and Sam Shirkey, that all but guaranteed success for Meanwell. Such a trio of talented and experienced players was rare in fall 1917. America had entered the First World War in April, and as the Army's rolls swelled, the university's shrank. Though many college-aged men were engaged in the war effort, the quality—if not quantity—of men available to Doc Meanwell was exceptional. Those men also proved adaptable, as the coach shifted their positions to put the best five on the floor at a time when reserves were rarely used. Campbell, a forward throughout his career, moved to center to replace the departed Fred Williams. Shirkey remained at forward and Slusher at "defensive guard," while Leslie Wackher, a forward on the 1917 freshman squad, took over at "floor guard" after the incumbent Harry Viner was called to duty in the Army early in the season. And while Meanwell undoubtedly benefited from these returning players (and they from him), it was the addition of one new player that helped push Missouri past its competition. Craig Ruby, a guard-turned-forward from Kansas City's Westport High, would become the team's floor leader and one of the greatest Tigers of all-time.

The Tigers appeared invincible early in the season, every bit as good as Meanwell's Wisconsin teams. The year began with a 52–12 thrashing of Henry Kendall College (now the University of Tulsa), followed by a fifteen-point win over Kansas City Polytechnic Institute. Mule Campbell led Missouri with twelve points against KC Poly in a game played in quarters (Poly's custom) in a first half officiated by John Miller and in one continuous second half (Valley standard) officiated by once and future Kansas coach Phog Allen, a frequent referee at Missouri games.

The conference slate began much the same as the Tigers manhandled Drake 27–8, one of three times they would hold an opponent to single digits. Campbell, with fourteen points, outscored the entire visiting squad, while the sophomore Ruby added eight. But any illusions of invincibility vanished in the second of the two-game set when the Tigers trailed until the last five minutes. Late buckets by Ruby, Shirkey, and Wackher gave Missouri a 19–17 victory. One narrow escape begat two more as the Tigers traveled to St. Louis and took a pair of three-point victories over Washington University.

Those wins put Missouri at 6–0 overall and 4–0 in the Valley, a half game ahead of second-place Kansas, which stood 4–1 as it prepared to host the Tigers for a pair of games. Despite trailing Missouri in the standings, the Kansans were confident. While the Tigers had squeaked past Drake 19–17, Kansas had annihilated the Bulldogs 64–24, and Jayhawks fans could hardly contain their glee at the prospect of handing Missouri twin beatings. In the process they gave the Tigers some primitive bulletin board material in the form of a quote from the *Kansas City Star*: "Missouri, although leading the conference is doomed to drop into third place [behind Kansas and Kansas State] next week when the Tigers invade Lawrence for two games in Robinson Gymnasium. At least that is the viewpoint of the Jayhawker followers."

But the Tigers offered an opposing viewpoint and swept Kansas on its home court. The Jayhawks surged to a 7–0 lead early in game one as the Tigers failed to hit a field goal until Mule Campbell, the agriculture major from Odessa, Missouri, sank a shot eleven minutes into the game. But once they got warmed up, the Tigers overwhelmed Kansas with short, precise passes. In the end, Campbell, Ruby, and Shirkey combined for thirty-four points in a 36–22 win.

Game two was a tighter affair and a study in contrasting styles, with Missouri moving the ball Wisconsin-style while the Jayhawks relied on the traditional long pass. For most of the contest, the old-fashioned method prevailed as KU's Rudolf

Uhrlaub shot his way to a game-high eleven points. But the Tigers pushed ahead late and won 25–21.

*Walter Meanwell was acknowledged as the game's greatest coach when he arrived at Missouri in 1917, and his stature only grew during his time in Columbia.*

With the sweep at Kansas, people around the league were forced to take notice of the Tigers' new coach and his unorthodox approach to the game, even if they could not fully appreciate it. Though Meanwell's reputation preceded him, he was still something of an enigma when he arrived in Columbia. And though observers had been introduced to the Wisconsin style by Van Gent, they had not experienced it as taught by its architect. Accordingly, Missouri's play in 1918 was a revelation to those accustomed to a style barely evolved from Naismith's early concepts. Like any innovation, it was resisted by those without the vision to see its possibilities. Notwithstanding the newfound success, some Missouri fans preferred the old system of long passes and half-court shots, which they found more exciting. But Meanwell believed the spectators would come around when they saw the results. "The long pass is a luck chance pure and simple," he said, "and when the Missouri crowds learn what the short method of play means[,] I believe they will see my point of view."

If the fans were slow to see Meanwell's point of view, the press was not. In fact, local writers practically fawned over Meanwell and his innovations. "Missouri's director of athletics is not a mere coach of the game," one wrote, "he is a student, a diagnostician of causes and effects of victories and defeats; his chosen game has become a study with him and the striving for perfection and perfect scores his hobby."

After the triumphs at Kansas, Meanwell and his undefeated Tigers swept a pair each from Nebraska and Iowa State. At 10–0, Missouri led the Valley with six games to play. Kansas State, in second at 5–1, posed the greatest threat to the Tigers' hopes for their first-ever conference title. And the Aggies would host Missouri for a crucial pair of games in the season's next-to-last series. But thoughts of revenge against K-State, which had wrested the championship from the Tigers the previous year, would have to wait. First, Missouri would host Kansas, a nemesis like no other.

If the Tigers were looking past the Jayhawks, it didn't show in the first game. Kansas opened the scoring with a free throw, but Missouri quickly captured the advantage and never let it go. A 39–21 win put the Tigers 13–0 overall and 11–0 in the league.

Perhaps the ease of that win caused the Tigers to underestimate the Jayhawks the next night. With the decisive K-State series on the horizon, Kansas stunned Missouri 28–23. Rudolf Uhrlaub and Howard Laslett played exceptional defense and held Shirkey and Ruby to a total of three field goals. Uhrlaub himself scored twelve to help KU hand the Tigers a bruising defeat. That same day, Kansas State beat Drake and improved to 9–1 in the Valley. The 11–1 Tigers remained in first place, but they were headed to Nichols Gymnasium, where Kansas State had not lost in two years, to play the team that had swept them in the late going the season before. A repeat of 1917 would cost Missouri its first conference championship.

Like most of Missouri's games, the series showcased contrasting styles, with Meanwell's precision versus Zora Clevenger's more haphazard approach. Meanwell thought two things favored the Aggies: (1) playing at home ("worth ten points to them," he said); and (2) a ninety-foot court, ten feet longer than Missouri's, which abetted Kansas State's wide open game.

Despite the coach's concerns, his squad—just a little tougher, more talented, and better disciplined than any previous Tiger team—came through. After game one, the local news summed up the game and its significance: "The Missouri Tigers practically clinched the championship of the Missouri Valley Conference here tonight by defeating the Kansas Aggies, 22–19, in forty of the most torrid minutes of basketball ever played in Manhattan." By modern standards, it is hard to imagine that a game that was scoreless for the first five minutes, one in which the teams combined for just forty-one points, could be described as "torrid." But it was hard fought and close throughout. The Tigers led 11–8 at intermission, but the Aggies rallied to even the score at 12. In the end, however, Sam Shirkey's foul shooting carried Missouri to victory.

As the newspaper said, the team had "practically" clinched the title, but there was still work to do to make it official. The Tigers did that work the next day in

*Sam Shirkey was among the fine players who awaited Walter Meanwell at Mizzou.*

a 28–24 win, the most important victory in the program's history to that point. The win wasn't just important; it was lucky. Kansas State frustrated Meanwell's vaunted offense, preventing the Tigers from moving the ball with their short passes. At the same time, K-State hit its own shots to open up a lead. But Missouri, ever resourceful, ditched its offensive scheme and began unleashing—and sinking—long shots. Missouri tied the game at 16 and then went on a five-minute tear that resulted in a 26–16 lead. From there, the Tigers eased to victory as Shirkey sank ten foul shots (and one field goal) and Mule Campbell added ten points. Ruby, the sophomore who made the crucial plays all season long, contributed six.

After years of near misses, Missouri finally had a champion. It also had a coach seemingly incapable of failing. After four Big Ten titles in seven seasons, Meanwell earned a Valley crown in his first try. His genius was unparalleled.

The champs still had a pair of contests to play. As anticlimactic as those games were, Meanwell's Tigers remained ferocious. Sam Shirkey, star against Kansas State, continued to shine as he scored eighteen in a 34–13 rout of Washington at Rothwell Gymnasium. Missouri was just as sharp the next day, holding the Pikers scoreless for the first nine minutes en route to a 20–4 halftime lead in the final collegiate game for Mule Campbell, Sam Shirkey, and Clyde Slusher. Meanwell cleared his bench in the second half, and the result was a 32–18 victory as the scrubs enjoyed mop-up duty. Craig Ruby, the youngest of Missouri's regulars, led the team with ten points as the Tigers closed out their finest season.

At 15–1, the Tigers easily outdistanced the second-place Kansas Aggies, who finished at 10–4. Missouri's dominance was such that two starters, Ruby and Slusher, were first-team all-Valley selections, while the others, Campbell, Shirkey, and Wackher, made the second team. One, however, could understand a fear that this success might be fleeting. After the breakthrough of 1918, Ruby would be the only starter returning in 1919.

## 1918-19

The most remarkable thing about the season of 1919 is that it happened at all. Though the war had ended in November 1918, many men still had military obligations. One was Dr. Meanwell, who was pressed into duty in the Army medical service. In his absence, John Miller returned to coaching basketball on an interim basis. In addition to service obligations, military regulations intruded. The Student Army Training Corps, established in summer 1918, allowed men subject to military service to train for war while continuing their studies (the program was "voluntary"; the alternative was conscription). Though its members remained in school, the SATC imposed rules making it hard for them to practice or play basketball.

The Great War provided a formidable obstacle to Miller's efforts, but it paled next to influenza. An epidemic rocked the campus (and the country) in fall 1918, taking the lives of many students and faculty members. The university closed for three weeks in October. All public events, including the entire 1918 football schedule, were canceled to prevent the spread of disease through assembled crowds. When classes resumed on October 31, students and faculty wore masks. Despite that precaution, the epidemic returned in late November, and the university closed its fall term in early December. When classes resumed again on January 1, 1919, the worst of the outbreak was over, but students still were required to wear masks. This included the basketball team, which wore them during practice. Notwithstanding the circumstances, the Tigers quickly coalesced into an impressive unit.

Under the conditions, preparing for the season would have been hard even for an experienced team. It was doubly difficult for a club virtually devoid of veteran leadership. Craig Ruby and Eric Schroeder, himself just back from military service, were the only players returning from the 1918 squad, and Schroeder had been little used by Meanwell. They were ably assisted, however, by a trio of talented alums of the previous year's freshman team, Phil Scott, George "Pidge" Browning, and Ralph "Doc" Coffey.

Perhaps the most valuable commodity in forging a team out of such a ragtag group is time, but Coach Miller had precious little of it. Flu and SATC regulations conspired to postpone the start of practice until just before the season began. Fortunately, though, the Tigers were skilled, and they were well versed in Meanwell's philosophies. They also were blessed with the services of Paul "Deerfoot" Vogt, the lanky center who returned to the team after a year's absence. Vogt's return was especially crucial because of the loss of Mule Campbell. Coach Miller could plug his sophomores into vacancies at the guard and forward positions, but without Vogt, he would have lacked a championship-caliber center. Still, Miller lacked a capable reserve at that spot. Thus, the Tigers' chances rested on Deerfoot's durability as much as his talent.

Ready or not, with the threat of influenza still quite literally hanging in the air, the Tigers opened the season just nine days after classes resumed. To combat the flu threat, the fans wore masks. And to keep order, Phog Allen officiated, just as he would at all of Missouri's home games of the year.

Despite the outbreak, Rothwell Gymnasium was packed with fans to see the Tigers take on Iowa State. Their presence, however, did little to create a home court advantage. In keeping with the gentility of the times, "players of both teams were applauded impartially."

The Tigers didn't need the help. Ruby and Vogt quickly established themselves as Missouri's leaders. Vogt used his looping "sleeper" shot to score twelve points, and Ruby added eight in a 34–16 win. In that opening game, Miller established a six-man rotation of mostly Kansas City boys, with Ruby and Browning starting at forward, Vogt at center, and Schroeder and Coffey at guard. Phil Scott replaced Coffey in the game's last ten minutes and would soon supplant him as a starter (when that happened, Scott moved to forward with Browning taking a spot in the backcourt). Miller's rotation remained intact the next day when the teams met again. Iowa State's long pass and shot style worked for twenty minutes and gave it a 16–15 halftime lead. But the Tigers steamrolled the visitors in the second half as Scott and Browning shouldered the scoring load in a 35–22 win.

The triumph of the opening weekend suggested that the Tigers had the stuff to repeat as champs, and they did nothing to dispel that impression over the next several games. Phil Scott emerged as the team's designated free throw shooter and a third scoring option (along with Ruby and Vogt), while Schroeder and Browning formed a nearly impenetrable defense. Missouri won its next five by an average of more than twenty points per game. Two of those wins came at Kansas, where even a slippery floor caused by a campus dance on the Robinson Gym court could not slow the Tigers, who prevailed by eighteen and twenty-two in a pair of games.

With all seven of their wins coming by double figures, the undefeated Tigers headed to Lincoln, Nebraska, at 6–0 in the league. Kansas State was second at 5–0, and Nebraska, at 6–2, was the only other team in the running for the Valley title.

Missouri did nothing to sully its reputation on its first night in Lincoln. It dominated nonconference foe Nebraska Wesleyan, 48–15, the Tigers' eighth straight lopsided win. Next up was a pair against Nebraska. And though the Cornhuskers were always formidable at home, Missouri, owner of a twelve-game win streak dating back a season, was a clear favorite.

That made what happened over the next two days so inexplicable. In game one, Nebraska smothered Ruby, Vogt, and Scott, holding them to a combined three field goals (Scott added five free throws) in a 21–14 Husker triumph. Missouri put up a better fight the next day, but the outcome was the same. A Tiger run turned a 16–11 deficit into a 22–16 lead. But Nebraska responded with a run of its own and surged ahead 23–22. Browning and Scott each scored to put Mizzou up by three late in the contest. But the Huskers reeled off the game's final five points to hand Missouri a heartbreaking 28–26 defeat. The Tigers had arrived in first place, seemingly unbeatable. They left in third, shaken.

The team returned home to host Kansas, which entered the series at 3–5 overall and just 1–5 in the Valley. In game one, Craig Ruby scored fourteen in a 34–20 Mizzou victory. The next day, however, Kansas stunned the Tigers with a 36–29 defeat that effectively eliminated them from title contention. The game was scoreless for the first six minutes, but a succession of Jayhawk baskets gave the visitors a lead they never relinquished. In the first half, with Kansas center Kelsey Mathews dominating Deerfoot Vogt, Coach Miller faced a daunting choice. He could stick with an ineffective player or bench the team's only quality big man. Miller opted to replace Vogt with the smaller Doc Coffey. Without a capable reserve center to fill the breach, the Tigers were forced to watch Kansas play a brand of make-it-take-it basketball as the Jayhawks consistently won the jump balls that followed each score. All five Kansas starters went the distance, with four chipping in three field goals each and one adding five. In Vogt's absence, Scott and Ruby carried the weight of Missouri's offense and combined for

*All-American Craig Ruby steadied the Tigers through war and a devastating flu epidemic.*

*Paul "Deerfoot" Vogt anchored the middle in 1919.*

twenty-three points. But two men could not defeat five.

After eight days off to fume, the Tigers returned to the court with a 56–15 blistering of Central College. But the next week, while they traveled to St. Louis and took two from Washington, Kansas State swept Nebraska to clinch its second Valley title in three years.

That turned the season's final series into an anticlimax. The Tigers, who should have been defending their championship, were reduced to playing for pride as Kansas State invaded Rothwell Gymnasium for a pair of games. The Aggies, in contrast, were playing for perfection. They brought a 16–0 record to Columbia. The local press gave K-State a 50-50 shot to sweep the Tigers, but found two Missouri victories nearly unfathomable. "An even break would be no surprise to followers of the champions, although it is highly improbable that the Aggies will slump to the extent of losing both games."

Perhaps it was that kind of doubt that inspired the Tigers. Perhaps it was pride. Or perhaps it was the presence of Dr. Meanwell, on hand thanks to a furlough. Whatever it was, it worked. The Tigers crushed the new champs as Phil Scott sparkled in game one. The Missouri forward, with twenty-seven points, outscored the entire Aggie squad in a 47–26 Mizzou victory.

And to prove it was no fluke, the Tigers did it again the next night. Kansas State held its own in the first stanza, even leading 15–13 at the break. But the Tigers came out blazing in the second half. John Allen Clarke, a rare high-scoring guard, led the Aggies with nine points. But he was no match for Ruby, Vogt, and Scott, who combined for thirty-six in a 38–23 Missouri win.

A look at the final Valley standings surely stung the Tigers. Despite sweeping the Aggies and winning more conference games than the champs, Missouri lost the title by percentage points. Kansas State played just eleven conference games, and its 9–2 record—and .818 winning percentage—gave it the crown over the Tigers, who posted an 11–3 mark and a winning percentage of .786.

Neither war, flu, nor the champion Kansas Aggies could stop the Missouri Tigers. But oddly enough, a three-day trip to Nebraska could. The midseason stumble in Lincoln cost the Tigers a title; even a split with the Cornhuskers would have earned Missouri the Valley crown. But the sting of losing helped to steel the players who would return the following year. Disappointment turned to determination as it became clear that the 1920 championship might be theirs to lose. Indeed, none of them would ever finish in second place again.

With war over and the Jazz Age beginning, the 1920s brought new hope for America and new challenges for Missouri basketball. For the Tigers, it was a decade in three parts. First came domination in a period of instability, when three coaches in four years led Mizzou to three league titles and nearly another. Next came a steep decline, when a hero of three championship teams presided over a fall from the top to the bottom of the conference. And finally came rejuvenation, when a player from the past came home, turned the Tigers back into winners, and began a tenure that would last twenty years.

Across the country, the early years of the decade came to be called the Roaring Twenties because of a new prosperity, explosions in culture and technology, and a more liberal social climate. In Columbia, Missouri, the roar came from the Tigers, who from 1920 to 1923 were the best basketball team in America.

# THE 1920s

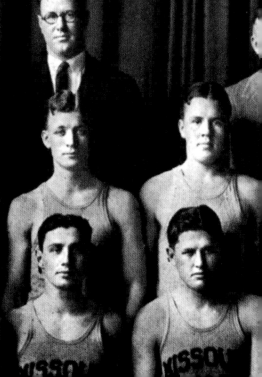

## 1919–20

As the decade began, there was cause for relief and delight in Columbia. The Great War and the deadly flu epidemic were in the past, and the football team clinched its first Valley title in six years by beating Kansas on Thanksgiving Day 1919. And when seasons changed, hopes were high that the basketball squad could match the football team's accomplishment.

the return of Doc Meanwell. Free from military duty, the Little Doctor hoped to take the team he saw dismantle Kansas State the previous March and turn it into champs. The pieces were in place: the game's greatest coach was back at the helm, and Craig Ruby, Missouri's greatest player, a two-time All-American, was back on the court. Phil Scott, Mizzou's surest shot, and Pidge Browning, the Tigers' most versatile player, were back, too. And though Deerfoot Vogt had been lost to graduation, a pivot player of even greater prowess arrived.

*The 1919–20 team was a who's who of Missouri basketball. Walter Meanwell (front, center) was the greatest coach of the era, and George Williams (middle, second from left) was among the finest players. Craig Ruby (front, second from right) and George Bond (middle, far right) each starred as players and went on to coach the Tigers.*

In the first week of 1920, the big story on the nation's sports pages was the New York Yankees' purchase of Babe Ruth from the Boston Red Sox. In Columbia, it was

George "Shorty" Williams, brother of All-American Fred Williams, immediately captured his coach's imagination. "When I first saw him," Meanwell said, "I knew that he would some day be the Van Gent of the Missouri Valley." High praise indeed, but in retrospect, comparisons between Williams and the Wisconsin star flatter Van Gent.

Meanwell's previous season at Mizzou had produced the best team in Tiger history, but that club, successful as it was, lacked the broad array of talent available to the Little Doctor in 1920. Meanwell, of course, was famous for his offensive innovations, and his team, with its many weapons, could score in waves. But the 1920 club would dominate with defense. Throughout the eighteen-game schedule, no foe would score thirty points against the Tigers, a mark Missouri would fail to surpass just three times.

The Tigers opened the season by twice demolishing Iowa State. The stifling defense of Missouri's guards—Browning and Leslie Wackher—freed Ruby, Williams, and Scott to dominate offensively. The sweet-shooting Williams, playing his first varsity game, scored twenty in a 55–20 rout, and Scott added three field goals and either seventeen or nineteen free throws (reports conflict). The next day, Scott scored twenty-seven in a 45–17 victory.

Two wins at Washington University put Missouri at 4–0 heading to Kansas to play the Jayhawks, also unbeaten in four starts. It marked the first meeting between Walter Meanwell and Phog Allen, who would become two of the seventeen charter members of the Basketball Hall of Fame. Allen, after ten years away from the University of Kansas, returned in 1919 to become athletics director and football coach. But when Karl Schlademan abandoned basketball after one game in 1920 to devote his full time to track and field, Allen resumed his basketball coaching career, a fortuitous turn for Kansas fans.

Meanwell and Allen were remarkably similar in some respects and distinctly different in others. Some historical revisionism has cast Phog as the avuncular sage who provided a good upbringing to Naismith's baby. But Allen was no saint, nor was Meanwell. Both were competitive and temperamental, prickly personalities prone to histrionics, teachers of a high order who were confident in their methods, brilliant ambassadors of the game on their best days, unrepentant bullies on their worst. But there was contrast even in their sameness, from their size (Allen was strapping, Meanwell slight) to their approaches to the healing arts. Meanwell was a medical doctor, Allen an osteopath. And despite their differences, it was probably good that two medics were on hand for the brutal battles that their teams waged.

Though Allen would go on to greater fame than any other coach in the first half of the twentieth century, Meanwell was still the acknowledged master in 1920, the standard-bearer for all coaches. As Blair Kerkhoff writes in his biography of the Kansas mentor, "A young Phog envied Meanwell's success. . . . Meanwell was who Phog wanted to be and beat."

Allen never came closer to beating Meanwell than he did in that first meeting. Early on, Missouri dominated. The Tigers held Kansas to just one field goal in the first half. But the Jayhawks rallied behind Marvin Harms and George Rody, who made four buckets apiece. The result was a 27–27 tie at the end of regulation. But the Tigers owned the extra period. Williams, Ruby, and Scott each scored as the Tigers prevailed 32–27.

Rarely have Missouri supporters been commended for fair-mindedness when it comes to Kansas. But the next day, *Kansas City Star* columnist C. E. McBride commented on their superior deportment:

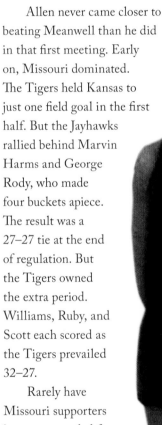

*George "Pidge" Browning was one of the best and most versatile players of his day.*

*In view of the attitude of certain downtown Lawrence citizens who were driven to a trembling frenzy and unclean letter writing because some of the officials in the late Missouri-Kansas football game lived in Missouri it is interesting to note that Columbia citizens assume no such attitude in reference to E. C. Quigley, who refereed the Missouri-Kansas basket ball game last night and will referee tonight's contest. Quigley was born in the state of Kansas and has lived there all his life. But more than this—Quig is a former K.U. football star whose long run enabled K.U. to tie a Missouri game years ago. All the greater tribute to the broadminded and sportsmanlike policy of the Missourians.*

Even had Quigley been prone to cheat, he could have done little for the Jayhawks the next night. Phil Scott blistered Kansas with twenty points in a 38–16 rout. Even Missouri's guards got into the act, with Browning and Wackher combining for ten. After two defeats at home, Allen was left frustrated, a frustration that would fester and resurface four weeks later in Columbia.

Next, Kansas State came calling, and the Tigers knocked the Aggies from the ranks of the unbeaten with a two-game sweep. From there, Phil Scott and reserve center George Bond starred as Missouri twice annihilated Drake, and Williams shone when the Tigers took two from Oklahoma. In the second OU game, a 53–18 drubbing, Williams, a hurdler and high jumper for Mizzou's track team, displayed a sensational offensive arsenal, even shooting free throws instead of Scott, who struggled from the line.

By the time the Jayhawks invaded Rothwell Gymnasium for a pair of mid-February games, the Valley race was all but over. The Tigers stood 12–0 with six games to play. Kansas State was 7–3, Kansas 5–3. But a title need not be at stake for the Missouri-Kansas rivalry to be compelling, as recognized by the Missouri students

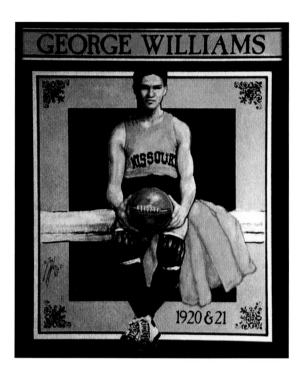

George Williams was the most dominant player the Valley had ever seen.

who snapped up all twenty-one hundred tickets the moment the box office opened. They knew that Tigers and Jayhawks will play riveting basketball for pride, for blood, for revenge, and for the pure pleasure of combat.

They played for all those things in the first contest, a game that saw the rivalry and rhetoric ratcheted up. Phog Allen began with some gamesmanship before the tip. The contest was to start at 7:15, but when the appointed hour came, Allen protested that it was not yet time. He succeeded in delaying the start to 7:20. Which is to say, he put off a beating for five minutes.

When the game finally began, it was all Tigers. Missouri won 36–21 as Scott and Ruby combined for thirty, but that was almost beside the point. Rough play and harsh words made for the bigger story. Howard "Scrubby" Laslett, a Kansas football player, applied his gridiron skills to the hardwood. His tripping and tackling led him to foul out less than fifteen minutes into the game. It also led Doc Meanwell to his feet, shouting to the official, "He's going to ruin a good man there!" Ever prickly, Phog Allen turned toward Meanwell and yelled, "Sit down, you big boob!" Rather than offer a retort,

Meanwell saved his feelings for after the game. "I would not let a man like [Laslett] play on a team of mine if I had to start with four men," he said.

Game two provided fewer fireworks but the same result. Missouri routed Kansas 31–13 as Phog fell to 0–4 against the man he wanted to be and beat. But the agitated Allen did not go quietly. He held court with the press at midnight and complained that newspapermen who described Laslett as a ruffian were biased. Changing the subject a bit, he said the reporters "did not take the trouble to find out that the Kansas team was denied the use of the ball before the game both nights and that we were shown other discourtesies." An uncommonly diplomatic Meanwell got the last word. "Neither Missouri nor Kansas touched the ball that was to be used in the game until the game started. I anticipated just such a charge and put the ball we were to use in the game into the hands of umpire E. C. Quigley as soon as he arrived at the gymnasium. It was not touched by Missouri, and Dr. Allen's charge regarding the ball is mistaken."

Amid far less drama, Missouri clinched the Valley championship the next week by twice defeating Washington University. With the title tucked away and two games to go, the 16–0 Tigers were playing for perfection, and the schedule added intrigue to the already heightened drama. Twelve months earlier, Kansas State invaded Columbia on the season's last weekend, Valley championship in hand, hoping to complete a perfect record. The Tigers played spoiler in spectacular fashion by twice trouncing the Aggies. With a chance to turn the tables, that disappointment must have been on the minds of Kansas State's players when Mizzou arrived in Manhattan with hopes of adding an exclamation point to a remarkable season.

The first game moved Missouri to within a game of its goal. Williams and Ruby, the two finest players in the first fifteen years of Tiger basketball, combined for twenty-one points in a 29–21 victory. Kansas State, however, understood better than anyone how to defend Meanwell's men. The Tigers' twenty-nine-point output marked just the second time they had been held below thirty. The first had come five weeks earlier in Columbia when the Aggies held Missouri to twenty-one points in a 21–19 contest, the closest the Tigers had come to defeat all season.

Still, when the Tigers burst out of the gate in the season finale, it appeared that the Aggies would fold. Missouri raced to an 11–1 lead and seemed destined to complete its mission. But the defending champs were resilient. G. S. Jennings and G. W. Hinds keyed a rally that cut the lead to 14–12 at the half. Then, the Aggies locked down a Tiger offense that had overwhelmed all comers throughout the year. George Williams, an irresistible force all season, tallied just three points, and when the clock struck zero, the dream ended. Kansas State prevailed 29–23, and Missouri finished the year 17–1.

When the momentary disappointment faded, the season's striking accomplishment shone through. The Tigers won their second Missouri Valley championship and years later were adjudged America's second best team (behind 22–1 Penn). They were 10–0 at home, where they played to capacity crowds all year long, and their twenty-two-game win streak (dating to 1919) was the longest in the first century of Missouri basketball. Phil Scott won the Valley scoring title at 15.2 points per game. Craig Ruby was all-conference. George Williams was All-America. A pipeline stocked with talent held great promise for future years, but an off-season development would let doubt creep in.

*Sure shot Phil Scott*

## 1920–21

It was an offer the University of Missouri could not match. In addition to a much larger salary, the University of Wisconsin promised to create a position to allow Walter Meanwell to use his medical training to improve the health and condition of its athletes. Not surprisingly, Wisconsin also invited him to coach its basketball team. And so Meanwell, the innovator who turned the Tigers into titans, returned to Wisconsin after coaching Missouri to two Valley titles in as many seasons and compiling a 34–2 record, giving him a .944 winning percentage, the best among all Tiger coaches and a mark certain not to be surpassed. His legend was cemented in 1959, when he became a charter member of the Basketball Hall of Fame.

Luring the game's finest coach away from Wisconsin had been a coup for the University of Missouri. Losing him back to the Badgers could have pushed the Tiger program back to mediocrity, especially given the dearth of accomplished coaches available to replace him. But rather than searching for a replacement of Doc Meanwell's stature, the university did something it would do four times over the next fifty years: it chose one of its own, a young former Missouri star.

As Missouri stars went, the university could hardly have chosen one younger or brighter. Craig Ruby, captain of Meanwell's last Tiger team, succeeded the Little Doctor—and matched his success win for win. Ruby achieved that success by adopting Meanwell's philosophies but not his demeanor, reflecting a maturity that belied his youth. Ruby's men displayed the familiar teamwork, ball movement, and lockdown defense developed by Meanwell, but the young coach was not prone to volcanic outbursts. When newspapers wrote of the Tigers in 1920, Meanwell was the story. In 1921 Ruby would be a footnote.

The new coach was blessed with an abundance of talented players. George Bond, a high jumper on the track team, filled one forward spot and became a star, scoring prolifically and drawing the toughest defensive assignments. George "Pidge" Browning,

*Craig Ruby followed Walter Meanwell as coach and matched his success.*

the team's captain, occupied the other forward position, while his younger brother, Arthur "Bun" Browning, became a key reserve, as did Johnny Knight, yet another gifted scorer. Leslie Wackher, a starter on the 1920 squad, returned at guard, while George Williams remained in the middle and elevated his play from simply All-American to entirely otherworldly. And to complement the irresistible force that was Williams, an immovable object named Herb Bunker joined the backcourt and began a storied career. Ox-strong, whip-smart, and barge-large, the sophomore proceeded to become a defensive presence of nearly mythic proportions. Even his name suggested defense. Bunker was the rarest of the rare, a four-sport letterman who also played football and baseball and used his superior strength as a shot-putter on the track team. In *Ol'*

*Mizzou*, his history of Missouri football, Bob Broeg writes, "Bunker was built like a blacksmith, with the brain of an egghead, and the soul of a Sunday school teacher." Bunker used all those traits and more to leave a lasting mark on the basketball program.

Though Craig Ruby's foray into coaching was a prominent subplot, the season's real story of individual achievement would be the play of George Williams, the lanky center who excelled defensively but whose legend was built on the offensive end, where he blossomed into a force unprecedented in the brief history of Missouri basketball. His tremendous size, touch, and ability to shoot with either hand from near or far helped him terrorize opponents and lead the Valley in scoring, often single-handedly outscoring the opposition.

For the third straight year, Missouri opened with two games against Iowa State. The Tigers, in their black shorts, black knee pads, black knee-high socks, and white high-top shoes, overwhelmed the Cyclones 30–11 in game one as Williams tallied sixteen points, then completed the sweep the next day. Never ones to shy from florid language, the student writers at the *Savitar* summed up the contests: "The Tiger, old at his game, licked his chops and lunched mincingly on the innocents from the North, taking the pair of scrimmages with ease." From there, it was off to the races. The Tigers hosted—and demolished—Washington University in a pair of games. Williams totaled thirty-six in the two contests, and Johnny Knight (playing in place of an injured Pidge Browning) knifed through the defense for twenty-six, but Missouri's most valuable player may have been Herb Bunker. Led by the rock-solid six-foot-three 190-pounder, the smothering Tiger defense held the Pikers to eleven points each day, routinely intercepting their long passes.

Pidge Browning returned to the lineup at Oklahoma, and he and George Bond put on a first-half shooting clinic. Williams dominated in the second half and finished with twenty-one points (Bond and Browning scored fourteen and ten, respectively) in a 47–24 win over the Sooners.

After beating Oklahoma once more for good measure, the Tigers returned home to face Kansas, which, like Missouri, entered the game with a 6–0 record. The Jayhawks fielded a remarkable array of talent—Paul Endacott, George Rody, John Wulf, Ernst Uhrlaub—but they had "no such outstanding player as Williams," or so said the *Kansas City Times*. Missouri's star tallied twenty-one in a 27–22 victory in game one. The scoring was more balanced the next day but the result was the same. Pidge Browning, still hobbled, left the game. In his place, brother Bun scored six in a 28–21 win that made the Tigers favorites to win a second straight Valley title.

Missouri continued to roll, propelled by Williams. He scored twenty-three in a rout of Washington and twenty-two in a 48–14 win over Kansas State. When Williams went to the bench after scoring twelve points against Drake

*George Williams, 1921's national player of the year*

in the Tigers' thirteenth contest (a 50–14 victory), it marked the first time all season that he had come out of a game. Williams had emerged as an unprecedented offensive force, frequently scoring more than twenty points, while others—most often Pidge—took turns as the Tigers' second option.

By the time they arrived in Lawrence, the Tigers stood 14–0, on the verge of clinching the Missouri Valley championship. Fans packed Robinson

Gymnasium to root on the Jayhawks, but Williams silenced them almost immediately. After Kansas took a 4–1 lead, Shorty caught fire, scoring from all over the court in a 33–17 victory. He was even more magnificent the next night as the Tigers all but locked up the championship. Williams, on his way to twenty-five points, broke the game open in the second half. Missouri cruised to a 41–30 triumph as Phog Allen fell to 0–8 against MU in his second stint as Kansas coach.

The Tigers took a 16–0 record into the season's final two games, again with Kansas State. Two differences from the previous year suggested that Missouri would avoid the disappointing fate of 1920. First, the games would be in Columbia, and second, the Aggies had shown little ability to compete with the Tigers. Earlier in Manhattan, Missouri easily swept the Aggies, who had no solution for Williams or the elder Browning.

Missouri overwhelmed K-State in game one at Rothwell. Though they led just 14–12 at the break, the Tigers exploded in the second half, racing to a 33–19 victory as Williams matched Kansas State's entire offensive output. At that point, the elusive perfect season seemed inevitable. Going into the final day, the Tigers again were Valley champs and again were 17–0. But on March 5, 1921, one year to the day after the Aggies foiled MU's try at a perfect season, they did it again.

Kansas State shocked the Rothwell Gym assemblage by doing what had seemed impossible. It shut down Williams. More precisely, Everett Cowell shut down the Tiger star. Cowell, like Herb Bunker, was an All-Valley guard who defended ferociously while scoring rarely, and he frustrated Williams throughout the game. In fact, Shorty failed to make a single field goal. While Cowell made Williams look entirely mortal, Kansas State's H. L. Bunger looked superhuman as he scored

*All-American Herb Bunker, a four-sport star, was an immovable object on defense.*

eighteen points in a 32–24 Aggie victory that put a bitter cap on the sweetest of seasons.

And like the year before, once the disappointment subsided, the size of the achievement was something to behold. The Tigers had won another title, this one for a rookie coach. Pidge Browning, Herb Bunker, and George Williams comprised three-fifths of the All-Valley team, with Bunker and Williams also earning All-America honors. And Williams, in addition to winning the MVC scoring title at 17.3 points per game, was named national player of the year—the only Tiger ever so honored. Mizzou even displayed some hubris at season's end by challenging Penn, the east's foremost power, to a three-game series to determine the nation's top team. Penn declined the challenge, and years later, historian Patrick Premo helped seal the Tigers' place in history by declaring them the nation's number one team for 1921, with Penn at number two (the Helms Foundation of Los Angeles would choose Penn as its mythical national champion). By the end of the 1921 season, the Tigers had emerged as college basketball's greatest power. Craig Ruby, already lionized as a player, sealed his legend as a coach by succeeding and surpassing Meanwell. A prodigious debut, it called for a spectacular encore.

## 1921-22

When the 1922 season opened, America was entering the radio age. Though only several thousand had owned receiving sets in previous years, it was estimated that one million Americans would have them by year's end. Still, broadcasts of basketball games were years away. Basketball had to be experienced in person, and more and more Midwesterners did just that. With major league baseball confined to cities from St. Louis eastward, Missouri Valley basketball was the big time across the plains, and thousands packed arenas to see the heroes of the newly popular game. Those who couldn't get tickets could read about the games on the local sports page, where they got equal billing with Babe Ruth, Jack Dempsey, and wrestling champ Ed "Strangler" Lewis, who regularly defended his title in the heartland.

The Missouri Tigers, two-time defending conference champs, received much of the spotlight, and rightly so. Still, despite their recent success, one could be forgiven for doubting Craig Ruby. After all, in his first year, he inherited a spectacular group of players who had been schooled by Meanwell. How could he have failed? In his second season, however, Ruby proved masterful, not simply the beneficiary of Meanwell's philosophies and existing talent.

He began by reconstructing his team, replacing starters Pidge Browning, Leslie Wacker, and George

Arthur "Bun" Browning earned All-America honors in 1922 and 1923.

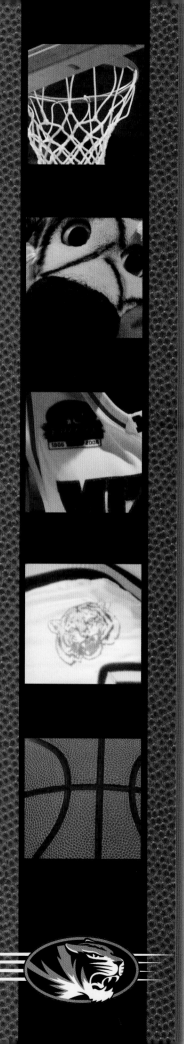

Williams, the finest player in the first fifteen years of Missouri basketball. Williams, who returned to his native Kansas City, would cement his reputation as one of the era's great players by leading both the Lowe & Campbell and Kansas City Athletic Club teams to AAU national championships, three times earning selection to the AAU All-Tournament team.

Ruby deftly manipulated the available talent. Herb Bunker nominally played center. The tallest Tiger, he jumped center and then retreated to play guard, trading places with George Bond who, though listed at guard, played an aggressive offensive game. Bun Browning replaced his brother at forward and surpassed him in almost every respect, and Johnny Knight—like Bunker, a four-sport letterman—completed the starting frontcourt. For the fifth spot in the lineup, Coach Ruby settled on a guard platoon of Bob Hays and Don Faurot. Neither scored often, but both were fierce defenders.

The Tigers began the year by beating the Rolla Miners. But there was much doubt about their ability to win another Valley title, partly because of the loss of George Williams and partly because of their perceived inability to hold onto the ball. The local press wrote that "fumbles have proved costly, and unless they improve in this department,

*Captain George Bond helped ignite Missouri's offense.*

they will have some mighty hard sledding in the next few games."

The sledding, it turned out, was easy for the Tigers as they rolled over a succession of Missouri Valley opponents by lopsided scores. The early success was ensured in part by Browning, who moved from key reserve to All-America, and by Knight, who became a potent scorer in his own right. Considerable credit also belonged to Bunker, who again earned All-America honors for his stellar defense. In fact, his play throughout the year inspired Leslie Edmonds, a Missouri Valley official, to wax poetic: "See the ponderous Bunker covering the back court with easy grace and guiding his huge strength ever toward the ball and never toward the man." A paradox of a man, Bunker was ponderous and graceful, hulking and intellectual, aggressive and gentle, so devoted to athletics that he lettered in four sports and so devoted to education that he later earned a Ph. D. Still, no player was more responsible for the Tigers' success than George Bond, an excellent ball handler and free throw shooter who scored twenty-three against Washington and sixteen against Nebraska.

The Tigers stood at 5–0 when they arrived in Lawrence for a single game against undefeated Kansas. The Jayhawk loyalists, hungry for their first title in seven years, had every confidence that their team would seize control of the Valley race, but that confidence was shattered by a Mizzou squad that had become a ruthless machine. The two hundred Tiger faithful who made the trip to Robinson Gymnasium saw their team race past Kansas with crisp passing and "marvelous long shots that seemingly couldn't stay away from the basket." Missouri, paced by Bunker, Bond, and Browning, led almost the entire way and took an easy win 35–25, thus establishing themselves as the team to beat in the Valley. Kansas had been much acclaimed for its defense, but it was the Tigers who put the clamps on the Jayhawks' stars. Hays held George Rody scoreless from the field, and future hall-of-famer Paul Endacott left the game with just two points when Phog Allen cleared his bench late in the game, conceding defeat.

As the Tigers left Lawrence, doubts about their ability to win a third straight Valley championship had vanished. They would have to play Kansas again, but that would be in Columbia, where the Tigers would have an advantage. First, though, the Tigers would have to deal with the rest of the league.

Deal they did. Johnny Knight and Bun Browning easily shot the Tigers past a string of six conference foes. Browning's touch against Drake was such that "several of his shots were made from the center of the court and dropped through the net without getting on familiar terms with the ring." But Kansas matched Missouri win for win, setting up the year's most critical game.

The Tigers stood 13–0 overall and 12–0 in the league when the Jayhawks came to town. A Missouri win would put the Tigers up by two games with three to play, while a Kansas victory would create a tie at the top of the standings. Kansas also had pride at stake. The Tigers had once been KU's whipping boys, losing thirty of thirty-two meetings from 1908 to 1915. But that trend reversed abruptly. Going back to 1916, Missouri had won twenty-one of twenty-five over Kansas, including nine straight against Phog Allen.

Allen got bad news shortly before game time when starting forward Armin Woestermeyer was declared academically ineligible. But Phog kept it to himself, sending Woestermeyer out for warm-ups and putting his name in the scorebook so Ruby, oblivious to the suspension, could make no adjustments. Once the game started, it was nip and tuck, and Kansas took a two-point lead at the break. But in the second half, George Rody, the league's leading scorer, shot Kansas to a 26–16 win that created a tie at the top of the standings. The game was a reverse image of the rivals' previous contest, with the Jayhawks shutting down Missouri's top scorers. Browning and Knight, so hot in recent games, were held to four points each as the Kansas defense forced the Tigers to take uncharacteristically long shots. Though disappointed, Missouri's mission was clear: win its final two games to ensure at least a share of the Valley championship for the third straight year.

The Nebraska Cornhuskers were in the wrong place at the wrong time. They visited Columbia just three days after Kansas left, and the frustrated Tigers scorched them 55–16. Missouri raced to a 31–6 halftime lead and didn't let up. Herb Bunker was just two points shy of being the fourth Tiger in double figures (Knight, Bond, and Browning scored twenty, sixteen, and ten, respectively), a feat almost unheard of at the time.

The only obstacle left was Kansas State. Kansas had won its final two games, and Missouri needed a victory in Manhattan to share the league crown. In one of the closest games of the year, MU squeaked past the Aggies 32–28, led by George Bond's fourteen points.

The season over, Missouri and Kansas had tied for the Missouri Valley title, each

*Johnny Knight helped the Tigers to league titles in 1921 and 1922.*

with a 15–1 conference record. Not satisfied to share, Missouri's committee on intercollegiate athletics challenged Kansas to a one-game playoff at a neutral site, Kansas City's Convention Hall. Phog Allen preferred a three-game series to be played in Columbia, Lawrence, and Kansas City, though he expressed concern that playing off-campus might smack of commercialism. He left the decision to KU's athletic board and chancellor.

Kansas declined the challenge. Though its team already had played eighteen games, the university objected to playing just one more, and used academic integrity as its excuse. Chancellor E. H. Lindley explained the decision. "We have kept in mind the fundamental that the university does not exist for athletics," he said. "Athletics are to be fostered as an important contribution to a broad education only when kept within reasonable bounds." The chancellor went on to say, "The basket ball season consisting of eighteen games is closed. It has been long and arduous enough. . . . We will play Missouri in basket ball next year."

The explanation was greeted with a measure of skepticism, especially among those who covered and followed sports in Kansas City. Some deemed KU's explanation an "alibi." Whatever it was, it put an anticlimactic end to a remarkable season.

The lack of a resolution yielded controversy. No true college basketball champion would be crowned until 1938 when the first national tournament was held. In 1936, however, the Helms Foundation, acting on its own authority, retroactively named mythical national champions. For the 1922 season, it picked the Jayhawks, and their win in Columbia has come to be regarded as the national championship game. The obvious question: why not Missouri? Each went 15–1 in the Valley, each won by ten points on the other's home floor, each defeated one nonconference opponent to start the season

(KU also lost a nonconference game, to the Kansas City Athletic Club, a formidable team of former collegians). Kansas may have gotten the nod based on the reputation of coach Phog Allen, whose stature grew through time; Helms selected him as the game's greatest coach in 1943. Whatever the reason, Kansas did not prove itself superior to Missouri on the hardwood, where the two clubs were dead even through two games against each other and fourteen more against the rest of the Missouri Valley.

Later, some balance was added to history. Years after Helms chose Kansas, historian Patrick Premo researched the game's early seasons and concluded that the Tigers were in fact the nation's best in 1922 (Premo and Helms agreed on the top team all but four times from 1911 to 1929; two of those times, Premo chose Missouri). The teams are as deadlocked in history as they were on the court. Nonetheless, Kansas continues to fly the banner of a mythical championship from the Allen Field House rafters, while Missouri fans have all but forgotten the great teams of the twenties, as men who knew glory in their day have been rendered anonymous by the passage of time.

Luckily, some record remains of their greatness. Bunker and Browning each were named All-America and first team All-Missouri Valley. George Bond and Johnny Knight made second team All-Valley, with Bob Hays earning honorable mention. Despite the loss of all-time greats George Williams and Pidge Browning (who led the Lowe & Campbell team of Kansas City to the national AAU championship in their first year out of school), Coach Ruby and company produced one of the most successful seasons in Tiger history. Valley official Leslie Edmonds offered these thoughts. "The 1922 basket ball team of Missouri was a credit to the university, to its coach, and to its personnel; yes, a credit to the ideals of sportsmanship that govern the play of gentlemen the world around and a tribute to the excellence of sports development in the Missouri Valley."

# 1922–23

After their 1920 championship, the Tigers lost Walter Meanwell, their greatest coach. After their 1921 championship, they lost George Williams, their greatest player. And after their 1922 championship, they lost the only person who could rival those men for their respective titles. Craig Ruby left Columbia for the University of Illinois, of the prestigious Big Ten conference. And though Ruby's Illini would have some success over the next fourteen years, it would be nothing like what he experienced with his Tigers.

In fact, Ruby's greatest contribution to college basketball while at Illinois may have been his indirect but crucial role in the birth of the dynasty at the University of Kentucky. A young Adolph Rupp was the coach at Freeport (Illinois) High School when Kentucky's coaching job came open. According to *The Winning Tradition: A History of Kentucky Wildcat Basketball*, Rupp "owed his hiring in large part to a recommendation from University of Illinois basketball coach Craig Ruby."

*Like Craig Ruby before him, George Bond went straight from team captain to head coach.*

Just as important, Ruby's system (learned from Walter Meanwell) became the blueprint for Kentucky's success. John Mauer, one of Ruby's earliest players at Illinois, coached Kentucky from 1927 to 1930 and became the father of its modern basketball tradition. Though the Wildcats had gone just 3–13 the season before he arrived, Mauer implemented Ruby's system and immediately turned them into winners. Kentucky posted a cumulative 40–14 record in his three seasons in Lexington, and the scheme he put in place became the foundation for the dynasty when it was adopted by his successor. As noted in *The Winning Tradition*, "It is ironic that the system Rupp employed at the University of Kentucky owed more to John Mauer and to the University of Illinois than to the man for whom Rupp had played at the University of Kansas, Dr. Forest [sic] C. 'Phog' Allen."

In replacing Ruby, the University of Missouri followed a tried-and-true formula. Like two years before, Mizzou hired the previous season's captain. And thus, George Bond became Missouri's new head basketball coach.

Luckily for the new coach, a strong nucleus returned, led by Bun Browning and Herb Bunker. Bob Hays and Don Faurot, who previously platooned at one guard spot, formed the starting backcourt. The only true newcomer in the lineup was sophomore forward Frank Wheat, a fine scorer who was counted on to replace Johnny Knight.

The story of the season again was the two games with Kansas. The Tigers swept their other fourteen conference games, winning most handily (50–22 over Drake, 41–13 over Grinnell, 50–20 over Oklahoma, 40–17 over Kansas State) and drawing large crowds nearly everywhere they played. Kansas enjoyed identical success, meaning that once again the Valley title would ride on the outcome of the two border battles.

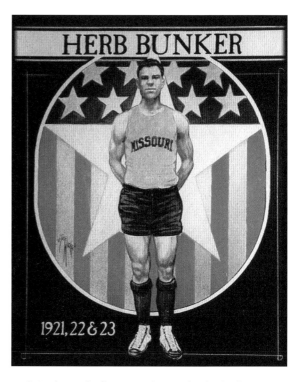

*Herb Bunker took All-America honors for the third time in the 1922-23 season.*

The teams featured contrasting styles. While the Tigers relied on the inside presence of Bunker and Browning, Kansas was built around a pair of remarkable guards, Paul Endacott and Charlie Black. Both teams were undefeated when the Jayhawks pulled into Columbia after a trip that featured a broken-down train, a broken-down truck, and a few miles of hoofing it into town. It would be the rivals' first meeting in Rothwell Gymnasium since the 1922 Kansas victory that cost the Tigers a perfect record and sole ownership of the league championship. All the elements for a great game were there: revenge, pride, preeminence in the Valley. There also was the curious case of Tusten Ackerman, a budding Jayhawk star. Ackerman had grown up idolizing KU multisport star Tommy Johnson, whose death from a kidney ailment had been hastened by a blow he received in a Missouri-Kansas football game. Legend has it that Phog Allen, master manipulator, drove Ackerman to frenzy before tip-off, convincing him that he could avenge Johnson's death by leading Kansas to victory.

The first half was a grinding defensive battle. Herb Bunker played a large part in holding Kansas to just six points before the break; still, a 6–6 tie was all Missouri could manage. The Tigers surged to a 16–10 lead in the second half before the Jayhawks made a surge of their own. Endacott, Black, and Ackerman keyed an 11–3 run that gave Kansas a 21–19 victory as Ackerman scored a game-high eleven points. As if the game weren't dramatic enough, Phog Allen propagated a myth about its end. According to the coach, the five-foot-ten Endacott sealed the win by allowing himself to be tied up and winning sixteen straight jump balls at a time when the jumper could control the tip. Game accounts don't support the tale, nor did Endacott's recollection, but Allen rarely allowed the truth to ruin a good story.

After a string of wins against Valley foes, the Tigers pulled into basketball-crazed Kansas City to face the Kansas City Athletic Club, an elite squad that would go on to win the AAU national championship. George Williams, Mizzou's former All-America center, anchored the Blue Diamonds, which also featured erstwhile Tiger star Pidge Browning.

The match-up drew the largest crowd ever to see a basketball game at Convention Hall as six thousand jammed inside. And though they were treated to some good basketball, they did not see a particularly close game. Bun Browning outscored his brother 14 to 6, but KCAC had its way with the Tigers, leading almost start to finish in a 32–22 win. While there may be no such thing as a good loss, some surely are better than others. The defeat did not count in the MVC race, thus leaving the Tigers just one game back of the Jayhawks, and it gave Missouri a good late-season test a mere nine days before the crucial rematch with Kansas.

Kansas remained undefeated when the Tigers arrived in Lawrence. A win would all but assure Missouri a tie for the Valley title, while a loss would guarantee the Jayhawks an undisputed championship. A record crowd of more than three thousand packed Robinson Gymnasium. They saw Missouri jump to a 3–0 lead on a trio of Browning free throws. But Kansas took over from there and raced to a 14–9 halftime edge. The Jayhawks extended it to 20–11 before Bunker, Wheat, and Browning all scored to trim the margin to 20–18 late in the game. But a Kansas field goal and free throw put the game away. Despite ten points from Frank Wheat, the Tigers fell 23–20.

Not just a defeat, the game marked a turning point. A win over Washington University to close the year was but a coda, the last notes of a majestic body of work that ended with all five Tiger starters making first or second team All-Valley and with Bunker and Browning again being named All-America. Missouri, so powerful over the past six seasons, would

*Forward Frank Wheat was a gifted scorer.*

never again win a Missouri Valley title. In fact, six decades would pass before the Tigers experienced a sustained success approaching what Dr. Meanwell and his disciples had wrought. The coaches and players of Missouri's first golden era cast long shadows over the program, but shadows turned to darkness as the greatness that had become habit faded from memory.

## 1923–24

After years of spectacular success, the Tigers were due for a decline. They got a collapse. George Bond coached Missouri for three more seasons. In each of them, the Tigers lost at least as many games as they had lost in the previous six seasons combined when they posted a 96–10 cumulative record.

The worst year came first. The Tigers won just four of eighteen games in 1924, and two victories came against Iowa State, which went 1–15 in the Valley. Surprisingly, one of the others came late in the season against an Oklahoma team that went 13–3 in the league. Despite the disappointing year, MU students turned out in droves for the upset of the Sooners.

A natural recipient of blame might have been the young coach. And while Bond may not have had the gift for coaching possessed by Meanwell and Ruby, he certainly didn't have the same kind of players. In recent years, Herb Bunker and Arthur Browning had replaced George Williams and George Browning, who had replaced Craig Ruby and Phil Scott, who had replaced Mule Campbell and Clyde Slusher. But there was no one of that caliber to continue the chain of excellence. The writers of the student yearbook, often apologists for bad results, gave a fairly accurate assessment: "No team can lose such players as Bunker and 'Bun' Browning and expect to come back the next year with a team equally as great or stars equally as brilliant." The only fault in their analysis is that it suggests that the team achieved some level of greatness and the players some level of brilliance. They did not.

Ironically, Missouri's decline coincided with the ascendance of Don Faurot, a towering figure in the history of MU athletics, to the team's captaincy. The smallish man from tiny Mountain Grove

*Don Faurot, a football legend, captained the basketball team in 1923–24.*

built his legend as a football player, coach, and athletics director, not on the basketball court, where he was a good, but certainly not great, player. And his ability as a basketball player was not enhanced by the responsibilities of leadership. "The cares of the captaincy seemed to retard his play," said the *Savitar*'s season recap.

## 1924–25

Bond's teams showed only marginal improvement over the next two seasons. By the time the 1924–25 season rolled around, Frank Wheat, who emerged as an upstart scorer in 1923, was Missouri's seasoned veteran, its best player, captain, and lone senior. But without a star like Bun Browning drawing opponents' attention, Wheat found the going much tougher.

The going also was slowed by the success of the football team, which robbed Bond of several players early in the season. After Wheat, perhaps the Tigers' best player was sophomore football hero Ted O'Sullivan, who, like Faurot before him, managed to be a multisport star at just 148 pounds. A guard, he was a fine ball handler with a deft touch from long range. He was joined on the basketball team by other footballers, including Carl Bacchus and Charley Tuttle.

Coach Gwinn Henry's football team went 7–1 (and shut out six opponents!) in 1924 to win the Valley. When the squad received a bid to play Southern Cal in Los Angeles on Christmas Day (in a bowl-like event called the Christmas Festival), Coach Bond lost several players for the early part of the season. Instead of joining the team just after Thanksgiving (the others had been practicing since October), they joined the squad just three days before play began.

Despite the difficulties of piecing together a team at the last minute, the Tigers won their first

*Football star Ted O'Sullivan was a good outside shooter.*

three games, including contests at Iowa State and Drake. But then, just as the football players began to be fully integrated into the team, the wheels came off. The Tigers won just four of their final fifteen games and finished sixth in the Missouri Valley, a mild and inconsequential improvement on the previous year's tie for seventh. The inheritor of a proud tradition, Bond had become the captain of a sinking ship.

## 1925–26

Coach Bond tried to right the vessel in 1925–26, the season in which the MVC expanded to ten teams with the addition of Oklahoma A&M. But again Bond's Tigers showed mild improvement without real success. They finished at 8–10, and half of their wins came in the season's last five games as captain Hugh McMillan and leading scorer Jimmy McDonough helped to salvage something from a season that started as miserably as the previous two had ended. That surge left Missouri at an even 8–8 in the Valley, good for fourth place. The season's result was respectable but unsatisfying, and it led to a change.

George Bond moved on after four seasons as coach. Initially reassigned to other physical education duties, he soon left the athletic department for a career at General Motors. The eight wins in Bond's last year gave him thirty-four for his career, tying Meanwell for most ever by a Tiger coach, one ahead of Ruby's thirty-three. But he concluded with thirty-eight losses—Meanwell and Ruby combined for just four—eleven more than any other Missouri mentor. Bond also committed the unforgivable sin of going zero for eight against archrival Kansas, which wrestled the mantle of the Valley's dominant team from Missouri during his time as coach.

Bond's four-year tenure was the longest in the program's twenty-year history. Ten men had served as Missouri's coach, and the lack of continuity made any sort of enduring success difficult, if not impossible. But the stability that had been lacking was just around the corner. Though Missouri had hired ten coaches in its first twenty seasons, it would hire just six in the next eight decades.

## 1926–27

In 1926, when it came time to hire a new basketball coach, the university employed an old formula with a new twist. For the third time in six years, it hired a former player to fill the job. But unlike before, it

did not ask a youngster to trade cap and gown for clipboard and whistle, nor did it choose a lineal descendant of the Meanwell tradition. Instead, the university picked a scholarly gentleman from the program's early years, a time before the Wisconsin style, the All-Americans, and the conference titles, and asked him to restore the program's glory.

At age thirty-six, Kansas City native George Edwards was positively ancient compared with Missouri's recent string of coaches. A high school teammate of baseball legend Casey Stengel, Edwards played several sports in high school and college, achieving the most acclaim on the basketball court. In three seasons at Missouri, he played for coaches Chester Brewer and O. F. Field. A defensive guard, he earned All-Valley honors in 1913, the same season he captained the Tigers to their first winning record in four years. In addition to playing sports year-round, Edwards earned a degree from the university's new journalism school. After leaving Columbia, he won three state high school basketball titles as a coach in Salina, Kansas, and he served a stint as basketball coach at Kansas Wesleyan. He then taught and coached at Kansas City's Westport High School, where his teams won state basketball titles in 1925 and 1926 and finished second in the national scholastic basketball championships in 1925. The man had experience.

Cleft-chinned and bespectacled, Edwards looked more like a banker than a basketball coach. He wore gray fleece on the practice court but was strictly gray flannel off of it, and his gentlemanly demeanor was a far cry from the fiery Meanwell, whose legacy he hoped to revive. A kind and quiet man who rarely reprimanded players, George Edwards brought with him a calm that suggested stability, yet no one could have envisioned just how much stability

*George Edwards returned to his alma mater in 1926 to coach the Tigers.*

he would bring to the Missouri program. Only one prior coach had stayed as long as four years. Edwards would stay for twenty.

In addition to his many other interests, Edwards was an amateur magician. His first trick upon arriving in Columbia in the fall of 1926 was to make the losing disappear. After three sub-.500 years, the Tigers closed the decade with three winning seasons, the first coming in 1927. Edwards had modest talent to work with that year, including Teddy O'Sullivan, a senior guard, team captain, ball handler, long range shooter, and first rate defender. Teddy's top accomplice was Kenneth Yunker, a forward from Sedalia who would rank fourth in the league in scoring. Still, without a quality center, the team had a hole in the middle.

Notwithstanding that glaring weakness, the Tigers were the surprise of the league for much of the season. Edwards debuted with a win over

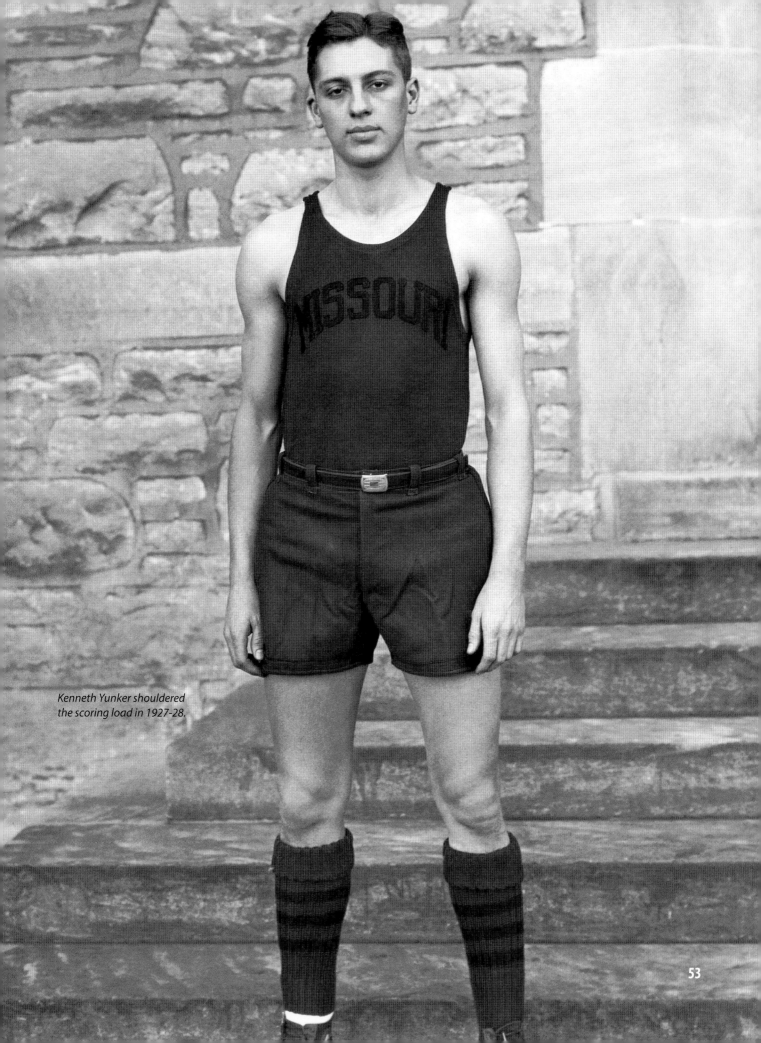

*Kenneth Yunker shouldered the scoring load in 1927-28.*

Kirksville Teachers College, coached by former Missouri star and future Missouri legend Don Faurot. Wins over Oklahoma A&M and Oklahoma on consecutive days put MU at 6–1 in the Valley and in first place with less than three weeks to play. But the Tigers lost five of their last six (to conference and nonconference foes alike) to fall to third at season's end. Nonetheless, they finished at 9–8. As he had done as team captain fourteen seasons before, Coach Edwards led the Tigers to their first winning record in four years.

Winning led to hope, a hope enhanced by a glimpse of the future every day in practice. Coach Anton Stankowski's freshman team held its own with the varsity, occasionally dominating the elder Tigers. With players like Marshall Craig and Wendell Baker set to join the A team in 1928, there was cause for significant optimism for the first time in a long while.

## 1927–28

By 1928 the enmity directed toward the University of Kansas was such that the spirit song "I'm a Son" ("I'm a son, a son, a son, a son of old Mizzou") contained the indelicate lyric "to hell with old K.U." In recent years, such sentiment was merely bluster when it came to basketball. The Jayhawks had beaten the Tigers eleven straight, dating back to Craig Ruby's final days as coach. One of George Edwards's most urgent responsibilities was to bring that streak to an end. Doing so would require the coach to shift responsibilities among his returning players while integrating newcomers into the lineup. With O'Sullivan graduated, Kenneth Yunker became the leader of the Tigers of old Mizzou, and George Flamank, a 210-pound football star, anchored the defense from his spot in the backcourt. Sophomore

*Defensive ace George Flamank*

Marshall Craig effectively filled the hole in the middle and became a dependable scorer.

The off-season optimism was rewarded when Mizzou won six of its first seven, including a 52–28 rout of Iowa State in which Yunker and Flamank combined for thirty-three. But two of the next three were against Oklahoma, and when the Sooners took them both, the conference race was all but over. From there, Oklahoma thundered to a perfect 18–0 in the Valley.

With the Sooner series behind them, the Tigers played for second place and pride. They moved toward the former and achieved some of the latter when they completed a season sweep of Kansas. Missouri's streak of eleven losses to the Jayhawks ended with a 32–30 win in Lawrence in January, but Kansas looked like a good bet to start another winning streak six weeks later in Columbia. The Jayhawks surged to a 12–4 lead before the Tigers closed the gap to two points at halftime. But Missouri dominated the second period and won 49–29 as Kenneth Yunker scored twenty. Four wins in the season's last six games put the Tigers second in the Missouri Valley, their best finish in five years.

# 1928-29

The end of the 1927–28 season marked the end of the original Missouri Valley Conference. When the league added Oklahoma A&M and expanded to ten schools, it caused problems, particularly in football, where teams played only five or six conference opponents in a year. At that time, the conference did not set schedules. Rather, the schools themselves arranged games with others in the Valley. Unfortunately, some were interested in scheduling only the league's weakest teams, a fact that threatened the legitimacy of conference championships. And so the Valley's larger schools—Missouri, Iowa State, Kansas, Kansas State, Nebraska and Oklahoma—left to form a new league. Though officially called the Missouri Valley Intercollegiate Athletic Association, it immediately became popularly known as the Big Six.

The birth of the Big Six simplified the schedule and stiffened the competition in basketball. In the Valley days, Missouri had mostly dominated Drake, Oklahoma A&M, Grinnell and, to a lesser extent, Washington. With those four gone, the conference schedule was shorter (just ten games), but it lacked pushovers. In the Missouri Valley's twenty-one-year history, five different schools had won basketball titles, and all were part of the new league (Iowa State was the lone member without a title).

The new arrangement suited the Tigers well in the season's opening weeks. Missouri won seven of its first nine, losing only at national powers Indiana and Butler, as Marshall Craig, Wendell Baker, Herb Ruble, and slick-shooting forward Harry Welsh took turns playing hero. Mizzou stood at 4–0 in the league when it hosted undefeated Oklahoma. The Tigers started fast but couldn't hold a halftime edge. Sooner star Tom Churchill took over the game and paced OU to a 40–34 win.

Missouri soldiered on, beating conference opponents, but losing to Washington University and Drake, two of the supposedly weaker teams booted to the curb when the Big Six left the little four behind. By the time the Tigers topped Kansas on February 20, they were 7–1 in the league with two games to play. Wins in those games—including the season finale at first-place Oklahoma—would secure at least a tie for the first Big Six championship.

Mizzou's hopes were dashed before getting to Norman. The Nebraska Cornhuskers, whom the Tigers had beaten six weeks before, came to Columbia and ended MU's title aspirations 39–33. With that, Oklahoma sewed up the championship, and the Tigers settled for second place. Despite the anticlimactic end, Missouri showed mettle by playing the champs to within a point in the year's final game. But Oklahoma proved its superiority throughout the year and finished with its second straight perfect conference record.

Still, the Tigers finished as league runner-up for the second straight year, junior defensive specialist Wendell Baker earned All-Big Six honors, and fellow junior Marshall Craig earned widespread acclaim. At the end of the decade, the program wasn't in the stellar shape it had been in at the beginning, but it was far better than when George Edwards inherited it. In ten remarkable years, the Tiger program had gone from highest heights to deepest depths to a steady rise. With Edwards firmly in control, a solid nucleus returning and a fancy new field house nearly completed, Missouri was poised to make a championship run at the dawn of the new decade—a dawn that would be darkened by a new national crisis.

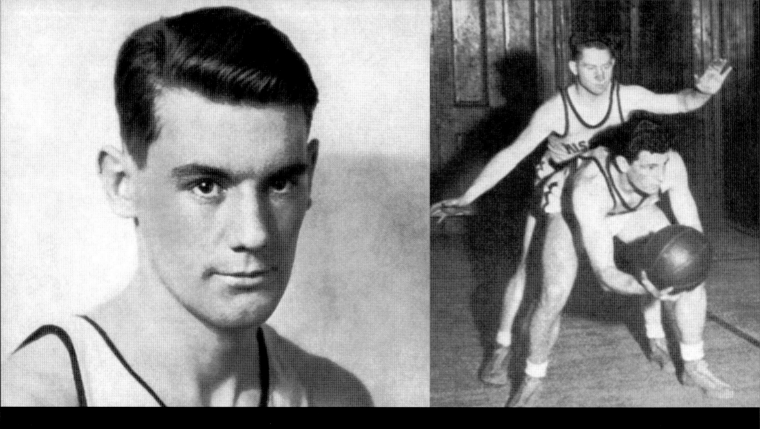

The 1920s stopped roaring on Tuesday, October 29, 1929, when the stock market crashed, signaling the start of America's Great Depression. While the nation struggled through economic crisis, the Thirties provided a new stability for the Missouri Tigers, as one coach led the team through the entire decade. But the consistency of George Edwards's leadership did not equal consistency on the court. It was an undulating decade, ten years of ups and downs. The series of peaks and valleys began on one of the higher pinnacles Missouri fans had ever seen.

# THE 1930s

## 1929-30

After the collapse of George Bond's final years, George Edwards had led the Tigers to three straight winning seasons, twice finishing second in the conference. The 1930 season gave him a chance to more fully restore the program's glory. His team was built for the present and infused with a sense of urgency. The deepest and most talented Tiger squad in years also was the most experienced. Of Mizzou's top seven players, five were seniors. The new season gave George Edwards his best shot yet at a championship. It gave his senior quintet its last.

That quintet was led by Wendell Baker, All-Big Six as a junior. On a team of stellar defenders, the standout was Baker, a big guard/center with a limited offensive repertoire. When the Tigers took the floor, Baker rarely scored; the man he guarded almost never did. The six-foot-six redhead from Kansas City also jumped center better than anyone in the league. When he went for the tip, the ball was all but conceded to Mizzou. What Baker was to the Tigers' defense, fellow senior Marshall Craig was to the offense. Craig, the league's most versatile player, led the Tigers in scoring. The remaining seniors were John Waldorf, another fierce defensive guard; Harry Welsh, a forward whose height and speed led to many Missouri points; and forward Richard Morgan, the team's third-leading scorer the previous year. Despite his experience, Morgan became a reserve in his final season, displaced by gigantic junior Charlie Huhn, who stood six foot six. The seventh key player was newcomer Max Collings, who played like a modern point guard with his ability to drive, pass and shoot.

Despite an array of capable scorers, these Tigers would forge their identity with paralyzing defense. In an age of lower scores, the Tigers held their foes to absurd

*Wendell Baker twice won all-conference honors for his fierce defensive play.*

point totals. In eighteen games, seven opponents would score twenty or less; only three would top thirty points. Mizzou, in contrast, topped thirty eleven times.

Less than two months after Black Tuesday, backed by a capacity crowd of fifteen hundred, Missouri welcomed Central College to Rothwell Gymnasium to open the season. In the second half, Missouri's defense rendered Central helpless. The Eagles managed just three points after halftime, as Mizzou won 24–17. The defense was equally effective in Missouri's second game, a nonconference tilt with Kansas in Kansas City just before Christmas. But the Jayhawks were even stingier, holding Mizzou to just two field goals in a 17–12 Tiger loss, one of the lowest combined point totals in Missouri's history. Before four thousand fans at Convention Hall, Jayhawk center Jim Bausch thoroughly outplayed Wendell Baker, repeatedly winning the tip from Mizzou's star. Though the game did not count in the standings, it established

Kansas as a favorite in the second season of the Big Six. As the Tigers later discovered, the road to the title would wind through Lawrence.

Mizzou found its offense in the season's third game, a 38–22 victory over a fine William Jewell team. Charlie Huhn keyed the scoring burst and helped control the ball simply by using a natural advantage; when he held the ball over his head, Jewell's players could not reach it. Huhn's effort aside, the night's top achievement belonged to George Edwards, who recorded his thirty-fifth career victory, moving him into first place on the all-time list of Missouri coaches. That total would more than quintuple over his tenure in Columbia.

After beating Washington University, the Tigers began conference play at Iowa State, where they made light work of the Cyclones. The next night, the Tigers eked out a 25–24 win at the University of Iowa before returning to Columbia and a home that was unfamiliar, yet fantastic.

When Chester Brewer returned to the University of Missouri in 1924 for his second stint as athletics director, he pledged to improve facilities. First came football. In 1926 the Tigers moved from humble Rollins Field to mammoth Memorial Stadium, originally constructed to hold twenty-five thousand spectators but designed to accommodate expansions that could take that number past ninety thousand.

Attention then turned to basketball. During the 1920s, schools across the country began to move away from gymnasiums and their small capacities and limited uses, and toward grand field houses that could hold larger crowds and stage more activities. In the summer of 1929, construction began on a field house for the Missouri Tigers.

That building opened in 1930. As America began to slip into crippling economic depression,

*The Tigers moved into state-of-the-art Brewer Field House in January 1930.*

the Tigers moved out of modest Rothwell Gym and into a lavish monument to indoor sports, a building that initially had no name. The field house, with its $225,000 price tag, hosted its first game on January 13 and drew rave reviews. Once inside, "spectators could sit back and admire the beauties and comforts of the building, its vast expanse and its perfect lighting arrangements." Tiny by today's standards, the field house was massive in its time, yet remarkably intimate. When configured for basketball, the action revolved around an elevated floor, with the closest fans peering out over the hardwood from seats below court-level. On the ends of the court, a few rows of bleachers backed up to walls of windows that let natural light pour in during the daytime, and allowed the exterior to glow on game night.

*The brilliant Marshall Craig led the Tigers to the 1930 Big Six championship.*

The field house provided a home that the Tigers could grow into; built to accommodate six thousand or more, it quadrupled Rothwell's capacity. On opening night, the thirty-five hundred on hand, sartorially resplendent in their suits, ties and hats, saw an impressive performance by their Tigers, who hosted Kansas State. But the next day most were talking about the night's near catastrophe, when a set of temporary bleachers collapsed, sending nearly three hundred fans tumbling. Remarkably, few were injured, none particularly seriously.

On the court, Mizzou handled the Wildcats (no longer the Aggies) with ease, even though Baker, who bruised his hip against Iowa State, was unable to control the tip. In the second half, Huhn—who led all scorers with twelve points—took over for his hobbled teammate and dominated jump balls to help Missouri control the game. The Tigers christened their new home with a 34–21 win that put them at 6–1 on the year and 2–0 in the Big Six.

Huhn again stood in for Baker when Mizzou hosted Nebraska. Marshall Craig starred in the 27–21 triumph by scoring nine points and holding Husker Don Maclay—the league's leading scorer—to eight. Missouri's defense was even tougher on Oklahoma's Tom Churchill, the defending Big Six scoring champ, who was held scoreless in his own gym, as Mizzou claimed a 37–20 win, made easier by Wendell Baker's return to form. Baker controlled the tip, stifled the Sooners and led the transition from offense to defense, dominating a game in which he did not score. Craig, in contrast, contributed thirteen points to an effort that moved Mizzou to 4–0 in league play.

After two nonconference victories against Creighton and a win over Iowa State at the new field house, Missouri, at 5–0, stood atop the standings, just ahead of 4–0 Kansas, with less than three weeks left to play. The Tigers started the stretch run in Manhattan, and took a 17–7 lead to halftime. But at the beginning of the second period, Missouri's stone wall defense sprung leaks, and the Wildcats rallied to tie the game at 17. The Tigers regained their composure and went on a run of their own to claim a 27–22 lead. But the defense faltered again and Kansas State took a late four-point lead. Only Harry Welsh's heroics gave Mizzou a chance. He sank three quick shots to put the Tigers up by two with a minute to play. But when K-State's Alex Nigro scored in the waning moments, the game went to overtime. In the extra period, Mizzou's sputtering offense produced but one Marshall Craig field goal in a 37–35 loss. The Tigers, who had held on to first place for so long, found themselves looking up at Kansas in the standings with just four games to play.

The loss in Manhattan made the next day's game in Lincoln even more important. Already fatigued by their fight with the Wildcats, the Tigers had little time to get from north central Kansas to southeast Nebraska, not an easy trip in those days. The Cornhuskers showed no mercy. Nebraska led by five at the break, and stifled Mizzou's comeback effort by trading baskets with the Tigers the rest of the way. With a 34–31 loss, the Tigers' championship chances were all but gone, or so said local papers in headlines like "Nebraska crushes Missouri title hopes," and "Defeat virtually eliminates Missouri from the conference race."

But as the *Chicago Tribune* would learn at the climax of a presidential election, it is unwise to prematurely report the demise of resilient Missourians. The Tigers were down, but not out. At 5–2 in the conference, the Tigers prepared to host 6–0 Kansas. A Kansas win would assure the Jayhawks of at least a tie for the title, while a Missouri victory would make it a race to the finish. The situation called for Mizzou to pull out all the stops.

The stops included speeches, music recitals and displays of folk dancing. On February 21, 1930, amid considerable pomp and circumstance, the University of Missouri's fancy new field house finally got a name. Before four thousand people, the largest crowd ever to see a basketball game in Columbia, the new structure was dedicated in honor of Chester Brewer "because of his tireless activity which made its construction and the building of Memorial Stadium possible."

Lengthy programs in Brewer's honor and in demonstration of the versatility of the field house preceded the game and entertained the crowd at halftime. The fans saw wall scaling, tumbling and dancing. In between, they saw some of the best basketball ever witnessed in Columbia. After Kansas seized an early 3–1 lead, Charlie Huhn hit a layup to tie the score, and Marshall Craig sank a long shot to give Mizzou a lead it never relinquished. Tactically, the glory belonged to George Edwards. Throughout the contest, the Tigers employed a "slow breaking offense" that allowed them to pick apart the Kansas defense. "It was a pageant of careful, cautious basket ball by Missouri," wrote the *Kansas City Times*. The Tigers employed patience and pounced on Jayhawk mistakes for easy scores, many by Charlie Huhn, who finished with fourteen points, most of them coming from point blank range. Kansas rallied in the second half to cut the deficit to one point, but when Huhn and Collings each drove for scores, Missouri began to pull away, turning the fans into "four thousand…mad men in ecstasy." The 29–18 victory raised Missouri's Big Six record to 6–2 and dropped Kansas to 6–1. The race was on.

While the Tigers waited for Oklahoma to come to town, Kansas ventured into Ames and limped away with a loss. Without lifting a finger, Missouri climbed into a tie for first place.

On March 1, the Tigers and the Jayhawks played their next-to-last games of the season. Kansas snuck past Nebraska, claiming a one-point win in Lincoln, while the Tigers rolled Oklahoma 36–20 as Welsh and Craig combined for twenty-two points. With one game to play, Missouri and Kansas each stood at 7–2.

It was Mizzou's biggest game in nearly a decade and the biggest yet in George Edwards's career. It

*"Giant" Charlie Huhn stood six-foot-six.*

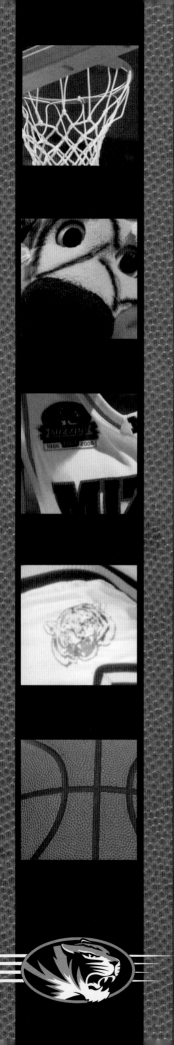

was a big game for Kansas, too, but big games were old hat to Phog Allen. Allen, forty-four years old and in the prime of his career, already had coached Kansas to eight conference titles. And while Kansas fans had grown accustomed to playing for championships, they were hardly blasé about it. They greeted the chance to win the Big Six crown with a fevered enthusiasm. The Jayhawks had recently moved to their new home in Hoch Auditorium, with its alleged capacity of three thousand. But a crowd of forty-two hundred—almost five hundred more than had ever seen a game in Lawrence—tested Hoch's limits and mocked fire codes, the spectators "frescoed on the walls, the floor, the chairs and everything else."

Once play began, the Kansas faithful witnessed a near-exact replica of the contest Missouri's fans had seen twelve days earlier. Amid claustrophobic conditions, with antagonistic fans close enough to touch, the Missouri Tigers dismantled Kansas, and they did it methodically, precisely, overwhelmingly. The key, as it had been so often, was Baker's dominance of the tip, as Mizzou's star exacted revenge on Jim Bausch, the Kansas center who had embarrassed him during the holiday season. Thanks to Baker's efforts, Mizzou monopolized the ball. And as had been the case in Columbia, the Tigers used a combination of icy patience and fiery decisiveness to stagger the Jayhawks' defense, exploiting cracks and then making shots, often from under the basket. Once inside the lane, Missouri's superior size rendered Kansas helpless, and the Tigers raced to a 10–3 lead in the first half. The lead stretched to 20–9 after halftime, and Mizzou eased to a 23–18 win. Baker, holding form, failed to score, but his teammates all chipped in, with Welsh, Huhn, and Craig doing the most damage. Once the game ended, word quickly spread in Columbia. The score was flashed on movie screens at local theaters, and exuberant students poured into the streets to revel in Missouri's first Big Six championship.

The Tigers reaped postseason honors that befitted their achievement. Wendell Baker headlined the All-Big Six team, the first Tiger honored in consecutive seasons since Herb Bunker and Bun Browning eight years before. Marshall Craig joined Baker on the first team, and John Waldorf—whose defensive prowess gained notice around the league—made the second squad. Craig and Harry Welsh were the league's fourth- and seventh-leading scorers, respectively, while Charlie Huhn finished ninth in the race. In retrospect, Patrick Premo rated the Tigers the nation's number seven team, a lofty position not dreamed of when the season began. In an era before postseason tournaments, these Tigers achieved almost all there was to achieve, providing a storybook send-off to Missouri's fine senior class. But success in college sports is ephemeral. After the season's end and subsequent commencement exercises, George Edwards had to ask himself the question on all Missouri fans' minds: where do we go from here?

# 1930–31

If the question was "Where do we go from here?" the answer was "down." The Tigers began a protracted stretch of mediocrity through most of the Thirties, never great, seldom bad, usually competitive. Still, mediocrity would have been a blessing early in the 1930–31 season.

In the Missouri Tigers' twenty-fifth year of college basketball, the game was still evolving. The latest conventional wisdom called for conservative play on offense. The style adopted throughout the Big Six slowed the game to the speed of cool molasses, as teams exhibited an extreme, hypnotic patience in efforts to lull defenses into drowsy mistakes. Defenses, in contrast, did their best to force action. Zones, once ubiquitous, all but disappeared, and extended man-to-man pressure became the rage. Passive offenses and aggressive defenses produced scores more appropriate for football. A typical game might end 28–27, with a missed free throw—not a missed extra point—making the difference.

*Max Collings earned All-America recognition for his play in 1931.*

For Missouri, the deliberate style helped mask a deficiency of talent. Coach Edwards had banked on being without Baker, Craig, and the other seniors who had carried Mizzou to the 1930 Big Six title. He had not anticipated losing Max Collings, but academic shortcomings put the budding star on the shelf through the first semester. When play began in December, Charlie Huhn was the only returning regular available.

Huhn was joined by fellow senior Hubert Campbell and a host of greenhorns, including a big sophomore forward named Norman Wagner, a disarmingly courteous and studious engineering major from Normandy High in St. Louis. The lack of experience showed early in the year, and the Tigers' defense of their conference championship began in disastrous fashion.

Mizzou dropped its first six decisions, three of them by a single point. One of the losses, however, was among the most lopsided ever for the Tigers, and it came at the hands of an old friend. The Tigers traveled to Madison, Wisconsin, to play Walter Meanwell's Badgers. In their only meeting ever with the architect of Mizzou's great teams of the World War I era, the Tigers were humiliated 37–9.

Despite the losing streak, twenty-five hundred Missouri fans filed into the field house to see the Tigers finally capture a victory 20–18 over Iowa State. Nine days later, the fans returned to Brewer, as did Max Collings, back from academic exile. Missouri immediately became a different team. Against Oklahoma, Charlie Huhn dominated in every phase. He controlled the tip and both lanes, and scored a game-high nine points. The Tigers grabbed an early lead and then retreated into their ball control offense. Collings scored four in his return, a 22–14 triumph that raised MU's conference record to 2–2.

Even with Collings, Missouri dropped decisions at Kansas and Iowa State, effectively eliminating the Tigers from Big Six contention. But they responded with their best basketball of the season, beating Nebraska and Oklahoma by thirteen and ten, respectively, and taking a pair of easy nonleague wins against Creighton and Washington University.

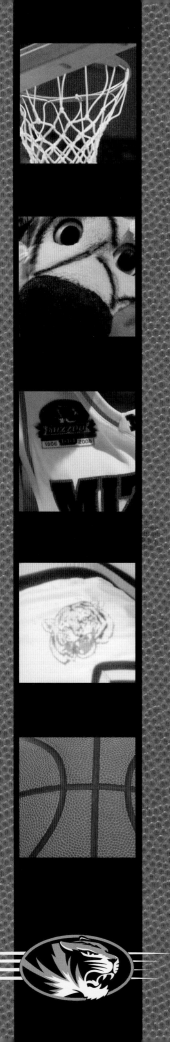

After the abysmal start, Missouri had crept toward respectability, standing 7–8 overall and 4–4 in the Big Six. An even better sense of the Tigers' quality was reflected in their 6–2 record with Collings in the lineup.

Still, a 21–14 loss at Kansas State ensured the first overall losing record for George Edwards in five seasons in Columbia. But Mizzou had one chance to extend the coach's streak without a losing season in league play.

*John Cooper, college basketball's first jump shooter, made the All-Big Six team as a sophomore.*

That chance came against the conference champs. At 7–2, Kansas already had clinched the Big Six title, but the annual meeting in Columbia provided ample drama even without title implications. The main plot twist came when Missouri ditched its slow-breaking offense for a game plan that saw the Tigers charge toward the basket. The switch had little early impact, and the teams went to halftime tied at 12. Coach Edwards continued to employ the aggressive style after the break, but it was Mizzou's defense that made the difference. Kansas failed to score for the first sixteen minutes of the second half. Norman Wagner scored eleven for Missouri, and Hubert Campbell held Jayhawk Tom Bishop, the league's second-leading scorer, to just four points in a 26–19 victory that helped redeem a season that had started so badly.

The 5–5 finish in the Big Six was good for a third-place tie with Kansas State. Charlie Huhn made the all-league first team, and Max Collings, a second team pick, was named to *College Humor* magazine's All-American team, a legitimate honor despite the source. With Huhn set to graduate, Collings and Wagner would form the foundation of yet another contender.

# 1931–32

Anyone who underestimates the home court advantage in college basketball should heed the tale of the 1931–32 Tigers. A schedule frontloaded with home games helped the Tigers build a lead in the Big Six standings, but a late road trip derailed them in a race that came down to the very last hours.

Max Collings, "one of the cleverest basket ball players in the country," returned for his senior season at guard, and six-foot-four junior Norman Wagner moved to Charlie Huhn's old spot at center and dominated tip-offs. Missouri also added a prominent new piece in sophomore forward/center John Cooper, who achieved a minor stardom almost immediately. Cooper was not the greatest Tiger player, but he was one of the best of his time. He was not the highest scorer the Big Six had seen, but he was close. And he would not lead his team to a championship, but he would help lead a revolution, changing the most fundamental thing in the game: the way players shoot the ball.

Since Naismith invented the game, shooting had evolved little. Shoulders squared to the basket, ball tucked under the chin, feet on the floor. The method proved accurate enough, but it was fairly easy to defend.

Enter the jump shooters. John Cooper began leaving his feet to shoot during his Kentucky high school days. But when George Edwards saw him practicing his shot as a freshman, the coach admonished Cooper to keep both feet planted. Edwards, however, came around when he saw Cooper go high in the air to catch a ball and then flip it into the basket when no teammate came open for a pass. More pragmatist than purist, Edwards never complained about the jump shot again.

Though he stood a hair under five-foot-eleven, Cooper's leaping ability (he could put both hands inside the hoop) allowed him to play center. Most opponents were bigger, but few could guard him. Cooper would hold the ball indefinitely inside the narrow free throw lane, and fake, spin, drive, spin some more, jump and shoot over taller defenders, hitting the target with enough frequency to cause consternation among traditionalists who viewed

Edwards, who used his position as secretary of the national coach's association to survey colleagues from across the country.

Despite having such a potent new weapon, the Tigers were nothing special in nonconference play, going just 3–5. A loss to Creighton was particularly tough to swallow. Late in the game, after Mizzou pushed to a 34–29 lead, Creighton scored six straight to steal a 35–34 win. Two of Creighton's earlier points had come in a most unorthodox fashion. A rowdy Missouri crowd heckled calls made by referee Ernest Quigley, who presided over a rough game.

*At practice, Max Collings defends Norman Wagner as John Cooper looks on.*

such foolishness as simply throwing up prayers. The writer who dubbed Cooper's move the "jack knife contortion shot" probably came as close as anyone to aptly describing it.

Cooper's shot was not just potent, it was pioneering. No other player in the conference used the jump shot, nor did any other player in the nation, at least according to the investigation of George

When the boos proved too much, Quigley slapped the crowd with a technical foul, and the two free throws provided Creighton's margin of victory. It marked the last time Quigley would work at Brewer Field House in 1932.

Nonconference struggles aside, the Tigers got off to a hot start in conference play, aided by a schedule that put them at home for five

of their first six league games. They won the home games, but lost at Iowa State. Their 5–1 record gave them the lead in the Big Six, with Oklahoma and Kansas tied for second at 4–3. Offensively, Mizzou was propelled by Cooper, a member of the all-conference team, and co-winner of the league's scoring title (with KU's Ted O'Leary).

The quirky schedule put Missouri on the road for its final four games. The trip started badly. Losses at Kansas and Oklahoma dropped the Tigers into third place. But Mizzou got a crucial win at Nebraska, as Wagner's defense and Cooper's offense (he scored fifteen) gave the Tigers a 32–28 triumph. At 6–3, Mizzou pulled into a tie with Kansas and Oklahoma. The Sooners and Jayhawks would face each other in Lawrence on the season's last night; at the same time, the Tigers would tangle with Kansas State. A win would mean a tie for the Big Six title, Missouri's second championship in three seasons.

It was not to be. The Wildcats shackled Cooper, holding him scoreless from the field in the second half. Kansas State packed its defense in around the basket, and declined to chase Missouri's shooters around the court. When the Tigers failed to knock down enough shots to force the Cats out of the lane, their offense bogged down. The 28–22 loss cost Missouri the conference crown. When Kansas beat Oklahoma, the Jayhawks had the title to themselves, as the Tigers missed their best chance at a championship for years to come.

## 1932–33

After nearly stealing the title in the closing days of the 1932 season, the Tigers had reason to believe that they could capture the 1933 crown. Though Max Collings was lost to graduation, Norman Wagner and John Cooper returned, as did a solid supporting cast, including Vic Davis, George Stuber, and Denver Miller. Cooper, however, moved to guard after dominating the league from the frontcourt as a sophomore. Perturbed by Cooper's unorthodox style, Phog Allen successfully petitioned for a rule that prohibited players from holding the ball in the free throw lane for more than three seconds. Stripped of his advantage over bigger players, Cooper moved to the perimeter where he modified the traditional two-handed set shot and became Missouri's first long-range jump-shooter.

The season began with some sadistic scheduling. The Tigers left Columbia on December 13, switching trains in St. Louis en route to Indianapolis, where they opened the campaign on December 14 and fell to perennial power Butler. After the game, the Tigers boarded a train for Washington, D.C., to meet George Washington University the next day. Snow and bitter cold delayed them for twelve hours, and they rushed to the court just before tip, without time for a meal or warm-ups. Nonetheless, they topped GW, and then managed to fit in some sightseeing, including a trip to the White House where they met President Herbert Hoover and Secretary of Agriculture Arthur Hyde, a former Missouri governor. The team hopped another

*Denver Miller blossomed into a star in his junior season.*

*An outstanding student and athlete, Norman Wagner earned the prestigious Big Six Medal for Athletics and Scholarship.*

train and arrived in St. Louis just in time to defeat Washington University, Mizzou's third game in three whirlwind days. Lucky to escape with a 2–1 record, the Tigers were equally fortunate to find an offensive chemistry absent the previous year, when the burden of scoring had fallen almost entirely on Wagner and Cooper. But at the dawn of this new season, Miller and Stuber emerged as near equals of the established stars, aided by a new double-post offense that called for the players to set frequent screens for one another.

Upon their return to Columbia, the Tigers got three days to rest before their first-ever meeting with the University of Illinois. It was also their first meeting with Illinois coach and Tiger legend Craig Ruby, who left Columbia for Champaign in 1922. After former teammates feted Ruby at a dinner in his honor, the Illini feasted on a Mizzou squad that missed high-scoring guard Denver Miller due to a recently fractured cheek bone. Despite the 36–24 loss, the Tigers stood 4–2 by the time they played their conference opener.

Big Six play followed a familiar pattern. Again, the Tigers won all five conference home games. And again, the only league foe they beat on the road was Nebraska. But unlike the previous year, the schedule sent them on a brutal early excursion. After beating Nebraska and Iowa State in Columbia, the Tigers lost every game on a three-game trip. The most crushing blow came at Oklahoma, where Mizzou took a 17–8 halftime lead, only to lose 31–26.

Upon returning home, Missouri began to claw back into the hunt. The Tigers engaged league-leading Kansas in a rough, physical game. Mizzou's intensity paid off on defense, as Denver Miller and Norman Wagner held Kansas stars Bill Johnson and Paul Harrington to a combined three points in a nip-and-tuck contest. Miller and Wagner also made critical plays on offense. With the game tied at 17, and less than three minutes to play, Wagner hit two free throws to give Mizzou the lead. Later, Miller slashed to the basket for the final two points in a 21–17 win that lifted the Tigers into third place. Six days later, Oklahoma, the new league leader, came to Columbia, where forty-two hundred Missouri faithful awaited them. The Tigers again pulled off the upset as Wagner, Cooper and Stuber combined for thirty-five points in a 40–30 win that dropped OU into a tie with Kansas and put Mizzou just a game out of the lead.

Standing 4–3 with three games to play, Missouri had a glimmer of hope in the conference race. That glimmer was extinguished at Iowa State. The Cyclones' Ralph Thomson sank a free throw with one second to play, breaking a 31–31 tie and giving Iowa State the win.

After a win at Nebraska, the Tigers returned home to cap the season against Kansas State. The game gave Missouri a shot at a winning record overall and in the conference, and it gave Norman Wagner, who was running neck-and-neck with KU's Bill Johnson, a shot at the league scoring title. In one of the year's most entertaining games, the Tigers trailed the Wildcats by two points with a minute to play, and Wagner trailed Johnson by one. Wagner's late field goal put the game into overtime and clinched the scoring crown. He scored four more in the extra period to give Mizzou a 37–33 win.

The scoring champ was named first team All-Big Six, an honor he had won in baseball the previous year, but the greatest tribute came from George Edwards, who said that, through dedication, Wagner developed "from a mediocre player to one of the most skillful in American intercollegiate basketball." Wagner also proved to be one of the most durable Tigers ever—in eighteen games, he spent just ten minutes on the bench. John Cooper, who earned second team honors, finished fourth in the scoring race at 8.8 points per game in ten Big Six contests. With Wagner on the verge of graduation, Mizzou's hopes in 1934 would rest with Cooper and Denver Miller, set to return for their senior season. For those hopes to be realized, the Tigers would need to find a way to win away from home.

## 1933-34

By 1933 the devastated United States economy had hit its lowest point, with one in four Americans unemployed. The effects were felt everywhere, including the University of Missouri, where enrollment dropped by 19 percent in the three years between 1930–31 and 1933–34.

Despite the exodus from campus, George Edwards continued to field a competitive team. His squad featured five sophomores, including the promising Evans Powell, but the stars were two seniors—Denver Miller and John Cooper—and a junior, Kenneth "Duke" Jorgensen. Cooper had become one of the most feared players in the league, and defenses blanketed him unlike any other player in the Big Six. That attention would drive down his production from previous years, while providing opportunity for Miller and Jorgensen.

Missouri continued the pattern established the prior two seasons. The Tigers were tough to top at home, easy to tame on the road. Among conference opponents, league champion Kansas was the only team to beat them at Brewer Field House, while Iowa State and Kansas State were the only to be conquered on their home floors (Missouri also won at Oklahoma in a game scheduled as a nonconference affair). Overall, the Tigers compiled their second straight 10–8 record, and their third consecutive 6–4 mark in the Big Six. They tied Oklahoma for second place behind a Kansas team that won its fourth straight title.

Miller, the team's captain, earned All-Big Six honors, and Cooper, a second team pick, graduated as one of the league's most respected players. Jorgensen, a fine long-range shooter, earned second team all-conference honors, and inherited the captaincy from Miller. For three years, Cooper and Miller had been keystones of the Tigers' limited success. Ever optimistic, the students at the *Savitar* wrote that "the development of five sophomores speaks well of Missouri's chances for a conference championship next year," but that was just wishful thinking. Without Cooper and Miller, the Tigers faced an uphill climb.

## 1934-35

In the 1934–35 season, the conference employed an unusual schedule. Iowa State and Nebraska played each of their five conference foes twice, while Missouri, Kansas, Kansas State, and Oklahoma played each other four times apiece. For the Cyclones and Cornhuskers, it meant a ten-game slate, while the others played sixteen times. For Mizzou, the expanded conference schedule meant a truncated nonleague slate. A pre-Christmas excursion to St. Louis provided the Tigers with their only two games outside the Big Six.

The new format, which cut down on travel, was unkind to Missouri. The Tigers opened the season with losses to St. Louis University and Washington U., then lost their first five league contests to open the season at 0–7. A one-point win over Nebraska stopped the losing streak. All-Big Six guard Duke Jorgensen scored twelve in the victory, while Evans Powell and Ralph Beer anchored Mizzou's defense. But the Tigers promptly resumed their losing ways on a short road trip that yielded one loss at Iowa State and two at Kansas State, and dropped their record to 1–10.

*Denver Miller prepares to shoot a free throw at the field house.*

The Tigers then began an amazing late-season turnaround, paced by Jorgensen and a surprising newcomer. It started with a trip to Lincoln, where sophomore forward Carmin "Chink" Henderson, who had made his Missouri debut just days earlier in Manhattan, teamed with Ralph Beer to score the bulk of the points in the 23–21 triumph over Nebraska. Back home, the Tigers hosted Kansas State for a pair of games. Jorgensen, Mizzou's best defender and leading scorer, tallied fifteen in the first game, a 44–31 victory, as Henderson and Powell contributed ten and nine, respectively. The next day, tight Tiger defense left the Wildcats resorting to futile long heaves at the hoop. Henderson, the midseason godsend, led the Tigers with eleven in an easy 34–20 win.

After splitting a pair at Oklahoma, the Tigers closed the year by hosting Kansas in two games at Brewer. A sweep could have given the Jayhawks their fifth straight conference crown. But the rejuvenated Tigers spoiled KU's season. A capacity crowd saw Mizzou win the first game 23–21 when Jorgensen held Ray Ebling, the league's leading scorer, without a point. Jorgensen was nearly as effective the next night, as Ebling scored just two points, and Kansas fell 21–18. Phog Allen went to his bench repeatedly, but George Edwards let his starters go the distance. That group rewarded him with an impressive, balanced effort. Gene Thompson, Lavere Strom, Chink Henderson, and Duke Jorgensen each scored four points, while Evans Powell chipped in five. Missouri's effort handed the Big Six title to

Iowa State, the Cyclones' first conference basketball crown.

After losing ten of their first eleven, the Tigers won six of seven to close the season, as Henderson earned honorable mention in the Big Six. The turnaround, impressive as it was, still left the Tigers with a losing record in conference play, a first in the

*Kenneth "Duke" Jorgensen earned all-conference honors in his senior year.*

Edwards era. Unfortunately, the late-season rally did not translate into momentum for the next year.

## 1935–36

The good news about 1935–36: so respected was George Edwards that his peers elected him vice president of the National Association of Basketball Coaches, a precursor to his election as president for the 1937–38 season. The bad news: just about everything else.

The Tigers had few stars, fewer compelling victories and a last-place finish

in the conference. Four of their five wins came by five or fewer points while many of their twelve losses were terribly lopsided. It was Missouri's worst season of the George Edwards era.

The Tigers lacked scoring punch. Senior guard Evans Powell led Mizzou with just 5.1 points per game. Nonetheless, Powell, the team's lone upperclassman, earned a spot on the All-Big Six second team. Lavere Strom and Chink Henderson struggled through the season, and each missed a number of games.

The Tigers opened the season with a one-point, last-minute victory over Westminster, but then lost seven of eight, including a 42–16 thrashing by Southern Cal in Kansas City, and a 51–24 loss to Warrensburg, Mizzou's most lopsided defeat to date at Brewer Field House. The sole win in that stretch came in the Big Six opener. The Tigers upset Oklahoma despite missing Henderson, sidelined by a tonsillectomy. Missouri got ten points from Powell, nine each from Strom and sophomore John Carroll (Chink's replacement at center), and six from Ralph Beer. But such performances came rarely. A win at Ames four weeks later would be Missouri's only other conference victory. A pair of nonleague wins over St. Louis and Washington University late in the year saw forward Allan Hatfield force his way into the lineup and emerge as a solid scorer, but it was not nearly enough to salvage the season.

While the Tigers struggled, the university convened a committee to address student behavior at basketball games. It seems that Mizzou students booed referees and heckled rivals a bit more lustily than their counterparts at other Big Six schools; even the band had played "Three Blind Mice" as officials of marginal competence exited the floor at halftime of a game. On campus, reactions varied. Basketball coach George Edwards was mostly bemused. While acknowledging some occasional rowdiness, he did not perceive the students to be much more rambunctious than their peers in Lawrence, nor did he believe that they unfairly affected the outcomes of games. Football coach Don Faurot, on the other hand, expressed indignation, saying that booing had no place in collegiate sports.

Though the committee of faculty and students focused mostly on how to limit booing, it also

*Captain Evans Powell led Missouri through the disappointing 1935–36 season.*

addressed complaints leveled by Phog Allen after the Jayhawks' mid-January visit to Columbia. Allen had taken umbrage at the Mizzou students and their desecration of that most sacred of Kansas chants. "Rock chalk dead hawk!" they yelled in unison. Most committee members expressed little concern about Allen's protest, and some even seemed amused, inclined to think that such conduct would be justified as long as Kansas partisans continued to holler, "Twist that Tiger's tail" and "Black that Tiger's eye" when the Missouri team visited Lawrence. For his part, George Edwards believed that Allen had brought much of the unfriendly treatment upon himself by his flamboyant conduct over the years in Columbia.

Decades later, it seems that the task was too large for the committee. Unrepentant Tiger fans continue to boo the Jayhawks from time to time.

## 1936–37

After the worst season in more than a decade, Missouri got off to a surprisingly good start in 1936–37, the season in which the jump ball following each score finally was eliminated. The Tigers went undefeated in December, knocking off four nonconference foes, including an overtime win against Colorado in Denver. But they knew things would get tougher as the season progressed. Chink Henderson, who had transferred to MU from Central College, would run out of eligibility between semesters.

Ralph Beer (the team's captain and leading scorer) provided senior leadership, but Edwards's squad was made up mostly of sophomores, including Kenny Brown, a big center from Lee's Summit. The inexperience showed when conference play began. Though Mizzou would better the previous year's last-place finish, it was thanks mostly to an Iowa State team that failed to win a single league game. Two of the Cyclones' ten losses came to Missouri, the only triumphs the Tigers would have in the Big Six.

With both Iowa State games coming early, Mizzou's fans might have been tricked into believing that their Tigers were contenders. Strong performances by Henderson and Brown against the Cyclones pushed Mizzou to 2–2 in the conference and 6–2 overall. But shortly thereafter, the schedule stiffened, Henderson departed, and the Tigers faded, winning only one of their remaining eight games, a nonleague tilt with St. Louis. In their losses, the Tigers often stayed close, but a 50–21 whipping by Nebraska exposed the team's many faults, and left fans to wonder whether there was any hope that things could be turned around. Hope, it turns out, had spent the season on the freshman team and was ready to move up to varsity.

## 1937–38

After bottoming out in 1936 and 1937, Missouri's 1937–38 season began a slight but perceptible upswing. The Tigers doubled the two conference wins recorded in each of the previous two seasons, and posted victories over three different Big Six foes, not just Iowa State. The difference was talent, but it was young talent. Team captain Kenny Brown was but a junior, and the squad was rounded out mostly by sophomores.

John Lobsiger came from Gary, Indiana, to pursue an education in journalism. A slender six foot

*Tiger guard Ralph Beer*

three inches, he played like a modern point guard. A fine one-handed set shooter, Lobsiger was also a deft ball handler and passer. Many of his passes would find their way to Bill Harvey, a terrific left-handed jump shooter who played mostly on the wing. Clay Cooper, brother of former Tiger star John, was a physical player who excelled defensively. Despite standing just five-foot-ten-and-a-half, he played forward and made good use of a one-handed jump fade shot. Blaine Currence put his athleticism and six-foot-five frame to good use in the pivot, though his skills allowed him to play on the wing from time to time. And six-foot-seven Haskell Tison, described as "a modern Goliath," backed Currence up at center. These five sophomores would provide the foundation for a Missouri basketball renaissance.

Their arrival on campus was a product of good luck, not precise planning. George Edwards resisted the growing movement toward active recruiting. He might send a letter to an athlete, but he would not visit, and he certainly would not make promises. Like all others who aspired to be Tigers, his prize sophomores paid their own way to school and earned spots on the team through tryouts.

The Tigers stood 4–3 when they opened league play in Lincoln against the Cornhuskers, who had shared the 1937 title with Kansas. Sophomores Harvey, Lobsiger, and Cooper started the game, along with junior Hal Halsted, and Kenny Brown, the only returning letter-winner among the bunch. Halsted, a guard, displayed a sharp eye from long range, while Lobsiger seemed to corral all of Nebraska's missed shots, denying the Huskers second-chance points. But Bill Harvey stole the show. His thirteen points led all scorers in a 28–18 win, Missouri's first conference road victory against someone other than Iowa State in almost three years.

Still, road wins would be tough to come by, especially shorthanded. Kenny Brown was out with the flu when the Tigers dropped a double-overtime heartbreaker at Kansas State. Mizzou returned home to win two of three (one a nonconference affair) before falling short on the road again, dropping a three-point decision to an Iowa State club that was little better than the previous year's winless squad.

At 2–3 in the Big Six, Missouri faced Nebraska at Brewer, and Bill Harvey scored fifteen points to

*Kenny Brown started at center in the late 1930s.*

propel the Tigers to a 38–30 win that leveled their league record. Next came a return engagement with Kansas State. Homer Wesche, the Wildcats' fine center, scored almost at will to give K-State a 24–21 halftime edge, but the Tigers erupted in the second half. At the final gun, Kenny Brown had tallied twenty-two points, as Missouri blitzed Kansas State to win 59–46. It marked the first time that the Tigers and an opponent had united to score in triple digits.

The win put Missouri at 4–3 in the Big Six, but the season's last three games would come against the league's two best teams. The first came at Oklahoma, where Haskell Tison scored sixteen points. But the Tigers fell just short, losing 41–39. The teams met again a week later in Columbia. The Sooners entered the game, their season finale, needing a win for a chance at the championship, while Missouri sought to secure third place. Harvey and Lobsiger paced Mizzou to an early five-point edge, but Oklahoma regrouped to take the lead in the second half. The Tigers rallied to tie the score at 47, but Oklahoma made the critical plays in the frantic waning moments to secure a 55–52 victory that was described as "the wildest scoring orgy in the Big Six history."

## 1938–39

After the Tigers won the 1930 Big Six title, they floundered through the next eight years, posting a cumulative 65–75 record, never better than 6–4 in conference play. A modern coach would fear for his job after such a stretch, but there was nothing particularly modern about George Edwards. At a time when winning wasn't everything, the gentlemanly deportment and scholastic commitment of Missouri's mentor guaranteed job security. Also, there's a real sense that the University of Missouri might have collapsed without him. Over the course of his career, Edwards also served as tennis coach, golf coach, golf course manager, sports information director, assistant football coach, physical education instructor, and, eventually, athletics director and head of the physical education department. George Edwards wasn't just a pillar of his community; he was the foundation.

He fielded a formidable squad in 1938–39, a time when basketball began to take on more national prominence. In 1938 the six-team National Invitation Tournament had become the first major college playoff, and the NCAA would initiate its own eight-team event in 1939. Mizzou's strength came not from an influx of new talent but from ripening veterans. The Tigers of 1937–38 had seen their share of triumphs, including a pair of wins over Colorado, the eventual runner-up in the inaugural NIT. But they also met disappointment, caused primarily by their inability to win close games on the road. Losses by three points at Iowa State, two at Oklahoma and one at Kansas State (in overtime) squelched any hopes for a Big Six title.

The sting of those losses helped transform a team of wide-eyed kids into a group of wizened vets. Seven players returned, including John Lobsiger, Missouri's catalyst on both ends of the floor, a sublime guard whose quality was not captured by the scant statistics then kept. Lobsiger's defense was such that Kansas State coach Jack Gardner called him the "human handcuff."

The talented Tigers stumbled early in the season, losing a pair of games on the road, and then falling to Wyoming at home. It would be Mizzou's only loss at Brewer all season.

*Bill Harvey's left-handed jump shot was a potent weapon.*

With one game to play, all that stood between Mizzou and a .500 league record was Kansas. All that stood between Kansas and sole possession of the Big Six title was Missouri. In addition to smelling a championship, the Jayhawks smelled blood when the Tigers took the floor without Kenny Brown, who had broken his thumb against Oklahoma. In the face of a hostile crowd and a motivated opponent, Mizzou never had a chance. Jayhawk Fred Pralle scored twenty-two to secure the conference scoring title, and Kansas won 56–36 to secure the conference championship.

Missouri finished 9–9 overall and 4–6 in the Big Six. The Tigers' rising fortunes weren't obvious from their record, but they were obvious from their play. Missouri had suffered through routs routinely over the previous two seasons, but they stood toe to toe with all comers in 1938. The season-ending loss at Kansas was the only lopsided defeat against Big Six foes. The other five losses had come by an average of less than three points per game. Missouri's newfound competitiveness combined with the expected return of every key player suggested that success was just around the corner. It was.

Missouri got well on a western swing. The Tigers christened 1939 with a 51–48 overtime win at the University of Denver and then whipped Greeley State. The trip ended with a six-point win at Wyoming, avenging the earlier loss.

*Clay Cooper, a fixture at Mizzou for years as an assistant football coach, was a stellar defender.*

With renewed confidence, Missouri opened Big Six play by routing Iowa State. Lobsiger led Missouri with thirteen points, and Clay Cooper came off the bench to score twelve. An impressive effort, but Mizzou's next performance revealed real championship mettle. A powerful Oklahoma team visited Brewer and took a 28–17 lead well into the second half. But the Bengal five (as they were often called) staged a tremendous rally. Tison, Halsted, Lobsiger, and Cooper all scored for Missouri, as the Tigers reeled off eleven straight points to knot the score at 28. A Clay Cooper free throw and a Bill Harvey field goal put Missouri up by three late in the game. But Oklahoma, led by All-American Jimmy McNatt, scored three quick points to force overtime. In the extra period, Harvey turned a pair of offensive rebounds into four points, the final margin in a 37–33 victory that put Missouri alone atop the Big Six standings.

The Tigers were not alone for long. They lost in Lawrence, where Jayhawk guard Dick Harp starred in a 37–32 Kansas win that dropped Mizzou into a tie with Iowa State. But Missouri returned home and picked up wins over Nebraska and Washington University. More than anyone, it was Lobsiger, despite a bum leg, who drove Missouri's improved play, especially on defense. At 8–4 overall and 3–1 in the Big Six, the Tigers stood poised for a title run.

But the hostile road awaited them. In Ames, Harlan Keirsey scored sixteen points, but husky Bob Harris countered with nineteen as the Cyclones prevailed by six. Then, in Norman, a 43–40 loss to Oklahoma dropped the Tigers into a three-way tie for third in the Big Six at 3–3, 0–3 on the road. By day's end, home teams held an 18–1 season-long edge in conference play.

On the verge of falling out of contention, the Tigers broke the road hex with a 46–36 win at Nebraska, behind twelve points from Clay Cooper. The win moved Missouri into a second-place tie with Kansas, just a game behind Oklahoma, and renewed hopes for a championship.

*John Lobsiger, Missouri's All-American floor general*

Those hopes got a boost at Kansas State as the Tigers stormed the Nichols Gymnasium court and raced to a 25–9 lead before easing to a 39–29 win. As usual, Missouri succeeded through team play. Currence led with nine points, followed by Lobsiger with eight, Tison with seven, and Keirsey with six. Then, in a rematch with Kansas State, Clay Cooper provided his typical spark off the bench, scoring ten, as Missouri won 46–37.

That same day, a rarity: Kansas aided Missouri. The Jayhawks beat Oklahoma and caused a dramatic shift in the standings. Missouri and Kansas found themselves tied for the league lead at 6–3, with the Sooners a half game back at 5–3. The day's results set up an event rare in recent years—a Missouri-Kansas game with title implications. The season finale between the Tigers and Jayhawks became a championship playoff, with the winner earning at least a share of the Big Six title. If Oklahoma faltered in either of its final two games, the victor would capture the crown outright.

The demand for tickets was overwhelming, greater than any game in the program's history. More than five thousand packed Brewer for the ninety-ninth or one hundredth meeting between the rivals, thirsting for the Tigers' first title in nine years. (The discrepancy dates to March 26, 1924, when the teams met in Kansas City and played a benefit game nearly a month after the season's end. The Jayhawks won 15–14, and Kansas counts the game as official, while Missouri does not). Hopeful as the home crowd was, it could not have foreseen the outcome. When John Lobsiger hit from the perimeter just eighty seconds into the game, the rout was on. The Tigers controlled the backboards, yielding easy scores and denying Kansas second chance points. Up 29–11 at intermission, the Tigers used the fast break to finish off the Jayhawks by a final of 54–30. Harlan Keirsey scored fourteen points in his last appearance at Brewer Field House. Mizzou's fans rewarded him with a thunderous ovation, as the Tigers rewarded their fans with a Big Six championship.

But Oklahoma, with a win over Kansas State four days later, secured a share of that title. Both teams finished 7–3 in the league, giving the Tigers their

*Big and athletic, Blaine Currence caused headaches for opposing defenses.*

first shared championship since they tied Kansas for the 1922 Missouri Valley crown. In past years, the season would have ended there. But with the dawn of the new NCAA Tournament, the possibility of postseason play loomed.

The first NCAA field would include one team from each of eight districts. The Big Six sat in district five, as did the Missouri Valley Conference. With Missouri and Oklahoma sharing the Big Six title, and Oklahoma A&M and Drake sharing Valley honors, the NCAA had four candidates for one berth. Preliminary plans called for a four-team playoff to break the logjam. But before details were finalized, Missouri did what would be unthinkable today: it declined a chance to play for a national championship.

The idea of a national tournament was novel and not entirely appealing. It extended the season for men who needed to devote time to their studies and who were not trying to catch the eyes of scouts from the NBA, a league that did not yet exist. It also involved significant expense, a fact not lost on frugal Don Faurot, Missouri's athletics director. Finally,

*"Modern Goliath" Haskell Tison lays one in.*

the tournament offered relatively little for fans. The games were to be played in faraway locations, against teams from other regions, in an age before television. Where's the fun in playing faceless squads from Wake Forest or Oregon when you've just brought the season to a rousing climax by whipping Kansas? That sentiment was an undertone when faculty athletics representative Sam Shirkey explained the university's decision. "We feel that our basketball season is over. Our team reached its peak for the Kansas game and another two weeks would carry on the season too far for our boys."

Just like that, it ended. Mizzou's players were unhappy, Clay Cooper recalled sixty-five years later, but powerless to do much about it. Still, for Missouri, there was more satisfaction than disappointment. As March rolled on, the Tigers found themselves in the classroom, conference championship in hand, and a rout of their chief rival fresh in their memories. Few teams could boast of a more successful 1939.

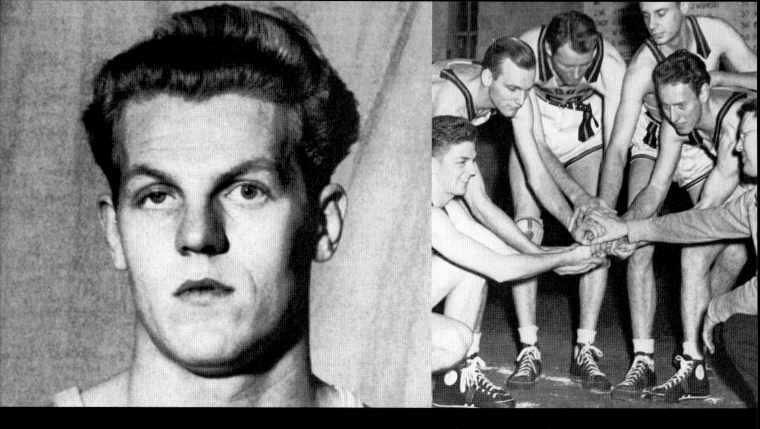

Most decades are about many things. The 1940s were about war—preparing for it, fighting it, winning it, celebrating victory, then turning the warrior's resolve to a domestic agenda. Like all aspects of American life, Missouri basketball was forced to navigate war's wake. Through the decade, one old coach and one young coach held the program together as young men passed through, played a few games, and then went off to war. Luckily, most came back. Several of them helped to write the chapter on one of the program's most fascinating decades. That chapter begins on a high note.

# THE 1940s

## 1939–40

The 1939 Big Six co-champs returned a lineup built for another title, with five talented seniors back for their final campaign. Basketball, however, provided just a fraction of the excitement pervading MU's campus.

It would have been hard to find a happier place in 1939 than Columbia. Though America still grappled with economic depression, the University of Missouri enjoyed high times. After dropping to less than thirty-five hundred students at the depression's depth, enrollment swelled to more than fifty-two hundred. The basketball team reigned as Big Six champs. And most notably, Mizzou celebrated its centennial, a tribute to early Missourians who brought public higher education to the expanding American West in 1839.

Still, the biggest excitement came from Don Faurot's football team. Led by quarterback Paul Christman, the Tigers posted their best record in thirty years, won the conference championship, earned their first invitation to a New Year's Day bowl game, and raised the centennial celebration to a fever pitch. Their meeting with Georgia Tech in the Orange Bowl would put an extraordinary cap on the year's revelry.

Though there had been little doubt about it, the success of 1939 reaffirmed that football was king at Mizzou. Basketball had grown in popularity, as evidenced by the fervor that accompanied the Tigers' drive for the 1939 league title. But to steal some spotlight back for themselves, the basketball Tigers needed another championship run. That quest would begin with the liberation of a pair of players from the football team.

Clay Cooper and Blaine Currence pulled double duty in the athletic department. Cooper, a halfback, and Currence, an end and punter, helped the football team to its Orange Bowl berth. Thrilling as that was for Cooper, Currence, and the university, it posed a problem for George Edwards. Typically, football ended around Thanksgiving. But with the season extended to January, Currence and Cooper would be occupied for a span that included Missouri's first six basketball games.

Faurot and Edwards compromised. The players would practice with both teams and would play in the season's first four basketball games. Then they would join the football team in Miami.

Notwithstanding the wealth of experienced leadership, the underclassmen starred on opening night at Brewer. Junior Arch Watson and sophomore Herb Gregg (a five-foot-eight forward) combined for eleven points in a critical rally, and Missouri beat St. Louis University 54–45. Two days later, the Tigers hosted Denver and again relied on a second-half rally. With under four minutes to play, Mizzou trailed 33–28. But Clay Cooper, Haskell Tison, and Bill Harvey led a barrage that gave the Tigers a 40–36 win as the seniors resumed command of the team.

Before Missouri's first road trip, the rigors of playing two sports at once caught up with Currence. During a basketball workout on December 20, he suffered a charley horse that threatened his ability to play in the Orange Bowl. The next day, while the rest of the football team boarded a train to Miami, Cooper and Currence were in St. Louis as the basketball Tigers beat the Billikens for the second time in a week. But the hobbled Currence scored just once from the field in the 48–34 triumph. Speculation about his availability grew the next night when he failed to play in a sluggish loss to Washington University.

While Cooper and Currence headed for the warmth of Miami, their teammates departed for colder climes to play New York University at Madison Square Garden. The Tigers walked into an ambush. A throng of 14,282 (three times the size of even a large Big Six crowd) awaited them, as did the hometown Violets, a perennial power. Furthermore, the Tigers found that the rules of the game were different in the Northeast. Back home, the Tigers set screens for each other, a style foreign to the eastern refs who repeatedly whistled Missouri for blocking. Taken out of their game by the crowd, the officials, and the absence of two starters, the Tigers were overwhelmed 68–47.

Missouri tried again the next night in Philadelphia against St. Joseph's. John Lobsiger, Bill Harvey, and Haskell Tison bore the scoring load in a nip-and-tuck affair that St. Joe's won 39–38 on a late free throw. The loss left the Tigers, once 3–0, at 3–3 as they returned home.

Most Missouri fans took little notice of the Tigers' frustrating eastern excursion. Instead, attention was focused squarely on Miami. But things didn't go Missouri's way in the Orange Bowl, as Georgia Tech took a 21–7 victory. Despite his injury, Blaine Currence was one of Missouri's few bright spots. He caught the key passes in Mizzou's lone scoring drive. He also punted magnificently, one of his efforts traveling fifty-eight yards. So much for the charley horse.

Back with the basketball squad five days later, Currence scored eleven in an easy win over Greeley State. Clay Cooper, also back, contributed eight. Its lineup finally intact, Missouri began its quest for another Big Six title. That quest would be

*Clay Cooper grabs a rebound.*

*John Lobsiger (center) eyes the action.*

witnessed by more fans than ever before. New bleachers increased Brewer's capacity to fifty-two hundred. Additional temporary seating pushed it past six thousand.

A sleet storm kept the field house's new limits from being tested in Missouri's first conference game, a tilt with Nebraska. Still, forty-five hundred observers—including Kansas coach Phog Allen, on hand to scout Mizzou—braved the weather. Allen got an eyeful. The black and gold raced to a 26–9 halftime advantage. When Nebraska rallied against Mizzou's reserves in the second half, Edwards reinserted his starters. Lobsiger, Cooper, and Harvey each scored in a thirty second span to put the Huskers away.

Two days later, the Tigers pulled into a first-place tie with Allen's Jayhawks by winning at Iowa State. In the three wins after the Orange Bowl, Missouri displayed its championship blueprint. The Tigers' success began with defense, the Big Six's best, a fierce man-to-man scheme that pressured the ball all over the court, with match-ups masterfully set by George Edwards. On offense, Mizzou attacked opponents from every angle. No Tiger scored a lot, but they all scored some. With dangerous shooters spread around the floor, Missouri relentlessly pressured defenses. The Tigers' solid play set up a showdown with the Jayhawks at Brewer with first place on the line.

The weather remained harsh when Kansas visited. A crowd of fifty-five hundred braved subzero temperatures, and the Tigers rewarded them. When Bill Harvey hit a pair of free throws midway through the first half, Missouri took a lead it never relinquished. The Tigers won 42–31 behind a balanced effort. Junior guard Martin Nash led the way with eight points, followed by Harvey with seven, Currence with six, Cooper with five, and Watson, Gregg, Tison, and Lobsiger with four apiece.

The Tigers led the league at 3–0, with OU and Kansas at 3–1. Opportunity presented itself at Brewer, where MU had won eleven straight, when the Tigers hosted fellow 1939 co-champ Oklahoma. A win could put Missouri in control of the Big Six race at the halfway point.

With cooperative weather, more than six thousand crammed into the field house, a second straight record crowd. But high-scoring Jimmy

McNatt and his teammates jumped on Missouri early. Oklahoma's defense left the Tigers resorting to errant long shots. At the break, Oklahoma led 22–10.

The second half saw more of the same. After four quick points, Missouri went scoreless for six minutes and trailed 29–14. But the veteran Tigers responded with an uncommon fury on both ends of the court. As usual, they did it as a team. Defensively, the key was Lobsiger, who switched assignments and shut down McNatt. Offensively, Currence, Cooper, Lobsiger, and Nash led an onslaught that put the Tigers up 34–33 with a minute to play. But with less than thirty seconds left, Bill Bentley, Oklahoma's backup center, got free under the basket and scored the game's final two points. When time expired, the Tigers sat on the short end of a 35–34 score with only themselves to blame. Their four-of-fourteen free throw shooting turned a crucial win into a painful loss.

The effects lingered three days later in Lincoln. Nebraska, just 1–4 in the league, staggered the Tigers and built a twelve-point first-half lead. With the season on the line, Missouri regained its composure and closed the gap to six at halftime. After the break, the Tigers evened the score and began trading the lead back and forth. Though Missouri's recent successes had been based on collective effort, John Lobsiger remained first among equals. The last of his team-high twelve points put the Tigers up for good in a 41–40 victory that felt more like relief than triumph.

Shaken to their senses, the Tigers went on a tear. Missouri rode Martin Nash's jump shot to an easy win at Kansas State, setting the stage for a rematch with league-leading Oklahoma at Norman.

*Haskell Tison breaks free for a score.*

The Tigers entered the game shorthanded after Haskell Tison was hospitalized with the flu. They faced a team with a weapon unlike any other in the league. Jimmy McNatt had broken his own conference record with thirty points against Nebraska in the Sooners' previous game.

Clay Cooper drew the daunting defensive assignment and made the most of it. He stifled McNatt, holding him to just four points on nineteen field goal attempts. With Cooper controlling McNatt, Lobsiger controlled the rest of the game. He fed Currence (who would join Lobsiger on the All-Big Six team) for point-blank shots, drained long shots of his own, and knifed through the Oklahoma defense in a 33–27 Missouri victory that shook up the standings. The Tigers ascended to the top at 6–1 with Kansas (4–1) and Oklahoma (6–2) close behind.

Tison remained flu-stricken when the Tigers returned home to host Kansas State, leaving Currence to go the distance at center again. If Currence was fatigued, it didn't show. He and Cooper combined for twenty-three in a 36–23 win.

The next contest would be the last at Brewer for Lobsiger, Currence, Harvey, Cooper, and Tison, who had recovered from his illness. Missouri's fans were treated to a remarkable display by the graduating class. The team rushed to a 23–5 lead over Iowa State and kept an enormous advantage until Coach Edwards cleared the bench, replacing his seniors with sophomores. But when Iowa State closed the gap to nine in the second half, the seniors returned and scored twenty-four in the game's final nine minutes to propel Mizzou to a 63–40 win. The Tigers' elder statesmen sparkled. Lobsiger scored fourteen, followed by Tison and Cooper with twelve each, Currence with ten, and Harvey with nine.

Despite the Tigers' stellar play, they could not widen their lead in the standings. Kansas and Oklahoma matched them win for win over the season's final four weeks. A win at Lawrence in the Tigers' last game would secure the championship; a loss would throw the race wide open.

*Coach Edwards with his 1940 Big Six co-champs*

Never ones to support the Kansas economy, the Tigers spent the night before the game at the Hotel President in Kansas City, Missouri. The next day, when they took to the floor, they were greeted by forty-three hundred fans crammed into Hoch Auditorium. Kansas rushed to a nine-point lead, but the Tigers rode a 14–4 run to a one-point halftime edge. The Jayhawks used a run of their own to open a 40–33 lead, sparked by Dick Harp's defensive play against Currence and Tison. Harp's blocked shots and rebounds helped Kansas build a nearly decisive edge. But the Tigers mounted a comeback. Currence and Cooper led Missouri to seven straight points to tie the game at 40.

With four and a half minutes to play, Kansas took a one-point lead when Don Ebling sank a free throw. When Missouri failed to score, Kansas froze the ball and exploited an experimental rule. While the Tigers fouled, Phog Allen chose to take the ball out of bounds rather than shoot free throws. His players successfully inbounded the ball three times in the last two minutes. Kansas played keep away as the Tigers tried in vain to steal the ball. Missouri committed one last foul as time expired. Adding insult to injury, Allen sent Dick Harp to the free throw line. As jubilant Jayhawk fans descended onto the floor, Harp scored the last point in a 42–40 Kansas victory.

The loss was bitter. Rather than winning the title outright, the Tigers were forced to root for Oklahoma the next week. A Kansas win at Norman would give the Jayhawks sole possession of the Big Six championship. An Oklahoma win would result in a three-way split, each team with an 8–2 conference record.

The Sooners did their part. Their 47–36 win over Kansas resulted in the only three-way title tie in Big Six history. It also left the league in a quandary, as the conference's commitment to the NCAA Tournament required a lone representative to be available for postseason play. The league arranged a three-team tournament in Wichita. The survivor would face a one-game playoff with Missouri Valley champ Oklahoma A&M to gain entry into the NCAA field.

Unlike the previous year, Missouri embraced the playoff, a two-game tournament with a lottery to determine which team would receive a bye into the title game. It went to Kansas. With the Jayhawks looking on, the Sooners took a 33–23 second-half lead. But like the teams' regular season meetings, this one featured a run. Missouri roared back. A Currence dunk and one-handed jumpers by Cooper, Harvey, and Lobsiger helped knot the score at 39–39 with seven minutes to play. But an unlikely Oklahoma hero emerged when Hugh Ford, a reserve center, entered the game and scored six unanswered points. Missouri's postseason hopes evaporated in a 52–41 loss.

With back-to-back titles (even if they were shared), Missouri experienced its greatest success in nearly twenty years, but things were about to change. The loss of the great senior class would leave the Tigers reeling in the short run, but events of far greater complexity would put a strain on the program for much longer. Missouri's seventh conference title had come in its thirty-third year of league play. Nearly two generations would pass before the Tigers captured an eighth.

## 1940–41

Without Lobsiger, Currence, Cooper, Harvey, and Tison, the Tigers had no shot at a third straight title. The struggle was merely to compete. Senior Martin Nash returned to captain the team, and he was supported by a cast that included Loren Mills, Herb Gregg, Arch Watson, and Keith Bangert, capable players all, but not of the caliber of the departed seniors.

The season started with a loss to Washington University, but Mizzou rebounded to win three straight against in-state foes. Then the Tigers hit the skids. A loss to Springfield Teacher's College preceded a five-game stretch that included one loss to each of Mizzou's Big Six rivals. The Tigers rebounded to win three of their last six, including a nonconference match-up with St. Louis University (a game in which Coach Edwards employed a zone defense for the first time) and a thriller against K-State that saw sophomore Roy Storm hit from

*Missouri's Martin Nash went on to be an alternate on the gold medal–winning 1948 United States Olympic basketball team.*

long-range at the buzzer to give Mizzou a 30–28 win. Still, Missouri went just 2–8 in league play (6–10 overall) and finished in last place. But that disappointment would seem small next to the crisis about to face every Missourian, every American.

## 1941–42

Just as the Tigers were making final preparations for the season, Japanese bombers struck Pearl Harbor and hastened the United States' entry into the Second World War. Despite a preoccupation with far weightier issues and despite that the Tiger squad was one of modest talent, the season started relatively well. On December 9, 1941, Coach Edwards used fourteen players in a 52–29 dismantling of St. Louis as Don Harvey scored ten. The Tigers then went to Spokane and topped Gonzaga as Harvey, George Constantz, Roy Storm, Loren Mills, and Ed Matheny each scored between eight and ten points.

Things began to fall apart in a visit to the University of Idaho. After Mizzou led 18–15 at intermission, the Vandals dominated in the second period and won 40–28. The team then traveled to Seattle for a pair of games and got clobbered by Washington and Washington State. Though the Tigers temporarily stemmed the bleeding with wins at California and at home against St. Louis, once conference play began, they got blistered.

Just as German U-boats began sinking ships off the U.S. coast, league play opened, and Mizzou's first four opponents handled the Tigers with relative ease; Kansas and Oklahoma each handed MU double-digit losses at Brewer Field House. A minor breakthrough came when the Tigers hosted Iowa State. Don Harvey's sixteen points helped Mizzou beat the Cyclones 45–41.

It was all downhill from there. Missouri's punchless offense left the Tigers helpless. They lost five of six to close the year and clinch their second straight last-place finish. Despite the disappointing season, the reality of Missouri basketball was far less grim than the reality about to face many of the Tigers on battlefields around the globe. With the military in need of able-bodied young men, George Edwards's program was about to be thrust into chaos.

## 1942–43

Though the emotional wallop of America's entry into World War II was felt most acutely at the beginning of the 1941–42 season, the practical effects on the college game were felt more strongly a year later. Some schools suspended athletics altogether. Those that carried on lost players to the draft, sometimes in the middle of the season. To compensate for the dwindling numbers of available men, the rule precluding participation by freshmen was temporarily lifted.

Another effect was the addition of armed services teams to the schedule. With military rolls swelled and collegiate ranks depleted, military trainees around the country competed head to head with NCAA schools. Some squads were like all-star teams, with so many talented players engaged in the nation's service. The Great Lakes Naval squad was a star-studded crew that annihilated Mizzou 92–45.

Missouri fielded an inexperienced team. Senior center Roy Storm returned as a reserve, and five-foot-eleven forward Ed Matheny worked his

way into the starting lineup midway through his second varsity season. The final returner was junior guard Earl Stark, the team's captain, who provided leadership on and off the floor.

The newcomers included a pair of sophomores who made immediate contributions. Pleasant Smith's scrappy style earned him substantial minutes off the bench, while powerfully built six-foot-two Thornton Jenkins was the most promising young Tiger in years. A forward from little Advance, Missouri, Jenkins immediately became Mizzou's best player and the most gifted Tiger scorer in memory.

His mettle—and that of his teammates—was tested early. Missouri's nonconference schedule was packed with tough military teams, plus an Illinois squad generally considered the nation's best. Known as the Whiz Kids, the Illini featured Andy Phillip, the game's top player. Despite a heroic defensive effort by Tiger guard Walter "Bubber" Robinson, who held Phillip in check, Mizzou fell 51–30.

The competition remained stiff when conference play began. Jayhawk All-American Charlie Black hung thirty-three points on Mizzou in an easy Kansas victory. A loss to Nebraska dropped Mizzou to 0–2 in Big Six play, 2–5 overall. But the Tigers reeled off three straight wins against conference foes, including a triumph over league power Oklahoma, a game in which Jenkins scored nineteen points.

Nebraska halted the winning streak, but the Tigers rebounded with a pair of wins, including one against Kansas State, played a day late after a misunderstanding saw Missouri pull into Manhattan on Saturday for a Friday tip. Those victories put Mizzou at 5–3 in the Big Six with two games to play. But the next game was against the Jayhawks, who remained unbeaten in the conference even after losing Charlie Black to pneumonia. The Tigers took Kansas to overtime before falling 47–44 despite sixteen points from Jenkins. Mizzou closed the year at Oklahoma, where the Sooners won with ease 52–37. Still, the young Tigers managed to finish 5–5 in the Big Six, good for a third-place tie, and Thornton Jenkins ranked second in the conference scoring race and earned first-team all-conference

*Herb Gregg passes to Don Harvey on the fast break.*

*Earl Stark provided leadership during wartime.*

honors. The pieces were in place for a bright future, but the realities of war made that future uncertain.

# 1943–44

In 1938, enrollment at MU had surged past five thousand. By 1943 it was down to fifteen hundred as men went off to war. But even as other activities around campus and the country were curtailed, college athletics—including Big Six basketball—carried on to help boost morale on the home front. Even so, Kansas coach Phog Allen undoubtedly was right in his assessment that "not many people will take a wartime championship seriously. With us here athletics are simply incidental to the war effort."

That effort had decimated the Tigers. Thornton Jenkins, Pleasant Smith, and others should have led Missouri's fight for a Big Six title. Instead, they were engaged in a fight of infinitely greater consequence. And with a dwindling student population, George Edwards's immediate challenge was not to win the conference; it was simply to field a team.

Edwards's challenge was far greater than that faced by Allen at Kansas, Louis Menze at Iowa State, or Bruce Drake at Oklahoma. Those schools hosted naval training units. Their teams drew from deep and talented pools of nascent sailors. Iowa State even acquired an All-American in the process when West Texas State's Price Brookfield, a high-scoring center, was shipped north by the armed forces.

In contrast, Missouri (like Kansas State and Nebraska) made do with civilian students—men too young to serve, unfit to serve or deferred from service. In assembling his team, Edwards started virtually from scratch. Ed Matheny, the only returning contributor, was set to graduate in December, meaning that by the holidays the starting five would consist entirely of players who had not before worn the Missouri uniform.

Edwards grabbed all manner of men to find four to start alongside Matheny. From the intramural ranks he snatched the Minx twins—Beauford, a guard, and Clifford, a forward—who were deferred to pursue civilian engineering degrees. From the 4-F rolls he snatched Paul Collins, a Tiger football star and future NFL player who, ironically, had been declared unfit for military duty. And from the cradle he snatched Dan Pippin, a six-foot-one coiled spring from Waynesville, Missouri, who started at center. At age seventeen, the freshman was too young for the draft and almost too good to be true. The wiry youngster was athletic enough to go toe-to-toe with much bigger players and skilled enough to dominate smaller ones.

Despite his skills, Pippin was literally a boy among men on most nights, and the schools with mature military men were clear Big Six favorites. Kansas had earned at least a share of the conference title each of the previous four seasons and had swept through the league undefeated in 1943. Oklahoma returned all-conference guard Allie Paine, who would soon rise to All-America. And Iowa State, in addition to Price Brookfield, had Roy and Ray, the talented Wehde twins.

Edwards's innocents were baptized by fire. Early on, as the coach tried to forge his grab bag of 4-Fs and baby faces into a team, the Tigers faced a steady diet of military men and accomplished collegians. Missouri showed some moxie by roughing up the 61st Troop Carrier Wing of Sedalia Air Base in a 49–29 season opening win. It then put a scare into defending Big Ten champ Illinois, leading by seven at halftime before fading.

*Thornton Jenkins began his brilliant career in the 1942–43 season and then went off to war.*

*Just seventeen years old, Dan Pippin (back row, second from right) starred on piecemeal team that enjoyed a remarkable and unpredictable season.*

The Tigers took their 1–1 record to Kansas City for a four-team tournament at Municipal Auditorium. On day one, Missouri played the Washburn Ichabods, a team of servicemen. After trailing for the first thirty-six minutes, the Tigers took a 26–24 lead when Lennie Brown, a speedy freshman, hit a running left-hander. Washburn regained the lead, but Missouri prevailed in the late stages on a tip-in by six-foot-five freshman beanpole Bob Heinsohn, his gangly appearance exaggerated by shorts cut high on the hips and socks that barely rose above the ankles. Dan Pippin led Missouri with eleven points and seemed to get every rebound.

Kansas routed K-State in the nightcap behind twenty-eight points from Don Barrington, setting up a showdown between ancient rivals in the tournament final. Coach Edwards assigned Pippin and fellow freshman Benny Arbeitman to hold Barrington in check, and they did as the Tigers shot to an 18–7 lead. But the green Missouri club faded, and Kansas pulled away for a 34–27 win in a game that did not count in the conference standings.

After defeating the military men of Westminster College at Fulton, the Tigers returned home to again face the Jayhawks, who had won twelve straight conference games. "Kansas figures to repeat its recent Kansas City victory over Missouri down at Columbia," declared the *Kansas City Times*. Missouri figured otherwise and stunned KU 35–28.

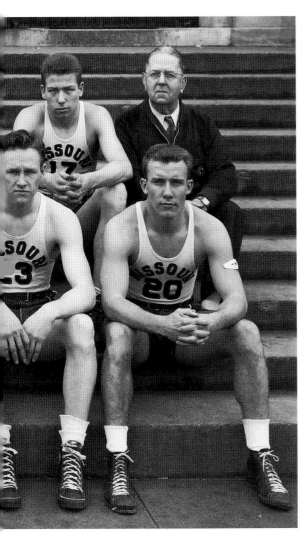

Paul Collins, already known as a fierce defender, led the Tigers with ten points and displayed open court skills that belied his inexperience. After a 14–14 halftime tie, Collins and Pippin led a decisive surge.

The high of that win subsided as the schedule stiffened. Double-digit losses to league leaders Oklahoma and Iowa State bracketed a defeat against the Olathe Naval Air Station team. Any Big Six title hopes vanished in painful fashion when Oklahoma visited Columbia. Missouri led most of the way, but the Sooners rallied and escaped with a 27–26 win. With the Sooners and Iowa State still undefeated, the Tigers, at 1–2, were playing for third place.

The schedule gave them a chance. Missouri's next three games came against the league's other nonmilitary teams. At Nebraska, Paul Collins recorded two field goals in overtime to push Mizzou past the Cornhuskers 36–32. Kansas State provided less resistance in Manhattan, as the Tigers cruised 45–30 behind eighteen points from Pippin. Then, in a rematch with Nebraska, the Tigers prevailed 44–29 as Pippin and Cliff Minx combined for twenty-three.

After avenging their earlier loss to the Olathe Clippers, the Tigers found themselves with a four-game win streak. Edwards's mismatched parts had blended into a surprisingly good unit, with Collins and Pippin playing at a particularly high level.

But tough challenges remained. Iowa State came to Columbia and stayed undefeated in conference play. Missouri's defense rendered Price Brookfield harmless and the Cyclones led by just two at halftime. But when Ray Wehde nailed three successive field goals in the second half, Iowa State pulled away. Next came a contest at Kansas, the winner guaranteed at least a tie for third in the Big Six. It was all Jayhawks. KU took the lead early and never looked back, prevailing 40–27.

With one game to play, the Tigers stood fourth in the league, ahead only of the other civilian teams. But the Jayhawks remained within reach. A Kansas loss to Iowa State, combined with a Missouri win over Kansas State, would leave the rivals deadlocked for third.

Iowa State did its part by whipping Kansas, and the Tigers capitalized by drubbing the Wildcats 38–14 in the season's most dominant performance. Missouri's defense stifled K-State, which hit its first field goal with less than a minute to play in the opening half. Cliff Minx and Dale Crowder scored eight points apiece to lead a balanced Tiger attack.

For Mizzou, the win secured the undisputed championship of Big Six civilians, but the Tigers remained far behind the best military teams. The final Big Six standings reflected a rare symmetry. Iowa State and Oklahoma tied for the title at 9–1, followed by Missouri and Kansas at 5–5 and Kansas State and Nebraska at 1–9. Given the circumstances, Mizzou's 9–8 overall record and third-place finish seemed like utter triumph. Still, unbeknownst to the Tigers, opportunity remained for greater glory.

As war played havoc with the NCAA Tournament, the big question was who would represent the Big Six in the eight-team field. The question was complicated because Navy regulations restricted the time that trainees stationed at Iowa State and Oklahoma could be away from their base.

If a team of trainees could win the western regional in Kansas City, the regulations might preclude them from traveling to New York for the finals.

The NCAA invited Iowa State, but the Cyclones declined the bid for fear that they could not keep the team together throughout the tournament. The NCAA then approached Oklahoma. But the Sooners also declined, citing the Navy's regulations. That raised speculation that Missouri, the league's top team not subject to the regulations, might receive the NCAA bid despite a mediocre record. But Iowa State reconsidered, thus ending Missouri's faint hopes.

Or so it seemed. On March 13, 1944, the University of Iowa withdrew from the tournament upon learning that its two leading scorers were to be drafted into the armed forces. In a pinch, the NCAA called on Missouri, with its proximity to Kansas City and its well-respected coach. After conferring with the other conference schools, the university accepted the bid.

Ten days after the season had ended, Coach Edwards reassembled his team. By then, Dan Pippin had been named first team All-Big Six by the Associated Press, while the United Press had bestowed the same honor on Paul Collins, remarkable achievements under the circumstances.

Missouri's late addition was not the last shake-up of the field. The Tigers should have played Arkansas in the first round, but tragedy intervened. The Southwest Conference champs were returning to Fayetteville after a scrimmage with a military team when a car carrying the starters suffered a flat tire. As the players changed the tire, a car rammed them at full speed, killing their faculty sponsor and seriously injuring two starters. The devastated Razorbacks withdrew from the field just days before the tournament was to begin.

That cruel fate provided opportunity for Utah, a team full of freshmen who spent the season as nomads after the Army commandeered their gym. Utah had declined an NCAA bid in favor of the NIT, but after Kentucky bounced them in round one, the NCAA called and asked the Utes to take Arkansas' place. Given a second chance at a national title, they cut short a New York sightseeing tour and hopped a train for Kansas City.

Dubbed the Blitz Kids, Utah was the only team to play in both national tournaments in 1944. Freshman forward Arnie Ferrin was their star, but much of their heart rested in five-foot-seven guard Wat Misaka, an American of Japanese heritage who absorbed opposing fans' bigoted taunts throughout the year.

The Tigers and Utes squared off before 4,622 fans in Missouri's tournament debut. At a time when two-handed set shots still prevailed, Utah flicked one-handers from every direction. The style frustrated the Tiger defense. Ferrin's shooting pushed the Blitz Kids to an 18–10 lead. Missouri closed the gap to 18–14, but a Utah spurt put the Tigers in a 27–14 hole at the half. Despite the deficit, the Tigers, and particularly Paul Collins, kept fighting. The two-sport star repeatedly forced his way through Utah's defense to score a team-high ten points. It wasn't nearly enough. Utah triumphed 35–25 before going on to win the NCAA Tournament.

The Tigers weren't finished. They would play Pepperdine in the

*Paul Collins, who would go on to play in the National Football League, earned all-league honors in his one and only season as a varsity basketball player.*

*Identical twins Beau and Cliff Minx went from intramural games to the NCAA Tournament during their time at Mizzou.*

regional consolation game. Six-foot-seven Nick Buzolich gave the Tigers fits, scoring twenty-three points before fouling out. But he got little help from his teammates, three of whom fouled out along with him. The Tigers, in contrast, got the usual steady performances from Pippin and Collins plus the game of Cliff Minx's life. He capped his intramural-to-varsity career by scoring twenty-one points as Missouri prevailed 61–46.

After some false endings, Missouri's 1943–44 season finally came to a close. The 10–9 record didn't sparkle, but the team's achievement did. The Tigers' play stood as a monument to George Edwards, who coaxed a lot from very little in the twilight of his career and helped to put Missouri on a national stage. It would be a very long time until Missouri played on such a stage again.

# 1944–45

In the time between Missouri's appearance in the NCAA Tournament and the start of the next season, the Allies seized control of the war. On June 6 the movement to reclaim Europe began with the D-Day invasion at Normandy. By the time the season opened, Paris, Brussels, Antwerp, and Athens had been liberated. Though the end was in sight, it would take a great effort to get there.

That effort required manpower, and the draft continued to suck talent from Missouri's roster. This time it took Dan Pippin, among others. And though players like Gene Kurash and Earl Stiegemeier joined the team and picked up some slack, the Tigers' challenge grew even greater when they lost Paul Collins to graduation at midyear. And unlike the previous year, when Pippin had arrived to take the sting out of Thornton Jenkins's departure, the Tigers had no new freshman star on whom to rely.

Still, they carried on. Stiegemeier, a floppy-haired set shooter, ascended to the team captaincy vacated by Collins, and Kurash earned praise around the league for his play, which included replacing Pippin's scoring almost point for point.

*The Tigers relied on Earl Stiegemeier during the war-torn mid-1940s.*

But Stiegemeier and Kurash couldn't fully replace the departed stars' contributions, a fact reflected in the *Savitar's* season recap: "As far as standout players were concerned, M.U. had none."

Despite again starting almost from scratch, George Edwards managed to produce a competitive club, though not as competitive as the 1944 squad. There were more lopsided losses, fewer nonconference wins. The high points were not quite as high (a come-from-behind overtime win against Nebraska, sparked by freshman Lane Bauer, was the year's signature moment); the lows were a bit lower (all ten losses were by at least fifteen points; seven were by more than twenty). But the Tigers found a way to win five conference games, as they again finished 5–5 in the Big Six and tied for third place. Unlike the previous year, third place wasn't good enough for an NCAA berth.

## 1945-46

By the fall of 1945, World War II was over, but military obligations were not. Consequently, George Edwards again scrambled to construct a team. His problems were exacerbated by a knee injury that hampered Earl Stiegemeier, his best returning player. But he got a boost from Kenny Bounds, a massive, mature ex-Marine and Tiger football player who joined the team and earned honorable mention in the Big Six at center. Newcomers Jim White, Wendell Moulder, and Richard Gwinn also contributed big offensive games at one time or another. But the most welcome contribution came from prodigal son Thornton Jenkins, who returned after two years in the Army Air Corps to join the team midway through the conference slate. Despite playing in just five games, Jenkins scored more points in league play than any other Tiger, including eighteen in his return (a win over Kansas State) and twenty in a loss to Kansas. In the end, there were fewer lopsided losses than the previous year, but there were also fewer wins. Missouri shuffled to a 6–11 record, 3–7 in the Big Six. It was the Tigers' worst finish in four seasons.

It was also the end of an era. After twenty seasons, genial George Edwards retired as basketball coach, having provided the first prolonged period of stability in Missouri basketball history. A paragon of commitment and service, the dignified and humble Edwards was not just a coach. After serving Mizzou in a multitude of positions, he remained in Columbia and continued to serve the university as head of the physical education department. He had also served his profession with a stint as president of the National Association of Basketball Coaches, composing its creed along the way. But Edwards's deeds off the court should not obscure his accomplishments on it, including three conference titles and 181 wins, more than five times as many as any of his predecessors. When he retired, George Edwards had served as Tiger coach for half of the program's forty-year existence and had presided over more than half of the games Missouri had ever played. His tenure may have lacked the brilliance of the Meanwell/Ruby years, but he infused the program with dignity and stability. Through his longevity and dedication, George Edwards became the personification of Missouri Tigers basketball.

As Edwards left his post, another man arrived in Columbia and began working to better connect the basketball program with the people of Missouri.

*Thornton Jenkins returned from war and gave the Tigers some badly needed scoring punch.*

Which is not to say that Sparky Stalcup wasn't successful in his own right. A native of Forbes, Missouri, Stalcup played on an Oregon (Missouri) High School team that won state and national basketball championships. From there, it was on to nearby Maryville State Teachers College, where he lettered in track, earned all-conference honors in football and basketball, served as student body president, and came under the tutelage of a young Iba. A brief career as a high school basketball coach ended in 1933 when Iba left Maryville for a short stint as the head coach at Colorado. At age twenty-three, Stalcup succeeded his mentor, and in ten seasons at Maryville, he won three conference titles and more than 70 percent of his games.

Then war intervened. In 1943 Stalcup found himself directing physical education programs in the Navy. After his discharge, he returned to Maryville briefly, but when George Edwards retired, Stalcup made his way to Columbia, where ultimately he would be a fixture for nearly as long as Edwards had been.

As a man, Stalcup was a gentle soul with a young family, a sensitive sort with deeply rooted principles, a warm

Mahlon Aldridge, an enterprising broadcaster, took over as station manager at KFRU radio and became the play-by-play voice of the fledgling Missouri Sports Network, which began with five stations. Under his leadership, the network would grow and touch every corner of the state, and for thousands of Tiger fans, Aldridge's voice would become the sound of the University of Missouri.

## 1946–47

Timing can be everything. Just as a gifted basketball coach named Wilbur Stalcup, known to his friends as Sparky, returned from the Navy, the top spot at his home state's flagship university opened up for the first time in twenty years. And just as that job opened up, Stalcup's mentor, Henry Iba, won his second straight NCAA championship at Oklahoma A&M. Undoubtedly, Sparky bathed in the glow of Iba's success.

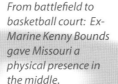

*From battlefield to basketball court: Ex-Marine Kenny Bounds gave Missouri a physical presence in the middle.*

and friendly ambassador for the university. As a coach, he was a a firebrand and hell-raiser, a rough-and-tumble son of a gun who relished trading barbs with officials, opposing coaches and unaccommodating fans. One friend in the press wrote that Stalcup "hate[d] losing worse than poison" and that he "wouldn't let his mother drive the lane." When he paced the sidelines, Sparky possessed a mean streak a mile

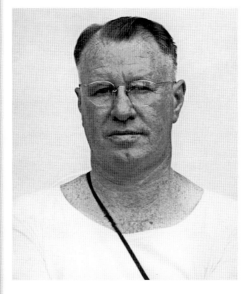

*Gentleman George Edwards served as coach for 20 years, winning 181 games and three conference titles, and becoming synonymous with Missouri basketball. Well respected on campus and around the country, Edwards served as president of the National Association of Basketball Coaches and wrote the Coaches' Creed.*

wide, and he expected his players to carry the same attitude onto the court. To play for Stalcup was to play for keeps. For two decades, Missouri fans had grown accustomed to the stoicism of George Edwards. Stalcup replaced it with fury.

Off the court, Sparky was a quick-witted charmer with a homespun style that played well across the Show Me State. Upon being hired at an annual salary of $3,700, he pledged to use his appealing manner to entice the best players from across the state to pursue their degrees in

*"He hated losing worse than poison." Wilbur "Sparky" Stalcup, the University of Missouri's twelfth head basketball coach.*

Columbia. "There's no reason these boys should go out of the state for their college education," he said. "Don Faurot has built top-flight football teams in Missouri with home state athletes, and I'm going to make every effort to do the same thing in basketball."

When the energetic and youthful Stalcup arrived at Mizzou, it marked the first time since Walter Meanwell left in 1920 that the Missouri coach was not a former Tiger player. For his part, Stalcup brought with him the grinding, possession-oriented style of play he learned from Iba. But what he found waiting for him in Columbia was equally critical to Missouri's hopes. With war over, Dan Pippin returned to school and teamed with Thornton Jenkins for the first time, giving the new coach a remarkable 1–2 punch. Stalcup moved Jenkins from forward to guard and called him the team's "coach on the floor." The ironically named Pleasant Smith also returned and cemented his reputation as the Big Six's toughest player, a competitor so ferocious that his own teammates dreaded practicing with him. The Tigers also added a gifted scorer in sophomore Darrel Lorrance, a six-foot-two guard who transferred from Kentucky. Sparky's new team had ammunition.

That ammunition powered Missouri to three straight wins to open the Stalcup era, including a 48–44 upset of St. Louis and budding star Ed Macauley. From there, the Tigers traveled to Kansas City for the first-ever Big Six Tournament, a December affair that included Arkansas and Southern Methodist to round out the eight-team bracket. Just before the tournament, Mizzou lost one key player but gained another. Earl Stark gave up basketball to focus on schoolwork, while big Kenny Bounds rejoined the team at the end of football season.

Despite fifteen points from Pippin, the Tigers stumbled in their opening game against SMU, a Southwest Conference club that, ironically, would go on to win the inaugural Big Six event. The next day they stumbled again as Oklahoma star Gerald Tucker tallied twenty-eight in a 61–53 Sooner victory. Mizzou gained some consolation on the tournament's final day, defeating Iowa State 56–55. Jenkins led the Tigers with seventeen points, and Pippin and Lorrance chipped in ten each, but it was the less-heralded Bob Wachter who secured victory by sinking a free throw with twenty-one seconds to play. Despite the win, the tepid overall performance inspired little confidence for the challenge awaiting Mizzou.

The Tigers remained in Kansas City for a neutral court contest with the reunited Whiz Kids of Illinois. In postwar 1946 four of the original Kids returned to the lineup, including superstar Andy Phillip, while the fifth spot featured Walt Kirk, who had earned All-America honors while the others were off at war. The Illini played to their considerable reputation to begin the season, and they arrived in Kansas City as twenty-four-point favorites.

With less than three minutes to play, the score stood tied at 48 when Missouri center John Rudolph, a player so little-known that his name failed to make the program, hit a shot to put the Tigers up for good. Missouri's defense held Phillip to just six points, while Lorrance scored eighteen, Jenkins fourteen, and Rudolph twelve in the stunning 55–50 upset. Many of the nearly forty-five hundred on hand poured onto the court after the final buzzer to help Stalcup's Tigers celebrate one of the biggest wins in years.

A few nonconference games later, Mizzou stood 8–4, and for a while the Tigers looked like the team that knocked off the Illini. After downing Iowa State in the league opener, the Tigers traveled to Kansas,

*Jumpin' Dan Pippin returned to Mizzou after two years of military service and earned a spot on the All-Big Six team.*

where they had not won since 1930, for the explosive first meeting between Sparky Stalcup and Phog Allen. Pleasant Smith, despite foul trouble, kept Charlie Black in check. With four minutes to play and MU leading 35–32, Smith and Black collided while chasing a loose ball. Smith was whistled for his fifth foul, a questionable call that brought Stalcup to his feet. As Sparky argued with the official, Allen rushed to the Missouri side of the floor, shouted, "Get off the court!," and shoved Stalcup toward the Tiger bench. The young coach cocked his fist before his players restrained him. "Get the hell back on your side of the court!," Stalcup shouted at Allen before play resumed without serious incident.

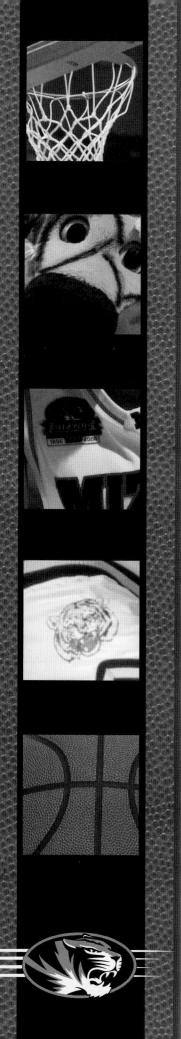

*Pleasant Smith scores against Oklahoma.*

After the fireworks, Missouri held on for a 39–34 win. Pippin, on his way to first team all-conference honors, scored seventeen points in his most impressive outing since returning to the team.

Three wins later (including one over nonleague foe Washington U.), Mizzou stood 4–0 in the Big Six. Perennial nemesis Gerald Tucker and his Oklahoma Sooners stopped the winning streak, but the Tigers rebounded and completed a season sweep of Jack Gardner's K-State Wildcats to stand at 5–1 in conference play, in prime position for a run at the championship.

Some questionable scheduling sent the Tigers to Des Moines to play a non-conference game against Drake (Missouri fell 66–52) just one day before a crucial contest at Iowa State. Though Mizzou already had beaten the Cyclones twice (once in the tournament, once in Columbia), Stalcup's men fell just short at Ames, 54–52, as Iowa State's Wehde twins combined for thirty-six points. Still, at 5–2 in the league with three games to go, Missouri was in the thick of the race and would play host to league-leading Oklahoma and archrival Kansas to close the season.

Mizzou began the home stretch by scoring an easy win at Nebraska, with Pippin, Jenkins, and Rudolph combining for forty-five points. That set the stage for a showdown with the Sooners. Oklahoma could clinch the title with a win, while a Missouri victory would create a first-place tie with one game to go.

A record crowd squeezed into Brewer, with another thousand fans turned away. Those inside saw another terrific performance by Gerald Tucker, whose seventeen first-half points propelled Oklahoma to a 24–20 edge. The Sooners extended the lead to seven points early in the second period, but Missouri drew within one following scores by Jenkins, Kenny Bounds, and Karl Pierpoint, a five-foot-ten sophomore who would become one of Missouri's all-time great defenders. From there, though, Oklahoma drew ahead to a 42–36 win, clinching coach Bruce Drake's fifth Big Six championship.

With the Tigers locked into second place, the season's final game might have been anticlimactic but for some intriguing subtext. First, it pitted Mizzou against its fiercest rival. Second, it was the first time the Tigers had met the Jayhawks since the near-fisticuffs between Stalcup and Allen (though Phog was absent; a concussion suffered in a January practice ended his season). And third, the game was played under the strangest of circumstances.

An early March flu outbreak pushed mid-Missouri hospitals beyond capacity and forced the university to shut down all public gatherings. Officials at Mizzou and Kansas agreed that the game would proceed in a virtually empty Brewer Field House. Though only reporters and radio announcers were supposed to witness the contest, a handful of local businessmen and varsity athletes made their way inside, while one hundred or so well-feeling students stood outside begging in vain to be admitted.

It was just as well that the students were excluded because the display inside was suitable only for mature audiences. The rugged, violent contest saw two Jayhawks and the entire Tiger starting five foul out. It also saw KU's Bill Sapp throw a punch at MU's Bob Garwitz, though he failed to connect.

The game itself was less compelling. Lacking a hostile crowd to contend with, Kansas led wire to wire and triumphed 48–38. And though the season ended with a pair of losses, Missouri's second-place finish in Sparky Stalcup's first season announced the arrival of a rejuvenated presence in the Big Six.

## 1947–48

The University of Missouri was hopping. During the war, enrollment plunged to fifteen hundred with most college-aged men at war. But with victory in hand, thousands of soldiers and sailors invaded campus to pursue deferred educations. More than eleven thousand students were enrolled at Mizzou during the 1947–48 school year, and they had a fine basketball team to support.

After declining an off-season offer from the University of Maryland, Coach Stalcup was rewarded with a hefty raise. In his second year, Sparky again was blessed with a nucleus of Thornton Jenkins, Dan Pippin, and Pleasant Smith, though the team lost Darrel Lorrance to the Springfield Squires of the Professional Basketball League of America, a short-lived and ill-fated association that came and went shortly before the birth of the NBA. Like the previous year, the Tigers looked sharp against nonconference foes, winning six of nine. Two of the three losses came to a tremendous St. Louis squad that went on to win the NIT at a time when that tournament's prestige rivaled the NCAA's; the third came against traditional power NYU at Madison Square Garden just after Christmas.

But success against nonleague opponents failed to translate to success in the conference tournament. Again the Tigers mustered just one win in three days. Jenkins and Smith paced Mizzou to a win over Iowa State that fell between losses to Nebraska and Oklahoma. That showing did not bode well for Missouri's chances in the conference race, especially given the arrival of a tough new contender.

The Big Six grew to the Big Seven in the 1947–48 season, and the newcomer was a powerhouse. The Colorado Buffaloes had enjoyed years of great success under coach Frosty Cox. They finished second in the 1938 NIT, the first-ever national tournament, and then won the 1940 NIT championship. The Buffs also made the NCAA final four in 1942 and earned a spot in the eight-team NCAA field in 1946, even after suspending play for two years during the war.

*Thornton Jenkins, a Tiger for all time, made the All-Big Seven team in his sensational senior season.*

The Tigers split their first four conference contests as Jenkins, Pippin, and center Bill "Red" Haynes alternated big scoring outputs. Their fifth game was against Kansas State, the surprise of the league at 4–0. Wildcat coach Jack Gardner's teams played disciplined ball-control offense and made opportunistic use of the fast break. A cerebral theoretician of the game who believed in intensive preparation, Gardner's meticulous approach began to pay dividends in the 1947–48 season.

Missouri hosted the Cats, needing a victory to remain in the Big Seven hunt. Dan Pippin scored twenty-four, but defense saved the day for Mizzou. The Tigers stifled K-State's fast break, and Red Haynes and Jerry Fowler held high scoring center Clarence Brannum to a single field goal in Missouri's 48–46 triumph. Many of the five thousand fans rushed the court to celebrate a win that breathed new life into the Tigers' season.

After stealing a three-point win over Kansas in Lawrence, Mizzou returned home to face Nebraska. Though the Huskers held Pippin and Jenkins in check, guard Don McMillen repeatedly connected from long range en route to fifteen points in the Tigers' 47–41 triumph. And as Missouri celebrated victory, Kansas State lost to Oklahoma. When newspapers hit the doorsteps the next morning, they showed the Tigers, at 5–2, with a half-game lead over both the Wildcats and Sooners.

*Rugged Pleasant Smith intimidated opponents and teammates alike.*

Mizzou's stay in first place was brief. Despite sixteen points from McMillen, the Tigers fell to Iowa State in their next game and dropped into second place. But a game at Kansas State would give them a chance to reclaim the league lead.

Instead of finding themselves in first, the Tigers found themselves on the wrong end of one of the wildest finishes ever. The contest was physical throughout, and officials ejected Wildcat Harold Howey for kicking Pleasant Smith after a violent collision. It was also tight throughout, and Howard Shannon gave K-State a two-point lead by sinking a shot with just eight seconds to play. Missouri inbounded the ball to Pippin, whose desperation half-court heave splashed home, tying the game with three seconds left. But Kansas State quickly got the ball to Clarence Brannum who unleashed a forty-five-footer as the gun sounded. The ball ripped the net, giving the Wildcats a two-point victory over Mizzou and a one-game lead over Oklahoma. Standing a game and a half back with three to play, the Tigers' title hopes hung by a thread.

That thread snapped in their next game. Colorado topped the Tigers in their first meeting as Big Seven foes. Buffs Carr Besemann, Bob Rolander, and Sox Walseth all broke double figures as Mizzou completed a one-week slide from first to fourth. The Tigers gained revenge when the teams met again in Missouri's next game, but it was too late to make much difference in the standings. Thornton Jenkins scored fourteen in the final home game of his stellar career, a 47–35 triumph. Mizzou wrapped up the season in impressive fashion, snapping Oklahoma's twelve-game home win streak 45–43 to secure a tie for second place in the league at 7–5. It marked the end for Jenkins, but Dan Pippin, who led Mizzou with twelve points, would be back for one more season. Unfortunately, he would not see that season to its end.

## 1948–49

Though Thornton Jenkins had gone, nearly everyone else came back, including seniors Dan Pippin, Pleasant Smith, Karl Pierpoint, and Bill "Red" Haynes, the twenty-eight-year-old center from Joplin. They were joined by a gifted quartet that included juniors Don McMillen and Don Stroot (at six-foot-eight, the tallest Tiger) and sophomores George Lafferty and Bud Heineman. On paper, Sparky Stalcup had yet another contender.

Despite the talent, Missouri won just two of six games leading up to the Big Seven tournament, which, for the first time, was played between Christmas and New Year's Day. Things got no better for the Tigers in round one when they fell to Kansas. But from there, things started to look up. Mizzou recorded a two-point win over a potent Nebraska squad and capped the week with a victory over Colorado.

The Tigers sustained their momentum by returning home and routing Northwestern before opening conference play with a 49–42 triumph over Kansas State, sealed by late buckets from Smith and Haynes. The momentum, however, came to a halt in a stretch that saw Mizzou lose three of four, including a nonconference game against St. Louis. But those three losses were nothing compared with a pair of losses that happened off the court.

Though the Tigers had started slowly, at 2–2 in conference play they still had a legitimate shot at the Big Seven crown. That is, until the university's registrar ruled George Lafferty and Dan Pippin academically ineligible. For Lafferty, a sophomore, it meant the end to a season. But for Pippin, Missouri's all-time leading scorer, it meant an unfitting end to a tremendous career. And for the Tigers, it almost certainly meant an end to their title aspirations.

*Dan Pippin starred for the United States team that won gold at the 1952 Olympics.*

But Missouri still had three seniors to lean on, two of whom lifted the Tigers to victory in their first game without Pippin. Red Haynes, one of the team's biggest players, dominated the first half, and Karl Pierpoint, one of its smallest, sank the crucial shots in a 40–34 win at Kansas State. The Tigers returned home only to be routed by Kansas, but rebounded when a last-minute Don McMillen basket gave them a one-point win over Colorado in Boulder. With league-leading Nebraska next on the schedule, the Tigers remained hopeful despite the fact that Dan Pippin had gone from starring for Mizzou to starring for Columbia's Semmons Furniture team in the Missouri independent league.

A crowd of ten thousand, huge for the time, packed the Coliseum and saw the hometown Huskers race to a 30–16 halftime lead. Mizzou chipped away throughout the second half until Pleasant Smith's shot from the corner with five seconds to play tied the score at 43-all. Before time could expire, Karl Pierpoint and Nebraska's Claude Retherford collided. The referee called a double foul, giving one free throw to each team.

Retherford, the league's top scorer, sank his, and Bill Haynes, standing in for his woozy teammate, buried one to send the game to overtime.

Bill "Red" Haynes starred at center in the post-war years.

In the extra period, after Nebraska took a one-point lead on a free throw, Don Stroot tipped in a rebound to put the Tigers on top. When the Huskers failed to score on their next possession, Missouri went into a stall and had the game all but salted away when Nebraska's Dick Srb stole a pass with five seconds left, sprinted the length of the floor and laid in the game-winner at the buzzer. In an excruciating heartbeat, the Tigers went from contenders to also-rans as the Huskers solidified their grasp on first place.

Mizzou bounced back to beat second-place Oklahoma as Haynes and McMillen delivered increasingly common strong performances, but it hardly mattered. The inconsistent Tigers had settled into a win-one-lose-one pattern that they maintained through the end of the year. Their final near-hurrah, in the season's last home game, came in a rematch with Nebraska. Karl Pierpoint, whose stellar play in Pippin's absence earned him second team all-conference honors, scored sixteen and held Claude Retherford to just six. And when he fouled out late in the game, the Missouri faithful rose to their feet and boisterously saluted him for more than two minutes. But as Pierpoint watched from the bench, the Huskers added the final two points in a four-point win that sealed a share of the Big Seven crown. A season that began with promise ended with the Tigers standing fourth in the Big Seven.

After opening the decade with a championship, Mizzou closed it in the middle of the pack, but no one could mind too much. The end of global war and economic depression allowed Americans to treasure trivialities like college basketball. Win or lose, it was nice to cram into the field house, to celebrate George Edwards, to welcome Sparky Stalcup, and to admire the brilliance of John Lobsiger, the precociousness of Dan Pippin, the poise of Thornton Jenkins. In the grand scheme, Missouri Tiger basketball may have been trivial, but it was far from meaningless. It had been a source of comfort and diversion in a time of pain and anxiety. It had given rise to minor triumphs at a time when any sort of triumph would do. And it had reinforced a sense of community at a time when no one possibly could have gone it alone. It was the best of things in the worst of times.

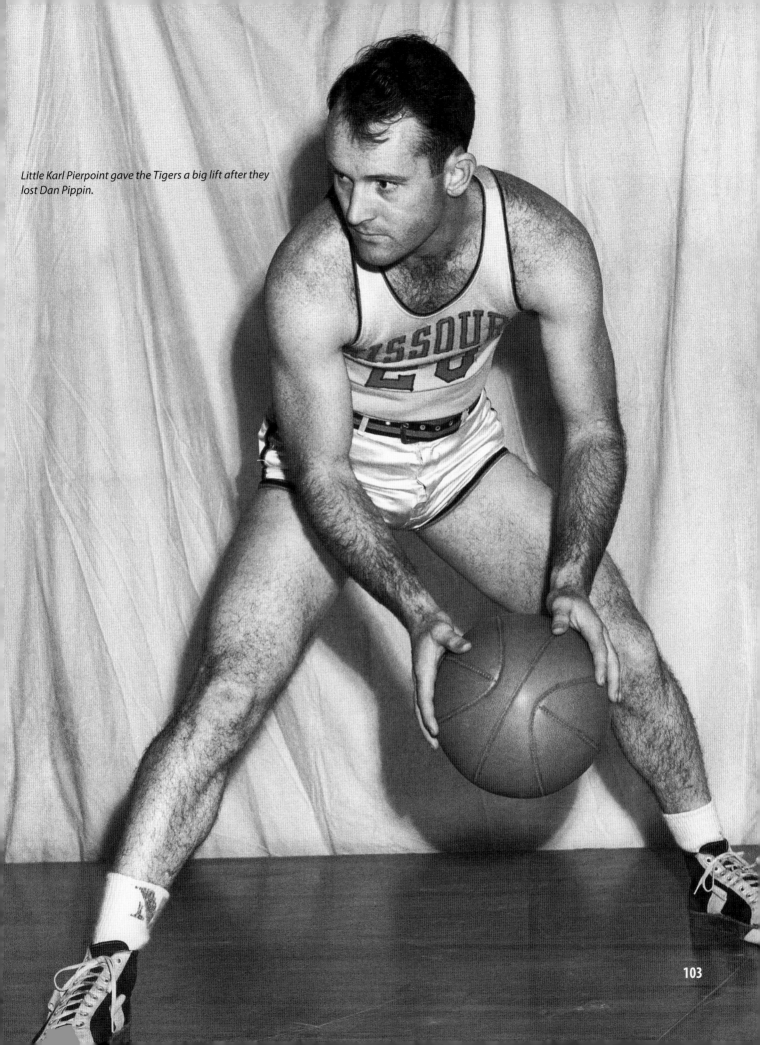

*Little Karl Pierpoint gave the Tigers a big lift after they lost Dan Pippin.*

For America, it was the decade of rock 'n' roll, DNA's discovery, and a deepening civil rights movement. For the Missouri Tigers, it was the Decade of the Near Miss, ten years that saw some of the best to don the black and gold come tantalizingly close to claiming titles, only to watch them slip away. It was a time that saw integration and prodigiously skilled giants radically reshape Big Seven basketball. And for Missouri fans, it was a time for hardwood heroes, individual players whose success eclipsed that of their teams. At the beginning of the decade, players like Bill Stauffer and Norm Stewart were anonymous. By its end, they were legends.

# THE 1950s

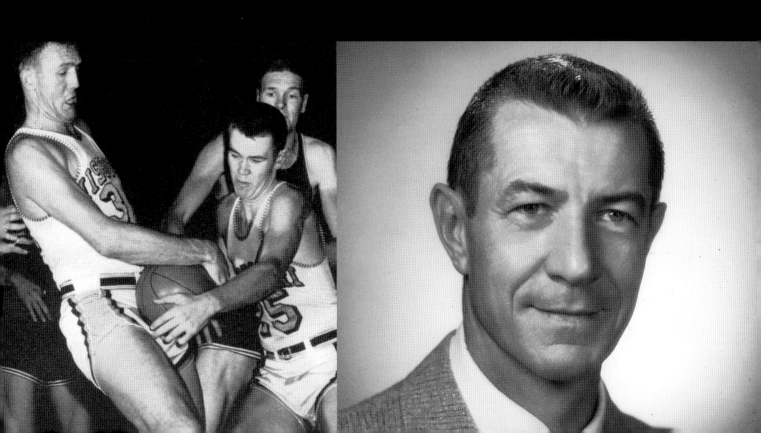

## 1949–50

He played with power, he played with finesse. He played a little guard and a little forward, but mostly, he played center. He went up against men a full head taller and destroyed them. At a time when six-foot-nine gazelles ruled the post, a six-foot-three bull overwhelmed them. He could pull up and shoot from the outside, or he could drive to the basket and score in traffic. But more than anything, he could rebound. In Missouri history, no one has made greater success out of others' failures. For Bill Stauffer, every errant shot meant opportunity. Cold shooters were his prey. He owned the glass.

Stauffer came to Columbia from Maryville, where, as a boy, he delivered newspapers to Sparky Stalcup's apartment and watched the coach direct basketball practices. When Stauffer made his way to the University of Missouri, he brought a friend, Dick Adams, his high school teammate. Together they provided Stalcup with young talent on which to build.

The Missouri Tigers had opened the 1920s, 1930s, and 1940s with conference championships. They looked like a good bet to do the same in the 1950s after a scorching start to the season. Following a loss to Texas Christian in the opener, Stalcup found a nickel and taped it inside his shoe for luck. The Tigers proceeded to go on their longest winning streak in years. Mizzou reeled off five straight wins leading to the Big Seven Tournament. There the Tigers' first opponent was Michigan, which had been invited to round out the eight-team field. In the final minute, Dan Witt came up with a steal, and Bill Stauffer hit a shot to give Missouri a 47–46 win. After topping Colorado in the semis, the Tigers faced Oklahoma for the title at Municipal Auditorium. In front of a sellout crowd of ninety-five hundred, junior guard George Lafferty carried the Tigers to a 44–42 upset victory. Late in the game, Lafferty came off a screen and hit a shot to tie the score at 40. Then he sank two free throws to give the Tigers a 42–40 lead. Finally, he made a layup with twenty seconds to play, giving Mizzou a four-point lead and its first tournament championship, a huge feather in the team's cap, especially at a time when

*Bill Stauffer, who began a legendary career in the 1949–50 season, takes a seat below the Brewer Field House court.*

the national tournaments had smaller fields and less prestige. The win also secured the Tigers' first national ranking as they placed twelfth in the first Associated Press poll of 1950 (the poll had come into being just a year before). Two weeks later, the entire campus celebrated the triumph at the Stalcup Stomp, a dance that drew more than one thousand people to Rothwell Gymnasium.

The hot start was surprising given the loss of several key players from the previous squad, including Don McMillen, who skipped his senior year to play professional baseball. But newcomers like Stauffer and Adams quickly melded with the rest of the team. After reaching new heights, however, Missouri went into free-fall. Over the next nine weeks, the Tigers won two nonconference games but lost eight of their first nine Big Seven contests, including a pair to Kansas and sophomore phenom Clyde Lovellette, a six-foot-nine scoring machine. The Tigers recovered in time to win their last three

*At 6'8," lanky Don Stroot was among the tallest Tigers to date.*

games to close the season at 14–10 overall and 4–8 in league play. Remarkably, half of their conference wins came at the expense of Kansas State, which went 8–2 against the rest of the Big Seven. Don Stroot, the gangly six-foot-eight, 185-pound center, starred in those victories, averaging eighteen points per game. Missouri's efforts forced the Wildcats to share the championship with Kansas and Nebraska.

In retrospect, the story of the season was the debut of Stauffer and a statistic tailor-made for him. For the first time, rebounds were officially tallied. Without the new statistic, the genius of Stauffer's play would have proved elusive. With it, there is some measure of the ferocity with which he fought for the ball. In his first year with the varsity, Maryville's favorite son averaged 9.5 boards per game to lead the team. But that was small potatoes compared with what would follow.

## 1950–51

For a moment, Missouri fans thought they would be looking for a new coach. Despite the sixth-place finish in 1950, Stalcup remained a hot commodity. Michigan State offered Sparky a big raise in an effort to lure him to East Lansing. While he mulled the offer, Michigan State prematurely issued a release announcing Stalcup as its new coach. He quickly quelled the uproar by announcing that he would be going nowhere. "I'm from Missouri and I like it here," he said. "I like working for Don Faurot, who is a real gentleman." Of course, Mizzou's decision to match the offer didn't hurt either.

The 1950–51 season followed a pattern similar to the previous year—a quick start, then a lull, and a strong finish. But the lull was shorter, the finish stronger, and the end result far more satisfying. The Tigers looked great against nonconference foes in December, but shaky play in the Big Seven Tournament and early conference slate left them at just 6–5 overall and 0–2 in the league. They began to

*George Lafferty's inspired play gave the Tigers their first conference tournament title.*

warm up in January, but didn't truly hit their stride until the following month. A loss to a tremendous Kansas State club left Missouri at 2–3 in conference play. But when nationally ranked Kansas came to Columbia, the Tigers' season turned on a dime. Though Missouri had trailed by eleven points in the second half, George Lafferty tied the score at 37–37 with a late field goal. Then, after KU's Bill Hougland

*Bud Heineman (left) and Bill Stauffer (right) were the great stars of Sparky Stalcup's teams of the early 1950s.*

sank a free throw, Lafferty struck again. His driving layup with less than thirty seconds to play gave Mizzou its first lead and the final margin in a 39–38 win. That victory propelled the Tigers to a stretch in which they won six of their last seven. Included was a twelve-point win over seventeenth-ranked Oklahoma as Bill Stauffer scored twenty-one despite going head-to-head with the Sooners' six-foot-ten Marcus Freiberger. That late-season surge gave Missouri a 16–8 overall mark, including 8–4 in conference play, good for a second-place tie with Kansas.

The Tiger team was Coach Stalcup's best to date and Missouri's best since the 1940 Big Six champs. The team's success was built on the strength of two impressive individual efforts. One was by senior Bud Heineman, a product of Versailles, Missouri, who played forward despite standing just five-foot-ten. Though small of stature, Heineman rode a deadly accurate left-handed jump shot to 283 points on the season, the most by a Tiger in thirty years. While Heineman controlled the perimeter, Bill Stauffer ruled the paint en route to all-conference honors. Stauffer used his powerfully built six-foot-three frame to wrestle 357 rebounds from bigger opponents, an average of 14.9 per game. His 261 points also ranked among the best outputs by a Missouri player. After the season, Stauffer was inducted into the prestigious Mystical Seven honorary. Coach Stalcup also was initiated into the secret society, his identity revealed at the ceremony by Don Faurot, a member since his days as a student.

Despite the achievements of the team and its stars, the season's most enduring story surrounds Missouri's second game of the year. Two days after dropping their opener to Washington University, the Tigers traveled to New York to play at Madison Square Garden. For a bunch of small-town Missouri boys, the venue alone was daunting. But the opponent was even more intimidating. The Tigers faced City College of New York, which had won both the NCAA Tournament and the NIT just eight months earlier. With most of their key players returning and at 3–0 on the young season, the Beavers had shown nothing to cast doubt on their ability to repeat the feat. As Bill Stauffer confessed years later, "We were scared to death."

But once the teams hit the floor, it was the tough City crew—and not the visiting bumpkins—who

looked like deer caught in headlights. Just hours after a dentist removed two teeth that had been knocked loose in the previous game, Bud Heineman sparked a shocking upset. He scored fifteen of his nineteen points in a decisive first half that included a 17–0 Tiger run. Missouri stunned eighteen thousand spectators by taking a 31–14 lead to the locker room, then cruised to a nearly unimaginable 54–37 win. Though matched against All-Americans Ed Warner and Ed Roman, Bill Stauffer dominated. He scored fifteen points, grabbed ten rebounds, and teamed with Dick Adams to limit CCNY's star tandem to a total of eighteen points. Mizzou's fierce defense held the Beavers to just 20 percent field goal shooting. Tiger fans from coast to coast celebrated. Missouri's athletic department sent Stalcup a telegram that said, "Congratulations on Greatest Win in Missouri Basketball History." The Associated Press ranked the Tigers number eight in the season's first poll; Mizzou even garnered two first-place votes. Missouri basketball had arrived as a national presence.

At least that's how it seemed on one remarkable evening in New York. But over the next few months, a series of arrests, confessions, and convictions revealed that something much more sinister happened that night. Gamblers had paid at least four CCNY players, including Roman and Warner, $1,500 apiece to ensure that the Beavers did not cover the spread against the Tigers. It was an early revelation in a far broader scandal that shook college basketball to its core.

From a Missouri fan's perspective, it is nice to believe that the Tigers may have won fair and square. After all, City College did not need to lose for the bets to pay off; rather, the Beavers simply needed not to win by more than the final line, which stood between six and twelve points. Even a student of the game as astute as Sparky Stalcup confessed that he was

*The defensive play of Dick Adams helped Missouri upset City College of New York, the defending national champion, though more sinister forces were at work that night in Madison Square Garden.*

"tremendously shocked" to learn that the fix was in. He had watched film of the game many times before the revelations and had never suspected a thing. But the 17–0 first-half run, abetted by the City players' duplicity, left the Tigers emboldened and the Beavers out of synch. Would Missouri have won without the gamblers' intervention? We'll never know. In the end, the Tigers were innocent bystanders, oblivious to their benign participation in one of the game's darkest chapters, an event that scarred college basketball for years.

# 1951–52

America's involvement in the Korean War siphoned men off college campuses, leading the Big Seven to suspend for one year the rule making freshmen ineligible. In truth, graduation proved more costly to Mizzou, with George Lafferty, Bud Heineman, and others lost to cap and gown. Freshmen Bob Reiter, Med Park, and Win Wilfong were forced to pick up the slack.

Freshman Win Wilfong was sprawled on his back when KU's Clyde Lovellette stepped on his gut and nearly started a riot.

With an inexperienced cast around him, senior Bill Stauffer wasn't exactly a one-man gang, but he wasn't far from it. Under Stauffer's leadership, Mizzou shot to a fast start, winning its first three before dropping games to Iowa, Tulsa, and Arkansas to enter the Big Seven Tournament with a .500 mark. Wins over Iowa State and Oklahoma put the Tigers in the championship game against Phog Allen's Jayhawks and their All-American, Clyde Lovellette. Kansas built a lead throughout the game and had it all but put away with just over three minutes to play. Win Wilfong, who scored a team-high seventeen, showed no fear in scrapping with the massive Lovellette, who had seven inches and sixty-five pounds on the youngster from Puxico. When the KU star grabbed an offensive rebound and scored with 3:02 left on the clock, Wilfong fell to the floor, flat on his back. Inexplicably, Lovellette stepped on the freshman's exposed torso, earning an ejection from the game and a cascade of jeers from the ten thousand on hand in Kansas City, and nearly igniting a brawl as Stauffer moved to exact revenge before the officials' timely intervention. The boos continued past the final buzzer (Kansas won 75–65) and through the trophy ceremony, creating chaos in the auditorium. A flustered Reaves Peters, executive secretary of the Big Seven, took the microphone and admonished the angry crowd. "I hope everyone here will remember where you are," he said. "This is America, not Russia." That spawned even more boos. Next,

*Three Tiger legends – Don Faurot, Sparky Stalcup, and Bill Stauffer – reminisce over Stauffer's jersey, the first to be retired at Mizzou.*

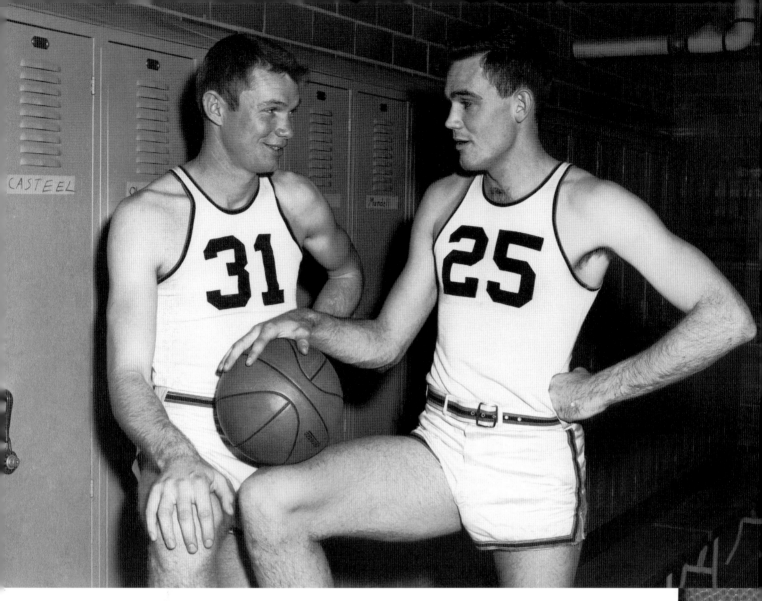

*Charles Oligschlaeger (31) and Gene Landolt provided leadership for a young Missouri team.*

Oklahoma coach Bruce Drake tried to calm the mob by explaining the tension present in a basketball game and the remorse shown by Lovellette. When that failed, he quoted a Bible verse, but to little avail. Finally, Coach Stalcup made a point to conspicuously shake Lovellette's hand. Then Sparky, who had nearly come to blows with KU's coach in a game just five years earlier, addressed the crowd and said, "The University of Missouri enjoys this rivalry with the University of Kansas. Doc Allen is a great coach." With that, Stalcup defused the hostility in the arena and earned Allen's lasting admiration. From then on, the rivals enjoyed a warm personal relationship.

After the spectacle of the Big Seven final, the Tigers muddled through a mostly unremarkable season, never again winning or losing more than two games in a row. Ultimately, they went zero for five against nationally ranked opponents, losing twice to Kansas State and three times to Kansas. When all was said and done, Missouri finished 14–10 overall and 6–6 in the conference, a distant third behind the Sunflower State superpowers.

Still, there was drama, most of which was provided by the Tigers' senior center and the Jayhawks' senior citizen. When Kansas visited Columbia, the elderly Allen put on a display that overshadowed a fantastic game. After falling behind by eighteen, Missouri rallied to take a one-point lead in the final minute, only to see KU's Dean Kelley sink a shot from the corner to win the game. Still, the real fireworks were yet to come. At the end of the first half, Kelley had hit a shot, but there was confusion over whether he beat the buzzer. The officials consulted with Chauncey Simpson, an assistant Tiger football coach, and the game's

timekeeper. Simpson said the shot should not count; the officials agreed, and Allen erupted. He regained his composure for the duration of the contest, but once the game ended, he let loose. Allen engaged in some fire-and-brimstone oration on the court, berating the officials, the press, and the fans. He made "unprintable remarks" about Simpson. Finally, Mizzou Athletics Director Don Faurot confronted Allen. "Now get out of here, Doc, you're causing enough trouble," he said. The bellicose coach held his ground, so Faurot took him by the arm and walked him toward the

*With a six-foot-eight frame and mile-long arms, Bob Reiter and his hook shot were hard to stop.*

Kansas locker room, and the two legends exchanged heated words along the way. Once inside, Allen continued to rant to no one in particular. Later in the evening, after heads cooled, Allen, Faurot, Stalcup, and others sat down to dinner together.

From that point forward, the season's main theme was Bill Stauffer's pursuit of history. Against Nebraska on February 2, he scored thirty-one points to set a Missouri single-game record. Two weeks later, he scored twenty-one against Colorado, giving him 313 points on the year and breaking George Williams's single-season record of 311 points. Then, on March 3 Stauffer played his final game as a Tiger. He scored nineteen to help Missouri secure a 68–53 win over Nebraska. At game's end, grateful fans hoisted Stauffer upon their shoulders and carried him off the court.

In his final season, the Tiger captain enjoyed a scoring and rebounding binge of epic proportions. Stauffer's 368 points shattered the season scoring mark. He also demolished his own rebounding record by grabbing 379 caroms, an average of 16.5 per game. In three varsity seasons, Stauffer averaged 13.6 rebounds, a figure that has never been seriously challenged. He also scored 813 points (11.4 per game) to surpass Dan Pippin as Missouri's career scoring leader. Bill Stauffer graduated as one of the greatest Tigers of all time.

## 1952–53

Gene Landolt and Charles Oligschlaeger provided veteran leadership, but precocious sophomores Bob Reiter, Win Wilfong, and Med Park provided the firepower in another season in which Missouri proved to be the best Big Seven team not from Kansas. Another sophomore, one with considerably more experience, pitched in as well. After four years in the Marines, St. Joseph native Gary Filbert returned to Columbia and provided a spark off the bench.

Reiter, the skinny center from Brentwood, Missouri, led the Tigers in scoring, with Wilfong second and Park third, and Wilfong earned all-conference honors. That kind of success for Wilfong had seemed written in the stars. He had been the best player on a Puxico High team that won the state title in his junior season. Puxico repeated in his senior year, going 40–0 while Wilfong amassed 941 points, making him the nation's top schoolboy scorer. Wilfong was the trigger man on a team that beat opponents by an average of forty-five points per game. He was named all-state and All-America. But once he got to Columbia, Wilfong had to remake his game. The wide-open style of Puxico was anathema to Sparky Stalcup, a true believer in ball-control offense and stifling defense. From day one of his freshman year, Win Wilfong became a stalwart of Missouri's lineup by excelling on the defensive end.

Wilfong and the Tigers followed a win-some, lose-some pattern throughout the year, including in the Big Seven Tournament, where Mizzou topped Yale (yes, Yale) to secure third place. From there, highlights included a 95–84 loss to fourth-ranked Kansas State (an astounding score for the time) in which the six-foot-eight Reiter scored twenty-seven, and a 77–73 overtime victory over Oklahoma in the year's next-to-last contest, a game that saw Reiter top himself with a school-record thirty-three points. A season-ending loss to Kansas left the Tigers with a 12–9 record and again at 6–6 and third place in the Big Seven.

After that loss, Missouri's sixth straight to the Jayhawks, the charismatic Stalcup made his way to Lawrence to speak at the Kansas basketball banquet. He left the crowd in stitches with a series of one-liners, many directed at himself in his trademark self-deprecating style. He also spoke from his heart, urging that the enormous new field house under construction in Lawrence be named for Phog Allen. Such a proposition had met resistance from some higher-ups who opposed naming the building for a living person. Ultimately, those in Phog's corner got their way.

## 1953–54

In the 1950s, long before the NBA stripped collegiate teams of talented underclassmen, coaches rarely worried about replacing prize sophomores. But that problem confronted Sparky Stalcup when Win Wilfong opened the 1953–54 season in the uniform of the United States Army. While Wilfong's play provided a boost for the Fort Leonard Wood Hilltoppers, his absence left quite a void for Mizzou. Fortunately, just as small Missouri towns like Maryville and Puxico had spawned players like Stauffer and Wilfong, the hamlet of Shelbyville produced Norman Stewart, a multitalented six-foot-four guard.

Stewart was shy and modest, a description that might surprise some who met him only years later. His blond crew cut and slender build made him look

*The most storied career in Missouri history began when Shelbyville's Norm Stewart made his varsity debut.*

like an ordinary college kid, albeit one who stood half a head taller than most of his peers. He was country, but he was no hayseed. In the local gym and dusty lots around Shelbyville, a natural savvy emerged, and remarkable athletic skills blossomed. He could throw a baseball like a bullet and shoot a basketball like nobody's business. In high school, Stewart scored more than two thousand points. He could nail jump shots from any angle, or he could drive to the hoop. He controlled the ball in a way that was foreign to men of his size at that time. Norm Stewart had an innate understanding of the game. Basketball was in his brain chemistry.

But he was just a sophomore, Reiter and Park were just juniors, and there were few senior contributors, leaving the Tigers' prospects as unremarkable as the austere uniforms they wore, which displayed their numbers but were devoid of script of any kind. Coach Stalcup spent much of the year trying different combinations to complement his emerging stars. Lloyd Elmore provided defense. Gary Filbert and his two-handed set shot provided an outside threat. Chuck Denny gave the Tigers

*Gary Filbert's two-handed set shot and relentless defense made him a valuable player.*

a physical rebounder, and Bill Holst, a senior forward, gave them toughness. Bob Schoonmaker, a five-foot-eleven football and baseball standout, gave them energy and the occasional offensive outburst.

Stewart scored seven in his debut, a 75–43 trouncing of Drake (Reiter and Park combined for thirty-seven), but the Tigers failed to string any wins together. They were just 2–2 headed into the Big Seven tournament, and they had not played well. Stalcup even seemed a bit desperate in Kansas City. In the semifinals against Kansas, Sparky employed a bizarre tactic by keeping Reiter on the bench for much of the game, hoping to gain an edge if and when B. H. Born, the Jayhawks' big center, fouled out. He never did. Ironically, Reiter was lost to fouls in limited play, and Kansas won by two. The Tigers regrouped to take third place, but after the tournament, a four-game skid dropped them to 4–7, with a trip to Manhattan, Kansas, looming. K-State had taken six straight from Missouri. Midway through the season, Mizzou's prospects seemed no more remarkable than they had at the beginning.

Surprisingly, the Tigers, led by Filbert's nineteen points, won their first game against Kansas State's new coach, Tex Winter. The Tigers made it two in a row with a win over Iowa State (Reiter scored seventeen) before losing a nonconference game to Iowa. They narrowly missed their third straight league victory when they dropped an 80–78 decision at Oklahoma despite the valiant effort of an ill Reiter who came off the bench to score thirty.

Before the stretch run, the Tigers took a break from league play to host Houston at Brewer. They won in a rout 96–62, a new record output for Mizzou. Bob Reiter tied his own single-game record with thirty-three points, while Norm Stewart contributed nineteen points and eighteen rebounds. The Tigers finally seemed to find their legs. They hosted Oklahoma and pasted the Sooners 66–51 behind twenty-eight points from Reiter. Then, Kansas State came to town and stole a one-point victory with a coast-to-coast drive in the closing seconds. Undeterred, Missouri recovered to win consecutive fifteen-point decisions over Nebraska and Iowa State. Reiter scored twenty-four points against the Cyclones and surpassed Bill Stauffer's season-scoring record as Missouri won its fourth

*Broad-shouldered Chuck Denny was a tenacious rebounder.*

game in five starts. Reiter and the Tigers were playing their best basketball of the season, but there was just one game left to play.

They entered that final game at 10–10 overall and 5–6 in the conference. To avoid their first losing season in five years, the Tigers would have to beat nationally ranked Kansas. The Jayhawks had clinched at least a tie for the league title with Colorado; a win in Columbia would secure the championship outright. But Stalcup's crew captured a surprising 76–67 win, keyed by Stewart (who scored twenty-two) and Reiter, who outscored B. H. Born twenty-eight to twenty-five, in a duel of two of the league's top centers. Missouri's victory allowed Colorado to grab a share of its first Big Seven title and ultimately a berth in the NCAA Tournament when Kansas drew the short straw in the lottery that determined the league's representative.

Despite their mediocre record, the Tigers had reason to be optimistic about the future. Reiter established a new scoring record with 411 points on the year, 19.6 per game, while Stewart averaged 12.2 points per game in his first varsity season. Both would be back, as would most other contributors, including the sensational Med Park, a bruising six-foot-two, 220-pound playmaking guard. And though they would fall short of their ultimate goals, the Tigers were about to have one of their most successful campaigns in thirty years.

## 1954–55

Sparky Stalcup had a dangerous ball club, one picked by many to win the conference championship. All five of his starters—Bob Reiter, Norm Stewart, Med Park, Redford Reichert, and sophomore Lionel Smith, a two-time all-stater at Madison (Missouri) High School—could score, and sixth man Gary Filbert was a defensive stopper. Reiter, with his fantastic hook shot, began the year with 809 career points, just shy of Bill Stauffer's all-time record, while Park's career total of 476 put him within striking distance of the exclusive 800 club. And despite playing alongside those two all-time greats, Stewart, who had helped pitch Mizzou's baseball team to the national title a few months earlier, already was recognized as the best player on the team, if not in the entire league; his ability to

*Powerful Med Park, a tremendous defender, went on to win an NBA title with the St. Louis Hawks.*

shoot, rebound, handle the ball and pass inspired whispers of "Stewart for All-American" shortly after the season began. Surprisingly, Illinois routed this formidable squad in the opener, temporarily dampening expectations. But those expectations were quickly and resoundingly revived.

The Tigers traveled to Indiana to face the sixth-ranked Hoosiers, allowing IU coach Branch McCracken, winner of two national titles, to see what he had missed. A friend of Norm Stewart's high school coach, McCracken had declined an invitation to recruit Stewart. Instead, he advised that Norm should play for Sparky Stalcup. McCracken came to regret the decision after Stewart scored sixteen points, including two late free throws, in a 64–61 Missouri upset. But Stewart didn't do it alone. While he and Reiter rode the bench with foul trouble in the second half, Park and Reichert (who combined for twenty-six points) kept the Tigers in the game and put Stewart in position to finish off the Hoosiers. Afterwards, McCracken told Stewart, "I lost this game two years ago when I didn't recruit you."

Next, the Tigers hosted fourth-ranked Iowa in the most breathless game ever at the field house.

The Tigers prevailed in a 97–94 thriller that saw Park, Reiter, and Stewart score twenty-six, twenty-four, and nineteen, respectively, while Smith and Reichert each chipped in twelve. After the Tigers beat Wisconsin behind twenty-six points from Stewart, they jumped from unranked to number six in the national polls.

*Bob Reiter finished his career as Mizzou's all-time scoring leader.*

An overtime loss at Houston provided a bump in the road to the Big Seven tournament, but once in Kansas City, the Tigers enjoyed a festive holiday season. They were never seriously challenged on their way to the title. Mizzou topped Nebraska by seventeen (Stewart scored twenty-six) in round one, then beat Oklahoma to advance to the finals. There they trounced Kansas State. Missouri led by as many as twenty-eight points in an 89–71 victory. Med Park scored twenty-four points in the title game, and Norm Stewart was named the tournament's most valuable player. Though they spent much of their careers as guards, Park and Stewart played most of the season at forward. And despite standing just six-foot-two, Park used his wide, powerful shoulders to muscle his way to the hoop, where he did most of his damage.

The title established Missouri as an early favorite in the Big Seven race, and the Tigers played like champions over the first half of the league schedule. They opened with their last-ever visit to Hoch Auditorium, the cramped and hostile room that Sparky Stalcup referred to without affection as "the Den of Noise." The Jayhawk fans made it a daunting venue, as did the Jayhawks themselves, who had won thirty-three straight games there. But Sparky's squad was fearless. The Missouri seniors made a statement with a 76–65 triumph. Reiter led the way with twenty-one points and twenty-four boards. Med Park was right behind with twenty points, and Gary Filbert came off the bench to score ten. Mizzou then returned home to defeat Nebraska, and the Tigers bounced back to number six in the Associated Press poll.

Peculiar scheduling set up back-to-back games with Kansas State. Reiter entered the first game,

*As a junior, Norm Stewart blossomed into the league's best all-around player.*

in Manhattan, with a sore knee. It did not slow him. He scored twenty-nine points and collected a Missouri-record twenty-seven rebounds in a 94–85 win. He also became the first Tiger ever to score one thousand career points. Though the Tigers stumbled in the rematch in Columbia, they won their next two games to take a 5–1 record to Boulder for a contest with high-scoring Burdette Haldorson and conference co leader Colorado. Haldorson and Bob Jeangerard combined for thirty-eight points and held Stewart and Reiter to just twenty-two as Missouri lost on the mile-high court 80–71. Nonetheless, the Tigers remained in the title hunt. They were just one game back with five to play, and one of those five would be a rematch with the Buffaloes in Columbia.

In the interim, Missouri took care of business by winning three straight Big Seven contests, as Park, Stewart, and Reiter continued to rack up points. But Colorado did the same, and when the Buffs invaded Columbia for the season's penultimate game, the Tigers needed a win to keep alive the dream of a Big Seven championship.

By the time the game came around, Reiter and Stewart had been named honorable mention All-America by the United Press. Close to six thousand fans packed Brewer to watch the Tigers try to stake a claim to their first title in fifteen years. It looked good for a while. Lionel Smith, who led Mizzou with fifteen points, helped the Tigers surge to a 44–37 lead early in the second half. But then they began to unravel. They turned the ball over repeatedly and failed to get second chances on offense. The Buffaloes thundered to the league crown with a 66–57 win.

The Tigers took out their frustration on Kansas in the year's final game, as the home fans bade farewell to seniors Reiter, Park, Filbert, Lee Fowler, and Lloyd Elmore. Med Park scored a career-high twenty-seven points in a 90–71 Missouri win that chagrined the Jayhawks' coach. When the student journalists of the *Savitar*, perhaps not on their best behavior, approached Phog Allen for comment at game's end, he gave them a terse "Get the hell out of here." According to the yearbook scribes, that's

*Redford Reichert possessed a deft shooting touch.*

when they knew Missouri's season had been a success.

Still, the win was bittersweet because it marked the end of two storied careers. Med Park, as fine a perimeter defender as there ever was, averaged better than fifteen points per game as a senior and finished his career with an even 800 points, making him Mizzou's fourth leading scorer to that point (Park would earn an NBA championship three years later with the St. Louis Hawks). Bob Reiter pulled down 14.3 rebounds per game as a senior—a figure topped in Tiger history only by Bill Stauffer—and finished his career with 1,188 points, far more than any previous Missouri player. Losing Park and Reiter was a terrible blow. But their junior all-conference teammate would return the next season for one valiant last stand.

## 1955–56

In his senior season, the Tiger team was indisputably Norm Stewart's. By the end of his junior year, Stewart already had been recognized as the best all-around player in the league, but he would have to be even better in his final year for the Tigers to contend for a Big Seven title. Without Park and Reiter, Stewart faced a titanic challenge in the fiftieth season of Missouri basketball. But he wasn't alone. Fellow senior Redford Reichert, with his dangerous jump shot, had averaged nearly eight points per game the previous year, and junior Lionel Smith, an exceptional shooter, had averaged better than ten.

The Tigers made an early season statement against eighth-ranked Illinois. Stewart scored twenty-seven second-half points to help Missouri overcome a fifteen-point deficit and win 74–73. He made another personal statement in a rout against Texas Tech when he tallied thirty-five points and broke Bob Reiter's single-game record. More recognition came Stewart's way over the holidays when he was named to the All-Big Seven Tournament team following Mizzou's third-place finish.

A less likely hero emerged when the Tigers visited Arkansas. Mizzou trailed by one in the closing seconds when Bill Ross, a six-foot-two junior, put up a last-second shot. He missed but was fouled. With no time left on the clock, Ross made two free throws to give Missouri a 51–50 triumph, the first of many wins in Fayetteville.

The Tigers stood 7–3 when Big Seven play opened at home against Kansas. Mizzou thumped the Jayhawks 76–54 behind twenty-four points from Ross and a twelve-point, eighteen-rebound performance by Chuck Denny. The win made for a nice start to the conference campaign, but the Tigers' hopes for a title were nearly dashed when Stewart injured his back early in a seven-point loss at Colorado. Stewart tried to play through the pain the next time out, and though he scored twenty-five points, he clearly was hobbled, missing his first eight shots in an 83–77 loss at Nebraska. By the time Missouri dropped its third straight game (58–54 to Kansas State), the senior captain was in traction at University Hospital.

A two-week break for exams gave Stewart a chance to heal. He scored twenty-three points in his return, a win over Oklahoma that put Mizzou at 2–3 in the league. The Tigers evened their record in Lawrence when Chuck Denny, Bob Reiter's replacement at center, scored twenty-three. After the game, the crowd pelted the Tigers with debris, but it felt like a ticker tape parade. The game marked Missouri's last confrontation with Phog Allen, who was forced from his job at season's end by a Kansas mandatory retirement age law. It was the only time the Tigers faced the legendary coach in the enormous new arena named in his honor. It also was the first time any opponent beat Kansas at Allen Field House.

Next came a return home and a meeting with Iowa State, a game that featured two of the league's top scorers, Stewart and the Cyclones' Gary Thompson. A capacity crowd saw a tremendous battle turn into a heartbreaking loss when Iowa State prevailed 88–85 in overtime. Stewart scored twenty-six points and Lionel Smith added twenty-five, but John Crawford, a six-foot-five center, lifted ISU to victory with seven points in the extra period. At 3–4, Missouri's hopes for a conference title were all but gone.

That didn't stop the Tigers—and especially Stewart—from trying. In Missouri's next game, Norm broke his own record with thirty-six points in a win over Colorado, and he became only the second Tiger to top one thousand points for a career. Two days later, the Tigers traveled to Ames and gained revenge on the Cyclones, as Stewart scored thirty-three. Missouri then made it three in a row as Stewart tallied twenty-nine in a win over Oklahoma. The win streak kept Missouri's faint title hopes alive. The Tigers trailed league-leading Kansas State by two games with two to play. The Wildcats would host Missouri in the Tigers' next game. A Kansas

*Scrappy Bill Ross hits the deck.*

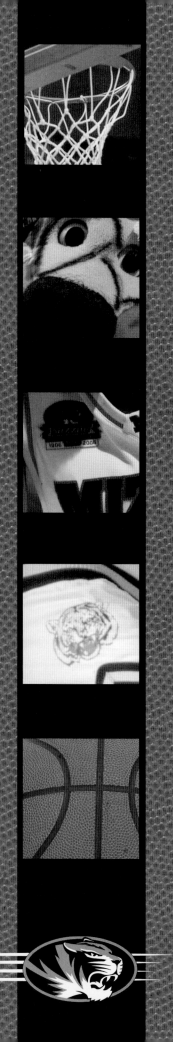

*Chuck Denny (left) and Lionel Smith fight each other for a loose ball.*

State victory in cavernous Ahearn Field House would clinch the Big Seven title, while a Missouri triumph would give the Tigers a fighting chance to win their first championship in sixteen years.

Before thirteen thousand fans, the Tigers closed the first half with a 14–0 run that gave them a sixteen-point lead at intermission. Offensively, the damage was done by Norm Stewart and Bill Ross while Chuck Denny dominated the backboards. Missouri took an 85–72 win as Stewart tallied twenty-four points and fifteen boards, while Ross added twenty-two points and Denny recorded ten points and twenty rebounds. With one game to play, the Tigers trailed the Cats by just one game. A Missouri win over Nebraska and a Kansas State loss at Kansas in the season's final week would give the Tigers a share of the Big Seven crown.

Missouri did its part two nights later in Columbia by topping Nebraska 88–80. In the last home contest for seniors Stewart, Denny, Reichert, and Kent Henson, the Tigers kept their title hopes alive. Denny, who came to Columbia from Fayette, Missouri, as a clumsy kid, left as a rugged inside presence. He led the squad with twenty-three points, followed by Lionel Smith with twenty-one, Stewart with twenty, and Bill Ross with eighteen. With their regular season completed, the Tigers were in the unusual and uncomfortable position of rooting for Kansas the next night. And the Tigers had reason for hope. Kansas had beaten the Wildcats seven straight times.

The Jayhawks let Mizzou down. After building a ten-point lead, Kansas faded in the final home game of Phog Allen's career. Kansas State clinched the Big Seven championship with a 79–68 victory, the first title for Tex Winter, who would succeed Allen as the league's dominant coach. With a postseason berth available only to the conference champ, Missouri's season ended on the Allen Field House court at the conclusion of a game between its two fiercest rivals.

The playing career of one of history's greatest Tigers ended as well. Norm Stewart won the Big Seven scoring title in his senior season and earned spots on the all-conference and All-America teams. He finished with 1,112 points, then the most by a Missouri player in a three-year career (121 of Bob Reiter's 1,188 career points had come in his freshman year). A revolutionary player, Stewart nearly averaged a career double-double by recording totals of 17.7

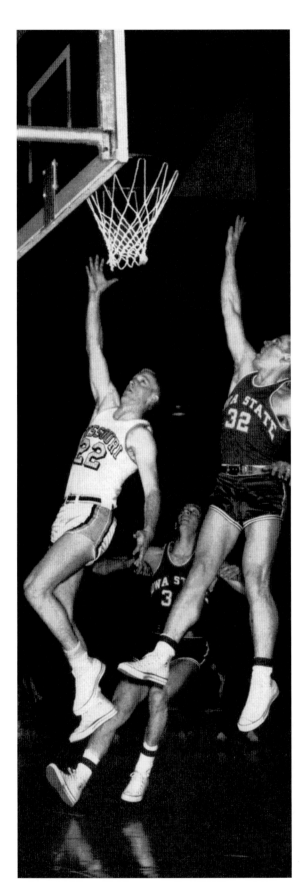

*Despite a bad back, Norm Stewart enjoyed an All-America senior season.*

points and 9.2 rebounds per game. But despite his greatness, Missouri was unable to capture the long-elusive conference championship in Stewart's three seasons, instead settling for two second-place finishes and one third, while Tiger fans wondered what might have been had Norm's back held up throughout his final year.

Given the context, the disappointment was especially acute. The 1955–56 season was Stalcup's last best chance to win a title. After Stewart's graduation, Missouri's talent level dropped off significantly, while rivals Kansas and Kansas State landed dominant athletes who would fundamentally change the way the game was played in the Big Seven and beyond.

## 1956–57

It was the start of a long, slow fade for Sparky Stalcup. In his first ten years at Missouri, his teams finished second in the conference five times. But after Norm Stewart's graduation, they would never again place higher than fourth. Though his clubs were not devoid of talent, Stalcup could not match the enormous firepower that found its way to Lawrence and Manhattan. Part of that was due to his personal fabric. When it came to recruiting, Stalcup was ethical to a fault and even a bit naïve to the way the game was changing. He believed to his core that basketball should be just one piece of the university experience. He believed in students who played basketball, not basketball players who dabbled in education. "A school like Missouri will not relax its educational requirements for the sake of getting an exceptional athlete," he said. "The era of the dumb athlete is fast drawing to a close." He abhorred the corrupt recruiting practices that became more prevalent in the 1950s and railed against them. He believed that under-the-table payments were being made to the best big men, the kinds of players that were changing the game. He blamed alumni for brokering deals and blamed coaches for turning a blind eye. He feared for the integrity of the game.

In addition to losing out on top talent, Sparky lost his biggest rival. Stalcup had been a foil to Phog Allen since their first meeting in 1947, when the Kansas coach stormed the Missouri bench. When Allen went into retirement, Stalcup's program

*Sparky Stalcup helped bring monumental change to the University of Missouri in 1956.*

went into decline. Still, in that time of remarkable cultural transformation, the greatest challenges facing Stalcup came off the court, where the veteran coach helped to remake the image of Mizzou and its athletics programs.

Throughout the first half of the twentieth century, the University of Missouri had many things to be proud of. Its record on racial integration was not among them. Missouri's Constitution of 1875 mandated "separate but equal" education that was anything but. White students were welcome at Mizzou while blacks were restricted to Lincoln University in Jefferson City. Black students who wished to take courses offered only in Columbia were not admitted to the university; rather, they were shipped out of state to integrated schools, with the state of Missouri paying their tuition. In fact, Mizzou was not integrated in any meaningful way until the 1954 United States Supreme Court decision in *Brown v. Board of Education of Topeka* ended segregation in public education.

This institutional prejudice extended to sports, where "Dixie" had served as Missouri's fight song until "Fight Tiger" debuted in 1946. The schools of the Big Six had informally agreed not to integrate their teams, and for a time the University of Missouri's official policy prohibited competition against teams that included nonwhite members.

In truth, Mizzou did not lag far behind other schools. Integration slowly moved across the country region by region. Most Midwestern schools first integrated their rosters in the 1950s, while southern universities took longer, with Mississippi State bringing up the rear in 1972.

The face of Missouri basketball, and all Mizzou sports, changed in early 1956. Alfred Abram Jr., a seventeen-year-old from Sumner High in St. Louis, became the university's first black scholarship athlete. Sparky Stalcup could hardly have chosen a better candidate to break Missouri's color barrier. At six-foot-five and 198 pounds, Al Abram was a model athlete and citizen. An exemplary student, Abram was president of his senior class, yearbook editor, choir member, and

*Al Abram made history when he broke the color barrier for Missouri athletics.*

National Honor Society inductee, and he compiled a perfect attendance record through all his years in high school. Abram even earned his diploma a semester early and enrolled at Mizzou in January 1956. In choosing Missouri, he turned down offers from Purdue, St. Louis University, and others. He did not make his choice to be a pioneer, but he did not shrink from that role either. "The chance to be the first of my race ever to be awarded an athletic scholarship at Missouri didn't sway me one way or the other," he said, "but now that I'm here, I'm going to try my best to be worthy of the honor." Because of freshman ineligibility, Abram had to bide his time on coach Clay Cooper's freshman team. His varsity career would have to wait until the second semester of the 1956–57 school year.

Just before that varsity career began, Sparky Stalcup found himself in a very public snit with an icon of wholesome Americana, the *Saturday Evening Post*. At a time when Mizzou was beginning to make strides toward equality, the *Post* ran an article that painted the university and Stalcup in an unflattering light. One semester before Al Abram enrolled at Mizzou, a young man-myth arrived at the University of Kansas. Before he ever suited up for the Jayhawks, Wilt Chamberlain was generally regarded as the most gifted player of his generation. Rumors swirled that the seven-foot kid from Philadelphia was lured to the dusty plains by something far greener than the scenery, and a consensus grew that he would turn Kansas into an unstoppable juggernaut. *The Post* sent sportswriter Jimmy Breslin to Lawrence to see what all the fuss was about.

Breslin's piece focused, in part, on how the eastern, urban black kid would be received in the conservative burgs that dotted America's midsection. Mizzou, in particular, received the back of Breslin's hand: "Testing points this year will be the Kansas away games with Missouri and Oklahoma—both in sectors where the prevailing attitude on the race question differs considerably from the Eastern outlook to which Wilt is accustomed."

While the article painted the university, in general, as a bastion of Jim Crow sentiment, it skewered Stalcup more specifically, suggesting that the coach had engaged in some opportunistic and perhaps unethical recruiting when Chamberlain came to the heartland to visit Kansas. The following, a quote attributed to Chamberlain, is the controversial passage exactly as printed in the *Post*: "The first time I went to Kansas, the Missouri coach"—Wilbur Stalcup—"met me at the airport—he was kind of cutting in—and asked me if I wanted to be the first Negro to play at his school."

When the article hit newsstands in late 1956, Stalcup was livid, and he had reason to be. At the time of publication, Sparky had never met Chamberlain, not in an airport, not on a basketball court, not anywhere. Stalcup immediately sent a telegram to the *Post* and demanded a retraction.

Chamberlain did not specifically identify Stalcup as the person he met in Kansas City's airport. Rather, Breslin inserted the Missouri mentor's name when Chamberlain referred to "the Missouri coach." In fact, the person Chamberlain encountered was William Toler, president of Kansas City's chapter of the Missouri Quarterback Club. When the controversy erupted, Toler explained that he was preparing to catch a flight when he bumped into a KU contingent, including Phog Allen's son, Bob, on hand to meet Chamberlain. When the group introduced Toler to Wilt, Toler asked him where he would attend college. Chamberlain replied, "It won't be the University of Missouri, Mr. Toler."

*With forty-four points against Marquette, Lionel Smith set a Missouri single-game scoring record.*

When the *Post* declined Stalcup's demand for a retraction, both Chamberlain and Kansas coach Dick Harp submitted letters confirming that Sparky had never met Wilt, and verifying Toler's account. And Phog Allen, who had great affection for Stalcup, said simply, "Whoever supports Breslin will be a sad sister." Still, the *Post* made no retraction, only an offer to print Stalcup's version of the incident. Sparky remained steadfast. "I have no version," he said. "I wasn't there."

While facing the challenges of integration, Stalcup confronted the challenge of replacing Norm Stewart. The man tagged with that daunting responsibility was a six-foot-three sophomore from Bayless High School in St. Louis. The job, of course, was impossible, but Sonny Siebert, with his soft shooting touch, gave an impressive effort.

Bill Ross returned after an impressive junior campaign, while baby-faced senior Lionel Smith was one of the most natural scorers of the Stalcup era. Ross, Smith, and Siebert formed a three-headed monster for the Tigers, who did most of their damage from the perimeter. Early on, Mizzou's assault from the edges paid dividends.

Siebert and Smith each scored twenty-two in a win over South Dakota, and Ross and Siebert scored nineteen apiece (Smith added eighteen) to beat Southern California. Game after game, Missouri leaned on the trio for the bulk of its offense. By the time the Big Seven tournament rolled around, the Tigers sported an improbable 5–2 record.

That was the season's high-water mark. The Tigers went winless in Kansas City, then traveled to Lawrence to face Wilt Chamberlain and the nation's top-ranked team. When Chamberlain recorded fifty-two points and thirty-one rebounds weeks earlier in his varsity debut, his aura of invincibility was cemented. By the time Mizzou faced Wilt and company, the goal wasn't to win, it was to avoid humiliation. Indeed, the day after Kansas topped the Tigers 92–79, the headline in the *Columbia Daily Tribune* didn't mention the outcome; instead, it read simply, "Tiger Zone Slows Wilt," as if holding Chamberlain to twenty-three points (eleven below his average) was a victory in and of itself. After Chamberlain scored thirty-two in the rematch, the writers at the *Savitar* recognized that "until someone comes up with an idea to stop Wilt, the Tigers are going to have to settle for some position besides first in the basketball race."

The insinuations surrounding the *Saturday Evening Post* controversy had been particularly troubling to Stalcup at a time when he was preparing

*Al Abram played in Wilt Chamberlain's long shadow.*

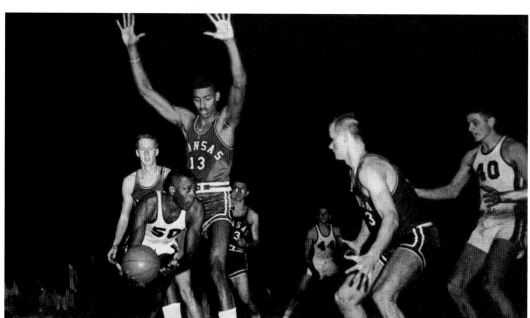

*Sharp shooting Sonny Siebert carried the Tigers before moving on to a long career as a major league pitcher.*

to add the first black athlete to the Tiger roster. In February 1957, Al Abram's year in the purgatory of freshman ineligibility came to a close. His arrival on the varsity came not a minute too soon. The Tigers had lost six of eight. Amid little fanfare, Abram made his debut in a 74–56 win over Oklahoma. He came off the bench with Mizzou trailing by three, and his eight points helped propel the Tigers to victory. "It has been a long time since a first-game sophomore got anything like the ovation which the M.U. student rooters gave Abram when he hit his first basket," wrote the *Tribune's* J. P. Hamel.

Unfortunately, Abram's arrival provided no real spark to the struggling Tigers. Missouri went on to lose five of its remaining seven games, stumbling to a 10–13 record and a sixth-place finish in the Big Seven. Still, that futile stretch provided one of the great individual displays in Tiger history. During the season, Lionel Smith had emerged from the long shadows of former teammates Stewart, Reiter, and Park, and on February 18, 1957, he delivered a performance that surpassed all that had come before. Smith lit up Marquette for forty-four points in a 98–76 Tiger win. Two weeks later, he finished his career with 992 points, then the third-highest total in Tiger history. His graduation would leave a mammoth void for a team that already found itself struggling to compete.

## 1957–58

A new season brought continued struggles. Like the year before, things went well before the conference tournament. Al Abram scored twenty-two in a rout of North Dakota, and Sonny Siebert poured in twenty-seven to propel the black and gold to a win over Indiana. Missouri stood 5–2 headed to Kansas City. And like the year before, the season slide started there. The Tigers won just once in three games, a twelve-point victory over special guest Princeton, in which Siebert and Cliff Talley scored twenty-three apiece.

Things got worse early in the league schedule. Already outmanned and outsized against enormous talents like Wilt Chamberlain and Kansas State's Bob Boozer, the Tigers were left virtually helpless when Al Abram, an undersized center but a good one, was lost midway through the year. His failure to earn enough credits during the fall semester rendered him ineligible, a fate that also befell reserve Don Hymer. Abram had been the team's leading rebounder throughout the year, and had averaged ten points per game. Sonny Siebert did his best to carry the team, and he scored thirty-one points in a surprising 74–53 win over twentieth-ranked Oklahoma. Still, wins were hard to find. Indignities, however, were easy to come by as fans around the league grew increasingly belligerent. Late in the year, the Tigers visited Kansas State to play the nation's top-ranked team, and they put up a spirited fight. More spirited, however, were the K-State partisans, who peppered the Missouri bench with apple cores, drinks, and coins. One fan in a balcony even dumped a soda on Stalcup. It was all insult added to injury in an 86–75 loss.

Siebert's 16.7 points per game helped earn all-conference recognition from the United Press. But in a league with two top-five teams (Kansas and Kansas State) and two others that spent time in the top twenty (Oklahoma and Iowa State), Mizzou tied for last with a 3–9 conference record. Unfortunately, things would get worse before they got better.

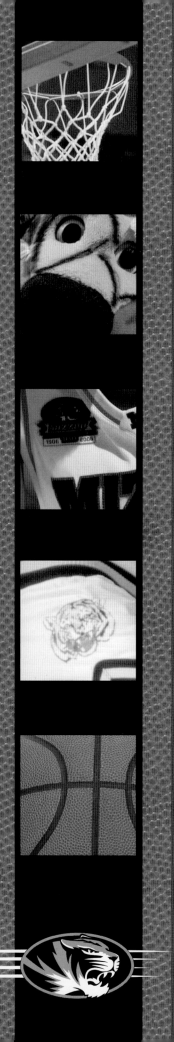

## 1958-59

The Big Seven became the Big Eight in time for the 1958–59 season as Oklahoma State joined the league. The Cowboys were coached by Sparky Stalcup's mentor, Henry Iba, who had won back-to-back national titles in 1945 and 1946 when the school still was known as Oklahoma A&M. And though they were not the dominant power they had been a decade earlier, Iba's teams remained formidable.

*Al Abram (50) was a bright spot in a difficult season.*

The class of the league, however, was Tex Winter's Kansas State team, the defending conference champ. Wilt Chamberlain left Kansas before his senior season to join the Harlem Globetrotters. When he did, he left the Wildcats with no serious competition for the first Big Eight title.

Like Kansas, Missouri unexpectedly lost its star player. Sonny Siebert skipped his senior season to begin his professional baseball career, and it's hard to quibble with his decision. The Cleveland Indians offered him $40,000. Having never seen that much money in his life, Sparky Stalcup gave the

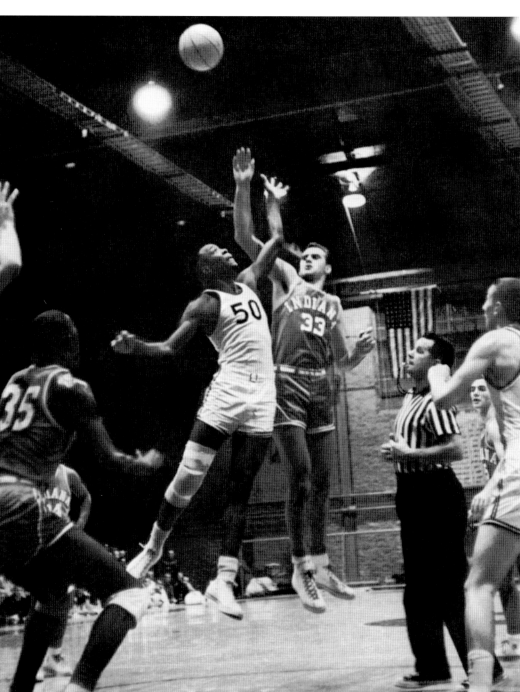

*Sparky Stalcup with his mentor, Henry Iba.*

only rational advice he could. "Go ahead and sign, Sonny," he said, knowing full well that Siebert's departure would spell disaster for Missouri's season.

With Siebert gone, the Tigers leaned on Al Abram, who regained his eligibility and played brilliantly, even while encountering the cruelty of being denied a hotel bed in Houston when Mizzou traveled to play Rice. Stalcup hastily arranged for a place for Abram to stay overnight. The next day, assistant coach Thornton Jenkins snuck Abram up the fire escape and into the offending hotel so he could rest before the game. Abram scored twenty-three in a 68–62 Missouri win. Throughout the season, Abram rose above the bigotry and averaged 16.1 points and 11.5 rebounds, but the Tigers were short on experienced talent. Sophomores Charlie Henke (a center) and Joe Scott (a guard) made solid contributions in their first year on the varsity, but their best days were ahead of them. First, they would suffer through one of the longest seasons in Mizzou history.

It didn't start out all bad. The Tigers won three of their first six, including overtime victories over Arkansas (Henke recorded twenty points and twenty rebounds in his varsity debut) and Vanderbilt. But then they collapsed, losing eleven straight and sixteen of their last nineteen. Most of the losses were by single digits, and the Tigers desperately missed an experienced scorer like Siebert. In the midst of the epic losing streak, the longest of Stalcup's career, things took an ugly turn on the home front.

The Tigers returned from a road trip to find that some of Missouri's more vituperative "supporters" had hung Sparky in effigy, a vile but not entirely uncommon practice on college campuses during that era. Stalcup, whose quiet nobility off the court matched his raging fury on it, was wounded by the act. He was the fiercest of competitors, but he believed that athletics should maintain an appropriate place within the broader context of the university's mission. He believed in the dignity of competition, in sportsmanship and fair play. But more than anything, Sparky Stalcup was a family man, and he ached at the thought that his daughter, about to enroll at Mizzou, might have to experience the hostility directed at her father.

Ironically, the longest losing streak of Stalcup's career ended when Henry Iba's Cowboys came to Columbia. The two coaches had maintained a close relationship through the years and had avoided playing each other until forced by the league schedule (they had met once previously, when Stalcup's Maryville squad beat Iba's Colorado team 17–12). Charlie Henke scored seventeen in the 51–44 Missouri victory, the Tigers' first win in conference play.

When, mercifully, the season ended (oddly enough, with a win), Missouri had earned the dubious distinction of becoming the first team ever to finish eighth in the Big Eight conference. The Tigers' nineteen overall losses established a new school record for futility.

It marked the disappointing end to a decade that tantalized Missouri fans but, ultimately, left them unsatisfied. The first seven years provided three second-place finishes and three thirds but no titles. The final three found the Tigers in the cellar. The very last season was Missouri's nineteenth straight without a conference title, far and away the longest such stretch in fifty-three years of Tiger basketball. But it was a streak destined to get much longer. The coming decade would extend the championship drought by ten years and would provide little but misery for the Tiger faithful.

The most tumultuous decade in America's recent history proved plenty tumultuous for the Missouri program. The modern history of Tiger basketball had known just two coaches. Calvin Coolidge occupied the White House when George Edwards took the helm. By the time Wilbur Stalcup retired, John Kennedy was commander in chief. Sparky's successor failed to outlast even the Johnson administration. Through the 1960s, Missouri basketball, long a model of consistent if not brilliant achievement, stumbled into a chasm of historic futility, only to be rescued toward decade's end by a prodigal son who returned to take the Tigers to heights not seen in a half-century.

# THE 1960s

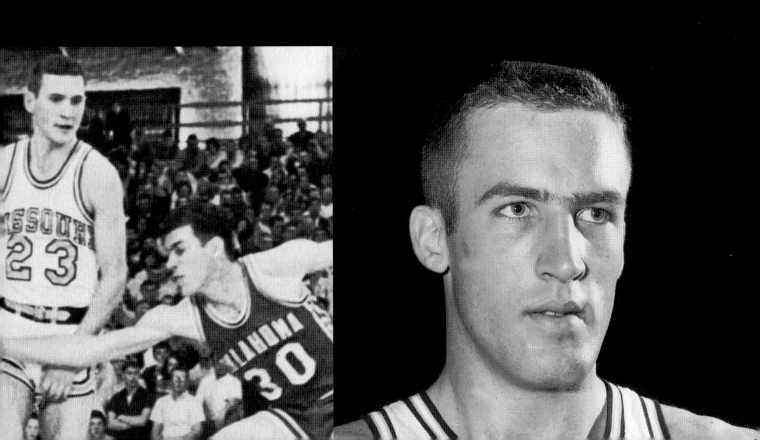

## 1959–60

As the program declined, witnesses to former glories sat nearby and tried to coax it back to life. Thornton Jenkins, arguably the best Tiger player of the 1940s, and Norm Stewart, arguably the fifties' finest, served as assistants to the man who had coached them both. Sparky Stalcup was in the twilight of his career, but he remained committed to winning, still recruiting like a man on fire. When, over the phone one morning, Cameron, Missouri, high school star Ray Bob Carey told Stalcup that he had decided to attend Kansas State, the coach responded, "The hell you have!" Four hours later, Carey was summoned to his principal's office, where Stalcup greeted him, looked into his eyes, and delivered an impassioned rant about state pride and wholesome virtues. By day's end, Carey was a Tiger.

Despite recent struggles, Stalcup's team gave him some hope. The 1959–60 Tigers had size, and they had it across the board. Missouri featured eleven players who stood six foot or taller, five who exceeded six-foot-five. Still, they had obstacles to overcome. Al Abram began the season burdened by a knee injury and the knowledge that he would not see the season to its conclusion. He had first become eligible to play midway through the 1956–57 campaign, and the rules then in place allowed him to play three full years. For Abram, it meant his career would end with the start of the winter semester. For the Tigers, it meant the loss of one of their best players during the season's most critical stretch.

They opened impressively and demonstrated their greatest strength, the one-two scoring punch of pivot man Charlie Henke and jump-shooting Joe Scott, one of the finest inside-outside combinations ever seen in Columbia. Scott scored twenty-six points and Henke added nineteen in a 70–62 win over Washington

*More than just a civil rights pioneer, Al Abram was one of the best players of his era at Mizzou.*

University, while sophomores Jackie Gilbert and Walt Grebing contributed nineteen and fifteen rebounds, respectively. Over the next few weeks, the Tigers reeled off a series of impressive victories, including a four-point triumph at Arkansas and a three-point win over Indiana. Against the Hoosiers, Scott scored thirty-one points, while Henke added twenty-four and Gilbert contributed eleven points and sixteen rebounds. The Tigers also held All-American Walt Bellamy to just six points. Wins over Wisconsin (Henke grabbed twenty rebounds) and Rice gave Missouri five straight wins to begin the season, the best start in thirty-seven years. By Christmas, the Tigers stood 6–1, matching the previous season's entire victory total. They were riding high as they headed for the Big Eight Tournament, but trouble loomed ahead.

Mizzou had built its gaudy record against nonconference teams, most of them in Columbia. Once the team hit the road against league opponents, things fell apart. The Tigers lost all three games in the Big Eight tournament. By the time they hosted Tulsa on January 23, they had lost seven of eight and stood just 1–4 in the conference. Though the Tigers beat Tulsa, the night was bittersweet as Al Abram played his last home game. The man who had overcome so much just to play at Missouri overcame the knee that had hobbled him throughout the season. He collected eighteen points and ten rebounds before leaving to a standing ovation with just over a minute to play. As the pioneering player made his way to the bench, tears welled in his eyes. Abram's stellar effort helped give Mizzou an 84–74 victory.

Abram's final game came the next week at Nebraska, and though he tallied twelve points to complement the twenty-nine scored by Charlie Henke, Missouri fell by five. From there, the Tigers rebounded with four wins in their last eight games, including a victory over Oklahoma in which Scott and Henke combined for sixty points.

On the season, conference co-champs Kansas State and Kansas swept the Tigers, but Sparky's squadron split with its other rivals to finish 5–9 in the Big Eight, good for sixth place. Charlie Henke, the six-foot-seven center from Malta Bend, Missouri, made the All-Big Eight team after averaging 19.3 points and 11.5 rebounds per game, while fellow junior Joe Scott was right on his heels with 18.4 points per game. Henke's 482 points on the season put him second in Tiger history behind the 506 that Norm Stewart tallied four years earlier, and his scoring average put him second in the conference to Wayne Hightower of Kansas. With two tremendous scorers coming back for their senior campaigns, Missouri fans held out hope that the string of losing seasons might come to an end.

## 1960-61

A season that started with hope appeared to be over shortly after it began. Following a 2–2 start, an eight-game losing streak all but doomed Missouri's year. The slide included the entire Big Eight Tournament and the first two games of the league schedule. After a loss at Iowa State dropped the Tigers to 2–10, Sparky Stalcup again was hung in effigy on the Missouri campus, as he had been two

*Mr. Inside, Charlie Henke . . .*

*. . . and Mr. Outside, Joe Scott*

*Fans flocked to see the Tigers play in Brewer Field House.*

years earlier. With twelve conference games remaining, Mizzou needed a dramatic change of fortunes. The Tigers would seek that change while three members of the program chased history.

Even as the team struggled, Charlie Henke sparkled. When he scored forty-one points against Nebraska in the conference tournament, his pursuit of Bob Reiter's career scoring mark was on. That pursuit did not come at the expense of the team. Rather, Henke's efforts helped revive Missouri's season. When he scored twenty-four in a win over Colorado, Henke propelled the Tigers to their third win in four starts, leveling their conference mark at 3–3. He moved past Norm Stewart into second place on the scoring list, sixty-three points behind Reiter. But the greater milestone that night belonged to Coach Stalcup, who became Missouri's all-time wins leader. With victory number 182, he surpassed George Edwards, whose career had followed a similar pattern—years of success followed by slow decline.

The Tigers made it four of five with a 94–78 triumph at Oklahoma, Mizzou's first conference road win in two years. Henke's twenty-six points moved him closer to Reiter. Still, it wasn't a one-man show. Joe Scott scored twenty-two, Don Sarver added seventeen, and Ken Doughty contributed thirteen points. After the abysmal start, Mizzou's hot streak put the Tigers at 4–3 in the Big Eight with a chance to make some hay. Their next three games would pit them against league leaders Kansas State (twice) and Kansas.

That's when Missouri's hopes came to a crashing halt. The Wildcats and Jayhawks had dominated the league, and the Tigers, for years. Mizzou had lost a combined nineteen straight games to their rivals over a span of five seasons. That streak extended to twenty-two games in a twelve-day span that eliminated the Tigers from title contention. First came an 88–73 setback in Lawrence, where the Tigers were greeted by an ugly, angry mob of eight thousand fans, incensed that their football team had been forced to forfeit its recent victory over the top-ranked Tigers for using ineligible running back Bert Coan. Kansas's fans greeted Mizzou with such hostility that pregame introductions were cut short to quell the abuse being heaped on Stalcup's players. Next, a crowd of twenty-five hundred in Brewer saw K-State trample the Tigers 99–70, a dismal

*Coach Stalcup and his senior stars, Joe Scott (22) and Charlie Henke*

*Joe Scott dropped forty-six points on Nebraska, the highest single-game total in the first century of Missouri basketball.*

result that dampened two milestones. Two minutes into the game, Joe Scott became just the fourth Missouri Tiger ever to score one thousand points in a career. Later in the first half, Charlie Henke scored point number 1,189 of his career, pushing him past Bob Reiter to the top of Mizzou's all-time list. Missouri's stars combined for fifty-two points in the game, but no other Tiger reached double figures. When, in their next game, the Tigers again fell to K-State (this time in Manhattan), the last flicker of hope for a run at the league title was extinguished.

After losing at Colorado, the Tigers returned home for three games to close out the season. They began with a thirteen-point win over Iowa State, then hosted Nebraska. The Cornhuskers had their eyes on Henke, who had hung forty-one points on them two months earlier. But Joe Scott did the damage this day. The skinny six-foot-four guard from Gainesville, Missouri, played like a force of nature in a 97–76 win. Sparky Stalcup, who didn't always approve of Scott's freewheeling shot selection, was relegated to watching as Scott fired at will. He unleashed a rainstorm of jump shots en route to forty-six points—a new Missouri record. A twenty-footer with forty-five seconds remaining pushed Scott past Lionel Smith's previous record and into history. "It was one of those times when everything absolutely clicks," Scott said more than forty years later, "when you can take a bad shot and it goes in."

Despite the achievements of Stalcup, Scott, and Henke, the season's best-remembered moment is almost certainly its last, a violent frenzy that illustrated the ferocity and occasional ugliness of the rivalry between Missouri and Kansas. When the Jayhawks rolled into Columbia, they were angry. A month earlier, the NCAA had hit them with sanctions for violations surrounding the recruitment of Wilt Chamberlain, and some Kansans believed that Mizzou Athletic Director Don Faurot had snitched on them. The Jayhawks were also determined. They entered the season's final day just one game behind Kansas State in the standings, still hoping to grab a share of the Big Eight title.

In addition to the usual rancor between teams, there was a game within the game. For the second straight year, Henke and Wayne Hightower battled for the league scoring crown. They stood one-two in the race, with Henke holding the edge. And with thirty-five hundred in the Brewer Field House stands and a nationwide audience watching on ABC, they went right at each other.

With Hightower and teammate Bill Bridges dominating the backboards and Joe Scott struggling from the field, the burden fell on Henke to play flawlessly. And he did, thoroughly frustrating Hightower. When Hightower gave him space, Henke looped hook shots over him. When Hightower played him close, Henke drove around him. By early in the second half, Henke had scored twenty points on nine-of-twelve shooting.

In typical fashion, the game featured bad blood and rough play. The crowd, riled up by tales of how Jayhawk fans had treated the Tigers a month earlier, littered the court with debris to protest the officiating, and Joe Scott earned a technical foul at the end of the first half for delivering a forearm shiver. With just over five minutes gone in the second half, it all came to a head. The animosity between the teams, the specter of Bert Coan, the battle between Henke and Hightower, the Jayhawks' probation, and

*Charlie Henke shoots over Wayne Hightower in Lawrence. When they met a month later in Columbia, their fistfight ignited a full-fledged riot.*

the Tigers' season-long frustration—those things were firewood. The rough play was kindling. And then, with 14:49 to play and Missouri leading by four points, came the spark. As Hightower went up for a shot, Henke fouled him hard and fell to the floor in front of the Missouri bench, which was along the baseline. As Henke stood up, Hightower punched him, prompting an explosion of violence unlike any previously seen in the rivalry. Henke and Hightower began trading blows. The Jayhawks rushed from their

bench on the other end of the court, and members of each team crashed in to the melee, fists and feet flying in a punching, kicking, whirling tempest. And then the ugliness grew exponentially. As America watched on television, what began as a rumble between rival gangs turned into chaos when hundreds of fans cascaded out of the bleachers. Some acted like marauding thugs, others like warriors for peace. Some looked for Jayhawk blood, others fought off the vigilantes. Missouri assistant football coach Harry Smith, a former All-America lineman at Southern California, stood back to back with KU's Bill Bridges and warded off would-be assailants. It took nearly three minutes to restore order and several more to resume play. Remarkably, few serious injuries were reported, though Kansas guard Nolen Ellison was bloodied and Henke walked away with a shiner.

Henke and Hightower each were ejected, making for a wildly inappropriate ending to Henke's brilliant career. The ejection, not only an ignominious end for Henke, marked a huge moment in the game. The Tigers had lost ten straight games to Kansas, and their slim 48–44 lead had been built on Henke's back. His absence should have portended disaster, but an unlikely hero came to the fore. Sophomore Howard Garrett, a six-foot-eight center from Poplar Bluff, picked up where Henke left off. He tallied fifteen points and eleven rebounds and recorded several blocks and steals. Garrett's effort helped the Tigers secure a 79–76 win in the most brutal game ever seen in Columbia.

In the days after the game, Don Faurot and Kansas Athletics Director Dutch Lonborg openly discussed the idea of ending the schools' athletics relationship. Hostilities, always at a simmer, had boiled over since Kansas was made to forfeit its football triumph. Faurot tried to be practical, but he also remained defiant, placing the blame squarely on Kansas. "If

*Poplar Bluff's Howard Garrett saved the day after Charlie Henke was ejected against Kansas.*

any bitterness exists, it has been brought about by the Kansas people on the Coan case," he said. He also pinned responsibility for the brawl on Hightower for throwing the first punch, and on the Kansas bench for rushing into the fray. In the end, it was just talk. The rivalry, in its full intensity, continued.

With the season over and the long championship drought extended, the highlights were the individual accomplishments of Charlie Henke and Joe Scott. Henke scored 591 points his final season, 24.6 per game. Both numbers eclipsed records set by Norm Stewart five years earlier. Henke also established a new record with 1,338 points in three seasons, and a new standard for career average with 18.1 points per game. Though not the biggest, strongest, or quickest player, Henke had worked hard to develop a vast arsenal of offensive weapons, one that made him the fourth-leading scorer in conference history, behind only Clyde Lovellette, Bob Boozer, and Wilt Chamberlain. Scott, for his part, wrapped up his career with 1,106 points, then fourth all-time at Mizzou. Still, Missouri managed only a 9–15 record (later changed to 11–13 after forfeits by Colorado for using an ineligible player). If that was the best the Tigers could do with Henke and Scott in uniform, what would the next season be like without them? It looked grim—and it was.

## 1961-62

In the first twenty seasons of Missouri basketball, the Tigers knew ten coaches. Over the next thirty-six, they knew just two, George Edwards and Wilbur "Sparky" Stalcup. But a change was at hand. After sixteen years at the helm, Sparky was set to retire to assume full-time duties as assistant athletics director.

Stalcup was respected nationally and served as president of the National Association of Basketball Coaches in his last season, a platform he used to urge the NCAA to hire more investigators to help eradicate corrupt recruiting. For most of Sparky's time in Columbia, the first ten years especially, he enjoyed a good run, but the failure to win a conference title stood as a disappointment. Still, there were many triumphant wins and spirited fights for the elusive championship. Ultimately, however, the Stalcup era is best remembered for the players who called Brewer Field House home: Pippin, Jenkins, Stauffer, Stewart, Reiter, Henke, and Scott, to name but a few.

Unfortunately, those names weren't available to Sparky in his final campaign. Nor was Howard Garrett, who, after six games of stellar play to start the season, was lost to a knee injury that effectively ended his career. In a year in which Stalcup started almost from scratch, the names were Doughty, Grebing, and Carey. Though gifted, they were relatively inexperienced, with little chance of matching the successes of their predecessors. Indeed, Missouri's fortunes had fallen so far that during the recruitment of a certain Crystal City, Missouri, phenom, the running joke was: "Fifty major basketball schools and the University of Missouri are after Bill Bradley."

The youngsters carried a heavy burden in Stalcup's twilight, but they seemed up to it early in the year. The Tigers stood 4–2 after six games and even managed a third-place finish in the Big Eight Tournament when Ken Doughty scored thirty-two points and Walt Grebing grabbed twelve rebounds in a win against Oklahoma. Five weeks after the tourney, a thirteen-point victory at Kansas (in which Doughty and Lyle Houston combined for thirty-eight points) gave Stalcup a unique distinction. He won in his first visit to Lawrence, in his last trip to old Hoch Auditorium, in his first visit to new Allen Field House, and in his final trip to KU as Missouri's coach. But that victory was Mizzou's only win in its first eight conference contests. After the 1–7 start, the Tigers scored back-to-back wins over Oklahoma State and Nebraska, but the triumph over the Huskers would be the 195th and last of Stalcup's career at Missouri. The Tigers lost four straight to close the year with sixteen losses, then the second most in school history. A tie for last in the league was Sparky's swan song.

The losses did not dampen the outpouring of affection for the coach. The student body gave Stalcup an engraved desk set, and the fans gave him a rousing ovation when he left the Brewer Field House court for the last time. The Missouri Quarterback Club gave him a new Oldsmobile,

*Ken Doughty captained Sparky Stalcup's final Missouri team.*

*Walt Grebing gave Mizzou a presence on the glass.*

took to podiums to pay tribute to him. At a dinner in Columbia, Norm Stewart, by then the young head coach at the State College of Iowa, captured his mentor in just a few words: "He's a hell of a man," said Stewart. Even President Kennedy got into the act, sending Sparky a letter of commendation for his efforts as NABC president.

The greatest honor of all came after the season, when Stalcup was inducted into the Helms College Basketball Hall of Fame in Los Angeles. He was only the third Tiger so honored, joining Herb Bunker and George Williams, the heroes of Missouri's glorious teams of the early 1920s. For more than thirty years, Sparky Stalcup had loved college basketball. In the end, it was clear, the game loved him back.

Despite the season's struggles, the old coach didn't leave the cupboard bare for his successor. Ken Doughty, the team's leading scorer, would be back for his senior year, and Ray Bob Carey, a long-armed

presented by Mahlon Aldridge, the voice of the Tigers, Stalcup's friend and partner on football radio broadcasts. Throughout the season, Sparky was honored in gyms around the league and dinners around the state. Phog Allen, Hank Iba, and others

*Wilbur "Sparky" Stalcup served with dignity, humor, and fury for sixteen seasons, and won more games than any previous Missouri coach.*

six-foot-six sophomore forward from Cameron, Missouri, looked like a star in the making. In a new era of Missouri basketball, Carey would be called upon not only to carry his share but to help replace the production of Walt Grebing, a good scorer and the team's leading rebounder. Fortunately for the Tigers, Carey was up to the task.

# 1962–63

Bob Vanatta, the University of Missouri's thirteenth head basketball coach, came to the job better credentialed than anyone since Walter Meanwell in 1917. An all-state basketball player at Columbia's Hickman High in the 1930s, Vanatta attended Central Methodist College in Fayette, where he earned varsity letters in a variety of sports, and he later began his coaching career there. But his greatest Show Me fame came as the head coach at Southwest Missouri State in Springfield. In three years at SMS, Vanatta compiled a 73–12 record and led the Bears to NAIA national titles in 1952 and 1953. Then, after brief stints at Army and Bradley, he took over at Memphis State and had a terrific six-year run, going 109–34 and leading the Tigers from Tennessee to four national tournament appearances. In 1957 Vanatta's MSU team—led by former Missouri star Win Wilfong, who transferred after his military service—came within a bucket of winning the NIT, which remained a prestigious event.

*Coach Bob Vanatta came to Missouri with impressive credentials.*

Vanatta brought an exciting, fast-paced brand of basketball to Columbia, and his first season at Missouri seemed to be the start of a successful rebuilding period. Ken Doughty, the six-footer with a linebacker's build and the only senior starter, gave the team stability while new stars blossomed. Ray Bob Carey, with low-post size and perimeter skills, emerged as Mizzou's top player, leading the squad with 14.2 points and 8.5 rebounds per game, and six-foot-two junior guard Bob Price finished the year just one point per game behind Carey. The starting five were rounded out by a pair of sophomores, Don Early and George Flamank. It was a team built for the future.

Still, its present wasn't without high points. Sure, Mizzou went just 10–15 and tied for sixth in the league, but it seemed that there was an excellent team inside the Tigers trying to burst out. In the Big Eight Tournament, Missouri had its first-ever one hundred-point game when it upended Oklahoma 104–82. In that wild affair, the Tigers pulled down seventy-four rebounds, twenty by Flamank. Mizzou also collected a pair of wins over top-ten teams. The

*Junior Ray Bob Carey emerged as the top player on Bob Vanatta's first team.*

Tigers beat eighth-ranked Indiana by one point in Columbia and handed number seven Colorado a 60–58 defeat when Carey, on his way to second team all-conference honors, intercepted a pass from the Buffs' Eric Lee, streaked down the court and laid the ball in with five seconds to play. Despite another losing season, optimism surrounded the Missouri basketball program for the first time in a long stretch. With a successful, energized coach and a stable of returning players, there was reason to believe that the Tigers could break into the upper echelon of the Big Eight for the first time.

## 1963–64

The Tigers began to realize their potential in Bob Vanatta's second year. Though they gave some uneven performances, they managed to post a winning record—the first Missouri team to do so in eight years.

Two weeks into the campaign, the Tigers had their fans dreaming of a championship. Though President Kennedy's assassination a week earlier cast a pall over America, Mizzou began the season in thrilling fashion, coming from behind to beat Air Force on a late long-range shot by Bob Price. Next, the Tigers took a two-point win over Arkansas behind the inspired play of five-foot-eleven guard Gary Garner and Ray Bob Carey, who combined for forty-seven points. An easy win over Washington University preceded a shocking eleven-point victory at eighth-ranked Ohio State, a game in which Carey, Price, and Garner combined to score sixty-five.

After the hot start, the Tigers cooled down, but still made themselves a factor in the Big Eight race. They swept Kansas in Dick Harp's last year as Jayhawk coach and beat Oklahoma State and Colorado in games that helped to knock those teams out of contention. But the Tigers didn't play at that level often enough. They finished 7–7 in conference play, tied for fourth place.

The middling finish notwithstanding, Mizzou's players collected plenty of honors. Bob Price finished second in the conference in scoring at 19.6 points per game and was named first team All–Big Eight. Ray Bob Carey joined Price on the first team after averaging 18.9 points and 9.9 rebounds and wrapping his career as Mizzou's fifth all-time leading scorer. With those two seniors set to leave the fold, much would be expected the next season of Gary Garner and George Flamank, both of whom earned honorable mention all-league recognition. They would deliver, but the team again would fall short of its ultimate goals.

*Bob Price elevates for a layup.*

*Ray Bob Carey, one of the Big Eight's best and most versatile players, finished his career as Missouri's number five all-time scorer.*

## 1964–65

Bob Vanatta fielded a small team in his third season. Ned Monsees and George Flamank made for an undersized frontcourt, and when Don Early, a six-foot-five forward, went down with an injury, they were forced to play the kinds of minutes that would have tested the endurance of larger men. But Vanatta was blessed with talented perimeter players, including senior Gary Garner, junior Charlie Rudd, and Ron Coleman, a sophomore guard from Jefferson City who ultimately would become one of the most prolific scorers ever to wear the black and gold.

In addition to their lack of size, the Tigers were hampered by Brewer Field House, which had become an impediment to success. When it opened in 1930, Brewer was a palace, but by the mid-1960s it was a pit. In those thirty-five years, MU's enrollment quadrupled, intramural programs expanded, and varsity sports grew in popularity, completely overwhelming the building. During the busiest part of the year, members of the basketball, baseball and track teams competed for space and kicked up dust that hung thick in the air. The place occasionally was overrun by birds that nested in the rafters and made dive-bombing runs over the court. Locker rooms were tiny. And most importantly to Bob Vanatta, the austere structure hurt recruiting efforts, as talented players opted for schools with more up-to-date facilities.

As with the previous year, it was hard to tell which Missouri team would appear from night to night. Three games into the season, the Tigers got blistered by top-ranked Michigan as Bill Buntin, father of future Tiger Nathan Buntin, led the Wolverines with fourteen points. But just five days later, they bounced back to hand fourth-rated St. Louis a 62–56 defeat, when Ned Monsees scored twenty-four points and collected twenty-four rebounds. Monsees, a bruiser at six-foot-four and 215 pounds, repeated the impressive rebounding feat in a loss to Kansas State in the holiday tournament—the Tigers' twenty-third consecutive defeat at the hands of the Wildcats, by far the longest losing streak to one opponent in the program's history.

Mizzou's schizophrenic play continued into the conference schedule, where the team played win-some-lose-some ball for six weeks. On January 16, the Tigers beat K-State to end the epic streak, the first time the Tigers had topped the Cats in Columbia in fifteen years. Only twenty-eight hundred long-suffering fans turned out, but those

*Tough as nails, Bob Price earned all-league honors as a senior.*

who did saw Missouri's miniature front line dominate. Flamank and Monsees combined for forty-two points and twenty-seven rebounds against Kansas State's far greater size. An 11–0 run late in the first half propelled Missouri to victory in a game in which Garner, Coleman, and Rudd each scored in double figures. Mizzou also took two of three from Oklahoma State in the Cowboys' only Big Eight championship season under Henry Iba. Still, with six games to play, Missouri stood just 8–10 overall and 3–5 in conference play.

The mercurial Tigers then staged their first great late-season run in nearly a decade. They won by eighteen at Nebraska when Garner and Coleman combined to score fifty. They beat Oklahoma back home at Brewer as Garner and Flamank each scored twenty-one and Monsees nabbed nineteen boards. They went to Colorado and topped the Buffs behind twenty-seven points from Monsees. They returned home for another eighteen-point victory over the Cornhuskers (Garner and Coleman scored twenty apiece), then went to Manhattan and extended their winning streak against Kansas State to two games, beating the Cats 67–58. That win, their fifth straight, gave them a chance to finish in a tie for second place if they could beat Iowa State in the season finale. Unfortunately, on the same day the first American marines arrived in Vietnam, a loss in Ames ended the season on a sour note. But Mizzou still managed to finish at 8–6 in Big Eight play and tied for third in the league—the Tigers' best finish in nine years. Three years into his tenure, Coach Vanatta had produced back-to-back winning seasons, success that spurred Mississippi State University, a perennial Southeastern Conference power, to try to lure him away. Vanatta turned down the offer, saying that he would never leave Mizzou for another coaching job. Finally, perhaps, the rebuilding was complete.

Or perhaps not. Mizzou's success was built around three seniors. Gary Garner, the team's top scorer and a second-team All–Big Eight pick, would not be back. Neither would first-teamer George Flamank, the pride of Albany, Missouri, and one of the most prolific rebounders ever at Mizzou. Nor would Ned Monsees, a scorer and rebounder on par with Garner and Flamank. In fact, Charlie Rudd and Ron Coleman would be the only lettermen

*Ned Monsees (below) and George Flamank (right) were ferocious rebounders.*

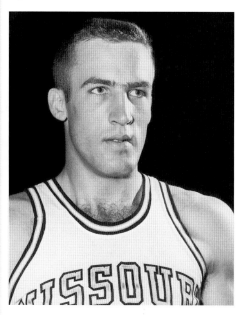

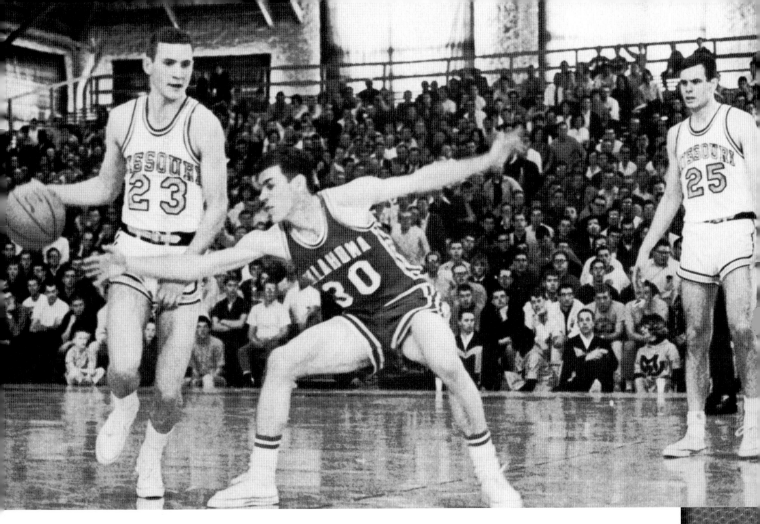

*Gary Garner led the Tigers in scoring in his senior season.*

returning for the 1965–66 season. With their roster so depleted, could Vanatta's Tigers continue their upward trend and compete for a Big Eight title? The answer would be an emphatic "no." The Missouri basketball program sat on the precipice of the most disastrous period in its existence.

# 1965-66

Abysmal. Dreadful. Excruciating. Pick an adjective. Pick two. Pick however many necessary to convey the abject misery of the Missouri Tigers' 1965–66 season, a year of cataclysmic and historic futility.

Mizzou went 3–21 on the year—and it could have been worse. The Tigers' second win of the season was a two-point overtime victory against Oklahoma State in the holiday tournament. Their third, and last, came two months later when Ron Coleman hit a twenty-footer in the final three seconds to give Mizzou a 64–63 win over Colorado in Boulder. In between, the Tigers lost twelve straight by an average of twenty points per game, including a forty-four-point drubbing at Kansas.

It is rarely a good sign when a six-foot guard jumps center and leads the team in rebounds. But that is the role that senior Charlie Rudd filled for Mizzou. Notwithstanding the occasional anomalous performance like Tom Officer's twenty-four-rebound effort against St. Louis, the lack of an inside game crippled the Tigers. Missouri's opponents simply owned the glass. A 58–36 rebounding advantage helped Loyola (Chicago) scorch the Tigers 108–85 at Brewer, while Iowa State outrebounded Mizzou by thirty-two in Ames. Forced to try to win from the perimeter, Vanatta gave Ron Coleman the green light to shoot, which he did more than nineteen times a game. In the process, he became just the third Tiger to top five hundred points in a season.

Coleman's historic production aside, it was the worst of times for Missouri basketball. The Tigers set dubious records by losing thirteen conference games and twenty-one overall. The silver lining in a season like 1965–66 is that it can't get much worse. Surely, the next year would have to be better. Wouldn't it?

## 1966–67

The new season started with promise. The Tigers added size, including Gene Jones, a high-flying six-foot-seven junior college transfer from Paducah, Kentucky, and sophomore Booker Brown, Mizzou's first seven-footer. They also added talent and depth in the form of junior college veterans Tom Johnson, Jim Chapman, and Larry Pierick. The new blood mixed with returning Tigers like Ron Coleman and Rob Vanatta, the coach's son, who joined Coleman in the starting backcourt. Before a crowd of forty-three hundred fans at Brewer, the Tigers opened the season with a win over Arkansas. Coleman led a balanced attack with fourteen points, followed by Tom Johnson with thirteen and Dave Bennett with twelve, and Gene Jones contributed ten points and seventeen

*Ron Coleman (left), Bob Vanatta, and Charlie Rudd led Missouri through a trying 1965–66 season.*

*Booker Brown (above), Mizzou's first seven-footer*

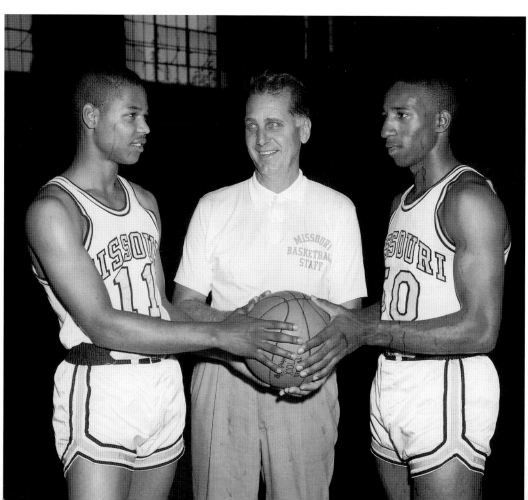

Ron Coleman, one of the most prolific scorers of his generation, skies for two of his 1,295 career points.

rebounds. Though no one was ready to predict a Big Eight title, the Tigers seemed much improved. Indeed, after four games, Missouri stood at 2–2, just one win shy of the previous season's entire total, and the losses caused no shame. The first came at eventual Big Ten champ Indiana, and the second came in overtime against St. Louis.

Mizzou displayed its improved interior play in its second win, a victory over Detroit, when Booker Brown collected twenty-four rebounds. Three days later, Gene Jones grabbed twenty-six boards—the second highest total in team history—in an overtime loss to Rutgers at Madison Square Garden, a game the Scarlet Knights secured with four free throws by Jim Valvano, who would later win a national title as head coach at North Carolina State. Though they stood just 2–3, the Tigers appeared to be turning things around.

Then came the slide. Mizzou fell to Seattle. Then to Santa Clara in two overtimes. Then to Oklahoma, then to Colorado. By the time the Tigers faced Oklahoma State on February 4, the losing streak had reached twelve games, and Gene Jones and Booker Brown had been ruled academically ineligible. Tom Johnson, the junior from St. Louis, scored twenty-three in a four-point win over the Cowboys, but it was the last gasp of a drowning team. Despite the customary twenty points per game from Ron Coleman, Mizzou closed the season with eight straight losses.

On February 23, halfway through the eight-game skid, Bob Vanatta announced his retirement, effective after the Tigers' last game. Though just forty-eight years old, Vanatta was completing his twenty-fifth year as a coach, and that was enough. "I have had a goal for a long time to give up coaching after 25 years," he said. "I know it may sound strange when I say that the record of the past two years has in no way influenced this decision. . . . Even if we had had Big Eight championship teams this

*Norm Stewart, just thirty-two years old, returned to his alma mater in 1967 and began a radical transformation of the basketball program.*

season and last, my decision still would have been the same." Athletic Director Don Faurot confirmed that Vanatta was under no pressure to resign. The earnestness of Vanatta's desire to exit coaching had been shown two weeks earlier when he declined an offer to become the coach and general manager of a team in the fledgling American Basketball Association. Instead, he went on to a lengthy career in athletics administration.

The Tigers' final mark of 3–22 eclipsed the prior year's record for futility. In a span of two seasons, Mizzou had won just six of forty-nine games. Vanatta's Tigers had strung together the two worst seasons in school history, a reality hard to fathom, especially given that the coach had been among the nation's most successful less than a decade earlier. But fortunately for Tiger fans, help was on the way.

# 1967–68

Columbia was football crazy in the 1960s, so much so that basketball was an afterthought on campus. In his first nine years at Missouri, coach Dan Devine had presided over nine winning seasons and had taken the Tigers to three New Year's Day bowl games. As such, mediocrity by the hoops squad might have been tolerated. Humiliation, however, was something different. And so it came as no surprise when a pair of football legends accepted Bob Vanatta's resignation. That was the easy part for Don Faurot and Devine, who was set to succeed the retiring Faurot as athletic director. The hard part was to find the right man to revive the program. They made their choice just four days after the end of the 1966–67 season. Missouri would wait thirty-two years to hire another men's basketball coach.

Norm Stewart, one of the best and most competitive athletes in Mizzou's history, was just thirty-two years old when he signed on to resurrect the moribund basketball program, but he possessed a wealth of competitive experience. After his playing career at Missouri, Stewart enjoyed a brief stop in the NBA as a member of the St. Louis Hawks, and he spent a season as a minor league pitcher in the Baltimore Orioles' organization. He then returned to Columbia to pursue a master's degree, and to serve as an assistant coach for Mizzou's basketball and baseball teams. After a four-year apprenticeship with Sparky Stalcup, Stewart was named head basketball coach at the State College of Iowa in Cedar Falls at the tender age of twenty-six. Six years later, after posting a record of 97–42 and winning two league titles, he moved back to Columbia with his wife, Virginia, and their three children to take on the challenge of a lifetime.

Over time he would become a towering figure in the athletic department, but when Norm Stewart arrived in 1967, he was just a kid compared with the pantheon in place. Though his tenure was winding down, Don Faurot was still in charge. A former three-sport star at Mizzou, he had won more games than any other Missouri football coach, and he became a college football immortal by developing the Split T offense. Dan Devine, in turn, had lifted the football program to national prominence with wins in the Orange Bowl and Sugar Bowl. Baseball coach John "Hi" Simmons, a fixture since 1937, had led the Tigers to a national championship and eleven conference titles. And Tom Botts, Mizzou's track coach since 1946, guided the Tigers to several conference titles and the 1965 NCAA indoor championship. Those four men comprised a Mount Rushmore of Missouri athletics.

The irony of Bob Vanatta's last season in Columbia had been evident in practice every day. While the varsity floundered, a rambunctious bunch of freshmen flourished. Kansas freshman coach Bob Mulcahy called the Baby Bengals the Big Eight's best freshman team in years. Under the tutelage of former Mizzou star Bob Price, the frosh won six of eight games. When players like Don Tomlinson, Pete Helmbock, and Theo Franks graduated to the varsity, they gave Norm Stewart a critical mass of talent with which to begin rebuilding.

In the autumn after the Summer of Love, the decidedly nonpsychedelic Norm Stewart coached his first game at his alma mater. His debut came against Arkansas in Fayetteville, and he immediately set a new tone. Gene Jones returned and scored nineteen, while Tom Johnson added seventeen in a convincing 74–58 victory that started the Stewart era on a high note. Still, turning around a program was difficult, and progress came slowly. The Tigers lost eight of their next eleven games, including their conference opener against Oklahoma.

Mizzou evened its conference record against Colorado, Stewart's first win in Big Eight play. Jones

*Power forward Gene Jones carried the Tigers in Norm Stewart's first season as coach.*

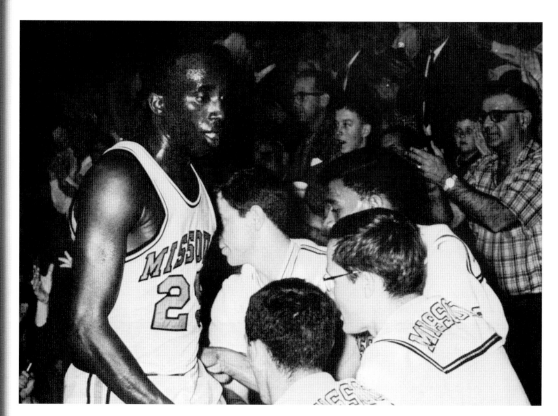

*Tom Johnson sealed his place in Missouri lore with two heart-stopping free throws at Allen Field House.*

recorded thirty points, thirteen rebounds, and several blocked shots. Sophomore forward Don Tomlinson, the most naturally gifted scorer on the team, contributed twenty-one points and began to establish himself as a new go-to player.

After a loss at Nebraska, the Tigers headed to Lawrence to renew hostilities with Kansas, which owned a seven-game win streak over Mizzou. The game served as a reunion for the Tigers' six-foot-four forward Tom Johnson and Kansas star Jo Jo White, erstwhile teammates at McKinley High in St. Louis. Each would figure prominently in the outcome of one of the most remarkable games in the series. White scored twenty-two points for the Jayhawks, who had a chance to win the game in the closing seconds. As the clock ticked toward zero, score tied at 65, Kansas held the ball. With just two seconds left, disaster struck for Missouri. Pete Helmbock hacked Rodger Bohnnenstiehl and fouled out. Bohnnenstiehl made a free throw to give Kansas a one-point lead, all but securing victory. Don Tomlinson desperately heaved the ball inbounds. Just beyond half-court, Jayhawk Phil Harman tried to deflect the pass but crashed into Tom Johnson. With no time remaining, the officials called a foul and sent Johnson to the free throw line to shoot a one-and-one. With the lane vacant, Johnson—who had already scored twenty-one—stood alone, Kansas supporters all around him. He sank the first shot, earning another. Amid the swirling hostility, Johnson made the second shot to give the Tigers a 67–66 victory. His jubilant teammates carried him off the Allen Field House court on their shoulders as thousands of Kansas partisans watched in stunned silence.

The Tigers posted wins over Iowa State and Tulane to put together their first winning streak of any kind in almost three years. But consistency proved hard to come by. Don Tomlinson scored thirty in his first trip to Manhattan, but a desperate last-second heave by K-State's Kent Litton gave the Wildcats a 69–67 win and started Mizzou on a seven-game skid. With two games left, the Tigers stood 3–9 in the Big Eight, only a marginal improvement over Bob Vanatta's last two campaigns.

The season was beyond saving when the Tigers visited Stillwater, but the program was ripe for resurrecting. The beginnings of a sea change had come when the university hired Norm Stewart, and glimmers of hope had been seen throughout the season, most notably in the preposterous win at Kansas. But the long-awaited turnaround began in earnest late in the second half at Oklahoma State. With less than four minutes to play, Missouri trailed by eleven. Headed for their eighth straight loss, the Tigers staged a wild rally. Don Tomlinson scored ten of his sixteen points in that decisive stretch to propel Mizzou to a stunning 60–58 victory.

Norm Stewart's team returned home for the season's final game and senior day for Gene Jones, Tom Johnson, and Henry Pinkney. And it truly was the seniors' day. Jones, Johnson, and Pinkney scored twenty-one, nineteen, and eighteen, respectively, to lead a 91–70 rout of Nebraska. Don Tomlinson chipped in fourteen to bring his season's total to 394 points, a new Tiger sophomore record. A two-game winning streak to cap a 10–16 season might not seem like much, but beginning with those two victories, wins would start to far outnumber losses for the first time in a long time.

By winning more games in his first season than the Tigers had won in the prior two years combined, Norm Stewart's debut was a qualified success. Still, he faced an uphill climb. Missouri's seniors had played a crucial role in the Tiger turnaround, especially Gene Jones, who led the team with 18.7 points and 10.7 rebounds per game. Continuing to improve while replacing a player of that caliber was a tall order, but Stewart and his Tigers were up to the task.

## 1968–69

In his first season, Norm Stewart relied solely on players inherited from Bob Vanatta. In his second, Stewart's recruiting began to bear fruit. The newest Tiger, five-foot-ten guard Dave Pike, made his presence felt in his first game. The Tigers again opened at Arkansas, and they won in dramatic fashion. Theo Franks and Don Tomlinson scored to cut a five-point Arkansas lead to one in the closing

*Newcomer Dave Pike gave Mizzou an immediate lift.*

seconds. Then, after an Arkansas turnover, Pike, a junior college transfer from Springfield, Missouri, hit a jump shot to give Missouri a rousing 60–59 victory. That success carried through most of the nonconference slate, a stretch capped by a 91–62 rout of St. Louis, a win that put Mizzou at 6–2 heading into the conference tournament.

But once the Tigers started Big Eight play, they began to backslide. They lost two of three in the tournament and then started the league race at 0–2,

with Kansas, the nation's fifth-rated team, next on the schedule.

Six thousand fans crammed into Brewer, with hundreds more turned away. Those inside witnessed one of the nerviest late-game tactics ever employed by a Missouri coach. With just under three minutes remaining and the Tigers trailing 46–45, Kansas turned the ball over and gave Norm Stewart an idea. He called time out, and when the Tigers returned to the floor, they had the guts of riverboat gamblers, willing to let everything ride on a single roll of the dice. They froze the ball. Theo Franks and Dave Pike played pitch-and-catch near the midcourt line. As Missouri stalled, the clock ticked below two minutes. No movement. Below ninety seconds. No movement. Below one minute. No movement. The tension built in the field house, everyone aware that something very good or very bad was about to happen. The clock moved below thirty seconds, the capacity crowd bristling with nervous energy. Still no movement. Below twenty. No movement. Then, finally, with fifteen seconds, movement. The Tigers started the offense. With ten seconds to play, the ball swung to Franks on the perimeter. He eyed the hoop, rose, and released the ball from twenty feet. The hushed crowd tracked its arc, then erupted into delirium as the ball splashed through the net with eight seconds left. Kansas tried to set up a play, but when Greg Douglas fumbled a pass out of bounds, the Tigers sealed victory 47–46.

With the losing streak over, the Tigers hosted Iowa State and improved their record to 6–0 at Brewer. The Cyclones simply could not guard Don Tomlinson. Unable to keep him from slashing toward the basket, they began to hack him, and Tomlinson made them pay. The junior forward made twenty of twenty-two free throw attempts in a 74–58 triumph.

But the Tigers never gained any traction in the Big Eight race. A loss at Brewer to league-leading Colorado effectively eliminated Missouri from contention, and wins on the road proved tough to come by. The one exception came in Lawrence, where Norm Stewart continued to inject fire into the rivalry with Kansas, a series that KU had dominated since Stewart's playing days. Before the game, Stewart exhibited a mischievous streak that would become famous. After the Jayhawks began pregame warm-ups on their favored end of the floor, he sent Don Tomlinson to inform Kansas coach Ted Owens that Mizzou preferred that end, then the visiting team's prerogative. Stewart hid behind the bleachers, watched, and laughed as Tomlinson delivered the demand to the indignant (but ultimately accommodating) Owens. The Tigers adopted Stewart's swagger and stood toe-to-toe with the Jayhawks. And though Kansas outplayed the visitors in most respects, the outcome came down to a carnival game, a free throw shooting contest. For Missouri, the key player was Don Tomlinson, who had an uncanny ability to get to the line. While Tomlinson made fifteen of eighteen charity tosses (as a team, Mizzou made thirty of thirty-eight), Kansas sank just thirteen of twenty-five. The Tigers' ability to hit the uncontested shot made all the difference in a 56–55 victory that gave them back-to-back wins in Lawrence for the first time in thirteen years.

In the end, the Tigers finished 14–11, their first winning record in four years. Mizzou's 7–7 conference record was good only for fifth place, but the Tigers came within three whiskers of a considerably better finish. Three of the seven losses came in overtime, two by one point and one by two points. Had they scored a few more points, the Tigers could have been conference champs. As it was, Don Tomlinson and Dave Pike were named first and second team All-Big Eight, respectively, a sign of newfound respect for Tiger basketball. The results of Stewart's first two seasons validated the decision to entrust the program to him. It was a program on the rise, though still flying below the national radar. That sort of attention was a few years away. But it was coming.

*Rough-hewn Don Tomlinson made the All–Big Eight team in 1969.*

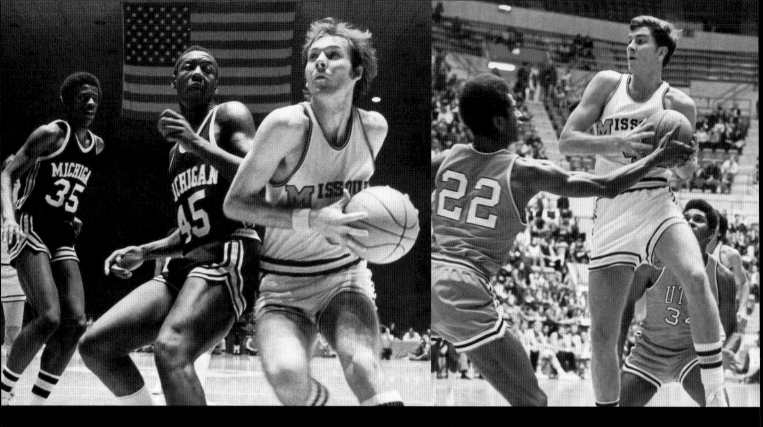

After the cultural fissures of the 1960s came ten years of self-indulgence. But for Missouri basketball, the Me Decade was the We Decade as the Tigers bonded together to move from the edge of oblivion to national prominence. It was a time for players to grow their hair, pull up their socks, move into fancy new digs, and chart a course for the top of the Big Eight.

# THE 1970s

## 1969-70

In the quest for a second straight winning season, Missouri relied on four seniors and one impressive newcomer. Dave Pike and Theo Franks comprised the backcourt, and fellow seniors Doug Johnson and Don Tomlinson filled the forward spots. The newcomer, a junior college transfer, was six-foot-seven center Henry Smith, who would become a keystone player in the program's rebirth. Norm Stewart was enamored enough of his team to quietly believe that a conference title was possible.

The Tigers played their first five games at home and won them all. More than fifty-two hundred fans saw them beat Indiana 109–96 as Tomlinson contributed thirty-two points, including eighteen free throws. But things were tougher on the road, where the Tigers lost a handful of games, including two of three in the conference tournament.

Mizzou returned home and beat Kansas in the conference opener. Playing on an injured hip, Don Tomlinson scored twenty-three in the three-point victory. Then the Tigers got a rare road win, a 60–56 overtime triumph at Oklahoma State, as Pete Helmbock scored the only four points for either team in the extra period. Still dominant at Brewer, the Tigers could contend if they could win away from home.

Unfortunately, they could not. A 64–63 loss at Kansas State dropped Missouri to 11–6 overall and 3–2 in league play. The Tigers struggled in close games on the road, a fact that may have been attributable to shaky chemistry. In his memoir, *Stormin' Back*, Norm Stewart recalls that four of his players were married "and their wives fought all the time." After that season, the coach instituted a new rule: "Don't recruit a married player."

The Tigers continued to win most games at home and to lose away from Columbia. They finished 15–11 overall, 7–7 in the league, good for a third-place tie. Despite Norm Stewart's higher hopes, his team recorded a second straight winning season, a small step from the previous year's 14–11 mark but a giant leap from where the program was just three years earlier.

Dave Pike and Henry Smith each made honorable mention All-Big Eight, while Don Tomlinson earned second team recognition. Tomlinson, the fiery forward, was the key player in Mizzou's abrupt resurgence and one of the most accomplished Tigers in a generation.

*Theo Franks was a fixture in Missouri's backcourt.*

He scored 1,198 career points, then third all-time, and displayed an unparalleled ability to get to the free throw line. Tomlinson attempted 650 free throws in seventy-seven career games—8.4 tries per contest—a rate unmatched in Missouri history.

Losing Tomlinson and three other seniors would hurt. But one player set to matriculate from the freshman team would kick the transformation of Missouri basketball into high gear.

## 1970-71

Coaches from far and wide visited little Dixon, Missouri, to see the six-foot-seven kid with uncommon intensity and uncanny skills.

*Henry Smith helped the Tigers to their second straight winning season.*

Missouri was not the most successful program to recruit John Brown, but it was close to home, and the Tigers had a young coach with whom he could relate, another tenacious blond from a small Missouri town who built his legend in Columbia. As Norm Stewart recuperated from back surgery in 1969, Brown visited the hospital and made a commitment that invigorated the Mizzou basketball program. "Brown may have felt some sympathy for me," Stewart later quipped, "but I was willing to have surgery again if it meant signing someone like John."

As a sophomore, Brown had a bright future, but hopes for Missouri's present rested with Henry Smith, the lone returning starter. The burden was especially heavy early in the season, with Brown sidelined by a sprained ankle. But others stepped up, including big Bob Allen, an interior scorer and rebounder; Mike Jeffries, a powerful swingman; Mike Griffin, a lightning-quick defender and playmaker; and Greg Flaker, a guard who made impressive use of the old-fashioned two-handed set shot.

While Brown healed, Smith sparkled. He recorded thirty-five points and twelve rebounds as the Tigers beat Arkansas in the season opener for the fifth straight year, and he contributed twenty-five points and thirteen rebounds in a two-overtime victory over Ohio. Thanks largely to Smith, Missouri stood 7–1 by the time John Brown was cleared to play.

Brown debuted at Pauley Pavilion, home of four-time defending national champion UCLA, coached by John Wooden. He scored fourteen, but the top-ranked Bruins claimed a nineteen-point win. Things got no easier in the Big Eight Tournament, where Missouri opened against a great Kansas team and fell 96–63.

But the Tigers came to life after the tournament. They defeated Oklahoma in Brown's home debut; a standing-room crowd saw him score twenty-three in an 84–78 win. They also beat Kansas State in Mizzou's first meeting with new Wildcat coach Jack Hartman. A balanced effort—Smith, Brown, Allen, and Flaker each scored at least fifteen—propelled Missouri to an eight-point victory.

The Tigers continued to play well through the heart of the schedule, and with one game left, they stood at 9–4 in the league. A win in their finale would assure them of sole possession of second place—success not seen in fifteen years.

It shaped up as the game of the year in the Big Eight. Missouri, undefeated at home, stood to secure a bid to the NIT, the reward for the league's runner-up, while fourth-ranked Kansas, undefeated in conference play, stood to make history in its last stop before the NCAA Tournament.

Considerable fanfare attended the contest, slated to be the last ever at the field house

*Don Tomlinson led Missouri's resurgence and graduated as one of the best players in the program's history.*

*John Brown's arrival at Mizzou inspired hope for the future.*

*Top: Big Bob Allen was a presence in the paint.*

*Bottom: Henry Smith's tremendous play in his senior season was rewarded with a spot on the all-conference team.*

as a modern new arena neared completion. Letter winners from all forty-one years of Brewer basketball commemorated the occasion. Six thousand fans packed the building, and they got what they came for—until the bitter end. John Brown's free throws with 2:47 to play gave Missouri a 62–58 margin. But two Tiger turnovers let Kansas forge a tie and send the game to overtime, where KU center Dave Robisch dominated. Kansas won 71–69 to complete the sweep through the league. In his final game, Henry Smith recorded twenty-four points and fourteen rebounds, capping one of the best individual seasons in Missouri's modern history. He averaged 22.3 points and 9.4 rebounds per game and earned a spot on the All-Big Eight team.

The loss spoiled Mizzou's perfect home record and dropped the Tigers into a second-place tie with Oklahoma. The NIT invited the Sooners, and Missouri was left home for the postseason. Mizzou's 17–9 overall record and 9–5 conference mark represented progress, but the Tigers fell short of their ultimate goals. Still, success in the short term seemed assured by John Brown, whose 14.9 points and 9.3 rebounds per game made him one of the most productive sophomores in Missouri history. With four starters returning and another tremendous freshman set to join the varsity, the Tigers stood poised for success not seen in thirty years.

## 1971–72

For the third straight year, the Tigers played their last season in Brewer Field House. Construction delays pushed completion of Mizzou's new arena two years past the target date and moved the program further into the dark ages. When Brewer opened in 1930, people marveled at its spaciousness, opulence, and lighting. By the end, they complained of its smallness, drabness, and darkness.

Still, Brewer retained a certain dog-eared charm. The austere, almost industrial, environment proved inhospitable to visiting teams. Players crossed a grimy track between the locker room and court, and navigated fences that surrounded the floor. And the crowds, when packed in tight, could be imposing. Fans stomped on bleachers, kicking up dust and creating an ear-splitting din.

A veteran team returned for Brewer's last stand, but senior center Bob Allen missed much of the year with a knee injury and was limited when he returned. Allen's absence moved John Brown to center and Mike Jeffries to forward, where he played alongside sophomore Al Eberhard, a physical six-foot-five farm boy from Iowa. The trio made for a small but quick frontcourt.

*Springville, Iowa's, Al Eberhard enjoyed a spectacular sophomore season.*

The Tigers were terrific in December. Eberhard debuted with twenty points and fifteen rebounds in a win against Michigan State, and Brown and Jeffries combined for forty-six points in a 74–73 victory over Arkansas. Missouri nearly pulled off a titanic upset at Kentucky in the Wildcats' own tournament. After John Brown scored twenty-three points to give the Tigers a two-point halftime edge, Kentucky (in coach Adolph Rupp's final season) switched defenses and took a two-point lead into the closing seconds. With a chance to force overtime, Brown drove the lane and drew contact, but the officials called a charge. Kentucky sank two free throws to seal an 83–79 victory that spoiled Brown's thirty-four-point, eleven-rebound performance. The next night, the Tigers beat California on Kentucky's floor, an important road win in advance of the Big Eight Tournament, where Missouri announced itself as one of the nation's best teams.

In Kansas City, Mizzou advanced to the final for the first time in seventeen years. There the Tigers met Kansas State in the first of three confrontations that would define the season. Since the Big Eight's inception, the Wildcats had been the league's dominant team, with seven titles in thirteen years. The tournament final helped ignite one of the decade's best rivalries, fueled by the personalities of Norm Stewart and Wildcat coach Jack Hartman. In the second half, Brown, Eberhard,

and Jeffries repeatedly scored on the inside to propel Missouri to a 67–58 triumph. "It was our mobility against their size," said Norm Stewart, explaining the difference in the game. Eberhard, the tournament's MVP, finished with twenty-one points, while Brown added eighteen points and ten rebounds, and Jeffries contributed eleven points and ten boards. Just five years removed from abject failure, the Tigers were champions.

Missouri continued to shine though January. Brown and Eberhard led the Tigers to a 4–1 start in Big Eight play, first place in the standings, and number fifteen in the polls. That success set up a second clash with Kansas State, which entered the competition just one game back of Mizzou. Playing in Manhattan, the Tigers began at a disadvantage, one made worse by the absence of Mike Griffin, out with a sprained ankle. Late free throws by Lon Kruger gave the Wildcats a 69–67 win, creating a tie at the top of the league.

Over the next month, as Kansas State continued to win, the Tigers took five of six, losing only at Kansas, where Jayhawk Bud Stallworth scored fifty. At 9–3 in league play, Missouri was positioned to make history. Two games remained, both at Brewer. The first came against K-State, which stood one game up. If the Tigers could win both games—and they had won all eleven at home on the season—they could do no worse than a tie for the title.

Round three against Kansas State, with its championship implications, marked the biggest game in memory for almost anyone inside Brewer. John Brown did his best to bring the crown home. When K-State denied him position in the post, he simply went out to the ball and burned the Cats with jumpers and drives to the hoop. But while Brown carried Missouri, Wildcats Lon Kruger and Steve Mitchell combined to score forty-one.

*Top: The brilliant John Brown led Missouri to its first post-season tournament in twenty-eight years.*

*Bottom: Greg Flaker sets and shoots.*

The Tigers fell 79–76 and saw their championship dreams go up in smoke.

Still, the Tigers played for second place and an NIT berth in the last-ever game at Brewer. They used a 23–5 run in the second half to beat Oklahoma 76–62 as Greg Flaker celebrated his final home game with nineteen points. It wasn't a title, but Missouri's first postseason bid since 1944 marked a watershed moment for the program. With a Big Eight Tournament trophy on the mantel and an NIT bid in hand, Norm Stewart's resurrection of Missouri basketball was complete.

In 1972, when the NCAA Tournament included just twenty-five schools, the NIT boasted an impressive sixteen-team field, including second-place finishers from the nation's top conferences. Played entirely at Madison Square Garden, the NIT remained a prestigious national spectacle. Missouri opened against hometown favorite St. John's and gave a shaky performance before the partisan crowd, turning the ball over and missing critical free throws. Still, despite foul trouble for John Brown, Mizzou managed to force overtime. In the extra period, Greg Flaker, who scored twenty-seven, led Missouri to a four-point lead with a layup and a pair of free throws. But disaster struck when Brown fouled out with 2:40 to play. Over the next minute and a half, St. John's capitalized on a series of Missouri miscues. The Tigers fell 82–81, ending a season fans had dreamed of for decades.

The 21–6 record was the best since the 1930 Big Six champs went 15–3. But a terrific year came close to being a season for the ages. Only one loss, a 93–80 defeat at Kansas, was lopsided. The other

*Norm Stewart shows off the Tigers' new home.*

five were nail-biters, two by a single point each and the others by two, three, and four points, respectively, leaving the Tigers to wonder what might have been had Bob Allen remained healthy. Still, as long as John Brown had eligibility, Mizzou had opportunity. Brown, who averaged 21.7 points and 10.5 rebounds per game, earned All-Big Eight honors in one of the finest individual seasons in Missouri history. He would come back for one last stand in hopes of pushing the Tigers to even greater glory.

## 1972–73

Between seasons, Mizzou mourned the losses of two former coaches. Losing George Edwards, who succumbed to cancer at age eighty-one, was not entirely unexpected. Losing Wilbur "Sparky" Stalcup, who suffered a heart attack at age sixty-two, was a shock. Stalcup had spent his "retirement" working in the athletic department and teaming with Mahlon Aldridge on radio broadcasts of Missouri football and basketball games. In 1971 he succeeded Dan Devine as athletics director, but it was a tragically short tenure.

*The Tigers christened the Hearnes Center with a win over Ohio University.*

*Mike Jeffries, John Brown, and Norm Stewart accept the Volunteer Classic trophy.*

By the start of Norm Stewart's sixth season, people understood that something was brewing in Columbia. Even Phog Allen heaped praise on Missouri's young mentor. "That fellow, Stewart, their coach, he's outstanding," said Allen. "He was a good player, too. We tried as hard as we could to get him to come to Kansas but we lost him." Further acclaim came when John Brown earned a spot on the U.S. Olympic basketball team, though a broken foot kept him out of competition. The break healed in time for him to have a tremendous senior season.

Brown's natural skills were undeniable, but his strength, work ethic, and basketball intellect set him apart. His powerful legs anchored him in the center of Norm Stewart's triple post offense, where he scored in a multitude of ways and passed to teammates for easy buckets. Despite gaudy individual numbers, John Brown was a team player. His potent skills allowed him to coast to twenty points on any given night. If angered, though, he could score a whole lot more.

Brown's final season was spent in a new home. The Warren E. Hearnes Multipurpose Building—built for $10.5 million and named for the governor who secured the funds—moved Mizzou into the

*Mike Jeffries (45) came up big in the conference tournament.*

modern world of athletic facilities. Brewer's wood and stone gave way to concrete and steel. Its cramped intimacy gave way to a vast expanse and a versatility befitting the new gym's unwieldy name, as the Hearnes Center hosted events from ice shows to rock concerts.

The need for a new building had taken a back seat to other campus concerns until 1966, when Governor Hearnes visited state-of-the-art Assembly Hall at the University of Illinois and came away committed to building something similar. Members of the basketball program already understood the need. The prospect of playing in Brewer Field House had convinced several recruits to go elsewhere, and it would have cost the Tigers John Brown but for the promise of a new arena. "I really liked Coach

Stewart, and I really liked the program," Brown said years later. "But as a young kid, material things were important, too. If I would have known I'd be playing in Brewer for my whole career, I wouldn't have come to Missouri."

The new building featured a space-age Tartan floor, an exotic gray court that the players loathed. The rubbery surface prevented them from sliding, and it dampened sound such that they could not hear the ball bounce, a disorienting experience for players who grew up on hardwood. Despite the new environment and crowds often well below the 12,600 capacity, the Tigers maintained the home-court edge that had become a hallmark of the Stewart era and rode it to the best start in half a century. Against Ohio, before a packed house, John Brown christened the building with a midrange jumper, and he and five other Tigers—Al Eberhard, Mike Jeffries, Orv Salmon, Gary Link, and sophomore Felix Jerman—tallied double figures. Attendance dropped sharply after opening night. Only 7,714 fans saw Brown collect thirty-five points and fifteen rebounds in a win over Purdue that moved the Tigers to 4–0.

At fifteenth-ranked Ohio State, the Tigers pulled an upset that vaulted them into the top twenty. Mizzou stayed on the road and won Tennessee's Volunteer Classic as Brown earned MVP honors. By the time they got to Kansas City for the conference tournament, the Tigers stood 8–0, ranked seventh in the nation.

After routing Colorado in round one, the Tigers faced nineteenth-ranked Oklahoma, which benefited from a monumental rules change. Beginning that season, freshmen became eligible for varsity play, and Oklahoma had one of the best in six-foot-nine Alvan Adams. With Brown, Eberhard, and Jerman smothering him, Adams scored twenty-seven points (one more than the Tiger trio combined)

*No one played through pain like Al Eberhard.*

and collected nineteen rebounds. But Mike Jeffries responded with the game of his career. The muscular guard recorded twenty-eight points, and Missouri advanced to the final with a 69–68 triumph.

There the Tigers faced sixteenth-ranked Kansas State. Al Eberhard, hampered by an ankle injury, could hardly walk and could not be stopped. With the score tied at 62, Mizzou reeled off eleven straight points, seven by Eberhard. His twenty-four points led all scorers, and Orv Salmon, who had been Norm Stewart's neighbor as a kid in Cedar Falls, Iowa, added twenty to secure an 82–72 victory and Missouri's second straight Big Eight Tournament title. "I want to tell you guys something," a joyous Norm Stewart said to the press after the game. "That Al Eberhard played a tremendous game, and we didn't know until game time if he could play."

The Tigers moved to number five in the polls, their highest ranking ever. Missouri's 12–0 start was the best since 1922. But Kansas State clobbered the Tigers in Manhattan, and Colorado stunned them in overtime, MU's first-ever defeat at Hearnes. At 0–2, Missouri had dug itself a hole in the Big Eight race, but the Tigers immediately began climbing.

Eberhard scored twenty-seven as the Tigers squeaked past Kansas in their next game. It was the first of three straight wins, including one at Oklahoma State that ignited a personal rivalry between John Brown and Cowboy sophomore Andy Hopson, a young rebounding machine. Missouri won easily, but Brown had an off-night, while Hopson collected seventeen points and twenty-seven boards. The performance prompted Hopson to boast that he was better than Brown, a slight that would be remembered.

Over the next two weeks, as Brown remained in a funk, Missouri won twice, lost twice, and fell out of serious title contention. But the Tigers continued to fight. They hosted Kansas State, which led the league at 8–1. While Norm Stewart and Jack Hartman bickered sporadically along the sidelines, Mizzou thumped the Wildcats. Brown, back to form, scored twenty points in the 80–66 victory.

At 6–4 in league play, the Tigers traveled to Lawrence. After trailing by eighteen, they staged an astonishing rally. In the second half, as a deluge of paper cups pelted the Missouri bench, the Tigers ran the Jayhawks out of their own gym. Brown and Eberhard combined for forty-nine points and thirty-seven rebounds in a 79–63 triumph. As he bounded toward the locker room, a jubilant Norm Stewart surveyed the projectile-hurling crowd and hollered, "The worst fans in America!" In the win, Brown moved into second place on MU's all-time scoring list, just twenty-three points behind Charlie Henke. A fairly ordinary effort in Mizzou's next game could secure the record. But Brown's performance was anything but ordinary.

Oklahoma State came to town, and with echoes still ringing in his ears, Brown destroyed Andy Hopson. While Charlie Henke watched, Brown unleashed his entire arsenal. Jumpers from the elbow, turnarounds from the baseline, finger rolls at the hoop. Eighteen minutes in, Brown had already scored twenty-two points. Then, shortly before halftime, he flicked a spinning jump shot from the

*In three fantastic seasons, John Brown rewrote the record book and rejuvenated Missouri basketball.*

free throw line. The bucket put Missouri up by fourteen and brought the game to a halt. The Hearnes Center crowd rose to salute the most prolific scorer in school history. After the delay, Brown continued to pour it on. He finished with forty-one points and nineteen rebounds in a 79–73 win, a historic performance on a historic day.

After dropping a game at Iowa State, the Tigers came home for senior day for Brown, Jeffries, and Salmon—and Brown went out fighting, literally. Early in the second half, Brown and Nebraska's Don Jackson exchanged a flurry of fists before being ejected. Junior forward Gary Link responded with twenty-one points and eleven rebounds to lead MU to an 86–70 win that secured a share of second place in the Big Eight and earned the 21–5 Tigers a spot in the National Invitation Tournament.

Mizzou opened against Massachusetts and suffered a terrible blow in the game's first minute when Felix Jerman crashed into a basket support and ruptured a tendon in his knee. John Brown, ever heroic, stepped up and made thirteen of sixteen shots from the field on his way to thirty-five points and sixteen rebounds. But he got too little help, and in the game's critical moments, Missouri faltered. Late misses from the field and the line spelled the end of the Tigers' season and Brown's career. Mizzou bowed out of the NIT 78–71.

In three seasons, John Brown's 1,421 points made him Mizzou's all-time scoring leader. His career averages of 19.7 points and 10.0 rebounds ranked in the top five in the program's first century. As a senior, Brown again made first-team All-Big Eight, and he earned spots on various second and third-team All-America squads. But Brown's time in Columbia meant far more than individual achievement. More than any other player, John Brown symbolized the rise of Missouri basketball. It didn't start with him and he didn't do it alone, but Brown was the central figure in the program's first two twenty-win seasons and back-to-back postseason tournament appearances. Before he arrived, such success seemed unfathomable. But with a player like John Brown, all things were possible.

# 1973–74

Life without John Brown got tougher when Felix Jerman transferred to Lincoln University before the 1973–74 season. Shortly thereafter, sophomore LaMont Turner and seniors Steve Blind and Charley Palmer left, too. In the face of such attrition, the Tigers leaned on seniors Al Eberhard and Gary Link plus junior guard Steve Dangos, a transfer from St. Louis University.

After starting at 2–2, the Tigers came to life, beginning with a win over Ohio State that featured a typical Al Eberhard effort. Mizzou's workhorse scored twenty-four points, grabbed twelve boards, and drew praise from Buckeye coach Fred Taylor, who had won a national championship with warriors like Jerry Lucas and John Havlicek. "It seems like when we get a rebound, it's a routine rebound," Taylor said. "When Eberhard gets one, it's a kind of a rebound that fires up everybody. Eberhard plays with such strength—you know he's going to play hard, and you're never going to lose in a situation like that."

Against Oklahoma in round one of the Big Eight Tournament, Eberhard posted twenty-one points and twenty-one rebounds, and Bill Flamank, a six-foot-six reserve center, contained Alvan Adams just enough to allow Mizzou to win 73–70. In round two, Eberhard, Dangos, and Link scored twenty-five, twenty-four, and twenty, respectively, and Flamank (son and brother of former Tigers George Sr. and George Jr.) scored most of his ten points late in the

*Steve Dangos came to Mizzou from St. Louis University.*

*In his senior year, Gary Link went from role player to high-scoring stalwart of the starting lineup.*

game to seal an 89–83 triumph over Colorado.

The next day, Norm Stewart's squad beat Iowa State to win its third straight tournament championship. Gail Wolf, a six-foot-eleven center who fought through an injury-plagued career, provided fourteen points off the bench, but Gary Link stole the show. The six-foot-five forward scored twenty-six points and sealed victory when he hit a jumper and two free throws to turn a 76–76 tie into an 80–78 Mizzou win. Eberhard again earned MVP honors, and Steve Dangos, who scored sixty-four points in the three games, joined him on the all-tournament team.

After winning three of four nonconference games, the Tigers played a rematch with Iowa State in the league opener. Eberhard (thirty-one points and twenty rebounds) and Link (twenty-seven points) singed the Cyclones in a 91–83 win. Mizzou appeared poised to contend for the Big Eight crown. Then things fell apart. After a surprising hot start, Mizzou suffered an equally stunning collapse.

Losses at Kansas State and Colorado gave cause for concern but not reason for panic. Panic came when the Tigers found that Hearnes held no magic. Mizzou lost at home to Kansas, Oklahoma, and Nebraska, blowing a fifteen-point lead against the Huskers despite twenty-eight points and seventeen rebounds from Eberhard. By the time Missouri hosted Colorado, the losing streak had grown to eight games, the longest since Norm Stewart took over. Despite playing with an injured shoulder and the effects of a concussion suffered in the previous game, Eberhard came up with twenty-five points and sixteen boards to help stop the streak, but the Tigers resumed their losing ways three days later against Kansas State.

In Mizzou's final home game, Norm Stewart tinkered with the lineup. Jeff Currie, a freshman who had played sparingly, replaced sophomore guard Kevin King, a starter for most of the year. The shakeup seemed to help. The Tigers handled Oklahoma State 87–81, and the senior co-captains gave fine efforts. Link scored nineteen, and Eberhard posted twenty-eight points and twelve rebounds.

From there, though, things continued to deteriorate. King, fresh from his demotion, quit the team just before the season's next to last game, the fifth player defection of the year. With King gone, Oklahoma routed the Tigers, then league champ Kansas humiliated them 112–76. Stewart acknowledged that the player attrition and attendant scrutiny had weighed on his team. "It was very difficult to prepare for our last ball game of the season because of all of the rumors going around," he said. "This team is close; the guys understand. But when you have that type of thing, it just tears them up."

The Tigers finished the year at 12–14 overall and 3–11 in the Big Eight. In part, the problem was defense. The Tigers gave up 78.2 points per game, the most since the end of Bob Vanatta's tenure.

*Bill Flamank was the third member of his family to be a Tiger.*

*With immeasurable heart, Al Eberhard graduated as one of Missouri's all-time greats.*

Mizzou lacked the offensive firepower to offset the defensive shortcomings. Only three players averaged more than six points per game. Steve Dangos contributed 14.3 and Gary Link chipped in 17.3, right behind Al Eberhard's 19.7. Eberhard also pulled down 12.0 rebounds per game and made first-team all-conference despite the Tigers' tie for last place.

Eberhard's 1,347 points put him second all-time, behind John Brown. His 10.1 rebounds per game made him one of only four Tigers (along with Brown, Bill Stauffer, and Bob Reiter) in the first century of Missouri basketball to average double figures over a career. Eberhard starred on three Big Eight Tournament champions and became one of the most accomplished Tigers ever. More than that, he became a sort of folk hero, the kind of player whose exploits grow over time. Surely today, some fan reminisces about the time that Big Al rode a tornado. But it's not all just fanciful recollection. Al Eberhard's ferocity was well-documented in his playing days, when he was described as "the blond torpedo who plays with such intensity that mere hustle pales into insignificance." Still, he seems

almost like a literary creation, a character named for his most important trait. More than anything, Al played Ever Hard.

With Eberhard and Link on the way out, things seemed destined to go from bad to worse, especially in the wake of what seemed like a mutiny. But in retrospect, it looked like a purge. The players who stayed, and the ones about to arrive, were proud to be Missouri Tigers, and they were committed to collective goals. Indeed, they proved to be the foundation of Mizzou's greatest success in half a century.

## 1974–75

Sometimes success comes by design. Sometimes it comes by luck. When Norm Stewart watched Willie Smith play in junior college, he saw defense. What he got was the finest scorer ever to wear a Missouri uniform, a player who helped the program make its next leap forward. Different as night and day, Stewart and Smith formed a bond over one common trait, a consuming passion for basketball. In his memoir, *Stormin' Back*, Stewart writes:

> When I met Willie . . . he approached me wearing a fur coat, and he had some kind of apparel on his head. When I walked up to Willie, he started giving me some unorthodox handshake. . . . "Willie, I don't have time for that," I said. "I don't understand it. I just don't know anything about it. I'm here to talk to you about you coming to the University of Missouri to play basketball."

Though Smith recalls that he tried to give the coach a conventional handshake, he appreciated the forthright style. While other coaches adopted hip façades, Stewart shot straight, which inspired trust. "It was refreshing," says Smith, who committed to Missouri shortly thereafter and brought a dynamic perimeter game to Columbia. With young players like Jim Kennedy and Kim Anderson, Mizzou could still battle on the blocks, but now, the Tigers could score from anywhere within thirty feet.

Playing before small home crowds, the kind that could have fit inside Brewer Field House, Missouri rode a soft schedule to a 6–1 start heading into the Big Eight Tournament. The Tigers failed to take a fourth straight title, but they made headlines both on and off the court. After losing in round one, Mizzou

Top: Willie Smith brought some unexpected offense to Mizzou.

Bottom: The pride of Sedalia, Kim Anderson emerged as an interior force in his sophomore year.

beat Colorado in the consolation bracket, then stunned eighteenth-ranked Oklahoma in two overtimes. Willie Smith entered the game intent on punishing the Sooners, who declined to offer him a recruiting visit, even though he attended nearby Seminole College. He scored thirty-seven points, and Scott Sims, a sophomore guard from Kirksville, made his first start and responded with eight points, ten rebounds, and eleven assists.

*Jeff Currie attacks the basket.*

The bigger news came in between the two victories, when word spread that Steve Dangos had been released from the team, an action "taken in the best interest of the ball club," according to a statement from Norm Stewart. Dangos shot back that he had quit, and had not been "released," because of conflict with the coach. Whatever the case, the move came after Stewart benched Dangos in favor of Sims, who drew the coach's praise for his heady play.

After splitting their remaining non-conference games, the Tigers dropped their first two Big Eight contests to fall to 9–5 overall and 0–2 in the league. Then they caught fire, starting at home against Iowa State. On a day when Willie Smith struggled, Gail Wolf, still recovering from knee surgery, made all seven of his shots from the field. With the score tied in the closing seconds, Missouri turned to a cold hand with a cool head. Despite missing fifteen of his first nineteen shots, Smith never hesitated. His jumper gave the Tigers an 87–85 win.

After a win at Oklahoma, the Tigers beat Nebraska behind twenty points from sophomore Jeff Currie, who made his first start of the year. A loss at Kansas State ended the winning streak, but the Tigers started another one, four games long, capped by an 87–72 win over Kansas in which Smith and Kim Anderson combined for fifty points. Missouri stood 7–3 in conference play, just one game out of the lead.

The Tigers' title hopes dimmed with a loss at Nebraska, but they still had much to play for. In 1975 the NCAA Tournament grew to thirty-two teams, and for the first time two squads from the same league could be invited. A second-place finish could mean Missouri's first NCAA berth since World War II.

The Tigers started the three-game stretch drive with a one-point win over Oklahoma. Then, in his last home game, senior Bill Flamank produced nineteen points and eleven rebounds to power Missouri past Kansas State as the Tigers finished their first perfect season at Hearnes and the first at home since 1930. At 9–4, Missouri and K-State each trailed Kansas by one game with one to play.

A win at Colorado, which was finishing a dreadful season, would have given the Tigers a solid claim to an NCAA berth and perhaps a share of the conference title. Instead, while Kansas and Kansas State won their games (and garnered NCAA bids), Mizzou limped out of Boulder with a 106–97 loss and a third-place finish.

The Tigers' consolation prize was a trip to the short-lived National Collegiate Commissioners Invitational Tournament, where they faced Purdue. Willie Smith scored thirty, and Kim Anderson added twenty-two, but the remaining Tigers combined for just twenty points. That lack of

*Jim Kennedy was tenacity personified.*

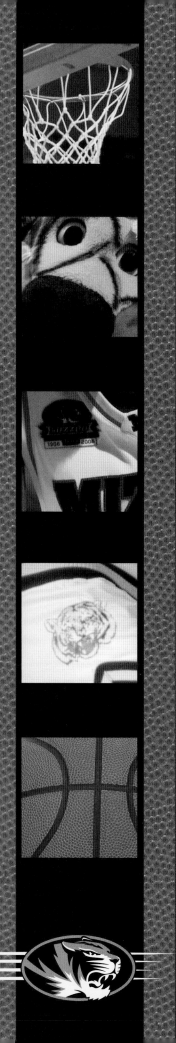

production, combined with foul trouble (Smith, Anderson, and Jim Kennedy each fouled out), sank Mizzou. The season ended in an 87–74 loss.

Back in November, no one thought the Tigers would be in NCAA contention in March, but they achieved success through unity. Gail Wolf called it the closest-knit team he had been around, and Norm Stewart said simply, "This has probably been my most enjoyable year of coaching."

More than just unity, the success was built on new blood and a full-throttle style of play. Led by Willie Smith, the run-and-gun Tigers scored a school-record 83.5 points per game. In his first year, Smith averaged 22.4 points and earned All-Big Eight honors, while sophomores Kim Anderson and Jim Kennedy emerged as stars in their own right. With three such fine players slated to return, long-suffering Missouri fans allowed themselves to ask, "Will next year be the year?" Finally, mercifully, triumphantly, it would be.

## 1975–76

When jazz fan Willie Smith asked Mizzou's pep band to learn Grover Washington's "Mister Magic," he simultaneously earned a theme song and a nickname that fit his ability to perform the paranormal with his left-handed jump shot. In Smith's final season, the magician's assistants were mostly the same as the year before, though a pair of newcomers countered the losses of Bill Flamank and Gail Wolf. Freshman Stan Ray, a center from Cape Girardeau, and forward James Clabon, a junior college transfer, matched the lost production point for point, rebound for rebound.

The Tigers won seven of nine before the holiday tournament, even winning at Hawaii with four players on the floor at the end after the other six members of the traveling squad fouled out. In Kansas City, Mizzou topped Oklahoma State and Kansas State to set up a rare event, a title

*As Stan Ray watches, Willie Smith schools another defender.*

game pitting Missouri against Kansas for the first time since 1951.

The Jayhawks, featuring stalwart forward Norm Cook and freshman seven-footer Paul Mokeski, towered over the Tigers. Still, before fifteen thousand fans at Kemper Arena, Missouri dominated the boards. Smith and Kennedy combined for forty-nine points in a 79–69 win that gave Mizzou its fourth title in five years. Smith earned MVP honors and some facetiously faint praise from his coach. "Willie Smith is a pretty decent ball player," said Norm Stewart.

Missouri readied for the Big Eight season with a pair of nonconference games, including a 106–34 demolition of little MacMurray College that set a Mizzou record for margin of victory. Norm Stewart tried to show mercy by lifting his starters early, but the reserves continued the carnage.

The MacMurray massacre revealed a mean streak, and when Kansas came to town, Mizzou savaged its archrival. Smith, Ray, and Kennedy each scored more than twenty points in a 99–69 rout that started a march through the league. After the Tigers drubbed Oklahoma State, Cowboy coach Guy Strong called Missouri "one of the best teams in the Big Eight that I've seen in several years." Willie Smith, in the midst of a sensational season, scored thirty-two points in a win over Iowa State and reached one thousand career points faster than any

previous Tiger. By the time the Tigers hosted Kansas State, they stood 5–0 in the conference.

The Wildcats, behind thirty-two points from Chuckie Williams, handed Missouri its first league loss. Undeterred, the Tigers collected wins at Colorado and Oklahoma State and whipped Iowa State before heading to Kansas. Down by one in the closing seconds at Allen Field House, Willie Smith rose above a sea of bodies, grabbed an offensive rebound, and scored at the buzzer. With four games to play, Missouri stood a game ahead of Kansas State.

But after Kim Anderson scored eleven in overtime to beat Nebraska, cold shooting and foul trouble derailed the Tigers at Oklahoma. That weekend, Kansas State won to tie the Tigers at the top of the standings, setting up a showdown in Manhattan. It would be, for all intents and purposes, the Big Eight championship game. And it would be played in a gym where the Tigers had lost ten straight. The title, once there for the taking, suddenly appeared in doubt. Nearly forty years of history worked against Mizzou. But that history vanished with the wave of a wand as a packed Ahearn Field House experienced a Magic show.

Willie Smith put up gaudy numbers throughout his career at Missouri, but he was never motivated by individual glory. He scored for the good of the team. Smith and his teammates came from diverse backgrounds, but they shared a blinding desire to win. Even more than he loved to win, though, Mr. Magic hated to be embarrassed. One of the proudest players ever to wear the black and gold, Smith took defeat personally. Late into the night before the Kansas State game, Smith and roommate Jeff Currie talked about the mission that faced them. K-State's guards Chuckie Williams and Mike Evans formed one of the nation's best backcourts, and they had humiliated the Tigers a month earlier by leaving the Hearnes Center with a win, the only time Smith ever tasted defeat in Columbia. Already keyed up for the challenge, Smith found further motivation during the walk from Mizzou's hotel to the field house. Kansas State's fans were out in force, taunting the Tigers along the way. Smith was incensed, but managed to keep a cool exterior. "Just wait till you get inside," he thought to himself.

*Top: Kim Anderson powers for two points.*

*Bottom: Freshman Stan Ray celebrates Mizzou's fourth conference tournament title in five years.*

Once inside, Smith erupted. He scored twenty-two points in the first half, but the Tigers could manage just a three-point lead. So he kept scoring. Missouri led 73–72 with ninety seconds to play when Smith flashed into the lane and sank a jump shot, and the Tigers pulled away to an 81–72 triumph. Smith, who scored thirty-eight points, felt vindicated. "We wanted this one," he said. "We had a lot of things we wanted to prove."

The Tigers proved plenty. They clinched a share of the conference title, their first since 1940, and gave themselves a chance to secure the championship outright for the first time since 1930. When Colorado visited on the season's final Saturday, the anxiety that preceded the K-State game gave way to dead calm. A confident Missouri team marched from the locker room to the floor, where they crushed the Buffaloes.

Five Tigers reached double figures in a game that was over by halftime. Mizzou led by twenty-nine at the break and won 95–60 in a performance so businesslike

*With the Final Four on the line, Jim Kennedy drives to the hoop against Michigan.*

that the team forgot to celebrate. Afterwards, Jim Kennedy said, "It wasn't until we were in the shower when someone said, 'Hey, we didn't even cut the nets down.'"

Norm Stewart and his team, having accomplished so much, had little time to savor their achievement. They had a national championship

*In his All-America senior season, Willie Smith shattered scoring records and took his place as one of the greatest Tigers of all time.*

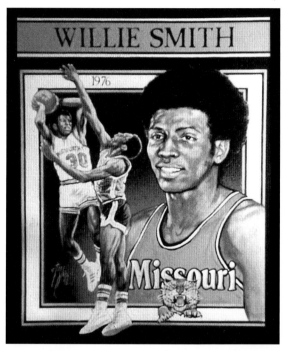

to play for. The experience was new to the Tigers, but the location was not. The Tigers opened NCAA Tournament play against the Washington Huskies in a familiar environment—Allen Field House on the campus of the University of Kansas.

In Lawrence, the composure that had marked Missouri's season evaporated. By the time the Tigers shook off the nerves, they trailed by eleven points. But they came back by going right at Washington's enormous front line. With the score tied at 65 and under a minute to play, Jim Kennedy drove to the basket and collided with seven-foot James Edwards. A controversial blocking call sent Edwards to the bench with five fouls. Kennedy sank two free throws to give MU a 67–65 lead. After that, free throws by Willie Smith and Scott Sims wrapped up a 69–67 win, and the Tigers were pleased to escape. "That was one of the worst games we've played all year," said Smith.

After a shaky effort against Washington, Smith starred against Texas Tech in the regional semifinal in Louisville. He sank long shots, crashed the glass, dished to Kennedy and Anderson for easy buckets, and finished with thirty points, ten rebounds, and seven assists. "Smith was everything we heard he was," lamented Tech coach Gerald Myers. The Tigers' 86–75 victory moved them to the verge of the Final Four. Kim Anderson captured the team's mood: "We're confident that we'll continue to play well, and we have nothing to be ashamed of—win or lose."

Despite their confidence, the Tigers came out flat in the regional final against Michigan. Willie Smith scored just two points in the first ten minutes, and Missouri trailed by eighteen. Then Smith began to warm up, and Mizzou cut Michigan's lead to thirteen at the break. Years later, Smith confessed, "We didn't think they could beat us at all . . . but their intensity level was higher." The intensity deficit vanished in the second half. The Tigers turned it up by turning to their All-American, who responded with the greatest twenty minutes ever played by a Missouri Tiger.

Smith shredded the Wolverine defense. He shot the ball arrow-straight and feather-soft. He hit turnarounds, floaters, and shots off the dribble. Each time down, his range expanded. He hit from twenty feet, then twenty-four as Michigan's lead vanished in a rainstorm of jump shots. With under eight minutes to play, Smith sank an unconscionably long jumper and got mugged by Michigan's Rickey Green. When Smith sank the free throw, Missouri led 76–71. The Final Four was within reach.

But then the wheels came off. The Tigers held the lead when Kim Anderson hurtled down the court on a fast break. He soared toward the rim and got undercut by a defender. In an instinctive effort to keep from falling, Anderson's layup turned into a dunk as he grabbed the rim for protection. But dunking had been outlawed in NCAA basketball. The officials waved off the hoop and called a technical foul, giving Michigan free throws and the ball and instantly changing the game. While Michigan capitalized on the controversial call, the Tigers, a 71 percent free throw shooting team, crumbled at the stripe in the final minutes and lost three starters when Anderson, Kennedy, and Currie fouled out. After thundering into the lead, the Tigers faded into history 95–88.

Still, all anyone could talk about was Willie Smith. His twenty-nine second-half points gave him forty-three for the game, the top performance in the entire tournament. More than two hundred media members cast ballots for the regional's most outstanding player award, and all but one voted for Smith.

Observers were mesmerized. "I can't think of any words to describe what he does," Kim Anderson confessed, while Michigan coach Johnny Orr called Smith's effort "one of the greatest shooting exhibitions that I have ever seen." "If there is a better [player]," said Norm Stewart, "I haven't seen him." But Smith, the ultimate competitor, took no solace in the recognition. "I cried," he says. "We should have won."

Though Jim Kennedy and Kim Anderson earned individual honors (first- and second-team All–Big Eight, respectively), the season belonged to Willie Smith. Even as he shot at a record rate, Smith displayed a knack for delivering the ball to teammates in position to score. His 138 assists established a new single-season record. He also managed to pull down 5.7 rebounds per game from the perimeter.

But more than anything, Smith scored. His 783 points and 25.3 point-per-game average established new single-season records, and his 23.9 career scoring average bettered John Brown's mark by more than four points per game. In just two seasons, Willie Smith rewrote the record book and redefined the program. He was a comet at the edge of the atmosphere, streaking in from nowhere, showering sparks, and disappearing, like magic, before anyone could make sense of him.

## 1976–77

The defending Big Eight champions persevered through a season marked by unexpected attrition. The first casualty was Jeff Currie, who missed the year with an illness. Still, the Tigers returned an impressive core led by seniors Kim Anderson, Jim Kennedy, and Scott Sims and augmented by Clay Johnson, a six-foot-four forward from Penn Valley Community College, who used an outrageous vertical leap to rebound like a madman and dunk with jackhammer authority, and by Larry Drew, a tough and talented guard from Wyandotte High in Kansas City, Kansas.

After some impressive play by Scott Sims and Stan Ray against nonconference foes, the Tigers entered the holiday tournament with a 6-2 record and advanced to the final against Kansas. There Missouri eked out a 69–65 win behind twenty-two points from Anderson and twenty from Kennedy. It marked Mizzou's fifth tournament title in six years, an unprecedented feat.

Then, after losing their league opener, the Tigers went on a tear, and they did it without Stan Ray, an academic casualty. They won in hostile settings like Manhattan and Stillwater and got stellar performances from their frontcourt stars. At Colorado, Clay Johnson shot fourteen of seventeen from the field and eleven of eleven from

*Scott Sims ran the show with precision passing and some surprising scoring pop.*

the line for thirty-nine points in a 90–83 win. At home, Kim Anderson scored thirty-eight to beat Kansas. Ten games into the conference schedule, the first-place Tigers stood at 8–2.

But with another title within reach, Mizzou lost at Nebraska and lost Jim Kennedy to a sprained ankle—a tough blow to a team with a short bench. After falling into a tie with Kansas State, the Tigers regrouped and routed Colorado as Scott Sims scored thirty. Then came the rematch with K-State. For the second straight year, the teams played a de facto title game in the season's next-to-last contest.

Kennedy, still in pain, helped the Tigers build a lead that they carried into the second half. Then Kansas State caught fire, making twelve straight shots to take a double-digit edge. Mizzou's hopes ended when Anderson and Johnson fouled out with more than seven minutes to play. Missouri dropped the game 88–77 and fell into a second-place tie with Oklahoma.

The Sooners lost their regular season finale, giving the Tigers a chance to take second for themselves. But they fell at Iowa State, and Kim Anderson aggravated an existing shoulder injury. In previous years, that might have spelled the end of the season. But for the first time, the Big Eight

*Gravity had little power over Clay Johnson.*

*Gritty Jim Kennedy played through injury in his senior season.*

held a postseason tournament. For nearly forty years, the conference had determined its NCAA Tournament representative through a two-month grind. Now, it would come down to a one-week sprint. Mizzou's hopes for a return to the NCAA's hinged on winning three games. But with Anderson and Kennedy nursing injuries, Missouri had few able bodies. Norm

Stewart, humor intact, said, "If we do manage to get to a postseason tournament, we'll be able to go in a Volkswagen."

The new tournament's format put higher seeds on their home floors in round one, with the winners advancing to Kansas City. Missouri hosted Oklahoma State and overcame ongoing injury problems. Anderson left in the first half because of his ailing shoulder, while Kennedy's balky ankle forced him to sit out much of the second half. Senior reserves James Clabon and Danny Van Rheen responded with twenty-two and fifteen points, respectively, while Larry Drew added seventeen in a 92–74 victory.

In Kansas City, Mizzou's small company of able-bodied men continued to cover for ailing colleagues. While Kim Anderson sat out against Oklahoma, Clabon, Drew, Johnson, and Sims each played the full forty minutes, with Kennedy and Van Rheen splitting time at the fifth spot. Clay Johnson's twenty-seven points and twelve rebounds spurred Missouri to a fifteen-point win as Scott Sims recorded ten assists for the fourth time on the year. "We thought Missouri would be a different team with Anderson hurt," said Oklahoma coach Dave Bliss. "They weren't."

The Tigers stood within one game of the NCAA Tournament. Kansas State stood in the way. So did fatigue. The Tigers had their legs early, racing to an eighteen-point lead late in the first half. Then they started to fade. The margin fell to ten at halftime, and the Cats continued to chip away after intermission. But Norm Stewart did his best to pump his team full of fire. Early in the second half, Scott Sims collided with K-State's Scott Langton and left him bloodied. The Wildcats claimed that Sims intentionally threw an elbow—a charge he denied. Soon, Stewart and Jack Hartman were standing nose to nose in front of the scorer's table, raging at each other until restrained by officials. After play resumed, the fierce battle continued. A long jumper by Mike Evans gave K-State a two-point lead with just under two minutes to play, but Clay Johnson responded with two free throws. Kansas State went into a stall and played for one final shot. When the Wildcats failed to score, the teams headed to overtime. Three minutes in, the game was still tied. Then Kansas State made some free throws, Sims missed the front end of a one-and-one, and it was over. The Wildcats prevailed 72–67, and the NCAA denied Mizzou an at-large invitation, a snub that Norm Stewart called unjustifiable. Missouri declined an invitation from the NIT. After advancing to the NCAA's Elite Eight the previous year, Stewart saw little sense in sending an injury-plagued, senior-laden team. "If we'd had a young ball club with something to prove, we might have done it," he said. "But I think our players have proven themselves to be one of the better ball clubs around." At 21–8, Missouri's season ended.

So did the careers of Kennedy, Anderson, and Sims, all of whom were selected in the NBA draft. Anderson's senior season was particularly impressive. His 18.3 points and 7.9 rebounds per game earned him the Big Eight player of the year award, an impressive feat for a center who

*The 1977 Big Eight Player of the Year, Kim Anderson*

stood just six-foot-seven. Both Anderson and Kennedy finished their careers in Missouri's all-time top ten in scoring and rebounding. Their departure left a giant hole in Missouri's front line and signaled a brief decline in the team's fortunes. The decline began with one of the stranger seasons in Missouri's history.

## 1977–78

It began plausibly enough. The Tigers fell to some good teams on the road and beat some bad teams at home. Then they traveled to face Florida State and got crushed 97–64. Things got worse when Kansas thrashed the Tigers 96–49 to open the holiday tournament. But in a small sign of the absurdity to come, Missouri bounced back to win twice and take fifth place.

After those ups and downs, the Tigers found consistency. They consistently lost. Through January, they lost every time they hit the road, and many of the times they stayed at home. The pattern continued into February. Mizzou jumped up and beat second-place Nebraska, but by then the team was just playing out the string. Decrying his team's lack of confidence, Norm Stewart said, "The way we've been playing is like missing an eight-foot putt by six feet."

The regular season finale showed the season in microcosm. After building a sixteen-point halftime lead at Hearnes, Missouri imploded and Iowa State rallied to win 67–63. For practical purposes, that should have been the end. An exit in the postseason tournament's first game would put an end to the misery as the seventh-seeded Tigers, who had not won on an opponent's floor all year, traveled to Ames for a rematch with Iowa State.

Then things got weird, starting with an unlikely promise. Stan Ray's career had been star-crossed. As a freshman, his play foretold an almost certain stardom. The league's rookie of the year, he nearly helped

*Clay Johnson (above) and Larry Drew (below) starred in a season that was headed nowhere until it took an unexpected turn.*

the Tigers into the Final Four. Then, with the world as his oyster, Ray lost his academic eligibility as a sophomore. His grades recovered in his junior year, but his game suffered, thanks to a broken hand suffered early in the season. While Larry Drew and Clay Johnson carried the team, Ray tried his best to contribute, but the cast on his hand might as well have been an anchor. Though he trudged through a tough year, Ray showed some surprising swagger as postseason approached. Before the conference tournament, Ray slid a note under his coach's door. "I know you don't have any confidence in me," it read, "but I'm going to prove everybody wrong and take this team to the NCAA Tournament."

The game at Ames followed a familiar pattern. Mizzou built a double-digit halftime lead, only to watch it vanish. But this time, the Tigers stiffened. With the score tied at 63–63 with less than a minute to play, and with the ball in Larry Drew's hands, Missouri played for one shot. As time ticked away, Drew found Clay Johnson on the baseline. The high-flying senior elevated and drilled a jump shot. By the time Johnson's feet hit the floor, the Tigers were in the second round.

Ray didn't look particularly prophetic yet, not with two games to go. But he began to seem positively prescient when Missouri met Nebraska in the semifinals. With the Tigers down by three points in the last two minutes, Ray took over. He stole a pass and sprinted the length of the court to cut the lead to one point, then scored again to put the Tigers on top. When the final buzzer sounded, Missouri owned a 61–58 win and a spot in the final.

There they met Kansas State, and the story turned stranger than fiction in a game that went to overtime. The score remained tied with 1:36 left in the extra period when Ray sank two free throws. Thirteen seconds later, he hit two more. Then, with forty-four seconds left, he made another pair to give Missouri a three-point edge. The Tigers won 71–68, and Ray, who recorded seventeen points and thirteen rebounds, was named tournament MVP. Missouri's sleeping giant, fully awakened, made good on his pledge and put his team in the NCAA field.

The inclusion of Missouri, with its 14–15 record, was anathema to those who deplored the rise of postseason conference tournaments, like the *Chicago Sun-Times* columnist who wrote, "Missouri's

*The Antlers, a frequently outrageous group of students, began heckling opponents from courtside seats in the late 1970s.*

*Stan Ray promised to take Missouri to the NCAA Tournament—and he did.*

presence in the tournament stands as an embarrassing tribute to college basketball's latest folly."

Despite their critics, the Tigers played like they belonged. Round one pitted them against fifteenth-ranked Utah, and the Tigers led 63–55 with just over six minutes to play, before the Utes rallied to force overtime. Clay Johnson, Larry Drew, and Brad Droy each scored in the extra period, but Utah matched Mizzou shot for shot. Sadly, Missouri's luck ran out in the second overtime. Utah's Buster Matheney scored ten quick points and the Tigers tumbled 86–79. Clay Johnson, in his final game at Mizzou, scored thirty. Stan Ray snatched twelve boards but managed just four points. Alas, he had not promised a national championship.

## 1978–79

After his improbable run, academic issues shelved Stan Ray for good. Without him, the Tigers returned two standout players—Larry Drew, the veteran leader, and six-foot-seven sophomore Curtis Berry, a rising star from Selma, Alabama. Senior

forward Brad Droy provided some scoring pop and junior Tom Dore, at seven-foot-two, provided size. More than anything, though, Mizzou's fortunes hinged on the production of a ballyhooed recruiting class headlined by Steve Wallace, an athletic junior college guard, and Lex Drum, a six-foot-ten center from Poplar Bluff.

Early in the season, Drum scored twenty-six points in a win over Eastern Kentucky, but soon thereafter Mizzou went into a tailspin. The Tigers dropped five of six heading into the thirty-third and final conference holiday tournament, where things got much worse. Missouri, which had dominated the event in recent years, lost all three games to fall to 4–8, and Lex Drum suffered a knee injury that effectively ended his career at Mizzou. He would make only a handful of appearances over the next two years before transferring.

When Missouri dropped its league opener to Oklahoma State, the season seemed headed nowhere. And then, for no apparent reason, things changed. At Hearnes, the Tigers broke a seven-game losing streak by beating Oklahoma as Drew scored twenty-three. But the big shock came four days later when the Tigers visited nationally ranked Kansas, and Berry posted twenty points and twenty rebounds in a 58–55 victory—Norm Stewart's 195th at Missouri, a total that tied him for first all-time with Sparky Stalcup. Stewart secured the record for himself the next time out in a win over Nebraska as Steve Wallace scored twenty-one.

Curtis Berry injured his ankle in a loss at Colorado, but the Tigers fought on. Drew, Wallace,

*Curtis Berry gave Missouri a budding star to build around.*

*Top: The electrifying, inexhaustible Steve Wallace*

*Bottom: Larry Drew, the first Tiger junior to reach one thousand career points*

Wallace poured in twenty-eight points. At 5–2, the Tigers moved into a first-place tie with Oklahoma, their next opponent.

Mizzou's bubble began to burst in Norman, where the Tigers fell by four. Two more losses dropped MU to 5–5 in the league and ended any championship aspirations. But the Tigers remained resilient. After winning at Colorado and losing at Nebraska, Mizzou traveled to Kansas State and won 67–63. Curtis Berry, back from injury, contributed fourteen points and thirteen rebounds to complement Steve Wallace's twenty-point effort. The Tigers closed the regular season with a win over Iowa State and finished tied for second place, renewing hopes that they might repeat the previous year's postseason performance.

The Tigers opened the tournament at home against Oklahoma State and won easily. All five starters scored at least fourteen points, including freshman Mark Dressler, who also collected thirteen rebounds, and Curtis Berry, whose twenty-four-point, twelve-rebound effort revealed him to be back in top form. But Missouri would advance no further. Kansas upended the Tigers in the semifinals. Larry Drew, who scored nineteen, finished the season with an even one thousand career points—the first MU junior to reach that milestone.

Despite the season's end, big news was around the bend at the Final Four in Salt Lake City. The Tigers weren't there, but Norm Stewart was. And while Larry Bird and Magic Johnson battled for the national championship, Stewart fielded a pair of phone calls that would change the face of Big Eight basketball.

and Droy starred in a triumph over Kansas State. Then, Mizzou got a lift from Tom Dore, the transfer from Davidson College. At Iowa State, he contributed twenty points and thirteen boards in Missouri's overtime win, a game in which Steve

From the beginning, every decade of Missouri basketball has produced moments of triumph and drama, but none quite like the 1980s, a decade of dominance and disappointments, ten years in which basketball became king on campus and Mizzou became the Big Eight's preeminent program. In the 1970s, Norm Stewart established a championship foundation. In the 1980s, a group of soon-to-be legendary players took Missouri basketball to an entirely different level.

# THE 1980s

## 1979-80

The first call came from St. Louis, the second from Kansas City. By the time Norm Stewart put down the phone, he knew his program was about to take a giant leap forward, but he did his best to contain his joy. "We're very pleased with both Steve and Jon," he said in an act of staggering understatement. He had just received commitments that would change the course of Missouri basketball.

Steve Stipanovich, a six-foot-eleven center from DeSmet High in St. Louis, was among the top recruits in the nation. Jon Sundvold, a sharp-shooting guard from Blue Springs, also was highly prized. A budding friendship helped convince them to pick Mizzou. "[Stipanovich] told me that if I went there, he'd go. And I told him the same thing," said Sundvold. And thus, the finest inside-outside combination in Missouri history was forged.

In the space between Stipo's low-post heroics and Sundvold's long-range pyrotechnics, a third new player would have equal impact. Ricky Frazier, a six-foot-five swingman from Charleston, Missouri, transferred to Missouri after a stellar freshman season at St. Louis University. The three newcomers joined experienced stars Curtis Berry, Steve Wallace, and senior captain Larry Drew to form as talented a top six as Missouri had ever known.

The new souped-up Tigers got off to a scorching start. Stipanovich scored twenty-three in his debut, a win over Southwest Texas State, and Larry Drew tallied twenty-five in an overtime victory at Illinois. Even after Mizzou dropped its league opener at Kansas, the Tigers stood 11–2, ranked thirteenth in the nation. But a huge loss loomed.

A day after the Tigers won a romp at Nebraska, they got rocked when Steve Wallace was ruled academically ineligible. A gifted scorer and oppressive defender, Wallace had been one of the top guards in the league, a player Norm Stewart called "inexhaustible." His loss moved Jon Sundvold into the lineup, further thinning an already wispy bench.

Without Wallace, the Tigers took time to get their bearings. After beating three of the league's lesser teams, they stumbled against Oklahoma and Kansas State to fall to 4–3 in conference play. But Mizzou found its championship form by forging a relentless interior attack, triggered by Larry Drew, who threaded passes to teammates for point-blank scores. For the season, Mark Dressler made 63.6 percent of his shots, followed closely by Ricky Frazier (63.5 percent), Curtis Berry (61.6 percent), and Steve Stipanovich (59.8 percent). As a team, Missouri would shoot 57.3 percent from the field—an NCAA record.

Berry kick-started Missouri's resurgence with nineteen points in a win over Nebraska, and twenty points and ten rebounds in a victory at Iowa State. Then came a statement game. In front of a record crowd at the Hearnes Center, Mizzou demolished Kansas. "We lost to Kansas the first time we played them, and reading the newspaper articles . . . you just want to go out there and kill them," said Stipanovich, who scored twenty-nine points in an 88–65 rout.

*Larry Drew was the leader of one of Mizzou's most talented teams.*

*Freshmen Steve Stipanovich (above, against Notre Dame in the NCAA Tournament) and Jon Sundvold (left) ushered in the most successful period in Missouri's modern history.*

After Berry and Frazier combined for forty-eight points in a double-digit win at Colorado, Missouri moved into first place by beating Oklahoma State. But it wasn't all good news. While fighting for a rebound against the Cowboys, Curtis Berry sprained his knee.

At 9–3 in league play, Mizzou hosted Oklahoma with a chance to secure Norm Stewart's second Big Eight championship. With Berry sidelined, the coach turned to Mark Dressler, a chameleon of a player, one who could take on any identity the team needed. In Berry's absence, the team needed an interior scorer, and Dressler responded with eighteen points in an 81–69 victory that secured the title and allowed thoughts to drift toward the postseason.

After closing the slate with a win at Kansas State, Missouri advanced to the semifinals of the Big Eight tournament. But there the Tigers not only lost to Kansas, but also lost Curtis Berry for the season. Playing for the first time since spraining his knee, he aggravated the injury, a blow to Mizzou's hopes for a run in the NCAA's. "It was a bad night all around," said Norm Stewart.

Despite the loss, the Tigers earned the number five seed in the Midwest region, where they opened against San Jose State and quickly found themselves in trouble. At halftime, a flu-stricken Stipanovich had as many fouls (four) as points and Missouri trailed by seven. With Stipo incapacitated by illness, Norm Stewart turned to Tom Dore in the locker room and said, "Do the job." Dore, with deadpan wit, stood before his teammates and said, "I will lead you to Notre Dame," the high-profile opponent that awaited the winner. He opened the second half with seven quick points to push Missouri into a 36–36 tie. Ricky Frazier did the rest, scoring twenty-four in a 61–51 victory. Dore finished with eleven points, five rebounds, and five blocked shots. "He did a heck of a job," said Stewart.

As Missouri prepared for its next game, Norm Stewart told his players not to fear the Fighting Irish, one of the nation's most talented teams. They

*High-flying, high-scoring Ricky Frazier played like a force of nature.*

a layup with just under a minute to play, giving Mizzou an 82–80 edge. Then Dressler, who had been a force all game long, iced it. With less than thirty seconds left, Notre Dame's Bill Hanzlik missed a jump shot. Dressler grabbed the rebound and was fouled. He hit both free throws for an 84–80 lead. Then he stole the ball from Orlando Woolridge, got fouled again, and hit two more. In the end, Dressler scored thirty-two points on thirteen of sixteen field goal attempts and six of eight free throws in the 87–84 triumph. "I would never have thought I could do it," he said. "But I did, and I am really proud."

Missouri's reward was a meeting with top-seeded Louisiana State in the Sweet Sixteen. The Tigers led 40–39 at the break, but LSU scored the first six points of the second half, then went into a stall. When Stipanovich picked up his fourth foul, things looked grim, and they were. With Stipo on the bench,

*Seven-foot-two Tom Dore makes creative use of manager Mike Noble.*

"don't walk around with halos on their heads," he said. Still, the Tigers would need an enormous effort to match Notre Dame's firepower. They would get one of the most improbable individual performances in school history.

Notre Dame led by six at halftime, but the Tigers chipped away and pulled even with a whirlwind of offensive motion. Larry Drew scored fifteen and fired laserlike passes that pierced the defense for easy shots. Stipanovich and Frazier cashed in on several of Drew's twelve assists, but a far less likely hero emerged. Mark Dressler, the six-foot-seven sophomore from St. Louis, stood among nine future NBA draft picks and dominated a game that went into overtime.

The teams traded baskets for most of the extra period. Drew fed Frazier for

Mizzou could not come back. Dressler again led Missouri with twenty points, but the Tigers fell 68–63. Larry Drew scored sixteen to close his career.

After a pair of losing seasons, the 1979–80 campaign renewed Missouri's momentum. The conference champs, at 25–6 overall, produced one of the program's finest seasons. Curtis Berry earned All-Big Eight honors, Steve Stipanovich was named the league's top newcomer, and Ricky Frazier matched those two point for point, rebound for rebound. All three were set to return, as were Jon Sundvold and Mark Dressler, giving Missouri a remarkable nucleus of talent. But for Larry Drew, it was the end. A first-team all-league pick, Drew finished his career with 1,401 points—then second only to John Brown—and established career records for assists and steals. In his senior year, Drew finally was surrounded with enough talent to let his gifts fully shine. Looking back, Jon Sundvold says that Drew "was one of the top point guards in the country, maybe the best," a player who failed to get his full due because he didn't play for a glamour program. But perhaps Drew's greatness became most fully appreciated when the Tigers learned what life was like without him.

## 1980–81

A bad moon seemed to rise over Missouri's quest for a second straight title. Voodoo first struck when Mark Dressler blew out his knee during an off-season pickup game, a jolt to a team already lacking depth. Then, after opening at number eleven in the polls, the Tigers suffered ugly losses to Arkansas and Illinois. Missouri regrouped and stood 8–3 headed into the holidays, but the strangest blow was yet to come.

Fate's haymaker struck just after Christmas when Steve Stipanovich accidentally shot himself with a pistol, resulting in a minor wound to his left shoulder but more serious injury to his pride. Embarrassed, Stipanovich initially claimed that a deranged assailant had burst into his home and fired the shot. He soon recanted, but not before providing fodder for rival fans to taunt him throughout the season.

When play resumed, Stipo scored ten points off the bench in a win over Oral Roberts, and Missouri later opened league play at home by

*Mark Dressler's effort against Notre Dame in the NCAA Tournament ranks among the legendary performances in Missouri basketball history.*

routing Oklahoma and Iowa State. But the road brought troubles, beginning at defending national champ Louisville and continuing at Kansas and Nebraska. The Tigers regrouped to win three of their next four, but after a subpar Oklahoma squad defeated them, they stood just 6–4 in the league.

Missouri's struggles were largely a matter of personnel. The Tigers lacked a floor general in

*Hall of Fame coach and broadcaster Al McGuire interviews Norm Stewart after Missouri's upset of Notre Dame, while an exuberant Tiger fan provides an expressive backdrop.*

Larry Drew's mold. Though recruited as a guard, junior college transfer Marvin "Moon" McCrary proved better suited to play forward, where he was a defensive powerhouse. Freshman guard Shawn Teague (who would transfer after the season) had skills but lacked experience. That placed the ball-handling burden squarely on Jon Sundvold while Ricky Frazier played beside him in a lineup of mismatched parts.

But the patchwork Tigers put together a charge. In Stillwater, Sundvold scored twenty-six to help beat Oklahoma State, pulling the Tigers into a second-place tie with Kansas and K-State, just a game back of Nebraska. Then, with a share of the lead at stake, Mizzou hosted the Huskers and trailed 45–44 before Curtis Berry hit an assortment of jumpers, dunks, and free throws to give Missouri a 55–45 victory. Kansas State beat Oklahoma to create a three-way tie at the top of the standings, while Kansas remained one game behind after a loss in Boulder.

At Colorado, Ricky Frazier scored twenty-six in a win that assured Missouri of a share of the lead headed into the final weekend. Meanwhile, Kansas State beat Iowa State, and KU routed Nebraska. The day's results left Mizzou and Kansas State to meet in a winner-take-all match in Columbia.

It is a game best remembered for a gambit by Norm Stewart that straddled the line between gutsy and crazy. With almost eight minutes to play, the score stood tied at 43. The Wildcats featured a stellar zone defense from which they rarely departed. At a time-out, Norm Stewart told his team, "If they won't guard us man-to-man, we'll wait until the end to win." And so the Tigers froze the ball, content to play for one last shot that seemed an eternity away. With twenty-two seconds left, Mizzou called a time-out, and Stewart drew up a play for Ricky Frazier. When Kansas State blocked Frazier's lane to the hoop, he improvised and took the ball to the baseline, where he elevated and released a rainbow that splashed home with seven seconds remaining. Fouled on the shot, Frazier sank a free throw to give Missouri a 46–43 win and another Big Eight

*Just a flesh wound: Stipo's mishap couldn't derail Missouri's season.*

*Often the only true guard on the floor, Jon Sundvold carried a heavy load as a sophomore.*

championship. Jon Sundvold, recalling the play, says that Frazier "was the absolute best I have ever seen on the collegiate level at scoring inside 14 feet."

Missouri opened tournament play against eighth-seeded Iowa State and got forty-five points from the bench (Moon McCrary, Ron Jones, and Carl Amos each reached double figures) in a 95–70 victory that advanced the Tigers to the semifinals in Kansas City. But despite a twenty-six-point, nineteen-rebound effort from Curtis Berry, Mizzou fell flat at Kemper Arena, trailing Kansas the entire way in a 75–70 loss.

Still, the NCAA extended an invitation, and the Tigers, seeded ninth in the Midwest, traveled to Austin to face eighth-seeded Lamar, a team they had run out of the Hearnes Center three months earlier. But Lamar slowed the pace and frustrated the Tigers. Curtis Berry scored twenty-one points in a 71–67 loss.

Berry finished his career as MU's number two all-time rebounder and number six scorer. It is never easy to lose such a productive player, but Missouri maintained high hopes for even greater success. Ricky Frazier earned first-team all-conference honors and headlined a group of players, including Sundvold, Stipanovich, and McCrary, that would comprise the foundation for one of the finest seasons Mizzou has ever known.

## 1981–82

This was it, the year above all years, the season in which Missouri broke from the pack and stood shoulder to shoulder with the nation's best. No longer just a regional power, Missouri, for the first time, was rated the top team in America, a true hoops heavyweight.

The Tigers got to the verge of national prominence on the backs of three All-America candidates. They joined the elite by adding role players who gave Frazier,

*Top: Ricky Frazier's clutch jumper beat Kansas State—and clinched the Big Eight crown.*

*Bottom: Curtis Berry capped a brilliant career with a second straight league title.*

Stipanovich, and Sundvold room to shine. Prince Bridges, an electrifying six-foot-one guard, came to Columbia after a year in junior college and relieved Jon Sundvold's ball-handling burden. Michael Walker, another junior college guard, boasted a linebacker's build, which allowed him to mix it up anywhere on the floor. Freshman Greg Cavener provided interior depth, as did Mark Dressler, back from knee surgery. The new arrivals allowed Ricky Frazier to return to his forward position, giving the Tigers a small but quick lineup. Among the starters, only Stipanovich stood taller than six-foot-six.

But more than just the right personnel, the Tigers had the right chemistry, beginning with seniors Frazier and Moon McCrary and trickling down through a roster of players who cared about nothing so much as winning. Cohesive, emotionless, almost cold, the team possessed a disposition akin to Norm Stewart's 1975–76 squad. The very thought of losing offended them.

After beginning the season ranked number sixteen, Mizzou began its assault on the polls. The Tigers topped Illinois in overtime 78–68 as Frazier scored twenty-eight points. In Los Angeles, Mizzou beat both Alabama–Birmingham and Southern California to win a four-team holiday tournament, and Jon Sundvold earned MVP honors with cerebral play that prompted USC coach Stan Morrison to remark, "Sundvold is one of the smartest guys to put on sneakers since Einstein." Then, after the

Point guard Prince Bridges provided the final piece to the best Missouri team in memory.

Marvin "Moon" McCrary menaced opposing offenses.

New Year, Missouri displayed a ruthless precision in a rout of Notre Dame, making twenty-eight of thirty-nine field goal tries and thirty-six of thirty-nine free throws.

By the time Missouri opened conference play against Colorado, the Tigers stood 10–0, ranked fourth, their highest position ever. That day while they manhandled the Buffaloes, second-ranked Virginia and number three Kentucky each lost. When the new polls came out three days later, Missouri sat at number two.

After beating Oklahoma State in Columbia, the Tigers faced a brutal weekend excursion that cemented their new stature. It began on a Saturday night at Nebraska, where Bridges sank a shot at

*"Einstein in Sneakers." Jon Sundvold took his genius-level play up a notch in the 1981–82 season.*

the buzzer to give Missouri a 44–42 win. The Tigers then raced to catch a flight to St. Louis, where they faced Louisville in a noon tip-off on Sunday. It was an accommodation for television as NBC gave the nation its first glimpse of the surging Tigers. Despite the circumstances, Missouri showed no signs of fatigue. Ricky Frazier scored twenty-two points, and Moon McCrary held Louisville star Derek Smith to seven as the Tigers rolled the Cardinals 69–55. While Norm Stewart's club dismantled a perennial national power, television commentator (and Hall of Fame coach) Al McGuire exclaimed, "Gang, Missouri is for real!"

When the new poll came out on January 18, Missouri checked in just behind top-ranked North Carolina for the second straight week. On January 20, the Tigers beat Kansas to run their record to 15–0. A day later, North Carolina fell to Wake Forest. And in Columbia, anticipation grew.

When Oklahoma visited on January 23, the weight of the moment did not faze the Tigers. Before a record crowd of 12,944, Norm Stewart's club stormed the Sooners. Missouri raced to a 14–4 lead, withstood a brief Oklahoma run, then put the game away. As the lead grew to thirty points in the second half, the delirious crowd chanted, "We're number one!" and the Tigers eased to an emphatic 84–64 triumph. Oklahoma coach Billy Tubbs would not dispute the fans' take on Mizzou's standing. "I'd be pretty stupid to say they don't deserve to be number one," he said. "What would the number one team do to us then?"

It became official on January 25. For the first time ever, the Missouri Tigers stood as the nation's top-ranked team. Mizzou's fans had taken time to warm up to big-time basketball, but they finally embraced it. The meeting with Oklahoma marked the first time that the Hearnes Center had been sold out for consecutive games. The national recognition validated a belief that had grown in Mizzou's most ardent supporters throughout Norm Stewart's tenure as coach. Indeed, as they already knew, Missouri was for real.

Still, the Tigers downplayed the ranking, aware that it would mean little without a strong finish to the season. While Norm Stewart acknowledged that "everybody likes a little recognition," Steve Stipanovich was more dismissive. "It's neat," he said, "but really, who cares?"

In their first game as the nation's top-ranked team, the Tigers won easily at Iowa State. Then, at fourteenth-ranked Kansas State, a late Stipanovich dunk sealed a 58–57 triumph. When they returned home to play before their fans for the first time since ascending to the top spot, the Tigers crushed Colorado. Stipanovich, Sundvold, Frazier, and Walker each scored in double figures, with Bridges (nine points), McCrary (eight), Cavener (seven), and Ron Jones (six) close behind. Mizzou's nineteenth straight win to start the season stood as a school record, as did the Tigers' twenty-ninth consecutive win at home. With just seven games to go, the prospect of an undefeated regular season seemed surprisingly plausible.

That is, until Nebraska visited. Before another sellout crowd, Missouri came out flat. The Tigers, who shot poorly, were outrebounded by a smaller team, and Ricky Frazier, a force all season long, scored just six points. After giving credit to an inspired performance by the Huskers, Norm Stewart explained the result succinctly. "We didn't have a good day, and they did."

Mizzou's reign lasted two weeks. The Tigers dropped to fourth in the next poll but resumed their winning ways at Kansas and Oklahoma State. And when they routed Iowa State behind eighteen points from Sundvold, the Tigers advanced their conference record to 11–1 and clinched at least a share of their third straight title.

A record crowd awaited the Tigers at Oklahoma, where they had won only once in their last twenty trips. But Jon Sundvold, unmoved by history, scored twenty-one points, including four late free throws, to lead Missouri to a 60–55 triumph. Again, the Tigers were the undisputed Big Eight champions, but Norm Stewart wasn't ready to celebrate. "We're pleased," he said, "but there's still two games that we have to concentrate on."

The first came at Georgetown's McDonough Arena, a tiny bandbox stuffed with fans eager to see Stipanovich face Patrick Ewing, the Hoyas' freshman center. After Stipo picked up his third foul in

"We're Number One!" Steve Stipanovich's low-post heroics helped Missouri to the top of the national polls for the first time ever.

the first half, the game began to slip away. Ricky Frazier posted twenty-four points and fourteen rebounds, but Georgetown won with relative ease 63–51.

Then, the Tigers returned home and lost by one to Kansas State in the closing seconds. Mizzou moved into the postseason riding the year's first losing streak, but Norm Stewart wasn't worried. "We've had a great year, and we've got a great bunch of guys," he said. "[Kansas State] shot the ball well from the outside in the last few minutes, and that was the difference."

The Tigers turned things around in the conference tournament, advancing to the final, where Ricky Frazier scored twenty-four points in a triumph over Oklahoma—Mizzou's third victory against the Sooners on the year. "We have won the conference [before] and come to Kansas City and not played well," said Jon Sundvold, a member of the all-tournament team, "but we were ready to play tonight." For the first time ever, the Missouri Tigers captured the Big Eight regular season title and postseason tournament championship in the same year. They entered the NCAA Tournament back on stride.

After a first-round bye, second-seeded Missouri met Marquette in the Midwest Region in Tulsa. On a day when jittery ball handling almost sank them, the Tigers rode their front line to victory. Frazier and Stipanovich combined for thirty-nine in a 73–69 victory that advanced them to the regional semifinals in St. Louis. To reach the long-elusive Final Four, Mizzou would need to win just two games before a local crowd.

In the Sweet Sixteen, Missouri faced a tremendous but relatively unknown team from the University of Houston. With players like Rob Williams, Clyde Drexler, and Akeem Olajuwon, the Cougars' anonymity would be short-lived. Houston's big, powerful front-court overwhelmed the smaller Tigers and forced Norm Stewart

*Conference player of the year Ricky Frazier broke John Brown's career scoring record.*

to give extended minutes to Greg Cavener, the six-foot-nine freshman. Down by ten points with 5:30 to play, the resilient Tigers mounted a comeback but could not catch up. Ricky Frazier scored a career-high twenty-nine points in a 79–78 loss. Afterwards, Missouri's players were mad at themselves. Their eighteen turnovers and eighteen-of-thirty-one free throw shooting cost them in a bitter end to a brilliant season.

The Big Eight player of the year, Ricky Frazier, concluded his career as Missouri's all-time leading scorer. From the moment they donned the uniform in 1979, Frazier, Stipanovich, and Sundvold had been the trinity of Missouri basketball, three players intertwined and inseparable from the Tigers' success. After three years of unprecedented achievement, Stipanovich and Sundvold would return, as a duo, hoping to remain the Big Eight's dominant force for one final season.

# 1982–83

Steve Stipanovich and Jon Sundvold entered their final season determined to be the first players to lead a team to four straight Big Eight titles. They began their quest in St. Louis against defending NCAA champion North Carolina. Ranked third, the Tar Heels featured superstars Sam Perkins and Michael Jordan, while Mizzou entered the game short-handed as injuries sidelined Prince Bridges and Michael Walker for several early season games, leaving Sundvold as the only true guard in the lineup.

Despite their personnel issues, the Tigers gave fine efforts on both ends of the floor. Defensively, Greg Cavener contained Perkins, and gritty Ron Jones held Jordan in check. Meanwhile, Stipanovich and Sundvold combined for forty points in a 64–60 triumph that erased any doubts about Missouri's ability to compete without Ricky Frazier.

Over the season's first few weeks, Mizzou reeled off seven straight wins and jumped to number six in the polls. But a loss at the University of Washington preceded a trip to the Rainbow Classic in Honolulu, where the Tigers advanced to the finals and again met North Carolina. The Tar Heels exacted revenge 73–58 as Michael Jordan scored nineteen.

*Three for three. The tremendous trio of Jon Sundvold (20), Steve Stipanovich (center), and Ricky Frazier led the Tigers to their third straight Big Eight championship.*

The Tigers returned home to face North Carolina State, coached by Jim Valvano, and Jon Sundvold scored seventeen in a 49–42 Missouri victory. Southern Cal's Stan Morrison had famously dubbed Sundvold "Einstein in Sneakers." But while Morrison admired the science of Sundvold's game, Valvano was captivated by its art. "Asking if Sundvold is more than a shooter is like asking if Van Gogh is more than a painter," he said after the game.

When Mizzou beat Dayton six days later, Stipanovich supplanted Ricky Frazier as Missouri's top all-time scorer, and the Tigers improved to 12–2. They then began their march to a fourth straight title. In the league opener, Stipanovich scored thirty-two as the Tigers routed eighteenth-ranked Oklahoma State. A week later, Stipo and Sundvold combined for forty-seven points in a win at Kansas, then Sundvold scored twenty-five points—and played fifty minutes—in a double overtime win at Colorado. By the time Missouri visited Iowa State, the Tigers stood 6–0 in the league and number ten in the polls.

Their momentum slowed at Ames. Barry Stevens hit a twenty-footer at the buzzer in overtime to give the Cyclones a 73–72 triumph that ISU

*Ron Jones puts the clamps on the world's greatest player.*

coach Johnny Orr called "the greatest win in Iowa State history." The loss turned Missouri's championship cruise into a horse race. At 6–1 in league play, the Tigers stood just one game up on Oklahoma, their next opponent.

The Sooners had a swagger unlike any other Big Eight team, and they had talent to match it. Wayman Tisdale, a supernaturally gifted freshman center, paired with senior forward David Little to give Oklahoma a sensational frontcourt. But it was coach Billy Tubbs whose brash style set the tone. Confident and unapologetic, the Sooners played at breakneck speed with no qualms about running up scores. When they forced opponents to run, the Sooners rarely lost. But when other teams slowed the tempo, they could get frustrated. After Missouri controlled the pace and won 48–41 at Hearnes early in conference play, Little said, "Wait 'til we get them in Oklahoma."

When the Sooners got the Tigers in Oklahoma, they got more of the same. Tisdale's arrival had given the Sooners visions of toppling Missouri's Big Eight dynasty, but Mizzou's seniors had none of it. Sundvold scored twenty-eight points, and Stipanovich, who scored twenty-six, punctuated an 84–79 overtime victory by dunking over Tisdale in the final seconds. With six conference games to play, Missouri opened up a two-game lead in the standings.

After beating Kansas to creep closer to the title, Missouri stumbled at Oklahoma State. Before closing out the championship, the Tigers took time for a marquee national event.

*Young Missouri broadcasters John Rooney (left) and Bob Costas with Stormin' Norman.*

In 1979 Steve Stipanovich was one of the nation's top high school basketball players. But Ralph Sampson was deemed the best in the country, a once-in-a-generation athlete who, at seven-foot-four, possessed skills unprecedented in a man his size. Stipanovich spent his college career devouring Mizzou's record book, while Sampson became the very face of the game, winning national player of the year honors three times at Virginia. With only about a month left in their college careers, the towering titans met in East Rutherford, New Jersey. Missouri's third game in seventy-two hours, it came just a day after the loss in Stillwater.

Stipanovich immediately knocked Sampson and the fifth-ranked Cavaliers on their heels. He scored sixteen of Missouri's first twenty points, mostly by taking Sampson outside and shooting over him. Mizzou maintained a slim edge well into the second half before fading. Virginia closed the game on an 18–4 run to hand the tired Tigers a 68–53 defeat. Still, the buzz was about the epic confrontation of senior centers. Sampson, dazzling as usual, posted twenty-one points, ten rebounds, and five blocked shots, but Stipanovich bettered him with twenty-seven points, twelve boards, and five blocks. Months later, they would be the top two picks in the NBA draft.

The Tigers returned to conference play with an 88–53 rout of Colorado and closed in on the title with a win at Nebraska. Missouri completed its historic mission in Manhattan. With the game tied at 47 and one second left, Jon Sundvold sank a long jump shot to beat K-State. "When it left my hands," Sundvold said, "I knew it was going in." The notoriously quotable Norm Stewart could barely summon speech. "Jon Sundvold. Great performer, great performer," he said, summing up a single play and an entire career.

With the fourth title under their belts, the Tigers turned to more elusive postseason goals. Mizzou advanced to the finals of the conference tournament against Oklahoma State, which held a 23–6 record. It was a bruising, exhausting affair. Steve Stipanovich received stitches in his lip thanks to an elbow from Leroy Combs, and seven players fouled out of a game that went into two overtimes. Oklahoma State won the battle of attrition 93–92.

*Jon Sundvold's buzzer beater at Kansas State clinched Missouri's unprecedented fourth straight Big Eight championship and cemented the legacy of one of the greatest Tigers of all time.*

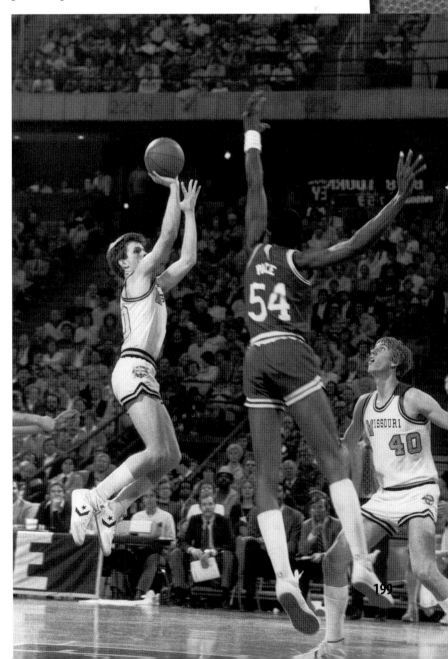

*Stipanovich by the numbers: one hundred wins, four conference titles, graduated number one in career points, rebounds, and blocked shots.*

Despite the loss, the tenth-ranked Tigers received the number two seed in the Midwest Region of the fifty-two-team NCAA Tournament. After a first-round bye, Missouri faced Iowa, with the winner advancing to the regional semifinals in Kansas City. A year earlier, the Tigers had missed an opportunity to march through their home state to the Final Four. They longed for the chance to try again.

Coach Lute Olson's Hawkeyes stifled Missouri in the first half and led 32–20 at intermission. With Steve Stipanovich shackled by foul trouble and Iowa's stifling defense, Mizzou turned to its other senior star. Despite facing a defense designed specifically to stop him, Jon Sundvold backed up and shot over the Hawkeyes. He scored twenty-three second-half points but got too little help. With the outcome decided in the last minute, Sundvold left the game to a standing ovation from the packed house, including thousands of Iowa fans. A remarkable era in Missouri history ended with a 77–63 loss. The disappointment was palpable, but the principals kept stiff upper lips. "It has been a great four years. I wish the season was another week longer," said Stipanovich. Sundvold acknowledged that "making the Final Four would have been nice" but added, "it's not like the end of the world or anything." Norm Stewart's thoughts were with his seniors. "It's a tough way to end the season for these guys who have been so great here. I can't say enough for what these guys have done here."

What those guys did, simply, was to redefine Missouri basketball. Under their leadership, Mizzou won four conference titles and one hundred games. Stipanovich finished number one in school history in scoring, rebounding, and blocked shots. Sundvold set new records for minutes played and free throw percentage and ranked second in scoring and assists. Both again were named first-team all-conference, and they earned consensus second-team All-America honors. Steve Stipanovich and Jon Sundvold remain intertwined in history and in the hearts of Missouri's fans. One kid from the state's eastern border met in the middle with one from the western edge, and together they unified the state, galvanized the program, and became enduring legends of Tiger basketball.

*Top right: From the moment he arrived on campus, Malcolm Thomas was Mizzou's go-to player.*

*Bottom right: With Stipanovich and Sundvold gone, Greg Cavener's role grew.*

## 1983–84

In the span of two seasons, Missouri lost its three all-time leading scorers to graduation with no obvious successors in place. Norm Stewart scrambled to rebuild his team, only to see it fall apart. Four freshmen joined the squad for the 1983–84 season, and none would return as sophomores.

Stewart had greater success with a pair of junior college transfers. Blake Wortham boosted a thin front line, while six-foot-seven forward Malcolm Thomas immediately became Missouri's top player. The national player of the year at Moberly Community College, Thomas made his Division I debut in Greensboro, North Carolina, against Michael Jordan, Sam Perkins, and the top-ranked Tar Heels. The first game of the post–Stipo/Sundvold era shaped up as a hopelessly unfair fight. But the Tigers acquitted themselves with a defensive effort that kept the game close. All five Missouri starters—Thomas, Wortham, Greg Cavener, Prince Bridges, and Ron Jones—scored in double figures in a 64–57 loss that could have been a titanic upset had the Tigers converted at the charity stripe. Missouri made just eleven of twenty-five free throws.

That moral victory preceded a string of real wins, keyed by Thomas, who recorded twenty-five points and thirteen rebounds to help beat Ohio State, and twenty-one points and nine boards in a victory against nineteenth-ranked Michigan State. His chief accomplice was Greg Cavener, who posted sixteen points, ten rebounds, and ten assists in a rout of Wisconsin–Green Bay, the only triple-double by a Tiger in the first century of Missouri basketball.

By the time Big Eight play started, Mizzou stood at 11–3. After falling to Kansas in the league opener, the Tigers beat Nebraska, then edged Iowa State when freshman Cecil Estes hit a twenty-footer just before the final buzzer. At 13–4 overall and 2–1 in conference play, the new era of Missouri basketball had begun more successfully than anyone could have imagined. But success was fleeting.

A rout of Colorado (Thomas scored twenty-eight) was the high point in a low stretch that saw Mizzou lose seven of nine games, then lose its best player. Just three regular season games remained when Norm Stewart dismissed Malcolm Thomas from the team for insubordination after an incident during practice.

Soon thereafter, Stewart commuted the dismissal to a suspension. Thomas was on the bench in street clothes when Mizzou hosted Oklahoma State. Ironically, the Tigers got a rare win in their first game without their leading scorer. Ron Jones drove for the winning bucket with two seconds left in the second overtime and Missouri prevailed 65–64. Afterwards, Stewart addressed Thomas's status, saying that his star player had "made a mistake" and remained indefinitely suspended.

While Thomas watched, Missouri lost twice and finished the regular season with a 5–9 conference mark in a three-way tie for sixth place. Tie-breakers made the Tigers the bottom seed in the tournament, sending them to play at Oklahoma, the nation's sixth-ranked team. Stewart reinstated Thomas, who fouled out while trying to defend Wayman Tisdale. Prince Bridges scored twenty-two points in his last game as a Tiger. Missouri fell 72–66, ending the season at 16–14.

In a transitional year, Mizzou's stranglehold on the conference title was broken and Oklahoma emerged as the league's top power. Between seasons, the team underwent a dramatic transformation. Malcolm Thomas and Greg Cavener remained as the team's anchors, but they would be joined by one of the finest recruiting classes in Norm Stewart's long tenure as Missouri's coach.

## 1984–85

He cut a striking profile, six-feet-seven inches of dramatic angles and long, coiled limbs that bounced to an oddly rhythmic gait. He spoke rarely but memorably, such as when he described the "erotic dunking" he used to impress the girls on the playgrounds of his native New York City or when he explained "face checking," a technique that involved staring into an opponent's eyes and defending with his mind. But no quirk was more famous than his ever-present Band-Aid, worn absent cuts and abrasions.

*A high school All-American from New York City, Derrick Chievous brought great expectations to Columbia.*

A rare character, but Derrick Chievous's basketball skills were rarer still. Effective inside and out and possessing a nearly supernatural ability to get to the free throw line, the high school All-American was born to score.

Fellow newcomers Dan Bingenheimer and Jeff Strong, both junior college transfers, joined Chievous in the starting lineup. Bingo, a six-foot-nine forward, played up front, and Strong, a six-foot-one guard, became a dangerous scorer. Lynn Hardy, a tenacious freshman from Detroit, came off the bench to solidify the backcourt, a role he shared with junior Bill Roundtree, who had seen limited action in his first two years as a Tiger.

Thomas, Cavener, Bingenheimer, Chievous, and Strong made for an unconventional starting five, essentially a shooting guard and four forwards.

The peculiar new lineup fumbled for direction at the beginning of the season and again at the start of the conference schedule.

After starting just 4–5, Mizzou came alive in paradise at the four-team Hawaii Pacific Invitational. Against Arizona, Thomas and Strong, the team's leading scorers, spent the first half on the bench as Norm Stewart tried to coax better effort from them. In their absence, Chievous scored twenty-one first-half points on his way to a game-high thirty-two. Missouri prevailed 76–73, breaking an eight-game road losing streak. Then, in the final, the Tigers shocked seventh-ranked North Carolina. Strong and Thomas, properly motivated, combined for forty-seven points in an 81–76 upset, and Norm Stewart let out a little emotion: "I hope our players are elated, because I sure am."

After finding their groove against heavyweights, the Tigers feasted on lightweights and took a six-game winning streak into conference play, where they would have to find their rhythm all over again. The Tigers lost their first four conference games and narrowly avoided a fifth straight loss when they hosted Oklahoma State. After MU built a twenty-two-point lead, the Cowboys roared back and nearly won when Bill Self released a shot just before the buzzer. It missed, and Missouri survived 66–65.

With that, the Tigers found their stride and began a five-game winning streak that included victories at Kansas State (Strong scored nineteen) and Iowa State (Thomas scored twenty-two), plus a 62–55 triumph over tenth-ranked Kansas. The stretch moved Missouri to 15–9 overall and 5–4 in the league, but the Tigers lost three of their last five regular season games and finished tied for third in the Big Eight.

The Tigers advanced to the semifinals of the conference tournament, where they met league

*Junior college transfer Jeff Strong made an immediate impact.*

Seniors Greg Cavener and Malcolm Thomas led Missouri to the National Invitation Tournament.

champ Oklahoma, the nation's fourth-rated team. Despite twenty-eight points from Chievous, Mizzou lost 104–84, ending any hopes for an NCAA Tournament berth. But the NIT called, and Missouri hosted St. Joseph's in the first round. Plagued by back spasms, Norm Stewart sat at a press table high above the floor, while assistant coach Gary Filbert ran the team from the bench.

*Bingo! Dan Bingenheimer breaks free for two.*

The Tigers trailed by seventeen points at halftime, but they made a huge rally, capped by Cavener's three-point play with just five seconds left. Missouri grabbed a 67–66 edge—its first lead of the game—but fell victim to a controversial finish. St. Joseph's inbounded and put up a desperate shot. As action continued, the final buzzer sounded and a St. Joe's player tipped the ball in. The confused officials looked at each other, then one signaled to count the bucket. Replay showed that the score came late. Nonetheless, St. Joseph's walked off as winners and Missouri's season ended in a moment of disbelief.

Malcolm Thomas, an All–Big Eight choice, finished his two-year career with 1,002 points, while the versatile Greg Cavener wound up in the top five on Missouri's career lists for rebounds, assists, and blocked shots. They kept the team competitive while the Tigers found their bearings in the wake of the great success of the early 1980s. Paced by Chievous, a roster of new faces would soon lead Mizzou to yet more glory.

## 1985-86

A stress fracture in Jeff Strong's right foot sidelined Missouri's top returning scorer for the season's first ten games. While Strong convalesced, Derrick Chievous, Dan Bingenheimer, and Lynn Hardy, along with freshmen Mike Sandbothe (a versatile swingman) and Gary Leonard (an enormous center), formed the team's core. Without Strong, Missouri was ordinary at best and something much less at worst, as shown in a disastrous trip to the Great Alaska Shootout. A blowout loss to top-ranked North Carolina preceded an embarrassing defeat at the hands of Alaska–Anchorage, a Division II school. Strong returned against Illinois, but the Tigers fell by double digits. At 7–4, with few impressive wins, Missouri was headed nowhere until a beach vacation helped salvage the season.

The highlight of the year came in Honolulu at the Rainbow Classic. Missouri opened with a nineteen-point win over Villanova, the defending national champion, as Strong scored sixteen. Next, Chievous scored twenty-four to carry the Tigers past previously undefeated Clemson. After the win, Norm Stewart lauded the play of his starting guards and handed out some uncharacteristically effusive praise. "I had some real good [guards] to complement Willie Smith," he said. "Then I had Jon Sundvold and Larry Drew, and then Sundvold and Prince Bridges, but Jeff Strong and Lynn Hardy complement each other about as well as any I have ever had."

In the final against Washington State, Strong and Hardy fed the Tigers' interior scorers. Dan

*Left: Detroit's Lynn Hardy gave Mizzou a tough, heady presence at the point.*

*Above: Jeff Strong scored one thousand points in just two seasons.*

Bingenheimer, often passive as a junior, became Missouri's top inside threat. Bingo scored twenty-one points and Chievous added twenty as Mizzou took the title. For the second straight year, the Tigers jelled over the holidays in Hawaii, but this time they used the experience as a springboard to more sustained success.

Mizzou maintained momentum on the mainland, winning three straight before conference play. The Tigers won three of their first four Big Eight games to push their record to 16–5, raising hopes for a return to the NCAA Tournament after a two-year absence.

But in the midst of their roll, the schedule turned torturous. In the span of ten days, Missouri faced three teams—Kansas, Memphis State, and Oklahoma—ranked number seven or higher, and lost to all of them. After the third loss, Norm Stewart candidly described his mental state. "I need a psychiatrist," he said. By the time Missouri played a rematch with Kansas, the Tigers had lost five of six and their tournament hopes had faded. The third-ranked Jayhawks did their best to crush whatever hopes remained. In Lawrence, KU pasted the Tigers 100–66 behind twenty-seven points from Danny Manning, the Jayhawks' great sophomore.

The loss dropped Mizzou to 4–5 in conference play as eighth-ranked Oklahoma prepared to visit Columbia. But with a stunning opening flurry, the Tigers took a giant step toward saving their season. Missouri blitzed the Sooners, scoring eighteen of the game's first nineteen points. The burst came largely from Jeff Strong, who scored twenty-nine in the game. Then, after Oklahoma cut the lead to six at halftime, Derrick Chievous took over. He scored twenty-seven of his twenty-nine points in the second half of a 101–88 victory. The win put Missouri's season back on track. It also helped Kansas open up a lead on Oklahoma in the conference standings. "Kind of like helping Satan," quipped Stewart.

Mizzou went on to win three of its next four games, including a 94–86 triumph at Colorado, where Strong, Chievous, Bingenheimer, and Hardy combined for eighty-eight points. The late-season surge lifted Missouri into a three-way for third place and back into NCAA contention.

But those postseason prospects took a blow at the Big Eight Tournament (by then played entirely in Kansas City), where the Tigers lost their first-round meeting with Oklahoma. At 21–13, Mizzou sat on the bubble of the NCAA field, which had grown to sixty-four teams. No more than three Big Eight teams had ever received invitations in the same season, but the league was growing in stature, a fact confirmed when the NCAA extended bids to Missouri, Oklahoma, Kansas, Iowa State, and Nebraska. The Tigers were shipped to the West Region, where they were the eleventh seed.

They met Alabama–Birmingham in a first-round game that went down to the wire. Down by two in the closing seconds, Jeff Strong tried to pass the ball inside to Chievous, but a sea of bodies converged. After a scramble, the ball popped out of the pile. The Tigers watched helplessly as it rolled away and time expired. Strong scored nineteen points in his final game, a 66–64 loss, finishing with an even one thousand for his career. His efforts had helped Missouri return to the NCAA Tournament, a big step forward for the program. But an even bigger step was on the horizon.

## 1986–87

Even after the NCAA appearance, no great expectations greeted the Tigers to start the 1986–87 season. The Tigers did nothing to raise hopes when they muddled through their nonconference schedule, going 10–6 without a single impressive win.

After six weeks of nondescript basketball, the Tigers showed signs of life in the league opener against eleventh-ranked Oklahoma. Missouri led by fifteen midway through the second half before Oklahoma rallied to take a six-point lead with less than three minutes to play. But the Tigers turned steals and clutch free throws into a 13–3 run and captured an 87–83 win.

Derrick Chievous, with thirty-four points and eleven rebounds, narrowly won the head-to-head battle with Sooner Harvey Grant, while Missouri's supporting cast made the difference. Lynn Hardy scored eighteen points, and six-foot-nine freshman Nathan Buntin contributed sixteen.

With that, Missouri was off and running, the surprise team in the Big Eight. A one-point loss at Kansas was the only blemish in the first six conference games, a stretch that saw big scoring performances from Chievous and Buntin. At 5–1, Mizzou stood in a three-way tie with Kansas and Oklahoma at the top of the standings. But just as quickly, the Tigers began to slide back to the pack. After losses to Iowa State and Oklahoma, Mizzou fell behind by two games. But the Tigers were about to impose their will on the rest of the league in a way that no one could have foreseen, beginning with one dramatic play.

On February 11 Kansas visited Columbia, and the score stood tied at 60 with under fifteen seconds to play when Mike Sandbothe took a pass from Chievous under the basket. Before he could shoot, Sandbothe got fouled and fell to the floor, incapacitated by leg cramps. Norm Stewart tapped

*Freshman Nathan Buntin gave the Tigers nearly twelve points per game.*

*As they marched through the league, the Tigers took time to rap their way through "The Cats from Ol' Mizzou."*

reserve guard Devon Rolf to shoot the one-and-one in Sandbothe's place. Rolf missed the first shot, but Greg Church, Missouri's consummate role player, grabbed the rebound and passed the ball out to Lynn Hardy, who swung it to Lee Coward in the corner. Coward, a freshman guard from Detroit, stood behind the three-point line, which was used throughout college basketball for the first time that season. He rose and let fly a shot that splashed home. The capacity crowd erupted as Missouri won 63–60, though it all seemed routine to Coward. "It wasn't hard. I have done that in high school all the time," he said. That same night, Oklahoma lost to Oklahoma State. MU, at 6–3, trailed the Sooners and Jayhawks by one game. The race was on.

Mizzou made strides in its next game, at Oklahoma State, using a 15–4 run in the final five minutes to win 69–68. That same day, Kansas beat OU. At 7–3, Missouri stood tied with Oklahoma, one game back of KU.

Before the Tigers' next game, the race tightened after Kansas lost at Iowa State. When Nebraska visited Columbia, Gary Leonard's fifteen-point, eleven-rebound effort paced Missouri to an 80–64 win and a three-way tie for first with three games to play. The unlikely contenders maintained the tie with a win at Colorado before traveling to Manhattan and taking control of the race.

On a day when Oklahoma lost at Iowa State, Missouri topped Kansas State; late free throws by Buntin and Church sealed an 80–75 win. When Kansas lost the next night at Colorado, Missouri stood alone in first with one game to play, assured at least a share of the championship.

Then, behind twenty-six points and twelve rebounds from Chievous and twenty-two points from Hardy, Mizzou beat Iowa State in the regular-season finale, securing the title outright with an 11–3 record. The Hearnes Center remained packed well past the final buzzer, transformed into a giant dance party. As speakers blared "Kansas City here I come," the Tigers cut down the nets. Norm Stewart was impressed with his young team's chemistry. "It's a good group of people and an interesting blend," he said. "For the most part, this group has been easy to encourage in games."

The Tigers entered the conference tournament as the top seed. At number nineteen in the polls, the champs had earned their first national ranking of the season. They survived an opening-round scare against Colorado, winning a game that was tied late. Before the game, Colorado forward Dan Becker said he had a strong feeling that the Buffs would win. "He

*Icy cool Derrick Chievous led Missouri to a surprising conference title.*

should have had a stronger feeling," quipped Norm Stewart.

In the semifinals against Kansas State, Buntin scored twenty-eight points and MU rallied from twelve down in the second half to win 72–69. After the game, Lon Kruger, K-State's coach, articulated what his peers around the league had begun to understand: "Missouri won the conference because they're tougher than anyone else." Nearly lost in the victory was a remarkable personal milestone. Derrick Chievous scored twenty and surpassed Steve Stipanovich as Missouri's career scoring leader. And he had a full season left to play.

The tourney final provided the rubber match in the season series with Kansas. The game was nasty and physical, even by the rivalry's standards. Early on, KU's Sean Alvarado caught Lynn Hardy with an elbow under the eye, opening a cut that required stitches. Norm Stewart stormed onto the court, where Kansas coach Larry Brown met him for an impromptu and impolite summit meeting. In the second half, some shoving between Mike Sandbothe and Jayhawk Chris Piper evolved into a full-scale scrum as players began to push one another. The entire game crackled with a dark energy. "We were all walking that thin line between competition and combat," said Gary Leonard, who expressed relief that the game wasn't marred by a full-fledged brawl. "We can fight later," he said.

The ending mirrored the earlier meeting in Columbia. With the score tied and less

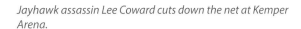

*Jayhawk assassin Lee Coward cuts down the net at Kemper Arena.*

than twenty seconds left, Sandbothe went to the free throw line to shoot a one-and-one. He missed the first shot, and bodies crashed for the rebound. Lynn Hardy grabbed it and found Lee Coward at the free throw line. The ruthless freshman hit the tournament-winning jumper with just four seconds left, an echo of the shot he sank at the Hearnes Center. With regular season and conference tournament trophies in hand, the confident Tigers strutted on to the NCAA Tournament.

Missouri, the number four seed in the Midwest Region, opened against thirteenth-seeded Xavier, a team about to make a big splash. After Mizzou rushed to an 11–4 lead, Xavier awoke. The Musketeers, led by thirteen boards from future NBA forward Tyrone Hill, dominated Mizzou on the glass. Xavier also dominated Missouri at the free throw line, where Byron Larkin converted sixteen shots. Meanwhile, Xavier's defense double-teamed Chievous, limiting him to sixteen points on eleven field goal attempts. The result was a shocking 70–69 loss. The tournament had barely begun and one of the nation's hottest teams was gone. After giving Xavier credit, Norm Stewart said, "We were just flat. Our legs were dead . . . We left part of ourselves in Kansas City."

It was a huge disappointment, but Missouri remained flush with hope for the next season. The entire team would return, including Chievous, who led the conference in scoring and earned spots on the All–Big Eight team and various second- and third-team All-America squads. The veterans would be joined by a talented crop of newcomers, making Mizzou a favorite in the conference and a preseason top-ten team. But things didn't go quite as planned.

## 1987-88

In winning the conference title in 1987, the Missouri Tigers had been greater than the sum of their parts as one star and a roster full of role players found a rare chemistry. In 1988, Mizzou brought all of its championship parts back and augmented them with a pair of emerging stars, but the chemistry vanished.

The missing mojo was obvious early when the Tigers struggled in the Show-Me Classic, a tournament stocked with hand-picked opponents. In the final against Eastern Michigan, Missouri needed a frantic rally to force one overtime and a miraculous coast-to-coast drive by Lynn Hardy to force another. Finally, Lee Coward sank a jump shot that gave the Tigers at 77–75 win, but the game set the tone for the season. Nothing would come easy.

Despite struggling, Missouri won eleven non-conference games, losing only at nationally ranked Memphis State and in St. Louis against Illinois. At home against Virginia Tech, Derrick Chievous scored forty-two points on a night when he became the Big Eight's all-time leader in free throws made. Still, the Tigers toiled to find the right mix of

*Byron Irvin could score from anywhere on the floor.*

players. Junior Byron Irvin, a six-foot-five guard who transferred from Arkansas, became a key cog in the offense, as did Doug Smith, a phenomenal six-foot-ten freshman from Detroit. At the same time, Nathan Buntin's role diminished. More critically, Lynn Hardy suffered a back injury that threatened his season. Norm Stewart was forced to tinker with the previous season's success, and he had little time to find solutions. "It's just not the same each year," Stewart would say later. "You try to get that mesh. But the makeup was an unusual one."

Compounding Stewart's problem was his frustration with Chievous's play. After Mizzou's star senior made just six of twenty shots against Illinois, the coach grumbled, "Chievous played by the postman's creed: I do solemnly swear to shoot and continue shooting until both arms are severed from my body no matter how many men are open." After the Tigers lost their first two games in league play, Stewart put Chievous on the bench to start Missouri's game against tenth-ranked Iowa State. The coach sought a spark but lit a blaze.

By the time Chievous set foot on the floor, Missouri led by twenty. He proceeded to score thirty. Mizzou played at lightning speed, fast-breaking to a 53–21 first-half lead before cruising to a 119–93 triumph. Smith and Irvin scored twenty-six and twenty-four points, respectively, while Buntin, Mike Sandbothe, and Lee Coward all reached double figures. Finally, the machine was firing on all cylinders.

The fire continued over the next three weeks as Missouri won four of five from conference foes, dropping only a 120–101 decision at Oklahoma as Sooner newcomer Stacey King scored forty points. Chievous scored thirty-nine in a rout of Colorado, and he and Coward combined for fifty-one in a 79–75 win that gave Kansas State its first conference loss. The real hero against K-State, though, was a flu-stricken Mike Sandbothe, who checked out of the hospital in time to play and make the game-winning free throws.

*The enigmatic Derrick Chievous scored far more points than any other player in the first one hundred years of Missouri basketball.*

*An injury to Lynn Hardy threatened Mizzou's hopes for back-to-back titles.*

A break from conference play gave Mizzou its stiffest test to date, a trip to Las Vegas to play seventh-ranked UNLV. Consistent with Sin City's sensibilities, UNLV featured a bombastic lineup introduction complete with fireworks—an experience that could rattle visitors. Norm Stewart had none of it, taking his team off the floor before the Rebels could be introduced amid the smoke and thunder. It seemed to work. The composed Tigers led by twelve at halftime. But after UNLV tied the game with just under two minutes to play, apparent disaster struck. Derrick Chievous, who scored twenty-six points, fouled out. UNLV took a one-point lead on a free throw, but the Rebels did not score again. Instead, Byron Irvin took control and sank the decisive free throws in an 81–79 win. "I wanted to come through in a big game situation," Irvin said after the game. "I wanted to prove to my teammates I could do that."

Suddenly, the mercurial Tigers were hot. They entered the national polls at number fifteen and looked like a lock for the NCAA Tournament. And then, inexplicably, they lost traction again. Missouri dropped three of its next four. At 17–8 overall and 6–6 in the Big Eight, Mizzou's momentum had ground to a halt.

But the news wasn't all bad. After missing seventeen games, Lynn Hardy returned for the stretch run, which began at Hearnes against fourth-ranked Oklahoma. Oklahoma entered on a twelve-game win streak, hoping to clinch the conference title. The packed house saw the kind of scintillating game that became the trademark of the Missouri-Oklahoma rivalry in the late 1980s. A three-pointer by OU's Ricky Grace forced overtime, where Chievous and Doug Smith finished tremendous efforts. They combined to score eight of Mizzou's nine points in the extra period and grabbed several key rebounds. Missouri stamped its ticket to the NCAA Tournament with a 93–90 victory, the Tigers' fourth win over a top fifteen team. Chievous's last performance at the Hearnes Center was one of his best—he tallied thirty-five points and eighteen rebounds, while Doug Smith added twenty-one points and eleven boards. Mike Sandbothe, with twelve points and ten rebounds, gave Missouri a third double-double on the day.

True to form, the Tigers followed a sensational win with a loss as they closed out the regular season at Kansas State. Missouri finished fourth in the league and opened the Big Eight tournament against Iowa State. The Tigers won by ten to give Norm Stewart his four hundredth victory at his alma mater.

In the semifinals, Missouri had another epic battle with Oklahoma. Down by fourteen points with eleven minutes to play, the Tigers closed the gap to one point in the last minute. But they couldn't catch the Sooners. Oklahoma prevailed 102–99 as Stacey King scored thirty-five.

*Doug Smith began to dominate as a sophomore.*

Despite the mediocre finish, the Tigers made the NCAA field, grabbing the number six seed in the East Regional, where they faced eleventh-seeded Rhode Island. Mizzou's up-and-down play through the season did little to inspire confidence among Tiger fans, nor did the team's recent tournament history. The Tigers had lost their last four NCAA games, three to lower seeds. The worst fears were realized when Missouri again felt the shock of a first-round exit. Rhode Island guards Tom Garrick and Carlton Owens combined for fifty-four points, and the smaller Rams out-rebounded the Tigers. Derrick Chievous continued his torrid scoring with thirty-five points, but it wasn't enough. Missouri fell 87–80.

Despite the disappointment, Norm Stewart praised his enigmatic senior star. "Derrick Chievous came to Missouri at a time when we were really changing over our program," he said. "We needed a great player like he is . . . He had a great day today."

In the process of leading his team to a conference title and three NCAA Tournament appearances, Chievous scored 2,580 points—far more than anyone else in the program's first century—and pulled down 979 rebounds, then second only to Steve Stipanovich's 984. Still, his tremendous accomplishments drew scant more attention than his peculiar personality. "I really don't know what makes him tick," said Stewart. "He's definitely been different. It's been fun. That's the great thing about college coaching. They're not all just coming off the assembly line."

## 1988–89

There has never been another season like it, none that flirted so closely with triumph and tragedy, none in which such intense pressure collided with such ferocious play. The 1988–89 Tigers played for their own pride, for the integrity of the institution, and for the coach they nearly lost along the way.

The chemistry absent the previous season returned with a vengeance. Byron Irvin emerged as the team's top player, Doug Smith blossomed into a star, and Lee Coward, Gary Leonard, Mike Sandbothe, Greg Church, Nathan Buntin, and freshman Anthony Peeler, a high school All-American with jaw-dropping skills, each played key

*Ultimate role players Mike Sandbothe (left) and Greg Church battle in practice.*

roles. Together, they were selfless, relentless, and unified, as fearless as the coach who guided them.

Early on, the Tigers ravaged lesser teams and ran a gauntlet of national powers. After opening the season ranked number fourteen, they advanced to the semifinals of the preseason NIT in New York, where Byron Irvin scored twenty-one points as Missouri easily handled fifth-ranked North Carolina. In the title game against sixth-rated Syracuse, the Tigers fell in overtime 86–84. Despite the loss, Mizzou vaulted into the top ten. A week later, at a four-team tournament in Charlotte, the Tigers rallied from sixteen points down to force two overtimes against Temple. Irvin scored seven of his thirty-three points in the second extra period as Mizzou buried the Owls. Norm Stewart called the 91–74 result "just your routine seventeen-point double-overtime victory." In the final, the Tigers met North Carolina for the second time in ten days and gave the season's first disappointing performance, turning the ball over twenty-eight times in a 76–60 loss.

Missouri's only other nonleague loss came by three points to fifth-ranked Illinois. The Tigers

completed their nonconference blitz with wins over Arkansas, Memphis State, and Maryland, among others. Mizzou maintained its winning ways into the Big Eight schedule and delivered an emphatic statement in Lawrence. In their first meeting with new Jayhawk coach Roy Williams, the Tigers crushed Kansas. Irvin, Coward, and Peeler scorched KU from the perimeter in a 91–66 triumph, the Jayhawks' worst-ever loss at Allen Field House. Missouri's tenth straight win—and the Tigers' thirteenth-straight game shooting over 50 percent from the field—moved the team to 5–0 in the league. After beating Kansas State to move to 20–3 overall, the Tigers rose to number three in the polls. And then all hell broke loose.

Shortly after arriving at Mizzou in the fall of 1988, P. J. Mays, a freshman from Cincinnati, was ruled ineligible to play basketball. His story was disappointing but unexceptional until assistant coach Bob Sundvold acknowledged lending Mays money for a flight home in an effort to clear up his academic record. The loan violated NCAA rules, and on the evening of February 8, Sundvold was suspended pending investigation. That left the Tigers with just two coaches—Stewart and assistant Rich Daly—as they prepared to play fifth-ranked Oklahoma the next day in Norman.

The team boarded two small charter planes late in the morning. Stewart and Daly traveled with the freshmen and reserves. As the planes neared their destination, Stewart became dizzy and pale, then passed

*Gigantic Gary Leonard anchored the middle.*

out. Daly feared that the coach was having a heart attack. The plane descended into Oklahoma City, and an ambulance took Stewart to a hospital, where he was diagnosed with a bleeding ulcer and kept overnight. While Stewart stayed behind, Rich Daly and a shaken team carried on to Norman. In less than a day, Missouri's coaching staff had dwindled from three to one.

Before a packed Lloyd Noble Center and a national television audience, the Tigers played like nothing had happened. In the late 1980s, Big Eight basketball moved like lightning, and no one played faster than Oklahoma. But the Tigers opened the game at warp speed, scoring on their first four possessions to take an 8–0 lead. Missouri extended the margin to 18–5 before Oklahoma coach Billy Tubbs earned a technical foul. The lead stood at 21–8 when fans began to litter the floor with debris. When the officials asked Tubbs to calm the crowd, the chronically cantankerous coach doused fire with gasoline, taking the microphone and saying, "The referees request that regardless of how terrible the officiating is, do not throw stuff on the floor." Tubbs drew another technical, and the fans gave him their thunderous approval. Byron Irvin made both free throws, but Tubbs's outburst had the desired effect. His fired-up team went on a 28–9 run, and one of the great regular season games played anywhere, ever, was on.

After a 53–53 tie at halftime, the teams sprinted toward triple digits in the second half. Stacey King, Mookie Blaylock, and Tyrone Jones carried Oklahoma, while six Tigers scored in double figures. Players flew up and down the floor, one tremendous play after another, none quite as spectacular as Anthony Peeler's sinister dunk over a thicket of Sooner hands.

Oklahoma led 102–101 with 1:12 to play when Stacey King went to the free throw line. After making his first attempt, he missed the second, but the rebound caromed out of bounds off a Missouri player. Oklahoma inbounded the ball and Mike Sandbothe fouled Skeeter Henry. Henry made his first free throw to give OU a 104–101 lead. He missed his next try, but King snatched the rebound, scored, and was fouled. When he made the ensuing free throw, Oklahoma led 107–101. After scoring five points in a decisive twenty-second span, the Sooners held on to win 112–105. It was a classic game, the drama heightened by the events of the previous twenty-four hours. On a night when Oklahoma would have beaten any team in the country, the Sooners were the only team in the country that could have beaten Missouri.

The next day, the off-court stories continued to develop as NCAA officials met with P. J. Mays's mother, and Norm Stewart was flown home and admitted to Columbia Regional Hospital. But on the court, the Tigers prepared to host Kansas.

Rich Daly's second game as head coach came against Mizzou's greatest rival. It wasn't as easy as it had been in Lawrence, but the result was the same. A record crowd of 13,706 saw the Tigers win 93–80 to move into a first-place tie with Oklahoma. Even as chaos reigned around them, the Tigers maintained their poise.

Byron Irvin's brilliance helped carry Mizzou through a tumultuous and thrilling season.

But then the strain began to show. Norm Stewart's diagnosis proved far more serious than first reported. On Valentine's Day, Stewart underwent surgery for colon cancer. The players learned of the operation shortly before playing at Iowa State, their third game in six strange days. A step slower than normal, the Tigers lost by seven.

It was the start of an erratic stretch. Leonard and Peeler combined for fifty-five points in an easy win over Nebraska, but the Tigers wilted in the final minutes of a loss at Oklahoma State. Then they hosted a rematch with Oklahoma, which had risen to number one in the polls. Missouri trailed by one at the half, when Stewart, who was watching on television, called to tell the team to loosen up and have some fun. The advice worked. The Tigers used a 20–2 run to secure a 97–84 win, led by Irvin (thirty-four points, nine rebounds, six assists) and Peeler (eighteen points, ten rebounds, six assists). It marked the first time Mizzou had ever beaten the nation's top-ranked team.

Four days later in Manhattan, Greg Church played the game of his life, scoring thirty-one points on ten of twelve shooting from the floor and eleven of eleven from the line. But when K-State's Tony Massop tipped in a shot just before the buzzer, the Wildcats won 76–75. Mizzou's play was up and down, and so was the team's attitude as players adjusted to their new circumstances. While Norm Stewart convalesced at home, word got back to him that players were testing Daly's authority. Stewart snuck out of the house and went to the Hearnes Center, where he assembled his team. In terse language, he told them to play basketball and keep their mouths shut. "If Coach Daly asks you to stand on your head and crap through your nose," he said, "you stand on your head and blow." With that, the mutiny was quelled.

Church gave another stellar effort on a senior day he shared with Sandbothe, Leonard, and Irvin. The Hammer scored Mizzou's last thirteen points in a 66–65 win over Colorado that ended the regular season and sent the Tigers to the league tournament as the number two seed.

Al Eberhard, the great player from the 1970s, had joined the team as a temporary assistant

Nathan Buntin hoists the 1989 Big Eight Tournament trophy.

coach, and his influence on Doug Smith became apparent over three days at Kemper Arena. Missouri routed Nebraska in the opening round, and Mike Sandbothe articulated the team's regained focus. "We played a great game together," he said. "Forget about the negative points. Bring out the positive. Let's play basketball."

That's what they did in the semifinal against Kansas State, where Smith scored twenty-two points to lead Mizzou to victory, setting up another match with Oklahoma. Again, the Tigers had no answer for Stacey King, who scored thirty-eight points, but they shackled the rest of the Sooners. Oklahoma, on the other hand, could not stop Byron Irvin (twenty-nine points) or tournament MVP Smith, whose twenty-two points and fourteen rebounds paced Missouri to a 98–86 win and their fourth Big Eight postseason tournament title.

The sixth-ranked Tigers were seeded third in the NCAA Tournament's Midwest Region. If Norm Stewart's cancer and the NCAA investigation did anything positive, it was to ease concerns about Mizzou's recent tournament history. Having withstood so much, the Tigers couldn't be bothered with fear of losing in the opening round. And while they started slowly against fourteenth-seeded Creighton, the Tigers smoked the Blue Jays in the second half to break Missouri's five-game tournament drought. Even after trailing by two at the break, Daly said his mind never wandered to earlier disappointments. "For some reason," he said, "there's a feeling about these players that somewhere along the line, somebody out there is going to start doing it for us." In this case, it was Byron Irvin, who scored twenty of his twenty-five points after intermission in the 85–69 win.

In the second round, Mizzou clobbered Texas 108–89 as Doug Smith scored thirty-two. The victory put the Tigers in the Sweet Sixteen, where they again met Syracuse four months after playing the Orangemen at Madison Square Garden.

Playing in Minneapolis, Mizzou put together a solid effort against a talented squad led by Sherman Douglas and Derrick Coleman. The Tigers led 42–40 at halftime and extended the lead to 47–40 before the wheels temporarily came off. While the Tigers took bad shots, committed fouls, and turned

*Interim head coach Rich Daly shares wisdom with Lee Coward at the NCAA Tournament.*

the ball over, Syracuse went on a shot-making binge and used a 16–2 run to take a 56–49 lead. Try as they might, the Tigers could not reel Syracuse in. Douglas made six free throws in the late stages to fend off Missouri's comeback attempt. The Tigers fell 83–80 to end the most dramatic season in their history.

The loss also ended the most dramatic decade in Mizzou's history, one that produced five conference championships, three conference tournament titles, and eight NCAA Tournament appearances. Never before had the Tigers sustained such a level of excellence over such a long period. Still, questions remained, including whether Mizzou's legendary coach would return to the bench. That question was answered with an emphatic yes at the dawn of yet another decade of championship Missouri Tigers basketball.

As the twentieth century raced to a close, Missouri basketball experienced a complicated, uneven decade with extreme highs and lows both on and off the court. The 1990s gave fans two of the best seasons ever and some of the most disappointing in a generation or more. The decade also gave them the final act of the most storied career in Tiger basketball history.

# THE 1990s

## 1989–90

For decades, glory and heartbreak have been the twin constants of Missouri sports. More than at any other time, those constants collided in 1989–90, a season that began with hope, peaked with triumph, and ended in disbelief.

The previous year's graduations stripped the team of depth, but the returning squad brimmed with talent and reinforced how central the state of Michigan had become to Missouri basketball. Four Detroit Tigers—Doug Smith, Lee Coward, Nathan Buntin, and John McIntyre—started alongside Kansas City, Missouri's, Anthony Peeler, who blossomed into a superstar.

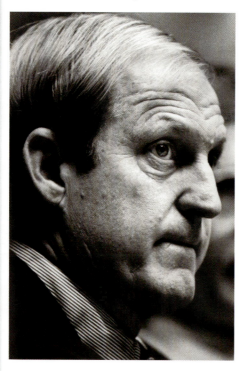

*Norm Stewart added cancer to the long list of opponents he defeated.*

The coach who returned was pretty impressive, too. Rid of cancer but not controversy, Norm Stewart came back fit and on fire. He presided over practice when it commenced in October, but he also faced an intensifying NCAA probe. Still, Stewart's brush with mortality allowed him perspective. "I was just happy to start the season on the right side of the soil," he later said.

With the investigation swirling around them, the Tigers bonded together like strands of carbon fiber, nearly unbreakable, almost unbeatable. They opened at the Maui Classic and made a national statement. Doug Smith scored twenty-four in a semifinal win over twelfth-ranked Louisville. Then, against seventh-ranked North Carolina, he tallied twenty in an 80–73 win that vaulted Mizzou to number five in the polls.

The Tigers continued their torrid start against seventh-rated Arkansas, where senior Nathan Buntin began a personal resurgence with twenty-four points and fifteen rebounds in a game the Tigers won 89–88 on a late jumper by Smith. Afterwards, Norm Stewart praised Buntin's play. "That could be his best game ever," the coach said.

The Tigers, ranked fourth, stood 9–0 when they headed to St. Louis for the annual meeting with fifth-ranked Illinois. The Illini took a 101–93 win, but a confident Norm Stewart shook off the loss. "We don't have to make any excuses," he said. "We're a good basketball team."

Stewart's team rewarded his confidence with a new winning streak. It began at Memphis State, where John McIntyre keyed a decisive rally, and continued through the start of Big Eight play. With a ravaged backcourt, the Tigers hosted Oklahoma State. While Anthony Peeler sat out ill and Lee Coward played through a cracked rib, freshman guard Travis Ford (himself flu-stricken) played thirty-eight minutes, dished seven assists, and iced the game with a steal and a pair of free throws. "It was just a tremendous effort from our guys," said Stewart.

Tremendous efforts—especially from Smith, Buntin, Coward, and Peeler—became the norm. At Nebraska, Smith scored thirty-one points, followed by twenty-nine from Peeler and twenty-one each from Buntin and Coward in a 111–95 victory, the Tigers' sixth straight win. Cornhusker coach Danny Nee was impressed. "I can't see anyone stopping them," he said. Another win over Oklahoma State stretched the streak to seven and set up a historic event.

When the Kansas Jayhawks arrived in Columbia, they stood 19–0, the top-ranked team in the nation. The Tigers, 16–1, were ranked fourth. For more than eight decades, Missouri and Kansas had battled in basketball. The clashes were personal, not just to the players and coaches but to fans, students, and citizens of the states, even ones who had never set foot in Columbia or Lawrence. It was a border battle with an almost nationalistic fervor, but it was, for the most part, locally contained. It mattered very much in the Heart of America but went largely unnoticed in the nation's extremities.

That began to change during Norm Stewart's tenure as coach, when college basketball became a national spectacle as television beamed games from coast to coast and stitched pockets of regional interest into one enormous patchwork. What mattered most, though, was the quality of the teams. Missouri had spent two decades becoming a power program, and never before had the Tigers met Kansas when each possessed such a lofty national reputation.

On Norm Stewart's fifty-fifth birthday, a day when second-ranked Georgetown and number three Oklahoma lost, Mizzou's fantastic four overcame a three-point halftime deficit and thundered past Kansas 95–87. Smith scored twenty-three, Buntin contributed twenty-two, and Coward added twenty. But more than anyone, Anthony Peeler dominated. Despite shooting just five of fifteen from the field, Peeler made all fourteen of his free throws and finished with twenty-four points, nine rebounds, seven assists, and three steals. "He is so talented, it's unbelievable," said Kansas coach Roy Williams. Talented, but also motivated. Having grown up on the border, Peeler understood the game's meaning. "All these Detroit guys told me that there wasn't really a rivalry for them," he said. "I was sitting there thinking, 'It's a big rivalry to me.' I didn't want to go home and have everybody on my case, talking about how they beat us."

For the first time since 1982 and just the second time ever, Mizzou ascended to the top of the national polls, but neither the players nor Norm Stewart made much of it. More than anything, the ranking put a bull's-eye on Missouri's back. The Tigers dodged bullets from Rutgers and Colorado

*Nathan Buntin elevated his play as a senior.*

and narrowly escaped at Iowa State as Peeler took his game into the stratosphere. He scored forty-two points—making all twenty of his foul shots—and grabbed nine rebounds. But it was the last of his five assists that made the difference. With the game tied and just four seconds left, Peeler dished to Travis Ford for the game-winning jumper. Norm Stewart called the 95–93 triumph, Missouri's twentieth win of the season, "a tremendous victory for us."

*Anthony Peeler took his game into the stratosphere and the Tigers to the top of the polls.*

when Missouri seemed to be on the ropes, Anthony Peeler put back an offensive rebound to give the Tigers a two-point lead. They never trailed again. Perfect free throw shooting in the final minutes secured a 77–71 victory. Norm Stewart called the effort a "tough, gutty performance," and Doug Smith added, "It was a great win because it was in the conference, it was against Kansas, and it was in their place." Missouri basketball had never known any greater glory, certainly not in the regular season. Top of the polls, top of the conference, twice knocking Kansas from the number one ranking. Even with the investigation looming, it was a great time to be a Tiger.

With the next poll not yet out, the Tigers remained ranked second when eleventh-rated Oklahoma visited Columbia. The Sooners led 90–89 with less than a minute to play when Doug Smith scored on the inside, got fouled, and sank a free throw, the final points in a 92–90 triumph. The

The win streak reached twelve games before the Tigers had their first bad outing of the year, a 65–58 loss at Kansas State. But they got back on track two days later and buried Nebraska 107–85 as Doug Smith scored forty-four points. "I wanted the ball today," Smith said. "Everything felt right." Nebraska coach Danny Nee called Smith "probably the most mobile 6-foot-10 guy this league has ever seen."

The K-State loss knocked Missouri to number two in the polls and allowed Kansas to regain the top spot. But the schedule gave the Tigers a chance to take it back. Missouri's next game, at Allen Field House, provided the first number one vs. number two meeting in the rivalry's storied history.

The Tigers played their typical game—offensively efficient, defensively aggressive, indifferent to the hostile environment. They built a ten-point lead in the second half, but Kansas caught fire and tied the game with a 10–0 run. Just

*Lee Coward prepares to bury another three-pointer.*

*Big Eight Player of the Year Doug Smith punished opponents all season long.*

win put the Tigers back at the top of the polls, but it brought more bad news than good and saw the start of an epic unraveling.

After three months of being tightly knit, threads started popping, one strand at a time. The first to snap was a bone in Lee Coward's left hand, a fracture that sidelined him for two games. And though the Tigers beat Iowa State 89–85, their effort troubled Norm Stewart. "At this point in the season, we ought to be really ready and get on the court and play better than that," he said.

Coward's absence took a toll on Peeler. Before the injury, Peeler had been like a second point guard, and his 5.8 assists per game on the year established a new MU record. But when Coward broke his hand, Peeler lost his game, struggling to score and handle the ball. In a rematch with Oklahoma, Peeler made just three of sixteen shots from the field, with six turnovers as the Sooners breezed to a 107–90 win. "I don't know if we've lost our stroke or what," said Stewart, "but the last couple of times out, we haven't been on top of our game."

The Tigers found their stroke, or at least enough of it, when they returned to Columbia for the season's last home game. Doug Smith collected twenty-eight points and seventeen rebounds as Missouri clinched the title with a 65–60 win over Kansas State. The Tigers cut down the nets, but not all was well. Coward returned and played twenty-five minutes, but Peeler continued to struggle, scoring just three points. Nonetheless, the team was jubilant. "There's nothing like it," Doug Smith said. "We're the Big Eight champs."

The champs took their number three ranking to South Bend, Indiana, to close the regular season, and controversy followed them. The Tigers' trip coincided with the publication of *Raw Recruits*, which detailed the dark side of recruiting. While the book examined programs across the country, it contained specific claims about Missouri's efforts in Michigan, allegations that Norm Stewart had repeatedly denied. NBC even asked Stewart to discuss the book and its claims at halftime, an invitation he declined.

Amid the controversy, the Tigers crumbled. After his starters lethargically plodded through the first half, Stewart called on the players at the end of the bench to start the second period. Notre Dame pulled away to a 98–67 win, a humiliating result for a team just a week removed from the number one ranking. Asked about his second-half lineup, Stewart said, "A person once told me that everyone deserves a chance to lose."

After closing the regular season with a resounding thud, the Tigers had six days to prepare for the Big Eight Tournament. But pressures intensified and threads continued to fray when NCAA investigators interviewed the coaching staff during the week. Physically fatigued from a long season with a short bench, and mentally distracted by outside issues, the Tigers entered the postseason on a low, even though they held the top seed in Kansas City.

History favored them in the opening round against Colorado; no eight-seed had ever won a game in the tournament. But history came crashing down on Missouri. The Tigers trailed by nine points with sixty-five seconds to play before Doug Smith led a run that forced overtime. For a moment, it appeared that the Tigers had finally shaken out of their slump. But the revival was only temporary. Colorado took a shocking 92–88 victory.

Missouri went reeling into the NCAA Tournament as the third seed in the Southeast Region. There they faced fourteenth-seeded Northern Iowa, and the game followed an all-too-familiar script. The sluggish Tigers trailed by double figures at halftime and struggled to make up ground after intermission. Down 67–55, hope faded when Doug Smith fouled out with under seven minutes to play. But the Tigers mounted a comeback, capped by Nathan Buntin's old-fashioned three-point play, which tied the score with twenty-nine seconds remaining. After a time-out, the Panthers got the ball to guard Maurice Newby in the waning seconds. As Peeler smothered him like a layer of thick smog, Newby heaved the ball toward the basket from twenty-five feet away. It fluttered through the air and then through the net just before time expired. When the buzzer sounded,

Missouri had fallen 74–71, a sledgehammer of a defeat that closed a once-fantastic season in stupefying fashion. Norm Stewart wasn't ready to immediately dissect the loss. "You have to keep things in perspective," he said after the game. "If you want to analyze the situation, you need a little time."

On February 24 Missouri stood 25–2, ranked first in the nation. On March 16 its season ended at 26–6 in round one of the NCAA Tournament. The last strands had finally snapped. But news delivered in the off-season would eclipse even that disappointment.

## 1990–91

On November 8, 1990, after nearly two years of scrutiny, the NCAA Committee on Infractions issued its report on the Missouri basketball program. The committee found several violations, including inappropriate recruiting contacts in Michigan. Penalties included a one-year postseason ban and recruiting restrictions. Norm Stewart bristled at the result, denying some allegations, acknowledging some inadvertent violations, and stressing the program's good faith cooperation with the NCAA. Still, the fallout was harsh. In addition to the NCAA's penalties, assistant coaches Bob Sundvold and Rich Daly tendered their resignations, effective at the end of the 1990–91 season (though Daly later was reinstated after a successful appeal).

That was just part of the bad news, which came in waves. Travis Ford, who would have been Missouri's starting point guard, transferred to Kentucky over the summer, and Anthony Peeler was ruled academically ineligible for the first semester of his junior year. Then, on the day that the NCAA issued its report, freshmen Melvin Booker, Jevon Crudup, and Lamont Frazier were injured in a mishap in their military science class.

Through it all, the constant bright spot was Doug Smith. Smith could have gone to the NBA after his junior season, when he was named Big Eight player of the year and second team All-America. But he stayed, knowing that probation was on the horizon. While others tried to find footing, Doug Smith was the pillar that propped up the program.

*Freshman Jevon Crudup was a rebounding machine until a broken wrist ended his season.*

But he was just one man, and the Tigers struggled through the season's first month, losing four of their first seven games, including one to Arkansas that snapped a record thirty-four-game home winning streak. The Tigers also lost to Illinois for the eighth straight year, despite thirty points and fifteen rebounds from Smith. "Whatever I said for the last eight years, just write that down again," Norm Stewart told reporters. "Just change the names."

Things got better when Peeler returned in late December. In his first game back, Peeler's eleven points, nine rebounds, and six assists complemented Mizzou's dominant inside play as Jevon Crudup scored twenty-four points in an easy victory over Grambling. It began a surprising seven-game winning streak that included MU's first three conference contests.

The first league victory came in Columbia against Oklahoma State. Cowboy Byron Houston tallied thirty points and fifteen rebounds, but Doug Smith countered with forty and fourteen, making

him the first Tiger ever to score forty points in a game twice in a career. Freshman guard Melvin Booker hit the game-winning shot in an 80–79 overtime thriller.

After the streak, the Tigers temporarily lost their way. Jevon Crudup, who had started all fifteen games, was lost for the year when he broke his wrist in a lopsided loss at Kansas. Things got worse when a knee injury shelved Peeler in defeats at Nebraska and Oklahoma. Doug Smith recorded twenty-seven points and sixteen rebounds in an overtime win at Colorado, but after losses to Kansas and Oklahoma State, Mizzou stood just 5–5 in conference play.

But then Missouri caught fire. Peeler scored thirty in a rout of fourteenth-ranked Nebraska. "If it wasn't our best game of the year," said Norm Stewart, "it was awfully close." Doug Smith, with twenty-two points, became only the second Tiger to surpass two thousand points for his career. He also moved past Steve Stipanovich to become Missouri's all-time leading rebounder.

The Tigers lost at Iowa State before mounting a historic charge. At Kansas State, sophomore center Chris Heller scored eighteen in an 84–75 win, and Doug Smith grabbed career rebound number one thousand, making him the third player in Big Eight history with two thousand points and one thousand boards, joining Wayman Tisdale and Danny Manning. Missouri closed the conference slate by routing Colorado as Smith collected twenty-three points and thirteen rebounds and Jamal Coleman, a war horse in Crudup's absence, added fourteen points and fifteen boards.

Next came revenge. A year after being humiliated at Notre Dame, Missouri hosted the Irish and returned the favor. Anthony Peeler scored twenty-five points in an 84–54 demolition, Doug Smith's

*Anthony Peeler's return started the Tigers on a roll.*

*Doug Smith's jersey was retired after his last game at the Hearnes Center, but he still had one more championship to bring home.*

last appearance at the Hearnes Center. Smith, who scored thirteen points and recorded a career-high nine assists, stood at midcourt after the game and watched his number thirty-four jersey ascend to the rafters. As fans saluted Smith, Norm Stewart reminisced. "What can you say about Doug Smith that hasn't already been said?" the coach asked. "He played a great game, and it was a great way for him to finish his career."

Mizzou went into the Big Eight Tournament on a roll, but the Tigers' presence irked some around the league. The tournament title came with an automatic bid to the NCAA field, but Missouri was ineligible for postseason play due to probation. If the Tigers could win, they might prevent an eligible team from advancing to the NCAAs.

After a cakewalk in round one against Iowa State, the Tigers walked a tightrope in the semifinals. Top-seeded Oklahoma State rallied from sixteen points down to force two overtimes. But Missouri endured in a 94–92 victory as Doug Smith played forty-six minutes on his way to twenty-nine points and ten rebounds.

The final pitted Missouri against thirteenth-ranked Nebraska. Late scores by Jamal Coleman opened up a decisive lead in a 90–82 victory. Peeler posted eighteen points, eleven rebounds, and eight assists and earned a spot on the all-tournament team. But the story of the weekend—and the season—was Doug Smith, whose thirty-one points helped him set records for scoring in a single tournament (ninety-two points) and in a career (207). Smith's play reflected the urgency he felt. "I knew this would be my last chance to play with my teammates," he said, "and I didn't want to go out with a loss." For Norm Stewart and the program, the victory was cathartic. "To have all the things that have gone on with us this season and still do this well [is] just very, very special," said the coach. True to their character, the Tigers played best when it was personal.

Fittingly, Doug Smith went out a winner, leaving a legacy among the very best in Missouri basketball history. The conference player of the year for the second straight season, Smith left Columbia as Missouri's all-time leading rebounder. He also stood number two in points scored, blocked shots, and steals and number eight in assists. Doug Smith may have grown up in Michigan, but in four scintillating years he proved to be a true son of old Mizzou.

## 1991–92

Unburdened by probation or expectations, Missouri entered the 1991–92 season with little to lose. With Doug Smith gone, the team consisted of Anthony Peeler and a group of relatively inexperienced teammates. Chris Heller's broken foot, which allowed him to play just a few minutes early in the season, contributed to the low expectations and exposed Missouri's paltry depth. Only seven Tigers would play many minutes, and of those seven, only Jeff Warren and Jevon Crudup stood over six-foot-five.

Mizzou's circumstances made the team's start all the more surprising. Entering the season unranked for the first time in five years, the Tigers went on a tear, winning their first eleven games, including one at eleventh-ranked Arkansas, where Peeler's thirty-two points led Missouri to an 87–76 victory. The Tigers also broke an eight-game losing streak against

*Sophomore Melvin Booker earned the league player of week award in February, the first of many honors.*

Illinois, prompting a playful Norm Stewart to declare, "Golly, there're no hills left to climb."

The winning streak ended at Memphis State, then the Tigers fell at home, in overtime, against sixth-ranked Kansas. But they regrouped and won seven of their next eight, including Mizzou's first win at Oklahoma since 1983 as Melvin Booker scored twenty-four points on his way to conference player of the week honors. When Peeler posted thirty-four points, eight rebounds, and seven steals in a rout of Nebraska, Missouri moved to 18–3 and solidified a spot in the top ten.

After getting humbled at Colorado, Mizzou bounced back to beat eighth-ranked Oklahoma State behind nineteen points from Jevon Crudup and eighteen from Jamal Coleman. The unassuming Tigers leaped to number six in the polls, then hit their high-water mark at Iowa State, where a 75–71 win lifted them to 20–4 overall. Jeff Warren scored twenty on ten-of-eleven field goal shooting, but the news was more bad than good. Coleman sprained his knee in the victory, a terrible blow for a reed-thin roster.

At Kansas State, the Tigers, minus Coleman, lost a game that was tied in the final minute. Coleman returned at home against Oklahoma but aggravated his injury in the first half. Though Jeff Warren made all ten of his shots from the field, the Sooners rolled 81–67. Anthony Peeler, who had previously experienced only three home losses in a four-year career, was shocked. "We got blasted at home," he said. "I never thought it could happen like this."

Still without Coleman, the Tigers closed the regular season at third-ranked Kansas. The Jayhawks held a big lead well into the second half and seemed poised to run away from the depleted Tigers. Then Peeler, in an effort recalling Willie Smith's performance against Michigan in the 1976 NCAA Tournament, put on a show for the ages. With under eight minutes to play, Missouri trailed 78–64, and Peeler led all scorers with twenty-four points. But he was just getting started. With the game all but out of reach, Peeler reeled Kansas in. He turned steals into dunks and carved up Kansas with his blinding speed. But more than anything, he put up shots with little conscience or consciousness and ripped the nets time after time. Peeler scored nineteen points down the stretch, the last nine on three successive three-pointers that cut KU's lead to 91–89 with forty-five seconds left. But Missouri could come no closer. Kansas converted free throws to win 97–89, but Peeler's forty-three-point performance was the story of the day. "He was unconscious," said Jayhawk Alonzo Jamison. Norm Stewart was proud in defeat. "Our effort was tremendous," he said.

Unfortunately, Peeler's heroic effort gave the Tigers no momentum in the conference tournament, where they lost to Iowa State in the first round. But Missouri was one of six Big Eight squads invited to the NCAA Tournament, a record for the league. Only Kansas State (which went to the NIT) and Colorado were left out.

Seeded fifth in the East Region, the Tigers traveled to Greensboro, North Carolina, where they met West Virginia in the midst of an apocalyptic thunderstorm. Lightning strikes knocked power out three times, resulting in long delays. With so little depth, the rest benefited Missouri, which won 89–78. Peeler led the way with twenty-five points, and Jevon Crudup, a second-team all-conference pick, chipped in eighteen, as did Jamal Coleman, back from injury.

The Tigers faced Seton Hall in the second round, but it was the end of the line. The Pirates

*Top: Jamal Coleman played like a warrior until a knee injury jeopardized his – and Missouri's – season.*

*Bottom: Conference player of the year Anthony Peeler did everything for the Tigers.*

*Melvin Booker (15) missed the dunk, but Lamont Frazier (22) cleaned up with authority.*

won 88–71. Anthony Peeler, the Big Eight player of the year, scored twenty-eight points to finish his career, but he was in no mood for reflection. "It probably hasn't hit me yet," he said, disappointed. "Right now I'm just thinking about what we could have done and what we should have done and what we didn't do" in the tournament.

In truth, there was little more Peeler could do. Among the most gifted performers in the first century of Missouri basketball, Peeler gave his all in his senior campaign. He finished his career as the Tigers' number three all-time scorer and established new records for assists and steals. A rare combination of explosive athleticism and hard-wired basketball instincts, the kid from Kansas City electrified fans through four spectacular seasons and left Mizzou as one of the best ever to wear the uniform.

## 1992–93

No names, no problem. Without a marquee player like Doug Smith or Anthony Peeler, Missouri fielded a fairly faceless squad that spent the season's first two months building a reputation. After the Tigers beat Illinois to give Norm Stewart his five hundredth win as Missouri's coach, Jevon Crudup recorded twenty-one points and eleven rebounds in a conference-opening win at Colorado, and Melvin Booker scored twenty in a victory over Oklahoma State that moved Mizzou to 12–4 overall and 3–0 in league play.

Following an overtime loss at Nebraska and a drubbing at Kansas, the Tigers bounced back with a double-digit win over nationally ranked Kansas State as Booker scored nineteen. At 4–2 in the league, Missouri looked like a title contender. But then the trap door fell open.

For the first time in nineteen years, MU lost seven straight games, some in agonizing fashion. In Stillwater, Jevon Crudup hit a three-pointer with four seconds left, giving Missouri a three-point lead and virtually assuring victory. But Bryant Reeves, Oklahoma State's seven-foot center, took an inbounds pass at half-court and launched a prayer. The ball bounced off the backboard and through

the net, forcing overtime. The Cowboys went on to win by four. Three days later at the Hearnes Center, Mizzou led Oklahoma by seven late in the game. But Oklahoma closed on an 8–0 run to win by one point. Night in, night out, the Tigers found new ways to lose.

The streak came to an end in the regular season finale, a 70–53 win over Colorado as Mark Atkins, a mad-bombing junior guard, scored eighteen on six-of-sixteen three-point shooting. Still, at 16–13 overall and 5–9 in the conference, Missouri entered the Big Eight Tournament as the seventh seed. Once there, though, Mizzou dished out some déjà vu to the league.

In 1978 the seventh-seeded Tigers won the tournament behind the inspired play of Stan Ray, a center who had struggled throughout the season. Fifteen years later, Chris Heller filled Ray's role. Heller, a six-foot-ten post player, had endured a frustrating season. But when the Tigers got to Kemper Arena, Heller and his teammates let it all hang out. "We had nothing to lose," he later said. "Everybody was loose." Heller began to find his game in a first-round rout of Oklahoma State. With twelve points and eight rebounds, he outplayed Bryant Reeves. But Heller was just one of three unlikely suspects to lead the Tigers to their 81–62 victory. Reggie Smith scored a career-high fifteen points to go with six assists, and Mark Atkins made four of seven three-pointers on his way to twenty points. "It was an alarm clock, and everyone woke up at the same time," said Smith.

Heller continued his stellar play in the semifinal against Iowa State, posting twenty points and seven rebounds in a 67–63 victory that propelled the Tigers into the final. "He's really showing some spunk," Norm Stewart said of Heller.

The Tigers caught a break when Kansas State upset league champ Kansas in the other semifinal. The Wildcats, with a bench even shorter than Mizzou's, relied almost exclusively on six players during the three-day tournament. And when the last five minutes of the game came around, Missouri was able to kick into a gear that K-State simply did not have. The Tigers took a 68–56 win that gave them a berth in the NCAA bracket. Heller, the tournament MVP, produced a modest nine points and six rebounds on a day when the Tigers got a balanced

effort from their top seven players. They also got motivation from Norm Stewart, who instilled belief in a team that had every reason to doubt itself. "We always tell our players that they can make things happen that other people don't think about," Stewart said, savoring victory. Years later,

*Top: Chris Heller wrote himself into Missouri lore with his effort at the 1993 Big Eight Tournament.*

*Bottom: For his career, Jeff Warren made 61.4 percent of his field goal attempts, a Missouri record.*

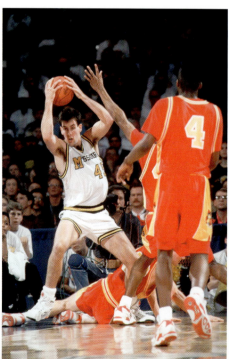

reflecting on the title run, Chris Heller stressed the team's achievement but admitted being pleased with his performance. "I felt good," he said, "because for three days I showed what I could do."

Seeded tenth in the NCAA's West Region, the Tigers opened against Temple, which employed a fierce match-up zone defense unlike anything Missouri had seen all year. Frustrated by the pressure, the Tigers turned the ball over twenty-two times. Despite Heller's twelve points and twelve rebounds, Mizzou fell 75–61. After the high of the Big Eight Tournament title, Missouri's lackluster performance was "like putting an olive on a dip of ice cream," said Norm Stewart. The bitter taste carried over briefly into the next season, but it quickly turned into a bowl of cherries.

## 1993–94

On the heels of a disappointing season redeemed only by a surprising run through the conference tournament, the Tigers began the year like a team hell-bent for last place. No one could have known that they would become one of the most accomplished teams in Missouri's modern history.

Mizzou opened against Central Missouri State, a Division II opponent, and the only bright spot was Kelly Thames, a freshman from Jennings High in St. Louis, who debuted with nineteen points and twelve rebounds. A game that should have been a laugher was a nail-biter to the end, and Missouri escaped with a 69–66 win, but that was nothing compared with what came next.

The Tigers traveled to Fayetteville, Arkansas, where they had won five straight times, but the setting they encountered was brand new. Mizzou faced the second-ranked Razorbacks in the dedication game for palatial Bud Walton Arena. With thousands in attendance, a national audience watching on ESPN, and the emotion of the occasion on their side, the Hogs gave Missouri an unprecedented beating. Arkansas was famous for its "Forty Minutes of Hell" defense, but the soul-scorching torture seemed to last much, much longer. With frenzied, turnover-producing pressure and lights-out three-point shooting, Arkansas poured it on from the opening bell to the final buzzer. The

*Lamont Frazier's "out-of-body experience" helped resurrect a season headed nowhere.*

score was 45–22 at half-time, and it kept getting worse. Scotty Thurman led seven Razorbacks in double figures, and Arkansas thundered to a 120–68 victory. Melvin Booker cringed at the realization that his family had watched on television. "I'm scared to call home and talk to my parents," he said.

The Tigers tried to put the night behind them, and though they won four straight games at home, they hardly covered themselves in glory, scrambling to beat the likes of Jackson State and Coppin State. When the Tigers traveled to St. Louis for the annual skirmish with Illinois, they may have been the least impressive 5–1 team in history. But history was about to take a stunning turn.

It didn't shape up as much of a contest, the struggling Tigers against the nationally ranked Illini in the final Braggin' Rights meeting at the old St. Louis Arena. But midway through the second half, the Tigers held a 61–48 edge. Then things got interesting. An Illinois rally keyed by guards Richard Keene and Kiwane Garris nearly finished off the Tigers as Jevon Crudup fouled out. With less than a minute to play, the Illini led 75–68. Then came the first in a series of miracles. Mark Atkins and Melvin Booker each hit shots to narrow the gap, and Lamont Frazier sank a three-pointer with four seconds left to tie the score at 79–79. Frazier later called the shot "an out-of-body experience."

In overtime, Atkins and Marlo Finner joined Crudup on the bench with five fouls apiece, and with forty-three seconds to play, the Tigers trailed by five. But late baskets by Kelly Thames helped forge an 88–88 tie and force a second overtime, where the game became the stuff of legend.

The Tigers didn't need another miraculous comeback, but they did need another miracle. With the score tied at 97–97 and the clock ticking down, Kiwane Garris drove to the basket. As time

*Paul O'Liney walked out of the mist and on to the floor for the Tigers.*

expired, the officials called a foul on Mizzou's Julian Winfield, his fifth. With no time left, Garris went to the line to shoot two, needing only one to give Illinois the win. "The only guy who didn't think the game was over was Coach Stewart," Lamont Frazier later said of the man who stood at midcourt berating the refs as Garris took the ball.

Garris, a freshman, had been sensational—he scored thirty-one points in the game—but he had never been in such a spot. He stepped to the line, the lane vacant, the other players reduced to spectators. Garris entered the game shooting 94 percent from the line, but as he stood there, nerves shot and legs spent, the basket might as well have been fifty feet away. He focused on the hoop. He breathed in and out. He put up his first shot. It hit the rim and bounced away. There were shrieks, moans, cheers. And then all of the air was sucked out of the building as Garris prepared to shoot again, feeling pressure like never before. He squared up and released. But after so much fight, the radar was gone. The ball bounced away harmlessly. On to a third overtime.

With four Tigers already fouled out, Missouri turned to Jason Sutherland and Derek Grimm, freshmen who had barely played to date. Inexperienced but fearless, Sutherland opened the third overtime with a three-pointer, and the Tigers never looked back. Melvin Booker, who finished with twenty-one points and a school-record thirteen assists, fouled out after playing fifty-two minutes and was replaced by Reggie Smith, forced into action after missing three weeks with a badly sprained ankle. But it was another senior, Lamont Frazier, who finally put the game away. He hit a series of free throws in the final five minutes, including two with 3.8 seconds to play to give Missouri a four-point edge. A three-pointer by Garris at the buzzer made no difference. Missouri won 108–107, and the Tiger players milled about in a euphoric mix of jubilation and exhaustion. Norm Stewart, as tired as his team, was just glad the game didn't last any longer. "We had the wounded in there," said the coach. "I guess the women and children would have been next."

One game changed an entire season. It inspired confidence by showing that every man on the roster could be counted on, and it proved what was possible through sheer tenacity. Frazier, who finished with twenty points, says simply, "It was always there. Illinois just brought it out."

The awakening was immediate. Over the next two weeks, the Tigers beat a series of nonconference opponents by lopsided scores and blistered Kansas State by twenty in the league opener. They also got a boost between semesters when a new player emerged from the mist. Paul O'Liney, a broad-shouldered scorer, had led his team to the junior college national championship the year before. He famously remarked that he had watched the debacle at Arkansas and figured he could help. O'Liney walked on to the team and became Missouri's sixth man, providing instant offense off the bench.

Though Mizzou produced a lackluster effort in a four-point loss at Notre Dame, the Tigers quickly regrouped and turned their attention toward dominating the Big Eight. Missouri slowly built up steam. Some nights, the Tigers overwhelmed opponents. They beat Iowa State by twenty-three in Columbia, and Nebraska by sixteen in Lincoln, and they used a second-half spurt to run away from third-ranked Kansas at the Hearnes Center. But on other nights, they employed a rare resourcefulness to pull out impossible wins. It was a trait borne of experience. Not only did the team have eight seniors—Booker, Crudup, Frazier, Heller, Smith, Atkins, and reserves Jed Frost and Derek Dunham—it was battle-tested. The Tigers' resiliency was displayed most vividly against Illinois, and assistant coach Kim Anderson says that the struggles the team endured the previous season paid dividends.

*Freshman Kelly Thames blended seamlessly into a veteran team.*

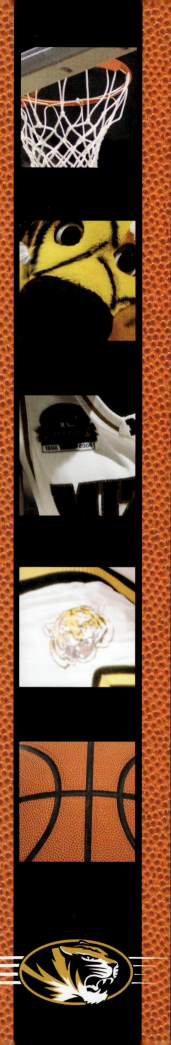

In the process of losing a succession of heartbreakers, the Tigers learned how small the difference between victory and defeat can be. Having seen every little thing go wrong, the Tigers were determined to make every small detail go right.

The first example came at Oklahoma State, where Mizzou trailed by fifteen in the second half. Jevon Crudup and massive Bryant Reeves pummeled one another in the post, but Crudup never wore down. While Mark Atkins and Paul O'Liney used fresh legs to give Missouri energy, Crudup led a surge with offensive rebounds and point-blank scores. In the end, the Tigers won 73–68, completing a twenty-point turnaround.

At Oklahoma, Mizzou scored on its last ten possessions to turn an 89–89 tie into a 104–94 win as Crudup recorded twenty-five points and fifteen rebounds. Sooner coach Billy Tubbs, incredulous after watching the newest Tiger score twenty points off the bench, sarcastically called O'Liney "a nice walk-on." Even when they played poorly, the Tigers proved resilient. Kelly Thames posted twenty-four points and twelve rebounds in a 79–72 overtime victory at Iowa State that moved Missouri to 10–0 in the league. Melvin Booker admitted, "We were flat," and Norm Stewart said, "I don't think we had it together tonight, but somehow we found a way to win."

By the time of that victory, whispers about a perfect 14–0 record in conference play had grown to a low roar. The feat had been accomplished only twice in Big Eight history (by Kansas State in 1959 and Kansas in 1971). For any Missouri team, the season's biggest test is the trip to Lawrence, and that's the obstacle the Tigers faced as they tried to move to 11–0.

Throughout the year, Melvin Booker had been Missouri's best player. At Kansas, he made a case for being the best in the league. Mizzou trailed by eight points with less than nine minutes to play when Booker took over. He scored ten points in a ninety-second span to bring MU even with the fourth-ranked Jayhawks. Then he kept scoring. Seventeen of Booker's thirty-two points came down the stretch of an 81–74 win that clinched at least a share of the conference title. After the game, Norm Stewart focused on the total team effort. "We dug ourselves a hole, and everyone had a part in getting us out," he said. But Kansas coach Roy Williams praised the kid from Moss Point, Mississippi, who had come to Missouri as an unheralded recruit less than four years earlier. "Melvin Booker was sensational," Williams said. "All those recruiting experts, it shows how much those guys know."

The Tigers clinched the title outright at home with a win over Oklahoma as O'Liney and Atkins

*With his granite physique and fearsome scowl, Jevon Crudup made for an intimidating presence.*

*Melvin Booker accepts his Big Eight Player of the Year trophy.*

combined for forty-six points. But the team, which had taken on a cold, businesslike demeanor, did not celebrate. "Coach said no net-cutting," Booker remarked. "It shows how serious coach is about it, how bad he wants it. Ain't no celebration going on here until we get to the NCAA." A week later, the Tigers beat Kansas State to move to 13–0 in the league, and Norm Stewart finally joined in the talk about a perfect record. "I want the players to have that," he said.

Missouri's last regular season contest was among the most highly anticipated games in Hearnes history. The Tigers hosted a surging Nebraska team, winners of three straight, including two over ranked opponents. The Huskers featured the long-range marksmanship of Eric Piatkowski, one of the league's top players.

Before a rambunctious overflow crowd, the Tigers played with their characteristic intensity but without their typical offensive efficiency. The score was close throughout, but when Nebraska opened up a three-point lead with one minute to play, Missouri drew on the resourcefulness that had sustained the team throughout the season.

Melvin Booker closed the gap to 78–77 with a jump shot. Then Piatkowski missed a baseline jumper with half a minute to play. Kelly Thames broke from the pack with the ball and had a clear path to the bucket until Piatkowski caught him and committed an intentional foul, giving Mizzou two free throws and the ball.

Thames, a 73 percent foul shooter, had a chance to give Missouri the lead. But he missed both shots, and the Tigers had the ball, down by one, with twenty-six seconds left. With seventeen seconds on the clock, Melvin Booker launched a leaner from the wing. As the shot caromed in, Booker crashed into Nebraska's Erick Strickland. One official called a block on Strickland, while another pointed to Booker for charging. The refs caucused and then compromised, rendering a decision that made little sense. They tagged both Booker and Strickland with fouls, waved the basket off, and gave the ball to Missouri thanks to the possession arrow.

Mizzou again got the ball to Booker, who flashed into the lane and knocked down another jump shot with twelve seconds remaining. Fouled on the play, Booker hit the free throw to give Missouri an 80–78 lead.

The Tigers stood twelve seconds from perfection, seeming to need only one defensive stop, but, in fact, needing one last miracle. With a deafening din inside Hearnes, Missouri's defense smothered the Huskers. As the clock ticked toward zero, the ball was forced way outside to Eric Piatkowski, who already had scored twenty-six. He squared and fired a three-point try from nearly thirty feet away. The ball traveled a perfect arc, right at the hoop, as the final buzzer sounded. It entered the rim, and for an instant, Nebraska had crushed the dream of the perfect season. More than thirteen thousand people gasped in unison. Then, inexplicably, impossibly, the ball popped out of the basket and fell to the floor. A momentary hush preceded delirium as the crowd exploded and players embraced. The finish seemed to provide evidence of a higher power. "Somebody tipped it out. I don't know who. But I want to thank him," said Melvin Booker, who had erased any doubt about the identity of the league's player of the year. "I thought it was fate," says Kim Anderson. And at a moment when most simply felt relief, Norm Stewart beamed. "I'm really proud of this group," he said. "This is a special team."

Three months after losing a game by fifty-two points, Missouri stood 24–2 on the year, 14–0 in the league, conference champions, the nation's third-ranked team. Unshakeable, unsinkable, nearly unbeatable, the Missouri Tigers achieved the impossible with a modicum of talent and monstrous amount of grit. They took on their coach's personality—stubborn, resilient, never giving a thought to losing—and became the very picture of mental toughness and competitive fire.

After the regular season achievement, with a high seed in the NCAA's assured, the Big Eight Tournament felt a bit anti-climactic, a feeling reflected in Missouri's play. In the opening round, the Tigers escaped with a 64–62 win over lowly Colorado, and in the semifinal, Nebraska got its revenge. The 98–91 loss ended Missouri's epic winning streak, but the Tigers were unfazed as they set their sights on the NCAA Tournament. "I'd rather lose before I go into the big dance," said Booker. "You lose here, and then you get back down to earth."

Rewarded with a number one seed for the first time ever, the Tigers were shipped to the West Region, where they opened play in Ogden, Utah, against Navy. In the first half, the Tigers' sluggish play continued, and they trailed the Midshipmen much of the way. With just under six minutes to go before the break, Norm Stewart replaced his starters with reserves from the far end of the bench. The move shook the Tigers back to life. Jevon Crudup tallied nineteen points and twelve rebounds as Missouri regained its edge in a 76–53 win.

Mizzou maintained its edge in the second round against Wisconsin, which featured the inside-outside combination of Rashard Griffith and Michael Finley. But Griffith languished in foul trouble, thanks in part to Tiger reserve Marlo Finner, who scored thirteen in the first half, and Missouri put on an explosive offensive show. The Tigers shot 68 percent from the floor and blew past the Badgers. Melvin Booker hit eleven of fourteen field goal attempts, plus all seven of his free throws to finish with thirty-five points. Missouri led by as many as twenty points in the second half before easing to a 109–96 victory. "We're back to ourselves," said Booker.

Back to themselves, and back to the Sweet Sixteen for the first time in five years, Missouri met fourth-seeded Syracuse. On a Thursday night in Los Angeles, Missouri looked like a number one seed for thirty-five minutes, leading by eleven points with five minutes to go, but a Herculean effort by Syracuse's Adrian Autry—he scored thirty-one points, all after halftime—forced overtime. That's when the Tigers made another typical stand. Booker opened the extra period with a three-pointer, and Frazier finished off the Orangemen with a long pass to O'Liney for an easy bucket. Missouri's 98–88 win put the Tigers in a regional final for the first time since 1976, on the precipice of their first Final Four ever.

Sadly, it was not to be. Against second-seeded Arizona and its powerhouse backcourt of Damon Stoudamire and Khalid Reeves, Missouri had its worst day since the trip to Fayetteville. The Tigers struggled from the field and flailed fruitlessly from three-point range, making just seven of thirty-three treys. The 92–72 loss awoke the Tigers from a long dream of a season and ended the careers of the seniors who dominated Missouri's roster. Melvin Booker spoke for the entire senior class when he expressed their disappointment at missing the Final Four, and his words spoke volumes about their character. "We came here on probation. We were trying to do it for everybody, the state of Missouri, the University," he said. "That would have been a great thing. First time in school history. But we came up a little short."

In truth, the Tigers came up huge, greater than anyone could have imagined. Booker and his overachieving colleagues became a team for all time, a source of pride for Mizzou fans everywhere, and a tribute to the coach who guided the team out of probation and back to national prominence.

*Versatile Julian Winfield filled many roles for the Tigers.*

# 1994–95

No other season is remembered for such a short span of time. After four months of overcoming obstacles, defying expectations, and nearly turning all of college basketball on its ear, the entire campaign was defined by its very last moment, the most heartbreaking 4.8 seconds in the history of Missouri sports.

When it began in November, there was little sense that the team could be special. Through the summer, fans had maintained high hopes for the season, based largely on the presence of Kelly

Thames, the 1994 Big Eight freshman of the year. But those hopes crumbled when Thames tore a knee ligament in practice, ending his season before it began.

Without Thames, senior Paul O'Liney became the focal point of the offense, and junior Julian Winfield was called on to score, as were Derek Grimm and Jason Sutherland, who had seen limited action as freshmen. The Tigers also received help from two junior college transfers who made for a peculiar sight when they arrived in Columbia. Sammie and Simeon Haley, skinny seven-foot identical twins, split time in the post and caused double-takes everywhere.

After opening with wins over Chicago State and Purdue, the Tigers fell to Arkansas, the defending national champs. But after that predictable loss, the Tigers went on a startling tear, highlighted by a 76–58 romp over twenty-third-ranked Illinois.

The winning streak stretched to eight games at nineteenth-ranked Nebraska, where Missouri's pregame warm-up was part sportsmanship, part gamesmanship. Just days after the Huskers had won the national football championship, the Tigers came out in red T-shirts commemorating the title, then tossed them to fans. Surprised by the display of good will, the capacity crowd found it hard to heckle the Tigers. With some of the home court edge dulled, O'Liney scored thirty-one and Missouri prevailed 82–74.

Mizzou lost to third-ranked Kansas the next time out, but immediately began a new streak, winning eight of nine games over the next month. By the time they hosted Oklahoma State in mid-February, the Tigers were one of America's hottest teams. Paul O'Liney scored twenty and Julian Winfield added thirteen points, ten rebounds, and six assists in an 81–79 victory that moved Mizzou to 18–3 overall, 7–2 in the league, and number nine in the polls, a ranking unfathomable when Kelly Thames blew out his knee. The surprising Tigers stood tied for first with just five games to play, but Norm Stewart warned against complacency. "If you go 'yee-haw' and figure we'll just keep on doing this," he said, "you're an easy target."

Despite the warning, the Tigers went into a tailspin, but the problem had less to do with complacency than with good opponents, bad luck, and hostile environments. Missouri lost four straight—including visits to Oklahoma, Kansas, and Colorado—as Julian Winfield was sidelined by a leg injury. But the Tigers bounced back in their regular-season finale, an overtime victory against Oklahoma, secured by a last-second bucket from O'Liney.

After the slide from first to fourth in the league, Mizzou's struggles continued in the Big Eight Tournament, where Iowa State pasted the Tigers in the first round. Despite the late-season fade, Missouri received an invitation to the NCAA Tournament and got a monster of a draw. Seeded

*Paul O'Liney emerged as Missouri's top player in his senior year.*

eighth in the West Region, the Tigers would face Indiana and its legendary coach Bob Knight in round one, with the winner advancing to play UCLA, the nation's top-ranked team. Notwithstanding his team's recent struggles, Norm Stewart remained curiously confident. "If we can get by Indiana," Stewart quietly told Mike Kelly, Missouri's radio play-by-play broadcaster, "we'll beat UCLA."

The meeting with Indiana produced the kind of intensity one would expect from teams coached by raging competitors with more than 1,300 wins between them. The Hoosiers got the better of things in the first half, but Missouri opened the second stanza on a 12–2 run, fueled by the play of Kendrick Moore, a freshman guard who had made big contributions to the team late in the season. Paul O'Liney hit crucial free throws in the waning seconds to secure a 65–60 victory and a date with the nation's best team.

UCLA, coached by Jim Harrick, fielded its best squad since John Wooden's teams ruled college basketball in the 1960s and 1970s, but the Tigers were not intimidated. Sharp shooting carried Missouri to a 42–34 halftime lead. And even when UCLA used a 15–0 run to take a six-point lead midway through the second half, the Tigers maintained their cool. On a day when Paul O'Liney, Jason Sutherland, and Derek Grimm combined to make twelve of nineteen three-pointers, Missouri fought back into the game.

In the final half-minute, Missouri had the ball, down 73–72. Kendrick Moore dribbled time off the clock. With fifteen seconds left, Norm Stewart wanted a time-out but could not get his team's attention. With a wry smile, he let them play. As time ticked away, Julian Winfield flashed to the basket. Moore rifled a perfect pass, and Winfield laid the ball in with 4.8 seconds remaining. Missouri 74, UCLA 73. Mizzou's fans erupted. One of the great wins in the program's history was just moments away.

The Bruins called time out, and Harrick told lightning-fast guard Tyus Edney to make the final play on his own. Missouri set up a full-court defense, and Edney took the inbounds pass ninety feet from the basket. With Moore and Sutherland shadowing him, Edney drove toward the left sideline and reversed field with a behind-the-back dribble. He

*Sophomore Derek Grimm averaged 10.8 points per game for Missouri's 1995 NCAA Tournament team.*

headed right, darting past Missouri's guards. Edney crossed the time line and sprinted toward the right side of the basket. Derek Grimm, playing despite a bad case of the flu, moved to the low block to cut off Edney's path to the hoop. As time dwindled below one second, Grimm stretched out his six-foot-nine frame, feet planted firmly to avoid the foul. Hurtling toward the baseline, Edney, off-balance, flipped the ball toward the basket with his right hand. As the buzzer sounded, the ball skimmed over Grimm's fingertips, bounced off the glass, and fell toward the rim. With just the faintest kiss off the iron, it dropped through the net. Final score: UCLA 75, Missouri 74.

At that moment, the world split into two. For UCLA, it was pandemonium. For Missouri, silence. Ecstasy turned to devastation in an instant. There was grief. There was disbelief. But mostly, there was quiet. Missouri's players milled about the court, eyes glazed over. Fans stood motionless. And on Missouri's radio broadcast, color analyst Jim Kennedy could find no words.

Over the next few hours, as denial receded into acceptance, it became clear that Missouri had suffered the most painful loss in a generation or more, maybe ever. Instead of a second straight Sweet Sixteen, the Tigers were left to sort out the scars.

## 1995-96

Tyus Edney's shot came to mark a bright line for Missouri basketball. In the ten years leading up to it, the Tigers made the NCAA Tournament nine times, missing only in 1991 because of probation. But Mizzou would fail to make it back to the field of sixty-four in each of the next three seasons, the longest drought since the 1970s.

Without Paul O'Liney, the Tigers lacked a dominant offensive player. Though Kelly Thames returned from injury, he lacked his prior explosiveness, leaving Jason Sutherland, the junior guard with a kamikaze's spirit, to emerge as Missouri's most dependable scorer.

The Hearnes Center continued to give the Tigers a substantial edge, but the road brought troubles. In the nonconference schedule, Mizzou beat substandard competition at home, but with losses at Arkansas, to Illinois in St. Louis, and to

*Kelly Thames returned from injury in the 1995–96 season and displayed trademark Missouri toughness.*

*Three players, twenty-one feet. The Haley brothers flank Monte Hardge.*

Southern California and North Carolina State in Hawaii, the tone was set for the season.

Mizzou opened conference play with two home games and won both, including a squeaker over Oklahoma in which Sutherland and Derek Grimm scored twenty-one and twenty points, respectively. But the team lost four of its next five games, all on the road.

After a demoralizing 104–68 loss at Oklahoma, the Tigers returned to Columbia and nearly blew a twenty-point second-half lead against Nebraska. A Cornhusker shot rimmed out in the waning seconds of a 99–98 Missouri win. "It'd have been a terrible loss," acknowledged Norm Stewart. Jason Sutherland made all fourteen of his free throws—extending his school record to thirty-two straight—and the Tigers needed every last one of them.

The Tigers were sharper when they hosted third-ranked Kansas, which, as usual, brought out Missouri's best. With Mizzou up 75–73 in the closing seconds, KU's Jerod Haase tried to force the ball inside but threw it straight to Simeon Haley, who covered the ball, got fouled, and sank two free throws to seal a 77–73 victory.

The Tigers would not play that well again. They closed the regular season by losing five of six games to enter the conference tournament at 16–13 overall, 6–8 in the league, good only for sixth place. Sutherland, Grimm, and Sammie Haley each topped twenty points in a win over Oklahoma in round one. But when Iowa State beat the Tigers the next day, all hopes for an NCAA berth disappeared.

Missouri accepted an NIT bid for the first time since 1985 and hosted Murray State in the first round. Sammie Haley's thirty-one points and fifteen rebounds paced the Tigers to an 89–85 win. But a trip to Alabama for the second round brought a predictable result. Away from the Hearnes Center, the Tigers suffered a humbling 72–49 loss.

*No one ever played harder than Jason Sutherland.*

Even one of the more disappointing seasons of the Norm Stewart era included recognition for what the coach had built at Mizzou. In 1958 the Big Seven evolved into the Big Eight, and after thirty-eight seasons, the league was set to grow to the Big 12, with the addition of Texas, Texas A&M, Texas Tech, and Baylor, refugees from the old Southwest Conference. In the nine seasons before Norm Stewart arrived as Missouri's head coach, the Tigers finished sixth or worse in the conference six times. In Stewart's twenty-nine seasons in the Big Eight, Mizzou won eight regular season titles and eleven conference tournaments. When it came time to reminisce about the old league, surveys by the Associated Press and the *Kansas City Star* confirmed what everyone already knew: Norm Stewart was the top coach in the history of the Big Eight.

## 1996–97

In college sports, rivalries still matter. Even in a season headed nowhere, beating a rival—especially one enjoying a tremendous year—can salve wounds and exhilarate fans. Overall, the 1996–97 season was disappointing for the Tigers. They posted Missouri's first losing record in eighteeen years, and their 5–11 mark in conference games placed them tenth in the new Big 12. But on one remarkable night in February, the Missouri Tigers walked like champions.

Kelly Thames (13.0 points per game), Jason Sutherland (12.6), and Derek Grimm (11.9) had productive seasons, but the team struggled, especially on the road, failing to win a single game on an opponent's court. A high point came when Thames scored twenty-five points and pulled down seventeen rebounds in a win over Oklahoma, but erratic efforts at home—Colorado broke a twenty-five-game Hearnes Center losing streak—caused Mizzou to slide toward the bottom of the league standings. Still, the Tigers showed some life in postseason play. After Norm Stewart's emphatic reminders that Kansas City is in Missouri, his players responded with three straight wins at Kemper Arena in the first Big 12 Tournament. A semifinal win over Oklahoma (Sutherland scored twenty-three) evoked memories of 1978 and 1993, when mediocre Missouri teams produced tournament titles and earned accompanying NCAA bids. But the Tigers faded in the final, their fourth game in four days. Gassed and outclassed, they fell to top-ranked Kansas 87–60 to end the campaign at 15–16. And despite all the losses, the season is best remembered for one remarkable victory.

The Kansas Jayhawks stood 22–0 and ranked number one when they visited Columbia on February 4. Led by Jacque Vaughn, Raef LaFrentz, and Paul Pierce, they were deemed nearly invincible. Missouri, by contrast, entered the game at 11–10, having lost eight of twelve. Even the Hearnes Center, a daunting venue for most opponents, didn't scare the Jayhawks. Kansas had won in four of its last six visits to Columbia.

*Big man Derek Grimm was an ace three-point shooter.*

*With a single jump shot, Corey Tate secured his spot in Missouri history.*

But the Tigers fed off the intensity of a ferocious home crowd and played a scintillating game. To the surprise of everyone—except Norm Stewart and his team—the Tigers stood to win as time ticked away. With fewer than ten seconds left, Missouri owned a 71–68 lead. In an effort to prevent Kansas from tying the game with a three-point shot, Tiger guard Dibi Ray fouled Jacque Vaughn. Vaughn went to the line and made his first free throw. But he purposefully missed the second shot, and LaFrentz, the All-American, spun around Derek Grimm, grabbed the rebound and laid the ball in to tie the score and force overtime.

After taking Missouri's best shot, Kansas should have pulled away, but the Tigers showed surprising poise. Though the Jayhawks scored on their first seven possessions of the extra period, Missouri matched them point for point by making twelve of twelve free throws, including a late pair by Corey Tate to force a second overtime.

Tate, a senior, came to Mizzou after playing one season in junior college and enjoyed a solid career

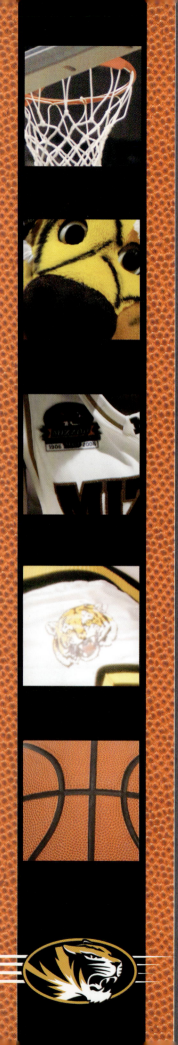

as a lunch-pail player who could distribute the ball, rebound, and score a little. With his steady demeanor, Tate could help a team win while remaining nearly invisible. But he was hardly invisible against Kansas. Instead, in an instant, Corey Tate sealed his place in Missouri lore.

Missouri held the ball, the score deadlocked at 94–94 with just seconds left in the second overtime. Kelly Thames and Derek Grimm, who combined to score forty-four points, had both fouled out. With two of their best offensive players on the bench, the Tigers called on Tyron Lee, a lanky slasher, to win the game. But before Lee could make his move to the hoop, Jacque Vaughn poked the ball free, setting off a wild scramble. While Lee and Vaughn fought for the ball, it rolled to Tate, who picked it up just beyond the free throw line. He rose up and shot. The ball ripped the net with 5.6 seconds remaining to give Missouri a 96–94 edge. Kansas still had a chance to win or tie the game, but the Tigers' defense prevented the Jayhawks from getting a shot off until just after the final buzzer. To the shock of nearly everyone nearly everywhere, Missouri gave Kansas its first loss of the year.

Tate, though, was not surprised. "No one expected this, except maybe the players and the coaches," he said. "No one except us, but we believed." Norm Stewart was just happy for his embattled players. "It was their night," he said. And it made their year.

## 1997-98

Once again, an inability to win on the road and a near invincibility at home defined Missouri's season. Early on, the Tigers got routed by Duke and Kentucky in Hawaii and by Arkansas in Fayetteville. They even lost to Coppin State in Columbia, and their 2–4 record marked Mizzou's worst start since Bob Vanatta's final year as head coach. But wins in six of the next seven games suggested that a turn-around was possible. Norm Stewart got his seven hundredth career victory in a 75–69 win over Illinois, a game that featured a sixteen-point, eleven-rebound performance by new Tiger Albert White, a gifted forward who had transferred from Michigan. The Tigers also upset twentieth-ranked

*New Tiger Albert White (44) fights for braggin' rights.*

Maryland when freshman guard Brian Grawer came off the bench to score fifteen points, and they routed Texas 91–69 as senior swing man Tyron Lee scored twenty-seven. But as much as the six wins provided hope, the lone loss in the four-week span suggested a darker fate.

On January 3 the Tigers traveled to Manhattan, Kansas, where they had often won during Norm Stewart's tenure. It was a game that could have provided a fairly ordinary win. Instead, it produced a historic loss.

Kansas State fielded a team with names like Josh Reid, Ty Sims, and Manny Dies. Their names might as well have been Jordan, Chamberlain, and Bird. Those three alone outscored the entire Missouri roster in a 111–56 blowout that ranked as the worst defeat in Missouri history.

It was impossible to see coming and just as hard to explain after the fact. Up 53–22 at intermission, Kansas State opened the second half on a 30–4 run and eventually stretched the lead to sixty-two points. For Missouri, Kelly Thames scored twenty-six points, but the rest of the team was nearly invisible. Norm Stewart diagnosed the result in the simplest possible terms: "They had an absolutely great basketball game," he said. "We had an absolutely terrible basketball game."

From then on, Missouri settled into a winsome, lose-some pattern. For the third straight year, the Tigers beat a tremendous Kansas team. Albert White scored twenty-three points in a 74–73 win that dropped the third-ranked Jayhawks to 21–3 on the year. The Tigers also won a crazy affair against tenth-rated Iowa. The Hawkeyes hit a three-pointer with two seconds remaining and took a 70–69 lead. After a time-out, Jeff Hafer launched a court-length pass to fellow sophomore Tate Decker, a big man dubbed "the Flying Aardvark" by Norm Stewart for his ungainly style. Decker corralled the ball and went for a layup that would have won the game, but he got clobbered by Iowa's Ricky Davis. With one-tenth of a second left, Decker went to the free throw line. He missed the first shot. With nerves eating up his insides, Decker's second shot rolled around the rim and fell through to force overtime, where Kelly Thames made two late free throws to give the Tigers a one-point win.

Despite those victories over highly ranked opponents, the inability to win away from home sabotaged Missouri's season. The Tigers lost all ten of their true road games (they were 3–3 on neutral courts), extending their road losing streak to twenty-three games over three seasons.

*Through a star-crossed career, Kelly Thames recorded some eye-popping numbers.*

But even as the season sputtered through its latter stages, Norm Stewart produced a signature moment in an overtime win against Nebraska. Late in regulation, the Huskers' Cookie Belcher, a marginal free throw shooter, got fouled. Supposedly injured on the play, Belcher was replaced by a better shooter, who knocked down both shots. When play resumed, Belcher immediately went to the scorer's table to check back in, to the dismay of Norm Stewart and the Hearnes Center crowd. While Belcher waited, Missouri brought the ball down the court, and Monte Hardge, the Tigers' enormous center, was fouled. Stewart insisted that Hardge, a 60 percent foul shooter, had been injured on the play. Hardge was summoned to the bench in favor of Kelly Thames, the fourth best free throw shooter in the conference. Thames made both shots and Missouri went on to win. Afterwards, Stewart deadpanned that Hardge had suffered a

"strained literal mitisimis dorsi," requiring immediate medical attention.

The season concluded with losses in the second round of the Big 12 Tournament and in the opening round of the NIT as Alabama–Birmingham handed the Tigers only their second loss all year at the Hearnes Center. The 17–15 record and third straight season out of the NCAA Tournament marked a twenty-year low for the program and provided a disappointing end for Kelly Thames, one of the most productive individual players of his generation. Despite the knee injury that transformed him from a dynamic inside-outside performer to a more conventional (and undersized) post player, Thames graduated as Missouri's number six all-time scorer and number nine rebounder. And despite his contributions, Thames's exit was nothing compared with the surprising and historic departure that came after the following season.

## 1998–99

Norm Stewart pulled off his biggest recruiting coup in years when he landed a pair of guards from Fort Lauderdale, Florida. Keyon Dooling was an ultra-athletic floor general; his best friend, Clarence Gilbert, a tenacious shooter. And while each would contribute as freshmen, the team's top player, indisputably, was junior forward Albert White.

Six feet five inches tall (and nearly as wide), White could rebound like a power forward and pass like a point guard. He scored at least sixteen points in each of Missouri's first eight games and nabbed at least ten rebounds in five of them. He just missed a triple-double against Arkansas–Pine Bluff with sixteen points, ten rebounds, and nine assists. Then, at Southern Methodist, White recorded twenty-eight points and sixteen rebounds to lead Mizzou to victory, ending the Tigers' road losing streak at twenty-three games.

His coach was impressed. "Those are big numbers," said Norm Stewart, "the kind John Brown and Al Eberhard used to put up." With White leading the way, the Tigers stood 7–1 as they entered the meat of their schedule.

Early in conference play, the Tigers looked like contenders. After routing Nebraska at Hearnes, they won at Kansas State to end an eighteen-game road losing streak in the league. A victory at Texas A&M moved the Tigers to 3–0 in the Big 12 and lifted expectations.

But then things got tougher. Kansas came to town ranked fifteenth in the nation, rather than the top three rating the Jayhawks had carried to Columbia in each of the previous five seasons. Though the Tigers had prevailed over four of those highly ranked KU teams, they could not handle a squad led by Ryan Robertson, a senior from St. Charles, Missouri, who had spurned his home-state school. Booed mercilessly by Missouri fans for

*Albert White opened the 1998–99 season on a tear.*

*Highly touted Keyon Dooling came to Columbia from Fort Lauderdale, Florida.*

four years, Robertson got his revenge in his last visit to the Hearnes Center, scoring seventeen points to pace the Jayhawks to victory. As they left the floor, Robertson and teammate Eric Chenowith taunted Missouri's fans, a fact noted by Mizzou's players.

After suffering a lopsided loss at Colorado, the Tigers had eight days off before a rematch with Kansas, and Norm Stewart got his team's full attention. One characteristic shared by all of Stewart's teams, no matter how good, was that they expected to win. The coach reinforced that expectation as his team ventured into Allen Field House, where no conference opponent had beaten Kansas since 1994. "We're gonna win the ballgame," Stewart told the Tigers, and he directed them to "walk off the court like you've been there before." He even had them practice leaving the floor in the days leading up to the game.

Norm Stewart may have been the only coach in the Big 12 who could tell his players that they would win at Kansas and make them believe it. Since Missouri's 1994 championship, Kansas had owned the league, winning four straight titles. In the previous three years, the Jayhawks had lost only four games to league foes. Three of those losses had come to Missouri.

Completely poised in an intimidating arena, the Tigers rewarded Stewart's belief. Unshakeable sophomore guard Brian Grawer scored eighteen points, and Keyon Dooling added fifteen as Missouri took a 71–63 victory. And true to Stewart's direction, the Tigers calmly walked off the floor. Reflecting back, Brian Grawer says, "The best noise I ever heard in my career was silence in Allen Field House."

That win started a roll. The Tigers won five of their next six, including a trip to Iowa State, where Clarence Gilbert scored thirteen points in his first start, a 77–61 victory. Then, against Colorado, Mizzou scored thirty straight points in the second half and moved to 9–3 in the league, tied for second.

But just when the Tigers seem poised to make a run at the title, they stumbled. In Columbia, Oklahoma scored twenty-two of the game's last twenty-five points to take a 69–57 decision that dropped the Tigers to fourth place. Then, with half the team fighting the flu and Dooling sidelined by a sprained ankle, Mizzou fell at Oklahoma State, extinguishing any remaining championship hopes.

But the Tigers regrouped at home on senior day for Monte Hardge and John Woods and whipped Iowa State behind twenty-seven points from Brian Grawer, who made all six of his three-point shots. Then, for the regular season finale, they traveled to Texas, which had clinched the league title. Albert White scored twenty-three points in a 54–47 win that moved the Tigers into a second-place tie and punched their ticket to the NCAA Tournament.

After a strong finish to the regular season, the Tigers fell flat against Kansas State in the conference tournament and lost 84–74. The effect was to bump Missouri down to the number eight seed in the NCAA's West Region, setting up a game with ninth-seeded New Mexico in Denver.

On a night when Albert White made just six of nineteen shots and Keyon Dooling just one of eight, Missouri stayed in the game with defense. But when Lamont Long hit a shot with six seconds left, New Mexico took a two-point lead. Though the clock should have stopped on the made basket, it continued to run, and more than a second elapsed before the Tigers frantically inbounded the ball and

raced up the court. Brian Grawer was forced to put up a wild shot that missed the mark. Missouri bowed out of the tournament 61–59.

Two weeks after the season ended, Albert White announced his intention to forego his senior year to turn professional. The decision was a surprise, but players come and go. Coaches, however, stay at Missouri for a long, long time. In the seventy-three years since George Edwards succeeded George Bond, only four men had served as head men's basketball coach at the University of Missouri, and Norm Stewart's thirty-two-year tenure was among the longest at any school in the nation. He decided that thirty-two years was enough.

Word started to trickle out on March 31, with a press conference slated for the next day. Given that it involved the irascible Stewart, many figured it for an April Fool's prank. But it was no joke. Norm Stewart was retiring.

He took the podium at the Hearnes Center and let the world know what had been on his mind for several weeks. Stewart said that he had heard Jayhawk fans repeat the time-honored chant, "Sit down, Norm" during his last visit to Lawrence and thought to himself, "I think I will." He sat down having won 731 games as a head coach at Missouri and Northern Iowa, then seventh-most in collegiate history. With a 634–333 record at Missouri, he won more games than all thirteen of his predecessors combined.

Norm Stewart coached Missouri to its first twenty-win season in 1972 and its seventeenth in 1999. He coached nine All-Americans and eighteen all-conference players. He filled Missouri's trophy case with regular season and conference tournament championships. Stewart also made his mark off the court, establishing the wildly successful Coaches vs. Cancer program that raised money for the American Cancer Society.

More than anything, Norm Stewart became the personification of Missouri basketball. He stamped the program with humor and fury, determination and pride. Though he successfully recruited all over the country, Stewart felt a deep kinship with the people of Missouri, from Shelbyville to St. Louis and all points in between. "I love this state," he

*Brian Grawer (right) was Norm Stewart's extension on the floor.*

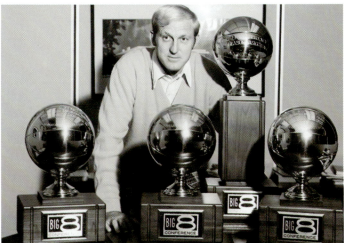

*Over thirty-two years, Norm Stewart turned the Tigers into champions and retired as Missouri's undisputed Man of the Century.*

said at his retirement announcement, "and I love this town." And somehow it was fitting that as the millennium drew to a close, Missouri's Man of the Century stepped down. Still, it was hard for Missouri's fans—many of whom could remember no other coach—to fathom. Oddly enough, Kansas coach Roy Williams seemed to speak for the entire community of fans, friends, and foes when he said, "I just can't picture Missouri basketball without Norm Stewart on the sideline."

After Norm Stewart's retirement, Missouri basketball looked to build a bright future in the shadow of a storied past. That process began with a glamorous hire that brought excitement and a fair share of success to Mizzou before off-court issues rocked the program and led to a decline. But a change at century's end brought a proven winner to Columbia and renewed hopes for a return to former glories.

# THE 2000s

## 1999–2000

He was a canvas onto which Missouri's fans could project their greatest hopes and see them reflected back in glimmers of endless possibility. His youth carried the thrill of the unknown, and his experience suggested that success was not only possible but inevitable. The scion of Duke University's basketball dynasty, his career had been filled with overachievement, from All-America player in high school to academic All-America performer in college, where he contributed to three Final Four teams. Ambition and curiosity took him on simultaneous but divergent paths after graduation as he earned a law degree and an MBA while also pursuing a career in coaching. He studied under two of the game's legends, briefly serving on Larry Brown's staff in the NBA, then assisting his own coach, Duke's Mike Krzyzewski. Telegenic and charismatic, he quickly became a rising star, the kind of coach on whom a program could pin its hopes. And when the University of Missouri introduced thirty-two-year-old Quin Snyder as its new basketball coach on April 7, 1999, Missouri's fans quickly and enthusiastically pinned their hopes on him.

As he stood at the podium, he acknowledged Mizzou's history with a nod to Norm Stewart. "I'm very fortunate to have an opportunity to be his successor," said Snyder, "to build on that foundation that his emotion and his sweat and his hard work laid." He also looked to the future and acknowledged the community that embraced him so warmly. When Snyder began looking for a head coaching job, Krzyzewski told him to find a place worthy of his passion. But upon being greeted in Columbia by fevered enthusiasm, he told the program's supporters "I'm convinced that it's my turn to show you that I'm worthy of your passion."

Snyder's passion proved contagious with Missouri's players, thanks in part to a style that emphasized freedom for individual players to make plays. With a small front line—Tajudeen Soyoye, a six-foot-nine junior college transfer, anchored the middle; converted swingmen Johnnie Parker and Jeff Hafer shared the power forward spot—Mizzou's personnel dictated that the plays would be made mostly from the perimeter. Keyon Dooling stood poised to become the team's top player, while fellow guard Brian Grawer provided a steadying presence. Missouri also got a lift from Kareem Rush, a six-foot-six freshman from Kansas City. A left-handed shooter with elegant form, Rush possessed the most potent offensive skills seen in Columbia in years.

*Though young, Quin Snyder possessed a sterling pedigree when he became Missouri's fifteenth head men's basketball coach. (MU Athletics/Sarah Becking)*

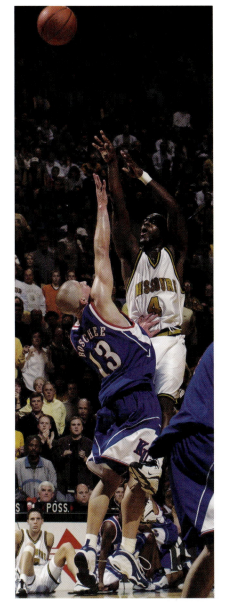

Left: With an avalanche of three-pointers against Kansas, Clarence Gilbert established himself as one of the Big 12's most explosive scorers. Reproduced with permission of The Kansas City Star © Copyright 2006 The Kansas City Star. All rights reserved. Format differs from original publication. Not an endorsement. (Julie Jacobson/Kansas City Star)

Above: Keyon Dooling ran the show for Quin Snyder's first Tiger team.

Early on, the team took to Snyder's style like a teenager to a stick shift, playing in fits and starts, lurching forward and then retreating, with moments of full-throttle action. After dropping its opener to Wisconsin, Mizzou won five straight as Dooling and Rush shouldered the scoring load. But losses to Indiana and St. Louis slowed Missouri's momentum, and a nine-game suspension handed to Rush by the NCAA (for his relationship with a summer league coach) threatened to throw the season off track.

Through the 5–3 start, no one struggled quite like Clarence Gilbert. Though he came billed as a scorching shooter, Gilbert shot poorly as a freshman and did little to rekindle his reputation early in his sophomore year. With Rush out, Mizzou needed Gilbert to produce, which he did by scoring thirteen points in a win over Iowa. But that barely hinted at what was to come.

When the Tigers met fifteenth-ranked Illinois, they rallied from fourteen points down to take a one-point halftime lead. Then, after intermission, Gilbert scored twelve straight points for Mizzou, and the Tigers opened a decisive edge. His twenty-four points on eight-of-eleven shooting (five of seven from three-point range) keyed Missouri's 78–72 victory. "It's one of those days when you feel it and you don't want to stop shooting," said Gilbert.

Still, the pattern of lurching and retreating continued with losses to Kentucky, little-known Winthrop University, and Iowa State. Then, without

Top: Gritty Jeff Hafer sacrificed himself for the good of the team.

Bottom: Even as a freshman, Kareem Rush had a sophisticated offensive game.

notice, the Tigers kicked into high gear. Dooling scored twenty-five in a win over Colorado, Gilbert matched that in a victory over Kansas State, and Jeff Hafer contributed fifteen in a triumph at Baylor that moved Mizzou to 3–1 in the league. Then, when the Tigers hosted seventh-ranked Kansas, Gilbert erupted again. With KU's Jeff Boschee clinging to him like a wetsuit, Gilbert fired shots from deep and connected with striking precision. With twenty-seven points on seven-of-ten three-point shooting, Gilbert led MU to a stunning 81–59 triumph.

Just as Gilbert began to emerge as a marquee player, Kareem Rush returned and played like a star in his own right. Rush's scoring led Missouri to three more wins and a 7–1 conference record at the halfway point. But the second half proved tougher, and Mizzou lost five games to nationally ranked teams even as Dooling and Rush continued to shine. Still, the 10–6 mark in the league was better than most had predicted.

After a second-round exit from the Big 12 tourney, the NCAA extended Mizzou an invitation but gave the tiny Tigers a disastrous draw, seeding them ninth in the South Region and pitting them against an enormous North Carolina team. The Tar Heels used their size to control the boards and take an 84–70 win that ended Missouri's season. Still, Quin Snyder felt fortunate. "It was a great first year for me to have a chance to coach this group," he said. As Snyder looked toward his second season, he knew that he would be without Keyon Dooling, the team's leading scorer, who entered the NBA draft. But the returning nucleus of Grawer, Gilbert, and Rush, combined with some stellar newcomers, suggested that even better things were to come.

## 2000–01

With Keyon Dooling gone, Brian Grawer returned to the point and led a team that combined veteran firepower with fresh talent. The newcomers came in a variety of shapes and sizes. Detroit produced two freshmen—Arthur Johnson, who at six-foot-nine and (at least) 275 pounds possessed agility rare in a man of his heft, and Rickey Paulding, a wiry purveyor of awe-inspiring dunks. Mizzou also added guard Wesley Stokes, a bantamweight with Barnum & Bailey hair, a wild mane that fans dubbed the Sideshow Bob. Pound for pound, though, two returning Tigers towered above all. Sophomore Kareem Rush took his place as one of the league's

*Brian Grawer earned praise for his poise and leadership.*

best players, and Clarence Gilbert brought his own sort of barely controlled fury to the table.

The Tigers shot to a hot start, including a win over St. Louis University sealed by Grawer, who grabbed a late loose ball, got fouled, hit two free throws, and earned the praise of his coach. "Brian Grawer right now is as good a leader on a team (as any) that I've ever been a part of," said Quin Snyder. Mizzou also won at Indiana when little Wesley Stokes twice ventured into the lane late in the game and sank crucial shots. At the semester break, the Tigers welcomed a fourth freshman, big man Travon Bryant, and they appeared to be a formidable (if young) team, with the scoring of Rush and Gilbert complemented by the interior defense of T. J. Soyoye and Arthur Johnson, who went on a shot-blocking binge early in his freshman year.

By the time the Tigers hosted Iowa State, the defending league champ, they stood 11–3 overall, 2–0 in league play. Jamaal Tinsley, a brilliant guard, led a balanced Cyclone squad that stood in contrast to Missouri's two-man gang of Rush and Gilbert. As the teams made plays and missed shots in lockstep, the game kept going. Tied 72–72 at the end of regulation and 82–82 after one overtime, the teams played on. After fighting to a 91–91 stalemate at the end of the second overtime, the teams moved to a third, where Iowa State tried to maintain its discipline while Clarence Gilbert opted for reckless abandon, hoisting wild shots that fell often enough

*Hard-working Tajudeen Soyoye roamed the paint for Mizzou.*

to keep Mizzou close. With the Tigers down 101–98 and less than twenty seconds left, Gilbert grabbed a loose ball behind the arc, drifted toward the corner, and drilled a shot that forced a fourth overtime, where Mizzou finally prevailed. Two free throws by Brian Grawer wrapped up an epic 112–109 triumph, the longest game in Missouri's history. Kareem Rush scored thirty-two points on thirteen-of-thirty-one shooting, while Gilbert made twelve of thirty-six field goal tries on his way to forty-three points. "You can't stop (shooting)," Gilbert said. "I don't care if you miss 10. You might make 11, you might make 12." Brian Grawer showed more restraint, making every shot he took—three of three from the field, two of two from the arc, four of four from the line—for a total of twelve points.

The victory was sweet but debilitating. The tired Tigers dropped three straight on the road, then returned home and eked out

*Clarence Gilbert, open twenty-four hours a day*

a 66–64 win over a mediocre Texas Tech team, an effort that left Quin Snyder frustrated.

A bout with Kansas is rarely good medicine for a staggering team, but no one ever made it work better than Norm Stewart, who was honored for his contributions as a player and coach when KU came to town. His number twenty-two jersey was retired, and the Hearnes Center floor was dedicated in his honor. When the third-ranked Jayhawks came out of the locker room, the Tigers made their first defense of Norm Stewart Court.

After Missouri took a 43–26 lead early in the second half, KU staged an 18–0 run to move ahead 44–43. Then Brian Grawer, the heart of the Tigers, drained three quick three-pointers to help Missouri take control of the game. Mizzou won 75–66, and no one was happier than the senior from St. Louis. "Every year you look forward to KU at Hearnes," said Grawer. "Three out of my four years I wasn't let down. And this one may be the best one of them all."

But Mizzou's joy was quickly muted on a somber night in Stillwater, where Oklahoma State played for the first time since several members of its basketball program, including two players, died in a plane crash. With heavy hearts, the teams played a spirited game that the Cowboys won 69–66 on a night that would have lasting repercussions for the Tigers. Late in the game, Kareem Rush fell on his left hand, the most valuable extremity on the Missouri roster. An examination revealed a bone chip and ligament tear in his thumb, injuries that required surgery. The news hit hard: Kareem Rush out for the season. Quin Snyder tried to be philosophical. "Anytime a team loses someone who is such a central figure in its collective identity," he said, "you have to come together even more."

Without Rush, Brian Grawer led the Tigers through trying times made harder when Gilbert was suspended for one game because of festering attitude issues. Still, the Tigers played well enough that when they beat Baylor in their home finale, they secured their ninth league victory, and, likely, an NCAA berth. But a lopsided loss at Texas reinforced how much they missed Rush's scoring touch. They wouldn't miss it much longer.

Despite the earlier declaration that his year was over, Kareem Rush returned for the regular-season

*Kareem Rush made a national splash with his performance against Duke in the NCAA Tournament.*

finale at Kansas, thanks to a specially made cast that protected his left thumb. But even with the protection, he managed just two points in a 75–59 loss that sent Missouri stumbling into the conference tournament. There, after a round-one win over Texas A&M, a resurgent Rush delivered a virtuoso performance against Oklahoma. He scored thirty-one points, and Mizzou had victory all but secured with thirteen seconds left when Sooner Nolan Johnson missed a free throw with the Tigers leading, 65–64. But Rush and Soyoye fought each other for the rebound and lost the ball out of bounds. Oklahoma got the ball to Johnson, who hit a shot to win the game. Still, Rush's performance drew much of the postgame attention. "Kareem Rush doesn't need an offense," said Oklahoma coach Kelvin Sampson. "He just needs the ball."

Despite the loss, the Tigers received an NCAA bid and the ninth seed in the East Region. In the first round against Georgia, Mizzou opened with a flurry, scoring the first fifteen points in a game marked by wild momentum swings. After Georgia rallied to take a 33–32 lead at the half, the Tigers regained control and led by eleven with under four minutes to play. But the Bulldogs thundered back to tie the score in the final minute, and Missouri's

Athletic swingman Rickey Paulding began to emerge as a star in his sophomore season. (MU Athletics/Sarah Becking)

Wild-maned Wesley Stokes helped the Tigers climb to number two in the polls early in the 2001–02 season. (MU Athletics/Sarah Becking)

history of tournament disappointments hung heavy in the air. Brian Grawer confesses that doubt crept in, but says, "Nothing was going to stop us from winning that game." With the score tied 68-68 and time ticking away, the Tigers played for one shot and put the ball in the hands of their best player. Kareem Rush moved toward the basket, drew two defenders, and dished to Clarence Gilbert on the baseline. From seventeen feet out, Gilbert delivered the knockout punch, a shot that fell with less than a second to play, giving Missouri a 70–68 victory and a trip to the second round for the first time in six years. "You've got to have confidence in yourself," Gilbert said. "I did. And I knocked it down."

The Tigers' next game provided them with their biggest stage in years, a national broadcast with a compelling story line. At Duke, Mike Krzyzewski had become the most successful coach of his generation, with two national championships to his credit. Quin Snyder had studied at Coach K's feet, first as a player and then as Krzyzewski's top assistant. The match-up between master and pupil made for good television, even if it caused some discomfort for the coaches.

Missouri's only shot against a top-ranked Duke team that featured Shane Battier and Jason Williams was to play flawlessly, and even that might not be enough. Early on, the game progressed as expected, with Duke leading by fifteen points late in the first half. But Mizzou used a 9–0 run to close the gap to 43–37 at the break. Then the Tigers, behind Kareem Rush's offense and some high-pressure perimeter defense, really made a game of it. Even with his thumb in a cast, Rush sank three-pointers, drove to the hoop, and unleashed his unstoppable turnaround jumper to help Missouri cut the lead to one point. And though the Tigers were playing brilliantly, it was only enough to keep the score close. In the end, the Blue Devils pulled away to a 94–81 triumph despite Rush's twenty-nine points. Still, Missouri earned respect. "That was the hardest anybody played against us all year," said Krzyzewski.

The loss ended the careers of seniors Grawer, Soyoye, and Johnnie Parker, but when Kareem Rush announced that the NBA could wait, he inspired hope of greater things for Missouri basketball. With the likes of Rush, Gilbert, and Johnson returning, expectations were sky high. But expectations would weigh heavy in a roller-coaster season that went from promising to disappointing to thrilling to nearly historic.

# 2001–02

In Quin Snyder's third year, the Missouri Tigers looked to fulfill the expectations that had arrived in Columbia with the young coach. Mizzou began the year ranked number eight and steadily climbed to the headiest regions of the polls. Early on, the Tigers advanced to the semifinals of the Guardians Classic tournament in Kansas City, where they faced nationally ranked Alabama in a tooth-and-nail affair that took a dramatic turn when an elbow to the head knocked Kareem Rush senseless late in the game. While Rush saw stars on the sideline, Clarence Gilbert willed the Tigers to a 75–68 victory.

In the final, against ninth-ranked Iowa, the drama rose even higher. Still feeling effects of the previous night's blow, Kareem Rush struggled, and Missouri along with him, trailing 73–62 with 2:15 to play. But wild defensive pressure and clutch shooting brought the Tigers roaring back. Rush nailed a three-pointer with thirty-six seconds left to close the gap to three points, and Rickey Paulding sank another trey twelve seconds later to tie the score at 77–77. Still, Iowa had a chance to win. But when Glen Worley missed a shot, Gilbert grabbed the ball and came screaming down the court. He stopped and tried to beat the buzzer with a jump shot, but Worley fouled him. With just eight-tenths of a second left, Gilbert went to the free throw line to shoot two, needing only one to secure an improbable victory. He missed the first shot. But he made the second, the last of twenty-seven points that helped earn him tournament MVP honors. "I thought our kids showed unbelievable character," said a proud Quin Snyder.

*Clarence Gilbert's move to the point helped resurrect Missouri's season.*

From there, the Tigers kept climbing, overwhelming a series of opponents before rising to number two in the polls and visiting the St. Louis Billikens for a game that was a fight to the finish. After SLU's Marque Perry tied the game with 4.8

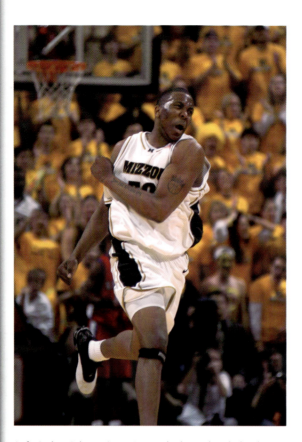

*Left: Arthur Johnson's scoring and rebounding helped Missouri advance to the 2002 NCAA Tournament. (MU Athletics, Sarah Becking)*

*Right: In his last season as a Tiger, Kareem Rush led Missouri deep into the NCAA Tournament.*

seconds to play, Mizzou inbounded the ball to Wesley Stokes, who hurtled down the court. Even as Rush and Gilbert called for the ball, Stokes pulled up just inside the three-point line and shot. The ball fell through the hoop at the buzzer to give Missouri a spine-tingling 69–67 triumph. When the Tigers beat Southern University by fifty points three days later, they moved to 9–0 on the season and looked like national title contenders. Then everything seemed to fall apart.

Iowa visited the Hearnes Center for a rematch of the Guardians Classic final, and the Hawkeyes came bent for revenge. They blistered Mizzou from start to finish, the 83–65 final score not fully indicative of the domination. "This one is going to sit heavy in our stomach," said Quin Snyder. The malaise continued through losses to Illinois and DePaul that knocked Missouri far down the polls.

The cohesiveness and relentlessness that marked Mizzou's hot start had vanished, and a big reason was porous perimeter defense. As the team scuffled to regain its form, Snyder took a gamble and moved Clarence Gilbert to point guard and slid Rickey Paulding into the starting lineup, making the Tigers bigger and more athletic. Putting the ball-hawking Gilbert at the point placed the Tigers' focus more squarely on defense even as it made for some awkward moments offensively. It also gave the vocal senior a more prominent podium. "When we lost Brian [Grawer] to graduation, it took almost a full season to replace his leadership," Quin Snyder says in retrospect. Moving Gilbert to the point was the first step in filling that void.

The Tigers won their first game with the new lineup (81–66 at Kansas State; Arthur Johnson posted twenty-three points and fifteen boards), but the transition wasn't easy. They beat most of the league's lesser teams but struggled against the top squads, including Oklahoma, which beat Missouri for the eighth straight time. And a one-point loss at perennial doormat Baylor threatened to dash MU's postseason hopes.

Yet even as the Tigers struggled to find consistency, they gave fans reasons for optimism. One came from Rickey Paulding, who began to grow into an offensive force as he played off Rush and Gilbert. Another was Gilbert himself, who made the move to the point without sacrificing his own explosiveness, evidenced by a win at Colorado, where he sank twelve three-pointers on his way to forty points.

Still, the Tigers stood just 8–6 in Big 12 play when they hosted twelfth-ranked Oklahoma State, needing a win to help secure an NCAA Tournament bid. They gave a breakthrough performance that showed how dangerous Missouri could be by trusting the full roster. On a night when Rush and Gilbert combined for just sixteen points, a new generation of Detroit Tigers carried the team. Rickey Paulding scored twenty-one points, and Arthur Johnson added eighteen points and fourteen rebounds in a 72–69 triumph. "Our backs were against the wall," said Kareem Rush. "Guys stepped up."

The Tigers got a similar effort but a less favorable result when they hosted Kansas to close the regular season. The Jayhawks, ranked number one, prevailed 95–92 despite twenty-seven points from Clarence Gilbert in his final home game. The loss dropped Missouri to 9–7 and sixth place in the Big 12. After a second-round exit in the conference tournament, the Tigers snuck into the NCAA field as the number twelve seed in the West Region, a position that did not bode well for their chances. In NCAA history, twelve-seeds had been good for the occasional first-round upset but little else.

But Quin Snyder still had faith in his team. He had seen his players' intensity rise—especially defensively—since they adjusted to Gilbert at the point. "This team can still be special," Snyder told his players before facing fifth-seeded Miami in round one. Then they went out and proved it. Mizzou raced to a 12–0 lead and never looked back. "We came out and jumped on 'em," said Clarence Gilbert, whose twenty points led six Tigers in double figures in a 93–80 victory.

Missouri met fourth-seeded Ohio State in round two and gave an even more impressive performance. The Tigers exploded to a 47–26 halftime lead and never let up, thanks largely to a ferocious effort on the boards. Rush, Paulding, and Justin Gage (a football star who had walked on to the basketball team) each grabbed nine caroms as Mizzou won the rebounding battle 52–28. Paulding also threw down two tremendous dunks on his way to twenty points in an emphatic 83–67 triumph. Ohio State coach Jim O'Brien was stunned by Missouri's play. "We kind of ran into a buzz saw," he said. Quin Snyder was far less surprised. "Today was a reflection of what's happened over the last month," he said. "That identity starts on the defensive end. First we had the will, and now our habits are coming." With their first Sweet Sixteen appearance in eight years on the horizon, the Tigers' timing was perfect.

In San Jose, Missouri met UCLA, and the game began badly when Clarence Gilbert dislocated his left ring finger in the first minute, but the Tigers recovered and led by two at halftime. Still, after UCLA opened the second half on a run, the Tigers trailed by eight points with fourteen minutes to play. But when Kareem Rush hit a three-pointer with

*Power forward Travon Bryant could score in the low post or step out and shoot the three-pointer. (MU Athletics/Sarah Becking)*

13:51 remaining, it began an avalanche. Mizzou used a 32–14 run to turn the deficit into a ten-point lead with just under four minutes to play. The Tigers won 82–73 as Gilbert—whom Justin Gage called "a maniac" after shaking off the dislocated finger—scored twenty-three points. Rush added twenty, Rickey Paulding contributed fifteen, and Arthur Johnson collected fourteen points and fourteen rebounds. With the win, the Tigers became the first twelve-seed ever to advance to the NCAA's Elite Eight. One more victory would put Mizzou into its first Final Four, but to get there, the Tigers would have to pass their toughest test against a familiar foe.

*Rickey Paulding's stellar play helped carry the Tigers through a tumultuous 2002–03 season. (MU Athletics/Sarah Becking)*

More than any other team, Oklahoma had become Missouri's great nemesis, with eight straight wins over the Tigers. At 30–4 on the year, Kelvin Sampson's Sooners had dominated opponents with high-pressure defense, relentless rebounding, and the stellar play of guard Hollis Price.

The Sooners took an eight-point lead to halftime, but Missouri rallied and cut the margin to three points with less than three minutes to play. The Tigers would get no closer. Despite twenty-two points from Paulding, Oklahoma won 81–75, ending Mizzou's miraculous run. The loss was particularly difficult for Clarence Gilbert, who, in his last game as a Tiger, made just one of sixteen field goal attempts. Gilbert kept a stiff upper lip, but Quin Snyder felt for his senior captain. "It was painful to watch that happen to Clarence," Snyder said. "He wanted it so bad. He's such a tough kid."

Still, the disappointment gave way to a sense of accomplishment. "I'm unbelievably proud of what this team became," said Snyder, who presided over the comeback from mid-season struggles. There was also a sense of momentum within the program. With Gilbert graduating and Kareem Rush skipping his senior year for the riches of the NBA, Missouri lost two of its ten all-time leading scorers. But Arthur Johnson and Rickey Paulding, who had become stars in their own right, would return. And though they would often perform brilliantly, Johnson, Paulding, and the rest of the Tigers were soon to experience some uniquely trying times.

## 2002–03

Even without Rush and Gilbert, Mizzou got off to a hot start in the new season, thanks largely to some off-season reloading, including the additions of Jimmy McKinney, a blue chipper from Vashon High in St. Louis, and Ricky Clemons, a high-scoring junior college point guard whose arrival induced Wesley Stokes to transfer out of the program. The team seamlessly adjusted to its new personnel, racing to a 10–1 start and the nation's number eleven ranking. Rickey Paulding and Arthur Johnson combined for forty-five points in a win over Memphis, and Clemons scored twenty-seven in an 88–82 victory at Iowa that prompted Quin Snyder to remark, "We're a team right now." When Arthur

Johnson racked up thirty points and fifteen rebounds to help beat Baylor, Missouri looked like a contender, and Johnson appeared to be the team's next star. "He's trying to become a great player," said Snyder.

A seven-point loss at eventual national champion Syracuse dropped Mizzou to 10–2. But all of the Tigers' goals remained achievable until an off-court incident threatened the team's success in the short-term and began a chain of events that led to more lasting consequences.

Ricky Clemons was arrested on January 17 and charged with assaulting his girlfriend. Quin Snyder noted that Clemons denied the allegations, but said that any player convicted of a violent act would face harsh discipline. With a game looming at nationally ranked Oklahoma State, Clemons was suspended. While he stayed behind in Columbia, Josh Kroenke, the team's sole experienced reserve guard, sat out with sore knees, leaving the team woefully short-handed. The Cowboys feasted on Mizzou's misfortune, winning by twenty.

Clemons returned to the lineup when Missouri hosted Iowa State, but it was the beginning of the end for him as a player. Before his arrest, he had been a fearless scorer and playmaker. After, he became an erratic, sometimes reckless, shooter. Though the Tigers beat the Cyclones, they were entering a period in which nothing would come easy as they tried to repair a fractured chemistry, with an increased burden on McKinney, the only other Tiger capable of playing the point. A month of inconsistent play culminated in a blowout loss at Colorado that dropped MU to 16–7 overall and 7–5 in the conference. The Tigers desperately needed a quality win to resuscitate their postseason hopes.

The revival began against Mizzou's toughest foe. Oklahoma had beaten Missouri nine straight times, most recently in the Elite Eight of the NCAA Tournament. The Sooners came to Columbia ranked third in the nation with a 20–4 record, a confident team intent on reaching its second straight Final Four.

Quin Snyder put freshman Kevin Young into the starting lineup, and Young rewarded his coach's confidence just sixteen seconds into the game when he took a pass under the basket and unleashed a seismic dunk, his enormous frame shaking the basket and shocking the crowd to life.

*Top: Arthur Johnson starred in Mizzou's run to the final of the 2003 Big 12 Tournament. (MU Athletics/Sarah Becking)*

*Bottom: Josh Kroenke's four three-pointers gave the Tigers a boost in an epic NCAA Tournament game against Marquette. (MU Athletics/Sarah Becking)*

Three-pointers by Ricky Clemons and Travon Bryant helped build an early lead, and the Tigers ran away with a 67–52 win. "This game proved that we can play with anybody in the country," said Rickey Paulding.

The Tigers split their next two games before hosting sixth-ranked Kansas to end the regular season. Mizzou stood on the precipice of victory, holding a 74–71 lead with a minute to play, when Kansas guard Aaron Miles, attempting to beat the shot clock, chucked up an awkward two-handed toss that skidded through the hoop to tie the score. Forty seconds later, KU iced the game with a similarly desperate clock-defying three-pointer by Kirk Hinrich. Though the loss was disappointing, the effort reaffirmed that the Tigers could go toe-to-toe with the nation's top teams.

But the Tigers could also wallow with lesser teams, as shown in the Big 12 Tournament against a Nebraska squad that took a 22–4 lead early in the game. With their NCAA hopes in jeopardy, the Tigers sprang to life. Johnson and Paulding combined for thirty-seven points and twenty-three rebounds in a 70–61 comeback win. The next day, Jimmy McKinney scored sixteen points and Travon Bryant hit a buzzer-beating jumper to give Missouri a 60–58 win over Oklahoma State. The victory advanced the Tigers to the semifinal, where Bryant again made his presence felt. He scored eighteen points in a win over Kansas that—to the surprise of most—put the Tigers in the final, where Oklahoma awaited.

While the Sooners had earned a first-round bye, the Tigers, playing their fourth game in four days, looked exhausted. Oklahoma used a 15–0 run to take a 37–18 lead at the break. Five minutes into the second half, the lead had grown to 46–24, but then the Tigers staged an epic comeback, fueled by tremendous defense.

Oklahoma crumbled under Missouri's pressure, failing to make a field goal in the game's final fifteen minutes. And with Arthur Johnson posting twenty-one points and eleven rebounds, MU stormed back. When Travon Bryant drilled a three-pointer with a minute and a half left, Missouri had closed the gap to one point, 48–47. Later, after a missed free throw by OU, Missouri had a chance to win. Rickey Paulding drove through traffic with less than five seconds to play and put up a shot that skimmed off the rim. An Oklahoma rebound and free throw finished the game. Missouri's 49–47 loss wasn't quite a moral victory, but it was close. "There was never any doubt we'd come back," said Paulding. "We had to." Quin Snyder echoed Paulding's comments and delved into his team's psyche, noting that the Tigers could have quit—they were tired, down by twenty, already a lock for the NCAA field. "To be champions, you have to refuse that logic," Snyder said. "The biggest thing for us was making the decision we were going to compete. I'm so proud of this team right now."

Missouri's performance lifted the Tigers to the number six seed in the Midwest Region of the NCAA Tournament, where they opened against Southern Illinois. And though they played poorly, the Tigers advanced with a 72–71 victory that put them in the second round against third-seeded Marquette.

The Golden Eagles, behind the powerhouse backcourt of Dwyane Wade and Travis Diener, built a ten-point halftime lead. Mizzou stayed in the game thanks in part to reserve guard Josh Kroenke, who scored fourteen points on four-of-six three-point shooting. But the Tigers pulled even with Marquette behind phenomenal efforts by the two juniors who carried them through the season's turmoil. While Ricky Clemons made just two of fifteen field goal attempts and Travon Bryant went scoreless on the day, Rickey Paulding and Arthur Johnson stood like giants. Johnson scored twenty-eight points and grabbed eighteen rebounds, and Paulding produced thirty-six points on nine of fifteen three-point shooting, though his most spectacular score came when he elevated beyond comprehension and put back an offensive rebound with a mind-bending dunk, one of the most sensational plays in a highlight-reel career. Missouri rallied to tie the score 80–80 at the end of regulation. Momentum was on the Tigers' side. But an unlikely hero was in a Marquette uniform.

Steve Novak, a six-foot-ten freshman with a stick-figure physique, had given the Golden Eagles a quality effort without giving any indication of what he would do in the season's most crucial five minutes. In overtime, Novak sank all three of his three-point attempts, leading a wave of perfection for Marquette. The Eagles made all six of their field goal attempts and all six of their free throws to pull away to a 101–92 triumph that tore the heart out of the Tigers. "I've never seen a team play as well as we did in overtime," said Marquette coach Tom Crean. In fact, Marquette was brilliant all game long, making twelve of eighteen three-pointers and nineteen of twenty free throws, the kind of excellence necessary to match Missouri's inspired play. "You're supposed to win when you play like that," Quin Snyder said of his team's effort. Even in his disappointment, Snyder recognized the character of the two juniors who had kept the team together. In a quiet moment, he told Paulding and Johnson, "I love coaching you guys." And with those stars set to return, optimism for the future abounded. Marquette's Crean said, "We just beat a team that's going to be one of the two or three best teams in the country next year." But it was not to be. The turbulence that had surfaced around Ricky Clemons would only intensify in the off-season, ultimately dragging down the entire program.

## 2003–04

It should have been a season to remember, a celebration of three decades of championship basketball at the Hearnes Center, and a coronation of Quin Snyder's best team yet. For thirty-two years, the sturdy Hearnes Center, with its cold concrete surfaces, had made for a hellacious home-court advantage, as deafening crowds helped the Tigers win 85 percent of their home games in an era that produced eight conference titles and twenty NCAA Tournament appearances. In the building's final season, as the university constructed a new arena fit for a king, Missouri hoped to join college basketball's royalty. Led by seniors Arthur Johnson, Rickey Paulding, Travon Bryant, and Josh Kroenke and ranked number five to start the year, Mizzou had designs on the elusive promised land of collegiate hoops, the Final Four. The elements for a storybook

*Over thirty-two seasons, the Hearnes Center was home to eight conference champions, twenty NCAA Tournament teams, and countless thrills for Tiger fans. (MU Athletics/Sarah Becking)*

*Even as the Tigers struggled, Travon Bryant shone early in his senior season.* (MU Athletics/Sarah Becking)

send-off for the Hearnes Center were in place, but fate wrote a far more complicated, difficult, and disappointing script.

The troubles began months before the season began. During the off-season, Ricky Clemons pled guilty to two misdemeanor charges for assaulting his former girlfriend and received a one-year suspension from the basketball team. Later, Clemons was dismissed from the program entirely and sent to jail after violating the terms of his sentence. During a tumultuous summer, Clemons and his ex-girlfriend made allegations of illicit payments and academic improprieties within the basketball program. And while those charges were ultimately discounted by the NCAA, they helped spark an investigation that dragged through the season and enveloped the team like a foreboding fog.

Still, hopes remained high, thanks to the strong nucleus of veterans plus an infusion of new talent. Linas Kleiza, a freshman forward from Lithuania, possessed a combination of refined skills and manic intensity, and swingman Thomas Gardner brought a deft shooting touch and a tenacious defensive presence. The Tigers also added junior college point guard Randy Pulley, and at the semester break they would welcome Jason Conley, a transfer from Virginia Military Institute, where he had led the NCAA in scoring as a freshman. Quin Snyder's team brimmed with talent, but blending the old with the new proved to be challenging.

The Tigers got off to a decent start while they tried to find the right mix. After opening with two wins, they visited Indiana and appeared headed for a loss. Missouri trailed by ten with 4:23 to play when Arthur Johnson fouled out. But Mizzou finished on a 15–0 run as Travon Bryant and Linas Kleiza dominated offensively, defensively, and on the glass. Bryant posted sixteen points and ten rebounds on the day, while his freshman cohort produced fifteen points and thirteen boards in a stunning 63–58 victory that moved the Tigers to number three in the polls and alerted everyone to Kleiza's unlimited potential and savage aggressiveness. "He's an animal," said Bryant.

But after that rousing win, controversy struck again, thanks to the release of some profoundly embarrassing tape-recorded jailhouse phone calls between Ricky Clemons and the wives of two university administrators. The tapes made headline news and stoked allegations of NCAA violations while suggesting a bizarre rift between the athletic department and the highest levels of administration. And though the conversations ultimately seemed to say more about the pathologies of the participants than any dysfunction in the department, they provided another enormous distraction for a team trying to find some sense of normalcy. The unsettled Tigers returned to the court and dropped an overtime decision to nationally ranked Gonzaga before rebounding to beat UNC–Greensboro as Jason Conley scored nineteen points in his debut. But the perplexing stretch that followed set the tone for a season in which nothing seemed to go right.

Missouri entered the annual Braggin' Rights affair as a favorite, but Illinois stormed to a twenty-one-point lead. Then, behind Travon Bryant's nineteen-point, twelve-rebound effort, the Tigers roared back, only to lose by one, 71–70. The same scenario played out four days later at Memphis, where Mizzou fell behind by fifteen, only to rally before losing by two. But rock bottom came when the squad returned home and dropped a four-point decision to Belmont, as anonymous an opponent as the Tigers would face all season. "It was an abysmal effort on our part," said a dejected Quin Snyder.

Then came an up-and-down spell, beginning with a rout of Iowa that raised hopes and ending with a lopsided loss to Syracuse that rekindled fears, as an awkward chemistry and shaky guard play conspired to sabotage the team. But the Tigers continued to fight, and they scored a huge road win, rallying from twelve points down in the second half to upset eleventh-ranked Oklahoma in overtime as Rickey Paulding scored twenty-three points. Then Missouri hosted sixteenth-rated Texas and learned that for a team in turmoil, even good plays can have bad consequences. MU led 61–58 with less than ten seconds to play when Texas guard Royal Ivey dashed through the lane and put up a shot that Arthur Johnson swatted away, his sixth block of the night. But the ball bounced outside to Longhorn Brian Boddicker, who calmly nailed a three-pointer to tie the game. Had Ivey's two-pointer gone in, Mizzou likely would have won in regulation. Instead, Texas went on to win in overtime, and the Tigers were left to wonder what they had to do to catch a break.

Even more chaos lurked around the corner. The Tigers dropped a decision to Colorado and lost Linas Kleiza for the season when he separated his shoulder late in the game. They also played without Randy

*Top: Jason Conley's all-around play lit a spark for a floundering Missouri team. (MU Athletics/Sarah Becking)*

*Bottom: The electrifying Rickey Paulding graduated as one of the highest-scoring players in Mizzou history. (MU Athletics/Sarah Becking)*

Pulley, who was suspended and ultimately dismissed from the team after skipping practices. By the time the Tigers lost at Nebraska on February 7, they stood 9–10 overall and 4–5 in the league.

Then, when the season looked lost, character kicked in. With the roster dwindling, Missouri's top six players were forced to play extended minutes and unfamiliar positions. Jason Conley, whose playing time had diminished since his debut, reinvented himself as an unorthodox six-foot-five point guard and gave the Tigers a desperately needed lift. After Arthur Johnson grabbed his one

*A dominant presence in the low post, Arthur Johnson collected more rebounds and blocked more shots than any other player in the first century of Missouri basketball. (MU Athletics/ Sarah Becking)*

thousandth career rebound in a win over Colorado, Conley propelled Mizzou to a 94–60 rout of Nevada–Las Vegas. With his seventeen points, eight rebounds, seven assists, and five steals, the junior guard didn't just give his team a spark, "it was a blowtorch," said Quin Snyder. After Jimmy McKinney scored twenty-one in a win over Iowa State and Conley posted twenty-four points in a victory over Baylor, the Tigers owned a four-game winning streak and the season's first surge of momentum. But things were about to get even better.

The Oklahoma State Cowboys visited Columbia for the penultimate game in Hearnes Center history. Ranked number six, the Pokes brought a 21–2 record, an eleven-game winning streak, and an air of invincibility to town. But the Tigers brought a newfound confidence and a wealth of pride on a night when their two stars reasserted control of the team.

Rickey Paulding and Arthur Johnson played their best basketball of the season, helping the Tigers build a 71–62 lead with five minutes left. But Oklahoma State staged an 11–2 rally that sent the game to overtime. With the game slipping away in the extra period, Thomas Gardner snared an offensive rebound and sank a three-pointer to force a second overtime. In those final five minutes, clutch free throws by Paulding and Johnson lifted the Tigers to a 93–92 triumph, their biggest of the season. Paulding scored thirty-one points and Johnson contributed twenty-nine points and thirteen rebounds in a victory that breathed life into a moribund season. "This season is a lifetime in and of itself," said Quin Sndyer.

The winning streak reached six games at K-State, where Rickey Paulding sparked a 16–0 Missouri run by jumping over Wildcat Frank Richards for a jaw-dropping dunk that was the buzz of water cooler talk for days. By getting white-hot at the right time, the Tigers rekindled hopes of making the NCAA Tournament and resurrected some of the optimism that had surrounded the season. But over the next several days, hope would come crashing down.

The Tigers traveled to Texas Tech and lost a game that ended the streak but not their NCAA hopes. When the team returned home for the regular season finale, conventional wisdom held that a win over Kansas would secure a spot in the tournament. Missouri's recent play and the emotion of the occasion were in the Tigers' favor. The last-ever game at the Hearnes Center was marked by remembrances and a tribute to the man whose name became synonymous with the success the Tigers had known in the building. At halftime, Chancellor

*The Tigers moved into spectacular Mizzou Arena in the 2004–05 season. (MU Athletics/Sarah Becking)*

Richard Wallace announced that the court in the new arena would bear Norm Stewart's name, an honor that visibly moved the former coach and his wife, Virginia, who were on hand for the festivities. The day also marked the last appearance at home for seniors Johnson, Paulding, Bryant, and Kroenke. Missouri's players, coaches and fans badly wanted a victory to stand as a tribute to Stewart, the seniors, and the building itself.

But under the weight of the occasion, the Tigers seemed tight, unable to let loose and play their game. Still, it was a see-saw affair until Kansas used a 9–0 run to take a 77–67 lead with just under five minutes to play. Then, Arthur Johnson, in the midst of one of his finest performances, scored eight points in two minutes to help cut KU's lead to one, boosting his total to thirty-seven points on thirteen-of-seventeen shooting. From there, Jason Conley took over, scoring six points in less than a minute, including a fast-break dunk after a steal. A 15–5 run tied the score at 82–82 with fifteen seconds remaining, but Kansas had the game's last shot.

The final play was designed for Keith Langford, a gifted slasher. But the Tigers cut off his path to the basket and forced him to pass to David Padgett, a freshman center who had scored only four points. With just two seconds to play, Padgett put up a shot from the baseline. The pancake-flat jumper slipped through the rim and stunned the crowd. Kansas had won 84–82, dampening the days' festivities and threatening Missouri's postseason hopes. After watching a tremendous rally fall just short, Quin Snyder expressed the exasperation felt by all Mizzou fans. "Throughout this year, things haven't gone the way they were supposed to go," he said. "There hasn't been a chapter that has ended storybook."

With a 15–12 record, the Tigers needed a good showing in the conference tournament to revive their NCAA hopes. Jimmy McKinney scored twenty to help beat Texas A&M in round one, setting up a rematch with Kansas in the quarterfinals. The Tigers trailed by just two points at the half, but the Jayhawks dominated the final twenty minutes, pulling away to a 94–69 victory that sent Missouri to the National Invitation Tournament for the first time since 1998.

The Tigers visited Michigan and fell to the Wolverines 65–64, a disappointing end to a devastating season. "There's nothing anybody can say right now to make anybody feel better," Quin Snyder said after the game, the last for Mizzou's four seniors. Rickey Paulding finished in Missouri's top ten all-time in scoring, while Arthur Johnson became the Tigers' fifth leading scorer and established new career records for rebounds and blocked shots. But in a season that began with such lofty team goals,

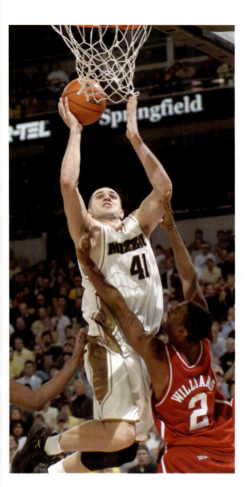

*Left: Lithuanian Linas Kleiza gave Missouri a ferocious interior presence. (MU Athletics/Sarah Becking)*

*Right: In his senior season, Jason Conley led Missouri to wins over nationally ranked teams from Gonzaga, Oklahoma, and Kansas. (MU Athletics/Sarah Becking)*

the individual milestones provided little consolation. Still, Quin Snyder appreciated the players who made up his first full recruiting class at Missouri. "The opportunity to coach them is something that I'm really grateful to them for."

## 2004–05

Nearly two years of turmoil came to a resolution on November 3, 2004, when the NCAA Committee on Infractions placed Missouri's basketball program on probation. Though the committee found no academic fraud, player payments, or unethical conduct, it did conclude that Mizzou's coaching staff had engaged in a pattern of excessive contacts with recruits, and it imposed penalties including recruiting limitations and scholarship reductions but no postseason ban. And while the sanctions stung, the end of the ordeal brought some small sense of relief for a program eager to move on.

In some ways, the new season marked a new beginning for Missouri basketball. With the investigation over, the Tigers—absent Johnson, Paulding et al—would forge a new identity while playing in a new home, a $75 million building (with luxury suites and state-of-the-art training facilities) that earned praise as one of the finest on-campus arenas in the nation. Originally christened Paige Sports Arena (for the daughter of Bill and Nancy Laurie, who donated $25 million to the project), it was soon renamed Mizzou Arena after a scandal involving the younger Laurie's academic record at another university. With an arched ceiling and windows welcoming natural light, the building recalled an old-time field house while providing modern amenities. For the young Tigers, it provided a chance to start over.

The new start was welcome for Linas Kleiza, who returned from shoulder surgery and played with the ferocity he had shown before his injury. A tough interior scorer, he was particularly valuable to a team that struggled offensively through a season of rousing wins and puzzling losses that translated into break-even play. Thomas Gardner recorded nineteen points and twelve rebounds as the Tigers opened their new palace with a win over Brown University, but the five-week funk that followed left Mizzou at 5–4 when the Indiana Hoosiers came to town. Early in the second half, the Tigers trailed 33–16 in a game short on aesthetic appeal. But Kleiza led a comeback that put Missouri on top 54–53 with thirty seconds to play. When Indiana's Bracey Wright lost the ball in the lane with six seconds left, freshman forward Marshall Brown streaked down the court and punctuated the victory with a 360-degree dunk.

In St. Louis, Kleiza scored twenty-five as the Tigers played top-ranked Illinois close before falling by six points. Then, back home, senior Jason Conley's sixteen points and thirteen rebounds helped Mizzou hold off twelfth-ranked Gonzaga 63–61, a victory forged with fierce defense. "Every time you turned around," said Quin Snyder, "someone was picking someone up, making a play."

Unfortunately, efforts like that came scarcely through the heart of the season. Wins over American University and Iowa State moved Missouri to 9–5, but losses in eight of the next nine games left the Tigers reeling.

When the Tigers welcomed Oklahoma to Norm Stewart Court, the teams were headed in opposite directions. The Sooners were on their way to a share of the conference title, while the Tigers were simply trying to win a game. Oklahoma led by ten points with less than six minutes to play, but with Snyder challenging his players simply to fight, the Tigers responded with one of the season's best runs. Jason Conley and Thomas Gardner hit key shots as Missouri rallied to tie the game at 59–59 and force overtime. Gardner drained two three pointers in the extra period, leading Mizzou to a 68–65 victory. Next, wins over Baylor, Nebraska, and Colorado gave MU the year's first four-game winning streak and pushed the Tigers' record above .500 for the first time in nearly a month.

But losses to Texas and Iowa State blunted the momentum and sent Mizzou into its regular season finale with a 14–15 record as seventh-ranked Kansas made its first visit to Mizzou Arena. After the Tigers used some sharp shooting to take a nine-point halftime lead, Kansas rallied to tie the game with

*Thomas Gardner's play buoyed the Tigers after the graduations of Arthur Johnson and Rickey Paulding.* (MU Athletics/Jon Brownfield)

*Jimmy McKinney carried Mizzou to victory over archrival Kansas in the 2004–05 regular season finale.* (MU Athletics/Sarah Becking)

under four minutes to play, and it looked like Missouri had run out of gas. But Jimmy McKinney, playing one of his best games, responded with a jumper that gave Mizzou the lead for good. The Tigers took a 72–68 victory that stood as the season's signature moment. McKinney scored twenty-one points on six-of-seven shooting. "Coach Q has been telling me to just go out there and shoot the ball and have fun and be comfortable and attack," he said. "That's how I played today."

After that climactic moment, the next three games played out like a coda. Missouri lost in the second round of the Big 12 Tournament, where Kleiza scored fifty-nine points in two games to earn a spot on the all-tournament team. A loss to DePaul in the opening round of the NIT ended Mizzou's season at 16–17, the first losing record of Quin Snyder's tenure. Still, the coach wasn't entirely displeased with the effort, especially after losing Johnson, Paulding, Bryant, and Kroenke. "In a year following losing that much production, we were proud to make postseason," Snyder says. But the Tigers were about to lose even more production with the graduation of Jason Conley and Linas Kleiza's early departure for the NBA draft. Quin Snyder would enter his seventh season trying to regain his footing after recent struggles. He would not make it to an eighth.

## 2005–06

The one hundredth season of Missouri Tigers basketball was a time of remembrances and celebration, but also a time of struggles and strife. After three difficult seasons, Quin Snyder desperately needed some success. But he was met with failure to begin the campaign, an 80–77 loss to Sam Houston State, Missouri's first defeat in a home opener in thirty-two years. "If we play like this, it's going to be an awfully long season," said Snyder. Long it was.

The season's discouraging first five weeks saw the Tigers rally to beat the likes of Northwestern State and Furman while being blistered by Davidson and Illinois. Mizzou entered the holidays with a 4–4 record and little confidence. Through the struggles, the lone bright spot was Thomas Gardner, who became the Tigers' go-to scorer thanks largely to the return of a three-point shooting touch that had abandoned him the previous year plus a newfound willingness to attack the basket.

Gardner and company finally gathered momentum at the end of the nonconference slate, easily handling three lesser opponents, including a 73–44 rout of Louisiana-Monroe that saw senior center Kevin Young produce one of his best games with twelve points and thirteen rebounds. Mizzou then carried that momentum through the start of Big 12 play.

When the Tigers hosted Oklahoma State, senior Jimmy McKinney recorded twenty-three points to propel MU to a 69–61 victory. Then at twenty-second-ranked Oklahoma, the Tigers held the ball in the closing seconds with the score tied. After a near steal by the Sooners, McKinney grabbed the loose ball and dished to Marshall Brown in the corner with two seconds to play. As Brown rose to shoot, OU's Taj Gray hurtled through the air and fouled him, sending Brown to the line for three free throws. Brown made two, giving Missouri a 71–69 triumph and a 2–0 record in league play.

*A tenacious offensive rebounder, Kevin Young was a fixture in the low post. (MU Athletics/Jon Brownfield)*

*Marshall Brown, an ultra-athletic forward, stepped up in his sophomore season. (MU Athletics/Jon Brownfield)*

*Quin Snyder's seven-year run came to an end on February 10, 2006. (MU Athletics/Sarah Becking)*

*High-flying, high-scoring Thomas Gardner led Missouri through a difficult 2005–06 campaign. (MU Athletics/Jon Brownfield)*

The Tigers returned home and lost a heartbreaker at the buzzer to Colorado before hosting Kansas in one of the most dramatic contests in the rivalry's history. Thomas Gardner scored twenty points in the first half, and the Tigers took a 37–32 edge to the break. The game continued much the

Melvin Watkins coached the Tigers for the final seven games of the 2005–06 season. (MU Athletics/Sarah Becking)

same early in the second half, and Missouri led 59–53 with nine and half minutes remaining. But Kansas staged a 19–4 run to take a nine-point lead with less than two minutes left, and fans began to stream out of Mizzou Arena. The Jayhawks led 74–67 with under forty seconds to play before Gardner hit a wild turnaround three-pointer to cut the margin to four. Kansas freshman Mario Chalmers sank a free throw before Jimmy McKinney nailed a jumper to make it 75–72. Then, after a held ball on the inbounds play, the Tigers got possession with seventeen seconds left. McKinney immediately drove to the hoop, scored, and got fouled. He missed the potential game-tying free throw and immediately grabbed KU's Russell Robinson, who, in turn, made two free throws to put the Jayhawks up by three. But the Tigers quickly got the ball to Gardner, who sank yet another long bomb to tie the score with five seconds to play. Kansas then rushed the ball up the floor, and senior big man Christian Moody ran to the rim, took a pass, and went up for a layup with less than a second left. But McKinney came out of nowhere to smother the shot, fouling Moody in the process.

Moody went to the line for two shots, needing only one to win it for Kansas. Despite the early departure by some fans, those who remained produced a jet engine roar. As the building shook, Moody missed one shot, then the other, and the game went to overtime. In the extra period, Gardner made a nifty feed to Marshall Brown for a dunk, and Gardner and McKinney hit crucial free throws to seal a spectacular, almost unfathomable, victory. McKinney scored nineteen on the night, and Gardner singed Kansas for forty points to secure a spot in the rivalry's lore. Quin Snyder, proud and exhausted, said, "I don't think we're a great team, but we were great at times tonight." At 3–1 in the

Jimmy McKinney (in a throwback uniform) was a throwback player, a guard who scored, distributed and rebounded. (MU Athletics/Jon Brownfield)

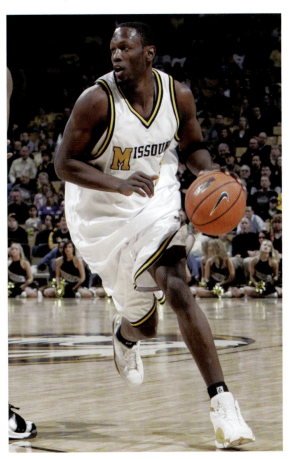

*Man of the Century: Norm Stewart headlined Mizzou's All-Century team. (MU Athletics/Jon Brownfield)*

Big 12 with wins over three of the league's traditional powers, the Tigers seemed to have turned a corner. And though thoughts drifted toward a first-division finish and a possible NCAA berth, the season was about to turn in a completely different direction.

When the Tigers traveled to Kansas State, the Wildcats revealed the blueprint for beating Missouri. They blanketed Gardner and McKinney and invited the rest of the roster to try and beat them. Mizzou's lack of interior scoring was exposed in a 79–64 loss that began a collapse. The Tigers returned home and got humiliated by Iowa State 82–58 as Snyder earned an ejection with two technical fouls. The downward spiral continued with three more double-digit losses, but rock bottom came when the listless Tigers ventured into Waco to play a Baylor team that stood just 1–7 on the year after having its entire nonconference schedule scrapped as a sanction for brazen violations of NCAA rules during Dave Bliss's tenure as coach. The Bears led 43–21 at the half and cruised to a 90–64 rout, one of the most embarrassing defeats in Mizzou's recent history. Still, after Missouri's sixth straight lopsided loss, Quin Snyder reaffirmed his intention to see the season through. "I'm down about losing," he acknowledged, but stressed, "my guys need to see me strong and committed."

Just three days later, though, it was over. On February 10, word spread that Snyder was out as Missouri's coach. Though there seemed to be confusion over whether he resigned or was fired, in the end it made little difference. With the program in free fall, a change was inevitable. Melvin Watkins,

*(L to R) Kim Anderson, Willie Smith, Ricky Frazier, and Steve Stipanovich were honored as members of Missouri's All-Century team. (MU Athletics/Jon Brownfield)*

"My goal is to win the national championship," Mike Anderson told Missouri's fans when he was introduced as the Tigers' coach on March 26, 2006.

Snyder's top assistant and a former head coach at Charlotte and Texas A&M, took over for the remainder of the season.

Amid the upheaval, the Tigers welcomed Kansas State to Mizzou Arena on a day when the program recognized its All-Century team, a collection of Missouri's twenty All-Americans, plus ten players added through fan balloting. At halftime, the lights dimmed, and titans of the Tigers' past descended on to Norm Stewart Court like guardians of the program on hand to see it through difficult times. The names included Charlie Henke, John Brown, Al Eberhard, Willie Smith, Kim Anderson, Ricky Frazier, Jon Sundvold, Steve Stipanovich, Byron Irvin, Doug Smith, Anthony Peeler, Kelly Thames, and, of course, Norm Stewart himself. Rising to the occasion, the Tigers broke their skid with a 74–71 victory as Marshall Brown scored eighteen. But it was just a momentary change of fortunes.

Missouri lost four straight leading up to the regular-season finale against Nebraska, senior day for Jimmy McKinney and Kevin Young. The Tigers rallied from eleven points back with under five minutes to play and won when Marshall Brown sank a jump hook with three seconds left in the game. The win moved Mizzou to 12–15 overall and 5–11 in the league. But a loss in the first round of the conference tournament capped a tumultuous season and the first century of Mizzou basketball, one hundred years of pride, passion, trials, and triumph that provided thrills, tested faith, and gave great joy to generations of fans who supported the Tigers through thick and thin.

The end of the century marked the beginning of a new era. The second century of Tiger basketball began on March 26, 2006, when Mike Anderson was introduced as the University of Missouri's new head basketball coach. During Anderson's tenure as an assistant at Arkansas, the Razorbacks reached three Final Fours and won a national title. Then he took over a struggling program at the University of Alabama–Birmingham and won more than twenty games in all four seasons as head coach, three times advancing to the NCAA Tournament with a full-throttle style that earned him a reputation as one of the nation's top defensive tacticians. When Anderson took the podium on Norm Stewart Court, Mizzou's newest true son recalled some furious battles between Arkansas and Coach Stewart's Tigers and spoke words that resonated with fans and alums who recall—and expect—a proud and winning tradition. "My goal is to win the national championship," Coach Anderson said. "I can get it done here."

# ACKNOWLEDGMENTS

Any project of this magnitude is, by its nature, a collaborative effort. A small army of people have helped this book along its way, and they all have my gratitude.

They include members of the Missouri basketball family who graciously shared their memories and insights. Thanks to John Cooper, Clay Cooper, Thornton Jenkins, Bill Stauffer, Gary Filbert, Joe Scott, Ray Bob Carey, Al Eberhard, Gary Link, Willie Smith, Jim Kennedy, Kim Anderson, Jon Sundvold, Chris Heller, Lamont Frazier, Brian Grawer, Quin Snyder, and Mike Kelly. Special thanks to the family of Wilbur "Sparky" Stalcup, particularly daughter Susan Stalcup Gray and her husband, Tom, and granddaughter Courtney Gaunt and her husband, Matt, who shared their memories and boxes full of materials essential to capturing a fascinating period in Mizzou hoops history.

Thanks to many members of the University of Missouri Athletics Department, including Athletics Director Mike Alden, Chad Moller, Kevin Fletcher, Dave Reiter, and Sam Fleury in the Media Relations office, Marketing Director Frank Cuervo, and former Director of Basketball Operations Lee Rashman. Thanks also to Linda Gilbert, the University's trademark and licensing program director, and to Bill Strickland at Collegiate Images, which administers the rights to the Athletics Department's photographs. Unless otherwise noted, all photographs appear pursuant to licensing arrangements with the University of Missouri and Collegiate Images.

This book was produced in partnership with the MU Alumni Association, and the entire staff and governing board have my gratitude. Executive Director Todd McCubbin and Jay Dade, my good friend and the Association's president in 2005–06, deserve special recognition.

Very special appreciation goes to everyone at The Donning Company Publishers, with particular thanks to Steve Mull, who gave his all to the book, Scott Rule and Lynn Parrott, who gave it its great look, and Kathy Sheridan, who gave it her meticulous attention through the editing process. Thanks also to Todd Donoho, whose guidance and marketing skills proved invaluable.

Thanks to all at the University of Missouri's Ellis Library, the Daniel Boone Public Library in Columbia, the Kansas City Public Library, the Mid-Continent Public Library (Independence branch), and the Missouri State Historical Society, to Gary Cox at the University of Missouri Archives, and to college basketball historian Patrick Premo.

Some special appreciation is reserved for my family, especially Sherri, Grace, and Evan, who rearranged their lives so this book could see the light of day, and for two longtime friends. Steve Owens helped this project take flight by sharing his wisdom and his contacts, and Art Hinshaw cheerfully slogged through many rough drafts, offering perspective and encouragement all along the way.

Finally, a deep, heartfelt thank you to Norm Stewart, the ultimate True Son of Old Mizzou, who graciously gave his time, memories, and words to this project, and who made the whole thing possible through a lifetime of fierce dedication to Missouri Tigers basketball.

# INDEX

## A
Abram, Al, 124–129, 132–133
Ackerman, Tusten, 48–49
Adams, Alvan, 164, 166
Adams, Dick, 106–107, 110
Advance, Missouri, 87
Ahearn Field House, 122, 173
Air Force Academy, 142
Alabama, University of, 17, 243, 261
Alabama–Birmingham, University of, 193, 206, 248, 279
Alaska–Anchorage, University of, 204
Albany, Missouri, 144
Aldridge, Mahlon, 95, 162
All-Century team, 278–279
Allen, Bob (Kansas), 125
Allen, Bob (Missouri), 157–158
Allen, Forrest C. "Phog", 15–16, 28, 31, 37–39, 42, 45–49, 62, 66, 69, 72, 82, 85, 88, 97, 99, 112–115, 119–120, 122, 124–126, 140, 162, 173
Allen Field House, 47, 121–122, 139, 150, 175, 214, 222, 249
Alvarado, Sean, 208
American Basketball Association, 148
American University, 273
Ames, Iowa, 98, 121, 145, 180, 197
Amos, Carl, 192
Anderson, Isadore "Izzy", 12, 14
Anderson, Kim, 169–170, 172–173, 175–176, 178–180, 235, 237, 278–279
Anderson, Mike, 279
Antlers, The, 181
Arbeitman, Benny, 90
Arizona, University of, 203, 238
Arkansas, University of, 92, 97, 112, 120, 129, 132, 142, 146, 149, 151, 157, 159, 189, 210, 214, 220, 225, 227, 232, 234–235, 240, 242, 246, 279
Arkansas–Pine Bluff, University of, 248
Army (United States Military Academy), 141
Army Air Corps, 94
Army Medical Corps, 31
Assembly Hall, 163
Associated Press poll, 107, 118, 193–195, 208, 221–222, 224–225
Association Park, 16
Atkins, Mark, 231, 234–235
Austin, Texas, 192
Autry, Adrian, 238

## B
Bacchus, Carl, 51
Baker, Wendell, 54–55, 58, 60, 62
Baker University, 12
Bangert, Keith, 85
Barrington, Don, 90
Battier, Shane, 261
Bauer, Lane, 94
Bausch, Jim, 58, 62
Bayless High School (St. Louis), 126
Baylor University, 244, 256, 258, 263, 265, 270, 273, 278
Becker, Dan, 208
Beer, Ralph, 68–70, 72
Belcher, Cookie, 247
Bellamy, Walt, 132
Bennett, Dave, 146
Bentley, Bill, 83
Bernet, Fred, 12, 14–15
Bernet, Milton "Snooks", 18, 20
Berry, Curtis, 181–183, 186–187, 189–190, 192
Besemann, Carr, 100
Big 12 Conference, 244, 248–249, 274, 278
Big 12 Conference Tournament, 244, 248–249, 256, 266, 274, 279
Big Eight Conference, 9, 128–129, 144, 149, 151–152, 157, 164, 166–167, 170, 172, 183, 187, 189, 205–206, 209, 212, 214, 224, 235, 244
Big Eight Conference Tournament (Holiday), 132–133, 139, 143, 145, 157, 159, 164, 166–167, 169–170, 172
Big Eight Conference Tournament (Postseason), 177–179, 187, 192, 196, 206, 216–217, 224, 227, 231, 238, 240
Big Seven Conference, 99–101, 108, 112, 116, 127–128, 244
Big Seven Conference Tournament, 101, 106, 108, 112, 115–116, 118, 120, 126
Big Six Conference, 55, 60–61, 73–74, 76, 85, 87, 91, 94, 98–99
Big Six Conference Tournament, 97
Big Ten Conference, 14, 21, 27, 47

Bingenheimer, Dan, 202, 204–205
Bird, Larry, 183
Bishop, Tom, 64
Black, Charlie (earlier), 48–49
Black, Charlie (later), 87, 97
Blaylock, Mookie, 215
Blind, Steve, 166
Bliss, Dave, 179, 278
"Blitz Kids", 92
Blue Springs, Missouri, 186
Boddicker, Brian, 269
Bohnnenstiehl, Rodger, 150
Bond, George, 36, 38, 40–41, 44–48, 50–51, 250
Booker, Melvin, 225–226, 228, 230–231, 234–238
Boozer, Bob, 127
Born, B. H., 116–117
Boschee, Jeff, 256
Botts, Tom, 149
Boulder, Colorado, 101, 119, 145, 170, 174, 190
Bounds, Kenny, 94–95, 97–98
Bradley, Bill, 139
Bradley University, 141
Braggin' Rights game, 234, 269
Brannum, Clarence, 100
Brentwood, Missouri, 114
Breslin, Jimmy, 125
Brewer, Chester "Chet", 6, 17–18, 20, 27, 52, 59, 61
Brewer Field House, 9, 59–61, 65, 68, 70, 73, 75–76, 82, 84, 86, 99, 116, 134, 136, 139, 143–145, 152, 156, 158, 160–161, 163
Bridges, Bill, 136, 138
Bridges, Prince, 193, 195, 197, 201–202, 204
Brodie, Francis, 20
Broeg, Bob, 41
Brookfield, Price, 88, 91
Brown, Booker, 146, 148
Brown, John, 9, 157–166, 168, 189, 248, 279
Brown, Kenny, 72–74
Brown, Larry, 208, 254
Brown, Lennie, 90
Brown, Loren "Red", 19
Brown, Marshall, 273–274, 276–277
Brown University, 273

281

Browning, Arthur "Bun", 40–41, 43–49
Browning, George "Pidge", 31–32, 36–38, 40–43, 47, 49
Bryant, Travon, 257, 263, 266–269, 271
Bud Walton Arena, 232
Bunger, H. L., 42
Bunker, Herb, 40–42, 44–48, 140
Buntin, Bill, 143
Buntin, Nathan, 143, 206–208, 210, 213, 216, 220–221, 224
Burress, Frank "Pete", 12, 14, 16–17
Butler University, 55, 66
Buzolich, Nick, 93

C

California, University of, 86, 159
Cameron, Missouri, 132, 141
Campbell, Hubert, 63–64
Campbell, Jesse "Mule", 23, 25–26, 28, 30–31
Cape Girardeau, Missouri, 172
Carey, Ray Bob, 132, 139–143
Carroll, John, 70
"Cats from Ol' Mizzou", "The", 207
Cavener, Greg, 193, 195–197, 201–204
Cedar Falls, Iowa, 149, 164
Central College (Central Methodist), 12, 22–23, 25, 33, 58, 72, 141
Central High School (Kansas City), 19
Central High School (St. Louis), 12
Central Missouri State University, 232
Chalmers, Mario, 277
Chamberlain, Wilt, 125–128, 136
Chapman, Jim, 146
Charleston, Missouri, 186
Charlotte, North Carolina, 213
Cheek, John, 20
Chenowith, Eric, 249
Chicago State University, 240
*Chicago Sun-Times*, 181
*Chicago Tribune*, 61
Chievous, Derrick, 202–206, 208–210, 212–213
Childs, Ida, 18
Christman, Paul, 80
Church, Greg, 207, 213, 216
Churchill, Tom, 55, 60
Cincinnati, Ohio, 214
City College of New York (CCNY), 109–110
Clabon, James, 172, 179
Clarke, John Allen, 33
Clemons, Ricky, 264–266, 268
Clemson University, 204
Clevenger, Zora, 30
Coan, Bert, 134, 136
Coffey, Ralph "Doc", 31–32

Cohen, Herman, 16–17
Coleman, Derrick, 217
Coleman, Jamal, 226–230
Coleman, Ron, 143–148
*College Humor* magazine, 64
Collings, Max, 58, 61, 63–65
Collins, Paul, 88, 91–93
Colorado, University of, 72, 99–101, 106, 114, 117, 119–121, 133, 136, 142, 144–145, 148–149, 152, 164, 167, 170, 173, 176, 182–183, 187, 190, 193, 195, 197, 199, 202, 205, 207–208, 210, 216, 221, 224, 226, 228, 230–231, 238, 240, 244, 249, 256, 265, 269–270, 273, 276
*Columbia Daily Tribune*, 15, 23–24, 126–127
Columbia Regional Hospital, 215
Combs, Leroy, 199
Conley, Jason, 268–274
Constantz, George, 86
Convention Hall (Kansas City), 46, 49, 58
Cook, Norm, 172
Cooper, Clay, 73, 75, 77, 80–82, 84–85, 125
Cooper, John, 64–68
Coppin State University, 234, 246
Costas, Bob, 199
Coward, Lee, 8, 207, 209–210, 213, 217, 220–222, 224
Cowell, Everett, 42
Cox, Frosty, 99
Craig, Cleo, 18
Craig, Marshall, 54–55, 58, 60–62
Crawford, John, 121
Crean, Tom, 267
Creighton University, 60, 63, 65, 217
Crowder, Dale, 91
Crudup, Jevon, 225–230, 234–236, 238
Crystal City, Missouri, 139
Currence, Blaine, 73, 75–76, 80–85
Currie, Jeff, 167, 170, 173, 175–176

D

Daly, Rich, 214–217, 225
Dangos, Steve, 166–168, 170
Davidson College/University, 183, 274
Davis, Ricky, 247
Davis, Vic, 66
Dayton, University of, 197
Decker, Tate, 247
Denny, Chuck, 115–116, 120, 122
Denver, Colorado, 72, 249
Denver, University of, 75, 80
DePaul University, 262, 274
Des Moines, Iowa, 98
DeSmet High School, 186
Detroit, Michigan, 202, 207, 210, 220, 256, 263

Detroit, University of, 148
Devine, Dan, 148–149, 162
Diener, Travis, 266
Dies, Manny, 247
Dixon, Missouri, 156
Dooling, Keyon, 248–249, 254–256
Dore, Tom, 182–183, 187–188
Doughty, Ken, 134, 139–141
Douglas, Greg, 152
Douglas, Sherman, 217
Drake, Bruce, 88, 98, 113
Drake University, 14, 17, 28, 38, 41, 45, 48, 55, 76, 98, 116
Dressler, Mark, 183, 186–189, 193
Drew, Larry, 176, 179–183, 186, 188–189, 204
Drexler, Clyde, 196
Driver, William, 12, 14, 18
Droy, Brad, 181–183
Drum, Lex, 182
Drumm, Manuel, 22
Duke University, 246, 254, 260–261
Dunham, Derek, 235

E

Early, Don, 141, 143
East Rutherford, New Jersey, 199
Eastern Michigan University, 209
Eberhard, Al, 158–160, 164, 166–169, 216, 248, 279
Ebling, Don, 85
Ebling, Ray, 69
Ebright, Mills, 14–15
Edmonds, Leslie, 45, 47
Edney, Tyus, 241–242
Edwards, George, 17–19, 52, 54–55, 58–59, 61–65, 68–70, 72–74, 80, 82, 84–86, 90–96, 134, 162, 250
Edwards, James, 175
"Einstein in Sneakers", 193–194, 197
Ellison, Nolen, 138
Elmore, Lloyd, 115, 119
Endacott, Paul, 41, 45, 48–49
ESPN, 232
Estes, Cecil, 201
Evans, Mike, 173, 179
Ewing, Patrick, 195

F

Faurot, Don, 44, 48, 50, 54, 70, 76, 80, 96, 108–109, 112, 114, 136, 138, 148–149
Fayette, Missouri, 12, 122, 141
Fayetteville, Arkansas, 92, 120, 149, 232, 238, 246
Ferrin, Arnie, 92
Field, O. F., 18, 20–21, 52
Filbert, Gary, 114–119, 204
Finley, Michael, 238

Finner, Marlo, 234, 238
Flaker, Greg, 157, 160–161
Flamank, Bill, 166–167, 170, 172
Flamank, George (Sr.), 54, 167
Flamank, George (Jr.), 141–144, 167
Florida State University, 180
Forbes, Missouri, 95
Ford, Hugh, 85
Ford, Travis, 220–221, 225
Fort Lauderdale, Florida, 248–249
Fort Leonard Wood, 115
Fort Riley, 13
Fowler, Jerry, 100
Fowler, Lee, 119
Franks, Theo, 149, 151–152, 156
Frazier, Lamont, 225, 230–231, 233–235
Frazier, Ricky, 8, 186–190, 192–197, 278–279
Freiberger, Marcus, 109
Frost, Jed, 235
Fulton, Missouri, 90
Furman University, 274

### G

Gage, Justin, 263–264
Gainesville, Missouri, 136
Gardner, Jack, 74, 98, 100
Gardner, John, 12, 14–15
Gardner, Thomas, 268, 270, 273–274, 276–278
Garner, Gary, 142–145
Garrett, Howard, 138–139
Garrick, Tom, 213
Garris, Kiwane, 234–235
Garwitz, Bob, 99
Gary, Indiana, 72
George Washington University, 66
Georgetown University, 195–196, 221
Georgia Tech, 80–81
Georgia, University of, 260
Gilbert, Clarence, 248–249, 255–258, 260–264
Gilbert, Jackie, 132
Gonzaga University, 86, 269, 273
Grace, Ricky, 212
Grambling University, 225
Grant, Harvey, 206
Grant Memorial Hall, 24
Grawer, Brian, 247, 249–250, 254, 256–258, 260–261
Gray, Taj, 274
Great Alaska Shootout, 204
Great Depression, 56, 59, 80
Great Lakes Naval basketball team, 86
Grebing, Walt, 132, 139–141
Greeley State University, 75

Green, Ricky, 175
Greensboro, North Carolina, 201, 229
Gregg, Herb, 80, 82, 85, 87
Griffin, Mike, 157, 159–160
Griffith, Rashard, 238
Grimes, Dorcet, 15
Grimm, Derek, 235, 240–246
Grinnell College, 48, 55
Guardians Classic, 261
Gwinn, Richard, 94

### H

Haase, Jerod, 242
Hackney, Ted, 16
Hafer, Jeff, 247, 254, 256
Haldorson, Burdette, 119
Haley, Sammie, 240, 242–243
Haley, Simeon, 240, 242–243
Halsted, Hal, 73, 75
Hamel, J. P., 127
Hanzlik, Bill, 188
Hardge, Monte, 242, 247, 249
Hardy, Lynn, 202, 204–212
Harman, Phil, 150
Harms, Marvin, 37
Harp, Dick, 75, 85, 126
Harrick, Jim, 241
Harrington, Paul, 67
Harris, Bob, 75
Hartman, Jack, 157, 159, 165, 179
Harvey, Bill, 73–75, 80–82, 84–85
Harvey, Don, 86–87
Hatfield, Allan, 70
Hawaii, University of, 172
Hawaii Pacific Invitational, 203
Haynes, Bill "Red", 100–102
Hays, Bob, 44–45, 47–48
Hearnes, Warren E., 162–163
Hearnes Center, 9, 162–164, 166–167, 170, 173, 180, 186, 195, 208–209, 212, 216, 227, 231, 235, 237, 242, 244, 247–250, 259, 262, 267–268, 270
Heineman, Bud, 101, 109–110
Heinsohn, Bob, 90
Heller, Chris, 226–227, 231–232, 235
Helmbock, Pete, 149–150, 156
Helms College Basketball Hall of Fame, 140
Helms Foundation, 42, 46–47
Henderson, Carmin "Chink", 69–70, 72
Henke, Charlie, 129, 132–138, 165, 279
Henley, Hezekiah "Zeke", 12, 14–16
Henry, Gwinn, 51
Henry, Skeeter, 215
Henson, Kent, 122
Hetherington, Clark, 12, 14
Hickman High School, 141

Hightower, Wayne, 133, 136–138
Hill, Tyrone, 209
Hinds, G. W., 39
Hinrich, Kirk, 266
Hoch Auditorium, 62, 85, 118, 139
Holst, Bill, 116
Honolulu, Hawaii, 197, 204
Hoover, Herbert, 66
Hopson, Andy, 165
Hotel President, 85
Hougland, Bill, 108
Houston, University of, 116, 118, 196
Houston, Byron, 225
Houston, Lyle, 139
Howey, Harold, 100
Huhn, Charlie, 58–64
Hyde, Arthur, 66
Hyde, Harley, 22–23, 25
Hymer, Don, 127

### I

Iba, Henry "Hank", 95, 128–129, 140, 144
Idaho, University of, 86
Illinois, University of, 47, 67, 87–88, 97, 120, 163, 186, 189, 193, 204, 209–210, 213, 220, 225, 228, 230, 234–235, 240, 242, 246, 255, 262, 269, 273–274
influenza epidemic, 31
Indiana University, 55, 117, 127, 132, 142, 148, 156, 241, 255, 257, 268, 272
Indianapolis, Indiana, 66
Iowa, University of, 14, 15, 59, 92, 112, 117, 200, 247, 255, 261–262, 264, 269
Iowa State University (Ames College), 14–15, 17–20, 23, 25, 29, 31–32, 37, 41, 50, 55, 59–60, 63, 67–68, 70, 72, 75, 82, 84, 86, 88, 91–92, 97–99, 112, 116, 121, 133, 136, 144–145, 150, 152, 167, 170, 172–173, 176, 180, 183, 186, 189–190, 192, 195, 197, 203, 206–208, 210, 212, 221, 224, 226–227, 229, 231, 235–236, 240, 243, 249, 255, 257, 265, 270, 273, 278
Irvin, Byron, 210, 212–217, 279
Ivey, Royal, 269

### J

Jackson, Don, 166
Jackson State University, 234
Jamison, Alonzo, 229
Jeangerard, Bob, 119
Jefferson City, Missouri, 124, 143
Jeffries, Mike, 157–160, 162–164, 166
Jenkins, Thornton, 87–89, 94–99, 129, 132
Jennings, G. S., 39
Jennings High School, 232
Jerman, Felix, 164, 166

Jesse, Richard, 15
Johnson, Arthur, 256–257, 262–271
Johnson, Clay, 176–177, 179–181
Johnson, Doug, 156
Johnson, Magic, 183
Johnson, Nolan, 260
Johnson, Tom, 146, 148–151
Johnson, Tommy, 16–17, 48
Johnson, William "Bill", 67
Jones, Gene, 146, 148–149, 151
Jones, Ron, 192, 195, 198, 201–202
Jones, Tyrone, 215
Joplin, Missouri, 12, 20, 101
Joplin (Mo.) YMCA, 12
Jordan, Michael, 197, 201
Jorgensen, Kenneth (Duke), 68–70

**K**

Kansas, University of, 8, 13–21, 23–25, 28–29, 32, 37–38, 41–42, 45–49, 54–55, 58, 61–63, 65–69, 72, 74–76, 82, 84–88, 90–91, 94, 97, 99–101, 107, 112–122, 125–126, 133–134, 136–139, 145, 150, 152, 156–158, 160, 165, 167, 170, 172–173, 175, 180, 183, 186–187, 189–190, 192, 195, 197–198, 201, 203, 205–209, 214–215, 221–222, 226, 228–231, 235–236, 240, 242, 244–249, 251, 256, 259–260, 263, 266, 270–271, 273, 277
Kansas City, Missouri, 14, 20, 44, 58, 70, 76, 85, 90, 92, 97, 112, 116, 118, 125–127, 159, 164, 172, 179, 186–187, 192, 196, 200, 206, 220, 224, 230, 244, 254, 261
Kansas City, Kansas, 176
Kansas City Athletic Club, 12–13, 44, 47, 49
Kansas City Polytechnic Institute, 26, 28
*Kansas City Star*, 28, 37, 244
*Kansas City Times*, 41, 61, 90
Kansas State University (Kansas State Agricultural College), 17–19, 21–24, 26, 29–30, 32–33, 38–39, 41–42, 46, 48, 55, 60, 65–69, 73, 75, 83–85, 87–88, 90–91, 94, 98, 100–101, 108, 113, 115–116, 118, 120, 122, 127–128, 133–134, 136, 143–144, 150, 156–157, 159–160, 164–165, 167, 170, 172–174, 176, 179, 181, 183, 186–187, 190, 195–196, 199, 203, 207–208, 210, 212, 214, 216–217, 222, 224, 226, 228, 230–231, 235, 237, 247–249, 256, 262, 270, 278–279
Kansas Wesleyan University, 52
Keene, Richard, 234
Keirsey, Harlan, 75–76
Kelley, Dean, 113
Kelly, Mike, 241
Kemper Arena, 172, 192, 217, 231, 244

Kemper Military Academy, 25
Kennedy, Jim, 169, 171–172, 174–176 178–180, 241
Kennedy, President John F., 140, 142
Kentucky, University of, 47–48, 92, 159, 193, 246, 255
Kerkhoff, Blair, 37
KFRU radio, 95
King, Kevin, 167
King, Stacey, 210, 212, 215, 217
Kirk, Walt, 97
Kirksville, Missouri, 170
Kirksville Teachers College, 54
Kleiza, Linas, 268–269, 272–274
Knight, Bob, 241
Knight, Johnny, 40–41, 44–48
Korean War, 110
Kroenke, Josh, 265–267
Kruger, Lon, 160, 208
Krzyzewski, Mike, 254, 260–261
Kurash, Gene, 93–94

**L**

Lafferty, George, 101, 106, 108–110
LaFrentz, Raef, 244–245
Lamar University, 192
Landolt, Gene, 113–114
Langford, Keith, 271
Langton, Scott, 179
Larkin, Byron, 209
Las Vegas, Nevada, 212
Laslett, Howard "Scrubby", 29, 38–39
Laurie, Bill and Nancy, 272
Lawrence, Kansas, 19, 21, 24, 28, 41, 45, 49, 54, 62, 75, 100, 115, 125, 134, 139, 150, 152, 165, 175, 205, 250
Lee, Eric, 142
Lee, Tyron, 246–247
Lee's Summit, Missouri, 72
Leonard, Gary, 204, 207–208, 213–214, 216
Lincoln, Nebraska, 32, 69, 73, 83, 235
Lincoln University, 124, 166
Lindley, E. H., 46
Link, Gary, 164, 166–169
Little, David, 198
Litton, Kent, 150
Lloyd Noble Center, 215
Lobsiger, John, 72–76, 81–85
Lonborg, Dutch, 138
Long, Lamont, 249
Lorrance, Darrel, 96–97, 99
Los Angeles, California, 193, 238
Louisiana–Monroe, University of, 274
Louisiana State University, 188
Louisville, Kentucky, 175
Louisville, University of, 189, 194, 220

Lovellette, Clyde, 107, 112–113
Lowe & Campbell, 44, 47
Lowman, Guy, 15–18
Loyola University (Chicago), 145

**M**

Macauley, Ed, 97
Maclay, Don, 60
MacMurray College, 172
Madison, Missouri, 117
Madison, Wisconsin, 63
Madison Square Garden, 9, 80, 99, 109, 148, 161, 217
Malta Bend, Missouri, 133
Manhattan, Kansas, 19, 23, 24, 30, 39, 46, 87, 91, 116, 118, 136, 144, 150, 160, 164, 173, 176, 199, 207, 216, 247
Manning, Danny, 205, 226
Marquette University, 127, 196, 266–267
Maryland, University of, 99, 214, 247
Maryville, Missouri, 106
Maryville Normal School, 23
Maryville State Teachers College, 95
Massachusetts, University of, 166
Massop, Tony, 216
Matheny, Buster, 181
Matheny, Ed, 86, 88
Mathews, Kelsey, 32
Mauer, John, 48
Maui Classic, 220
Mays, P. J., 214–215
McBride, C. E., 37
McCracken, Branch, 117
McCrary, Marvin "Moon", 190, 192–195
McDonough, Jimmy, 51
McDonough Arena, 195
McGuire, Al, 190, 194
McIntyre, John, 220
McKinley High School, 150
McKinney, Jimmy, 264–266, 270–271, 274, 277–279
McMillan, Hugh, 51
McMillen, Don, 100–102, 107
McNatt, Jimmy, 75, 83–84
Meanwell, Walter, 6, 21, 27–31, 33, 36–40, 63, 141
Memorial Stadium, 59
Memphis State University, 141, 205, 209, 214, 220, 228, 264, 269
Menze, Louis, 88
Miami, Florida, 80
Miami, University of, 263
Michigan, University of, 106, 143, 175, 246, 271
Michigan State University (Michigan Agricultural College), 17, 27, 108, 159, 201

Miles, Aaron, 266
Miller, Denver, 66–69
Miller, John, 25, 28, 31, 32
Mills, Loren, 85–86
Minneapolis, Minnesota, 217
Minx, Beauford "Beau", 88, 93
Minx, Clifford "Cliff", 88, 91, 93
Misaka, Wat, 92
Mississippi State University, 124, 144
Missouri Athletic Club, 13
Missouri football, 15, 16, 20, 36, 51, 80–81
Missouri Quarterback Club, 125, 139
Missouri School of Mines (Rolla Miners), 15, 44
Missouri Sports Network, 95
Missouri State University, 12
Missouri Valley Conference, 14–16, 19–20, 22–26, 30, 32, 39–41, 43, 45–47, 49, 54–55, 75, 85
Missouri Valley Intercollegiate Athletic Association, 55
"Mr. Magic", 172
Mitchell, Steve, 160
Mizzou Arena, 9, 271–273, 277, 279
Moberly Community College, 201
Mokeski, Paul, 172
Monsees, Ned, 143–144
Moody, Christian, 277
Moore, Albert, 12, 14, 15
Moore, Kendrick, 241
Morgan, Richard, 58
Morrison, Stan, 193, 197
Moss Point, Mississippi, 236
Moulder, Wendell, 94
Mountain Grove, Missouri, 50
Mulcahy, Bob, 149
Municipal Auditorium, 90, 106
Murray State University, 243
Myers, Gerald, 175
Mystical Seven, 109

## N

NAIA, 141
Naismith, James, 13, 15, 16
Nash, Martin, 82–83, 86
National Association of Basketball Coaches (NABC), 70, 94, 139–140
National Basketball Association (NBA), 99, 117, 149, 199, 209, 264, 274
National Collegiate Athletics Association (NCAA), 86, 92, 136, 139, 175, 214–215, 220, 255
National Collegiate Commissioners Invitational Tournament, 170
National Invitation Tournament (NIT), 26, 74–75 92, 99, 109, 157, 161, 166, 179, 203–204, 243, 248, 271, 274

Navy (United States Naval Academy), 238
NBC, 194, 224
NCAA Committee on Infractions, 225, 272
NCAA Tournament, 26, 74, 85, 91–93, 99, 109, 157, 170, 175, 178–181, 187, 196, 200, 205–206, 209, 212–213, 224–225, 229, 232, 238, 240, 249, 256, 260, 263, 266, 279
Nebraska, University of, 14, 17, 19, 24, 25, 29, 32, 45–46, 55, 60–61, 68, 73, 75, 82–83, 87–88, 91, 94, 99–102, 114, 116, 118, 120, 122, 133–134, 136, 139, 144, 150-151, 167, 170, 173, 176, 181–183, 186, 189–190, 193, 195, 201, 206–207, 216–217, 220, 222, 227–228, 230, 235, 237–238, 240, 247–248, 266, 270, 273, 279
Nebraska Wesleyan University, 32
Nee, Danny, 220, 222
Nevada–Las Vegas, University of (UNLV), 212, 270
New Mexico, University of, 249
New York, 92, 109–110, 202, 213
New York University, 80, 99
Newby, Maurice, 224
Nichols Gymnasium, 23, 29, 75
NIT (preseason), 213
Noble, Mike, 188
Norm Stewart Court, 258, 271, 273, 279
Norman, Oklahoma, 83, 183, 215
Normandy High School (St. Louis), 63
North Carolina, University of, 194, 196, 201, 203–204, 213, 220, 256
North Carolina–Greensboro, University of, 269
North Carolina State University, 148, 197, 242
Northern Iowa, University of (State College of Iowa), 27, 140, 148, 224, 250
Northwestern State University, 274
Notre Dame, University of, 187–188, 193, 224, 226, 235
Novak, Steve, 267

## O

O'Brien, Jim, 263
Odessa, Missouri, 28
Officer, Tom, 145
Ogden, Utah, 238
Ohio University, 157, 162, 164
Ohio State University, 142, 164, 166, 201, 263
Oklahoma, University of, 38, 41, 48, 50, 54–55, 60, 63, 66–68, 73, 75–76, 82–88, 91–92, 97–102, 106, 109, 112, 115–116, 118, 121, 127, 133–134, 139, 148–149, 157–158, 161, 164, 166-167, 170, 173, 179, 181, 183, 186–187, 189–190, 194–196, 198, 202, 204–207, 210, 212, 215–217, 221–222, 224, 228, 231, 236, 240, 242–244, 249, 260, 262, 264–266, 269, 273–274
Oklahoma City, Oklahoma, 215
Oklahoma State University (Oklahoma A&M), 51, 54–55, 76, 85, 95, 128–129, 139, 144–145, 148, 151, 156, 165, 167, 172–173, 179, 181, 183, 187, 190, 193, 195, 197–199, 202–203, 207, 216, 220, 225–227, 230–231, 236, 240, 249, 258, 263, 265–266, 270, 274
*Ol' Mizzou: A Story of Missouri Football* (Strode Publishers, 1974), 40–41
Olajuwon, Akeem, 196
Olathe Naval Air Station, 91
O'Leary, Ted, 66
Oligschlaeger, Charles, 113–114
O'Liney, Paul, 234–236, 238, 240–242
Olson, Lute, 200
Oral Roberts University, 189
Orange Bowl, 80–81
Oregon, University of, 77
Oregon (Mo.) High School, 95
Orr, Johnny, 175, 198
O'Sullivan, Ted, 50–52
Ottumwa, Iowa, 21
Owens, Carlton, 213
Owens, Ted, 152

## P

Padgett, David, 271
Paducah, Kentucky, 146
Paige Sports Arena, 272
Paine, Allie, 88
Palfreyman, George "Pip", 18–20, 22, 23
Palmer, Charley, 166
Park, Medford "Med", 110, 114–120
Parker, Joe, 18
Parker, Johnnie, 254, 261
Paulding, Rickey, 256, 260, 262–264, 266–267, 269–271
Pauley Pavilion, 157
Peeler, Anthony, 213–216, 220–222, 224–230, 279
Penn Valley Community College, 176
Pennsylvania, University of, 39, 42
Pepperdine University, 92–93
Perkins, Sam, 197, 201
Perry, Marque, 261
Peters, Reaves, 112
Philadelphia, Pennsylvania, 81, 125
Phillip, Andy, 86, 97
Piatkowski, Eric, 237
Pierce, Paul, 244

285

Pierick, Larry, 146
Pierpoint, Karl, 98, 101–103
Pike, Dave, 151–152, 156
Pinkney, Henry, 151
Piper, Chris, 208
Pippin, Dan, 88, 90–93, 96–102, 114
Poplar Bluff, Missouri, 138, 182
Powell, Evans, 68–71
Pralle, Fred, 74
Premo, Patrick, 42, 47, 62
Price, Bob, 141–143, 149
Price, Hollis, 264
Pulley, Randy, 268–270
Purdue University, 125, 164, 170, 240
Puxico, Missouri, 112, 114

Q
Quigley, Ernest "E. C.", 23, 26, 38–39, 65

R
Rainbow Classic, 197, 204
*Raw Recruits*, 224
Ray, Dibi, 245
Ray, Stan, 172–173, 176, 180–181, 231
Reeves, Bryant, 230–231
Reeves, Khalid, 238
Reichert, Redford, 117–118, 120, 122
Reid, Josh, 247
Reiter, Bob, 110, 114–120, 168
Retherford, Claude, 101–102
Rhode Island, University of, 213
Rice University, 129, 132
Richards, Frank, 270
Ristine, Carl "Curly", 12, 14–16
Robertson, Ryan, 248–249
Robinson, Russell, 277
Robinson, Walter "Bubber", 87
Robinson Gymnasium, 28, 32, 40–41, 45, 49
Robisch, Dave, 158
Rody, George, 37, 41, 45–46
Rolander, Bob, 100
Rolf, Devon, 207
Rollins Field, 59
Roman, Ed, 110
Rooney, John, 199
Ross, Bill, 120–122, 126
Rothwell Gymnasium, 9, 12, 13, 15, 16, 18, 20, 23, 25, 26, 30, 31, 33, 38, 42, 48, 58, 60, 107
Roundtree, Bill, 202
Ruble, Herb, 55
Ruby, Craig, 6, 28, 30–33, 36–37, 39–44, 46–48, 67
Rudd, Charlie, 143–146
Rudolph, John, 97–98
Rupp, Adolph, 47–48, 159
Rush, Kareem, 254–264

Rutgers University, 148, 221

S
St. Charles, Missouri, 248
St. John's University, 161
St. Joseph, Missouri, 114
St. Joseph's University, 81, 204
St. Louis, Missouri, 15, 18, 24, 28, 33, 63, 67–68, 124, 126, 148, 150, 186, 188, 194, 196–197, 209, 220, 232, 234, 242, 250, 258, 273
St. Louis Arena, 234
St. Louis Hawks, 117, 120, 149
St. Louis University, 68, 70, 80, 85–86, 97, 99, 101, 125, 143, 145, 148, 151, 166, 186, 255, 257, 261
Salmon, Orv, 164, 166
Salt Lake City, Utah, 183
Sam Houston State University, 274
Sampson, Kelvin, 260, 264
Sampson, Ralph, 199
San Jose, California, 263
San Jose State University, 187
Sandbothe, Mike, 204, 206–210, 212–213, 216–217
Santa Clara University, 148
Sapp, Bill, 99
Sarver, Don, 134
*Saturday Evening Post*, 125–127
*Savitar*, 15, 41, 50, 68, 94, 119, 126
Schlademan, Karl, 37
Schoonmaker, Bob, 116
Schroeder, Eric, 31, 32
Scott, Joe, 129, 132–136, 138
Scott, Phil, 31–33, 36–39
Seattle, Washington, 86
Seattle, University of, 148
Sedalia, Missouri, 52
Sedalia Air Base, 88
Self, Bill, 203
Selma, Alabama, 181
Seminole College, 170
Seton Hall University, 229–230
Shannon, Howard, 100
Shelbyville, Missouri, 115, 250
Shirkey, Sam, 23, 28, 30, 31, 77
Show-Me Classic, 209
Siebert, Sonny, 126–129
Simmons, John "Hi", 149
Sims, Scott, 170, 175–176, 179
Sims, Ty, 247
Simpson, Chauncey, 113–114
61st Troop Carrier Wing, 88
Slusher, Clyde, 28, 30
Smith, Derek, 194
Smith, Doug, 210, 212–213, 217, 220–227, 279

Smith, Harry, 138
Smith, Henry, 156–158
Smith, Lionel, 117, 119–122, 125–127, 136
Smith, Pleasant, 87–88, 96–101
Smith, Reggie, 231, 235
Smith, Willie, 9, 169–170, 172–176, 204, 278–279
Snodgrass, Harry, 18
Snyder, Quin, 27, 254–258, 260–274, 276–279
South Dakota, University of, 126
Southeastern Conference, 144
Southern California, University of, 70, 126, 138, 193, 242
Southern Illinois University, 266
Southern Methodist University, 97, 248
Southern University, 262
Southwest Conference, 92, 244
Southwest Missouri State University, 141
Southwest Texas State University, 186
Soyoye, Tajudeen "T. J.", 254, 257, 260
Speelman, Jake, 22, 23, 25
Springfield, Missouri, 141, 151
Springfield Teachers College, 85
Sproull, Ralph "Lefty", 19, 23
Srb, Dick, 102
Stalcup, Wilbur "Sparky", 95–97, 99, 101–102, 106, 108–110, 112–118, 123–129, 132–136, 139–140, 149, 162, 182
Stallworth, Bud, 160
Stankowski, Anton, 54
Stark, Earl, 87–88, 97
Stauffer, Bill, 106–110, 112, 114, 117, 120, 168
Stava, William, 12, 14, 15
Stevens, Barry, 197
Stewart, Norm, 6, 8, 9, 27, 115–123, 132–133, 140, 148–149, 151–152, 156–157, 159–162, 164–165, 167, 169–170, 172, 174–175, 178–180, 182–183, 186–188, 190, 193–196, 199–206, 208–210, 212–217, 220–221, 224–230, 232, 234–238, 240–242, 244–251, 258, 271, 278–279
Stewart, Virginia, 149, 271
Stiegemeier, Earl, 93–94
Stillwater, Oklahoma, 150, 176, 190, 199, 230, 258
Stipanovich, Steve, 9, 186–190, 192–193, 195–201, 208, 213, 226, 278–279
Stokes, Wesley, 256–257, 260, 262, 264
Storm, Roy, 85–86
Stoudamire, Damon, 238
Strickland, Erick, 237
Strom, Lavere, 69–70
Strong, Guy, 172

Strong, Jeff, 203–206
Stroot, Don, 101–102, 108
Stuber, George, 66–67
Student Army Training Corps (SATC), 31
Sumner High School (St. Louis), 124
Sundvold, Bob, 214, 225
Sundvold, Jon, 9, 186–187, 189–191, 193–201, 204, 279
Sutherland, Jason, 235, 240–244
Syracuse University, 213, 217, 238, 265, 269

## T
Taaffe, George, 18–20
Talley, Cliff, 127
Tarkio College, 22
Tartan floor, 164
Tate, Corey, 245–146
Taylor, Fred, 166
Teague, Shawn, 190
Temple University, 213, 232
Tennessee, University of, 164
Texas, University of, 25, 217, 244, 247, 249, 258, 269, 273
Texas A&M University, 244, 248, 260, 271
Texas Christian University, 106
Texas Tech University, 120, 175, 244, 258, 270
Thames, Kelly, 232, 234–237, 239–240, 242, 244, 246–248, 279
Thomas, Malcolm, 201, 204
Thompson, Gary, 121
Thompson, Gene, 69
Thomson, Ralph, 67
Thurman, Scotty, 234
Tinsley, Jamaal, 257
Tisdale, Wayman, 198, 202, 226
Tison, Haskell, 73, 75, 77, 80–85
Toler, William, 125–126
Tomlinson, Don, 149–153, 156–157
Tubbs, Billy, 194, 198, 215, 236
Tucker, Gerald, 97–98
Tulsa, University of (Henry Kendall College), 28, 112, 132–133
Turner, Lamont, 166
Tuttle, Charley, 51

## U
UCLA, 157, 241, 263
Uhrlaub, Ernst, 41
Uhrlaub, Rudolf, 29
United State Olympic basketball team, 86, 162
University Hospital, 120
Utah, University of, 92, 181

## V
Valvano, Jim, 148, 197
Van Gent, Eugene "Gene", 21–25, 27, 37
Van Rheen, Danny, 179
Vanatta, Bob, 141–146, 148–149
Vanatta, Rob, 146
Vanderbilt University, 129
Vashon High School, 265
Vaughn, Jacque, 244–246
Versailles, Missouri, 109
Vietnam, 144
Villanova University, 204
Viner, Harry, 28
Virginia, University of, 193, 199
Virginia Military Institute, 268
Virginia Tech, 209
Vogt, Paul (Deerfoot), 25, 31–33
Volunteer Classic, 162, 164

## W
Wachter, Bob, 97
Wackher, Leslie, 28, 31, 37–38, 40, 43
Waco, Texas, 278
Wade, Dwyane, 266
Wagner, Norman, 63–68
Wake Forest University, 77, 194
Waldorf, John, 58, 62
Walker, Michael, 193, 195, 197
Wallace, Richard, 270–271
Wallace, Steve, 182–183, 186
Walseth, Sox, 100
Warner, Ed, 110
Warren, Jeff, 227–228, 232
Warrensburg Normal School, 13, 18, 70
Washburn University, 18, 90
Washington, University of, 86, 175, 197
Washington, D.C., 66
Washington State University, 86, 204
Washington University (of St. Louis), 12–16, 18–21, 23–25, 28, 30, 33, 37, 39, 41, 45, 49, 55, 59, 63, 67–68, 70, 75, 80, 85, 98, 109, 132, 142
Watkins, Melvin, 277–278
Watson, Arch, 80, 82, 85
Waynesville, Missouri, 88
Wear, John, 22–24
Wehde, Ray, 88, 91, 98
Wehde, Roy, 88, 98
Welsh, Harry, 55, 58, 60, 62
Wesche, Homer, 73
West Virginia, University of, 229
Westminster College, 70, 90
Westport High School (Kansas City), 28, 52
Wheat, Frank, 48–50
White, Albert, 246, 248–250
White, Jim, 94
White, Jo Jo, 150
"Whiz Kids", 87, 97
Wilfong, Win, 110–112, 114–115
William Jewell College, 19, 59
Williams, Chuckie, 173
Williams, Fred, 22–26, 28
Williams, George, 36–42, 44, 47, 49, 114, 140
Williams, Jason, 261
Williams, Rob, 196
Williams, Roy, 214, 221, 236, 251
Winfield, Julian, 234, 239–241
*Winning Tradition: A History of Kentucky Wildcat Basketball, The* (University Press of Kentucky 1998), 47–48
Winter, Tex, 116, 122, 128
Winthrop University, 255
Wisconsin, University of, 17, 21, 22, 27, 40, 63, 117, 132, 238, 255
Wisconsin–Green Bay, University of, 201
"Wisconsin style", 22, 24, 29
Witt, Dan, 106
Woestermeyer, Armin, 45
Wolf, Gail, 167, 170, 172
Wooden, John, 157, 241
Woods, John, 249
Woolridge, Orlando, 188
World War I, 28, 31
World War II, 86, 93–94
Worley, Glen, 261
Wortham, Blake, 201
Wright, Bracey, 273
Wulf, John, 41
Wyandotte High School, 176
Wyoming, University of, 74–75

## X
Xavier University, 209

## Y
Yale University, 115
Young, Kevin, 265, 274–275, 279
Yunker, Kenneth, 52–54

# ABOUT THE AUTHOR

Photo by James Yates courtesy of *Mizzou Magazine*.

Michael Atchison received his bachelor's degree in communications from the University of Missouri in 1990 and earned a law degree from Mizzou three years later. In the course of practicing law in Kansas City, he helped earn freedom for a man wrongly convicted of murder, appeared on stage with the Blue Man Group with his head in a gelatin mold, swapped clothes with veteran rocker Sammy Hagar, and aided basketball coaches who ran afoul of NCAA rules. A lifelong college hoops fan, Mr. Atchison let his curiosity about the history of Missouri basketball run wild, and the result is this book, a true labor of love. He lives in Parkville, Missouri.